British Railways
LOCOMOTIVES & COACHING STOCK
1993

The Complete Guide to all
Locomotives & Coaching Stock
Vehicles of British Railways
(excluding Departmental Stock)

Peter Fox

ISBN 1 872524 49 4

Printed in England by Nuffield Press, Hollow Way, Cowley, Oxford and Double S Printers, Unit C4, Enterprise Way, Five Lane Ends, Idle, Bradford, BD10 8EW.

CONTENTS

This book lists details of all BR locomotives and coaching stock vehicles in service on 2nd January 1993, together with vehicles on order which may be delivered during 1993. 08700 and 47541 are included, as, although not in service on 2nd January, they were reinstated shortly afterwards. Departmental coaching stock vehicles are excluded. In addition, information is provided on vehicles of light rail systems, plus the stock of Eurotunnel.

1. LOCOMOTIVES

The following notes are applicable to locomotives:

LOCOMOTIVE CLASS DETAILS

Principal details and dimensions are given for each class in metric units. Imperial equivalents are also given for power. Maximum speeds are still quoted in miles per hour since the operating department of BR still uses imperial units. Since the present maximum permissible speed of certain classes of locomotives is different from the design speed, these are now shown separately in class details. In some cases certain low speed limits are arbitrary and may occasionally be raised raised when necessary if a locomotive has to be pressed into passenger service.

Standard abbreviations used are:

ABB	ABB Transportation Ltd.	kV	kilovolts
BR	British Railways	kW	kilowatts
BREL	British Rail Engineering Ltd. (later BREL Ltd.)	lbf	pounds force
hp	horse power	mph	miles per hour
kN	kilonewtons	RA	Route availability
		t	tonnes

LOCOMOTIVE DETAIL DIFFERENCES

Detail differences which affect the areas and types of train which locos work are shown. Where detail differences occur within a class or part class of locos., these are shown against the individual loco number. Except where shown, diesel locomotives have no train heating equipment. Electric or electro-diesel locomotives are assumed to have train heating unless shown otherwise. Standard abbreviations used are:

a	Train air brakes only
c	Cab to shore radio-telephone fitted.
e	Fitted with electric heating apparatus (ETH).
r	Fitted with radio electronic token block equipment.
s	Slow speed control fitted (and operable).
t	Fitted with automatic vehicle identification transponders.
v	Train vacuum brakes only.
x	Dual train brakes (air & vacuum).
y	ETH equipped but equipment isolated.
+	Extended range locos with Additional fuel tank capacity compared with others in class.

NAMES AND ALLOCATIONS

All official names are shown as they appear on the locomotive i.e. all upper case or upper & lower case lettering.

(S) denotes stored serviceable and (U) stored unserviceable. Last known allocations of stored locomotives are shown, but readers should note that locomotives may not necessarily be stored at their home depots.

After the locomotive number are shown any notes regarding braking, heating etc., the livery code (in bold type), the pool code, the depot code and name if any. Locomotives which have been renumbered in recent years show the last number in parentheses after the current number. Where only a few locomotives in a class are named, these are shown in a separate table at the end of the class or sub-class.

Thus the layout is as follows:

No.	*Old No.*	*Notes*	*Liv.*	*Pool*	*Depot*	*Name*
47673	(47593)	§	**IO**	IGJA	BR	Galloway Princess

GENERAL INFORMATION ON BRITISH RAILWAYS' LOCOMOTIVES

CLASSIFICATION & NUMBERING

Initially BR diesel locomotives were allocated numbers in the 1xxxx series, with electrics allotted numbers in the 2xxxx series. Around 1957 diesel locomotives were allocated new four digit numbers with 'D' prefixes. Diesel electric shunters in the 13xxx series had the '1' replaced by a 'D', but diesel mechanical shunters were completely renumbered. Electric locomotives retained their previous numbers but with an 'E' prefix. When all standard gauge steam locomotives had been withdrawn, the prefix letter was removed.

In 1972, the present TOPS numbering system was introduced whereby the loco number consisted of a two-digit class number followed by a serial number. In some cases the last two digits of the former number were generally retained (classes 20, 37, 50), but in other classes this is not the case. In this book former TOPS numbers carried by converted locos. are shown in parentheses. Full renumbering information is to be found in the 'Diesel & Electric loco Register'. This is at present out of print, but a new edition may be published in the future.

Diesel locomotives are classified as "types" depending on their engine horsepower as follows:

Type	*Engine hp.*	*Old Number Range*	*Current Classes*
1	800 – 1000	D 8000 – D 8999	20
2	1001 – 1499	D 5000 – D 6499/D 7500 – D 7999	26, 31.
3	1500 – 1999	D 6500 – D 7499	33, 37.
4	2000 – 2999	D 1 – D 1999	47, 50.
5	3000 +	D 9000 – D 9499	56, 58, 59, 60.
Shunter	Under 300	D 2000 – D 2999	03.
Shunter	300 – 799	D 3000 – D 4999	08, 09.

Class 14 (650 hp diesel hydraulics) were numbered in the D95xx series.

Electric and electro-diesel locomotives are classified according to their supply system. Locomotives operating on a d.c. system are allocated classes 70 – 79, whilst a.c. locomotives are allocated classes starting at 80.
Departmental locomotives which remain self propelled or which are likely to move around on a day to day basis are classified 97.

WHEEL ARRANGEMENT

For main line diesel and electric locomotives the system whereby the number of driven axles on a bogie or frame is denoted by a letter (A = 1, B = 2, C = 3 etc.) and the number of undriven axles is noted by a number is used. The letter 'o' after a letter indicates that each axle is individually powered and a + sign indicates that the bogies are intercoupled.

For shunters and steam locomotives the Whyte notation is used. The number of leading wheels are given, followed by the number of driving wheels and then the trailing wheels. Suffix 'T' on a steam locomotive indicates a tank locomotive, and 'PT' a pannier tank loco.

HAULING CAPABILITY OF DIESEL LOCOS

The hauling capability of a diesel locomotive depends basically upon three factors:

1. Its adhesive weight. The greater the weight on its driving wheels, the greater the adhesion and thus more tractive power can be applied before wheel slip occurs.

2. The characteristics of its transmission. In order to start a train the locomotive has to exert a pull at standstill. A direct drive diesel engine cannot do this, hence the need for transmission. This may be mechanical, hydraulic or electric. The current BR standard for locomotives is electric transmission. Here the diesel engine drives a generator or alternator and the current produced is fed to the traction motors. The force produced by each driven wheel depends on the current in its traction motor. In other words the larger the current, the harder it pulls.

As the locomotive speed increases, the current in the traction motors falls hence the *Maximum Tractive Effort* is the maximum force at its wheels that the locomotive can exert at a standstill. The electrical equipment cannot take such high currrents for long without overheating. Hence the *Continuous Tractive Effort* is quoted which represents the current which the equipment can take continuously.

3. The power of its engine. Not all of this power reaches the rail as electrical machines are approximately 90% efficient. As the electrical energy passes through two such machines (the generator/alternator and the traction motors), the *Power At Rail* is about 81% (90% of 90%) of the engine power, less a further amount used for auxiliary equipment such as radiator fans, traction motor cooling fans, air compressors, battery charging, cab heating, ETH, etc. The power of the locomotive is proportional to the tractive effort times the speed. Hence when on full power there is a speed corresponding to the continuous tractive effort.

HAULING CAPABILITY OF ELECTRIC LOCOS

Unlike a diesel locomotive, an electric locomotive does not develop its power on board and its performance is determined only by two factors, namely its weight and the characteristics of its electrical equipment. Whereas a diesel locomotive tends to be a constant power machine, the power of an electric locomotive varies considerably. Up to a certain speed it can produce virtually a constant tractive effort. Hence power rises with speed according to the formula given in section 3 above, until a maximum speed is reached at which tractive effort falls, such that the power also falls. Hence the power at the speed corresponding to the maximum tractive effort is lower than the maximum.

BRAKE FORCE

The brake force is a measure of the braking power of a locomotive. This is shown on the locomotive data panels so that railway staff can ensure that sufficient brake power is available on freight trains.

TRAIN HEATING EQUIPMENT

Electric train heating (ETH) is now the standard system in use on BR for loco-hauled trains. Locomotives which were equipped to provide steam heating have had this equipment removed or rendered inoperable (isolated). Electric heat is provided from the locomotive by means of a separate alternator on the loco., except in the case of and classes 33 and 50 which have a d.c. generator. The *ETH Index* is a measure of the electrical power available for train heating. All electrically heated coaches have an ETH index and the total of these in a train must not exceed the ETH power of a locomotive.

ROUTE AVAILABILITY

This is a measure of a railway vehicle's axle load. The higher the axle load of a vehicle, the higher the RA number on a scale 1 to 10. Each route on BR has an RA number and in theory no vehicle with a higher RA number may travel on that route without special clearance. Exceptions are made, however.

MULTIPLE AND PUSH-PULL WORKING

Multiple working between diesel locomotives on BR has usually been provided by means of an electro-pneumatic system, with special jumper cables connecting the locos. A coloured symbol is painted on the end of the locomotive to denote which system is in use. Class 47/7 used a time-division multiplex (t.d.m.) system which utilised the existing RCH (an abbreviation for the former railway clearing house, a pre-nationalisation standards organisation) jumper cables for push-pull working. These had in the past only been used for train lighting control, and more recently for public address (pa) and driver – guard communication. A new standard t.d.m. system is now fitted to all a.c. electric locomotives and other vehicles, enabling them to work in both push-pull and multiple working modes.

1.1. BR DIESEL LOCOMOTIVES

CLASS 03 BR SHUNTER 0-6-0

Built: 1960 at BR Doncaster Works (03079) or 1962 at BR Swindon Works (03179).
Engine: Gardner 8L3 of 152 kW (204 hp) at 1200 rpm.
Transmission: Mechanical. Fluidrive type 23 hydraulic coupling to Wilson-Drewry CA5R7 gearbox with SCG type RF11 final drive.
Max. Tractive Effort: 68 kN (15300 lbf).
Brake Force: 13 t.
Weight: 31 t.
Max. Speed: 28 mph.
Length over Buffers: 7.92 m.
Wheel Diameter: 1092 mm.
RA: 1.

Formerly numbered 2079 & 2179 respectively.

03079 v NKJD RY
03179 x **N** NKJD RY

CLASS 08 BR SHUNTER 0-6-0

Built: 1953 – 62 by BR at Crewe, Darlington, Derby, Doncaster or Horwich Works.
Engine: English Electric 6KT of 298 kW (400 hp) at 680 rpm.
Main Generator: English Electric 801.
Traction Motors: Two English Electric 506.
Max. Tractive Effort: 156 kN (35000 lbf).
Cont. Tractive Effort: 49 kN (11100 lbf) at 8.8 mph.
Power At Rail: 194 kW (260 hp).
Brake Force: 19 t.
Design Speed: 20 mph.
Max. Speed: 15 or 20* mph.
Length over Buffers: 8.92 m.
Wheel Diameter: 1372 mm.
Weight: 50 t.
RA: 5.

Non standard liveries:

08500 is red lined out in black & white.
08601 is London Midland & Scottish Railway black.
08642 is London & South Western Railway black and also carries its former number D 3809.
08721 is blue with a red & yellow stripe ("Red Star" livery).
08730/867 are BR black.
08793 is London & North Eastern Railway apple green.
08907 is London & North Western Railway black.
08933 is as 'D' but with two orange cabside stripes.
08938 is grey and red.

n – Waterproofed for working at Oxley Carriage Depot.
z – Fitted with buckeye adaptor at nose end for HST depot shunting.
§ – Fitted with yellow flashing light and siren for working between Ipswich Yard and Cliff Quay.

Formerly numbered in series 3000 – 4192. 08600 was numbered 97800 whilst in departmental use between 1979 and 1989.

CLASS 08/0. Standard Design.

08388	a	F	FSNI	IM
08389	a		FSNL	NL
08390	a		FSWL	LE
08393	a	D	MSSS	SF
08397	a	F	MSNA	AN
08401	a	D	FSNI	IM
08402	a	D	MSNA	AN
08405	a	D	FSNI	IM
08407	a	F	MSSS	SF
08410	a	D	MSSA	BR
08411	a		FSNY	TE
08413	a	D	MSSS	SF
08414	a*§		MSSS	SF
08415	x		MSNA	AN
08417	a	D	MSSS	SF
08418	a	F	FSCD	DR
08419	a		MSNU	CL
08428	a		MSNB	BS
08441	a		FSCN	TO
08442	a	F	FSCD	DR
08445	a		FSNI	IM
08447	a		MSNU	CL
08448	a		MSNB	BS
08449	a		FSCN	TO
08451	x		MSSW	WN
08454	x		MSSO	OC
08460	a	F	MSSO	OC
08466	a	FO	FSNI	IM
08472	a		MSNC	CD
08480	az		MSSO	OC
08481	x		FSWK	CF
08482	a	D	MSNA	AN
08483	a	D	MSSA	BR
08484	a	F	MSSB	BY
08485	a		MSNA	AN
08489	a	F	MSNA	AN
08492	a		FSCN	TO
08493	a		FSWK	CF
08495	x		MSSM	MR
08498	a		MSSS	SF
08499	a	F	FSCK	KY
08500	x	O	FSCK	KY
08506	a		FSNY	TE
08507	a		MSSR	RG
08509	a	F	FSNT	TI
08510	a		FSNT	TI
08511	a		FSCN	TO
08512	a	F	FSCK	KY
08514	a		FSCD	DR
08516	a	D	FSCK	KY
08517	a		MSSM	MR
08519	a	BS	MSSB	BY
08521	a		MSNA	AN
08523	x		MSSR	RG
08525	x	F	FSCK	KY
08526	x		MSSS	SF
08527	x	D	MSSS	SF
08528	x	D	MSSM	MR
08529	x		MSSM	MR
08530	x	D	MSSS	SF
08531	x	F	MSSS	SF
08532	x		MSNA	AN
08534	x	D	MSNU	CL
08535	x	D	MSNB	BS
08536	x		MSNE	DY
08538	x	D	MSSM	MR
08540	x	D	MSSM	MR
08541	x	D	MSSS	SF
08542	x	F	MSSS	SF
08543	x	D	MSNB	BS
08561	x		FSSM	ML
08562	x		FSCD	DR
08565	x		FSSM	ML
08567	x		MSSB	BY
08568	x		FSSM	ML
08569	x		MSNA	AN
08571	xz		FSSM	ML
08573	x		MSSO	OC
08575	x	BS	FSNL	NL
08576	x		MSSL	LA
08577	x		FSNH	HT
08578	x	R	FSNH	HT
08580	x		MSSM	MR
08581	x		FSNL	NL
08582	a	D	FSNY	TE
08583	x		FSCK	KY
08585	x		MSNC	CD
08586	a	F	FSSA	AY
08587	x		FSNH	HT
08588	xz	BS	FSNL	NL
08590	x	BS	FSNH	HT
08591	x		FSSA	AY
08593	x		MSSS	SF
08594	x		MSSC	CA
08595	x		FSCD	DR
08597	x		FSCN	TO
08599	x		MSNC	CD
08600	a	D	NKJD	EH
08601	x	O	MSNB	BS
08603	x		MSNB	BS

08604	x	G	MSNE	DY
08605	x		FSCK	KY
08607	x		FSCN	TO
08609	x		MSSW	WN
08610	x		MSNB	BS
08611	x		MSNL	LO
08613	x		MSNA	AN
08614	x		MSSW	WN
08615	x		MSNA	AN
08616	x		MSNB	BS
08617	x		MSSW	WN
08619	x		MSNL	LO
08622	x		FSSM	ML
08623	x		FSCN	TO
08624	x		MSNL	LO
08625	x		MSSW	WN
08627	a		MSSS	SF
08628	x		MSSB	BY
08629	x		MSSB	BY
08630	x		FSSG	GM
08632	x		FSNI	IM
08633	x	RX	MSNC	CD
08634	x		MSSO	OC
08635	x		MSNC	CD
08641	xz	D	MSSL	LA
08642	x*	O	NKJH	EH
08643	xz	D	MSSA	BR
08644	xz	M	MSSL	LA
08645	xz	D	MSSL	LA
08646	x	F	FSWL	LE
08647	x	G	FSCD	DR
08648	x*	D	MSSW	WN
08649	x	D	NKJH	SU
08651	xz	D	MSSO	OC
08653	x*		MSSO	OC
08655	x*	F	MSSS	SF
08656	a		MSSB	BY
08658	x		MSSN	NC
08661	a		FSNL	NL
08662	x		FSCK	KY
08663	a	D	MSSL	LA
08664	x		FSWK	CF
08665	x		FSNI	IM
08666	x		MSNL	LO
08668	x		FSWK	CF
08670	a		MSSO	OC
08673	x	IO	MSNL	LO
08675	x	F	FSSA	AY
08676	x		MSNL	LO
08677	x		MSSW	WN
08682	x		FSCD	DR
08683	x		MSSW	WN
08685	x		MSSC	CA
08689	a		MSSS	SF
08690	x		MSNU	CL
08691	x	G	FSNT	TI
08692	x		MSNC	CD
08693	x		FSSM	ML
08694	x		MSNA	AN
08695	x		MSNC	CD
08696	a	D	MSSW	WN
08697	x		MSNE	DY
08698	a		MSSS	SF
08699	x		MSNC	CD
08701	x	RX	FSNH	HT
08702	x		MSNC	CD
08703	a		MSNA	AN
08705	a		MSSM	MR
08706	x		FSCK	KY
08707	a		FSCK	KY
08709	x		MSSS	SF
08710	x		FSSM	ML
08711	x		MSSC	CA
08713	a		MSSM	MR
08714	x		MSSC	CA
08715	v		MSSS	SF
08718	x		FSSM	ML
08720	a	D	FSSM	ML
08721	x	O	MSNL	LO
08723	x		FSCN	TO
08724	x		MSSS	SF
08727	x	F	FSSA	AY
08730	x	O	FSSM	ML
08731	x		FSSG	GM
08733	x		FSSM	ML
08734	x		MSNB	BS
08735	x		FSSM	ML
08737	x	F	MSNC	CD
08738	x	D	FSSM	ML
08739	x		MSNC	CD
08740	x	F	MSSS	SF
08742	x		MSNC	CD
08743	x		FSNL	NL
08745	xz	BS	FSNL	NL
08746	x	D	MSNB	BS
08748	x§		MSSS	SF
08750	x		MSSS	SF
08751	x		MSNB	BS
08752	x	C	MSSS	SF
08753	x		FSSM	ML
08754	x		FSSI	IS
08755	x		FSSM	ML
08756	x	D	FSWL	LE
08757	x	D	MSSC	CA

08758	x		MSSS	SF
08759	x		FSNY	TE
08762	x		FSSI	IS
08765	xn	D	MSNB	BS
08767	x		MSSS	SF
08768	x		MSNU	CL
08770	a	D	FSWK	CF
08772	x	G	MSSS	SF
08773	x		FSCN	TO
08775	x		MSSS	SF
08776	a	D	FSCK	KY
08780	x		FSWL	LE
08782	a		FSCK	KY
08783	x		FSCK	KY
08784	x		MSNC	CD
08786	a		FSWK	CF
08788	x		MSNE	DY
08789	a		MSSB	BY
08790	x		MSNL	LO
08792	x		MSSL	LA
08793	a	O	FSSB	AB
08795	x	D	FSWK	CF
08798	x		FSWL	LE
08799	x		MSNA	AN
08800	x	I	MSSA	BR
08801	x		MSSL	LA
08802	x		FSNH	HT
08804	x		FSWK	CF
08805	x	FO	MSNB	BS
08806	a	F	FSCK	KY
08807	x		MSSB	BY
08809	x		MSNA	AN
08810	a		MSSN	NC
08811	a*		MSSO	OC
08813	a	D	FSCD	DR
08815	x		MSNA	AN
08817	x	BS	MSNA	AN
08818	x		FSWK	CF
08819	x	D	MSSL	LA
08822	x		FSWK	CF
08823	a		MSNC	CD
08824	a	F	FSCD	DR
08825	a		MSSO	OC
08826	a		MSNU	CL
08827	a		MSNU	CL
08828	a		MSSS	SF
08829	a		FSCN	TO
08830	x*		FSWK	CF
08834	x	F	MSSS	SF
08836	x		FSWK	CF
08837	x*	D	MSSO	OC
08842	x		MSNE	DY
08844	x		MSNU	CL
08845	x*	D	FSNX	EH
08847	x*		NKJD	EH
08849	x		MSSL	LA
08853	xr		FSSM	ML
08854	x*		NKJH	SU
08855	x		FSSB	AB
08856	x		MSNA	AN
08865	x		MSSC	CA
08866	x		FSCD	DR
08867	x	O	FSNY	TE
08869	x	G	MSSN	NC
08870	x		FSCK	KY
08872	x	D	MSNA	AN
08873	x	M	MSSS	SF
08877	x	D	FSCD	DR
08878	x		MSNB	BS
08879	x		FSNT	TI
08880	x		FSNT	TI
08881	x	D	FSSM	ML
08882	x		FSSB	AB
08883	x		FSSM	ML
08884	x		MSNA	AN
08885	x		FSCD	DR
08886	x		FSNH	HT
08887	x		MSSO	OC
08888	xz	R	FSNH	HT
08890	x	D	MSSW	WN
08891	x		MSNL	LO
08892	x*	D	NKJD	EH
08893	x	D	MSNB	BS
08894	x		MSNA	AN
08895	x		FSWL	LE
08896	x		FSWL	LE
08897	x	D	MSSA	BR
08899	x		MSNE	DY
08900	x	D	MSNA	AN
08901	xn		MSNB	BS
08902	x		MSNA	AN
08903	x		FSCD	DR
08904	x		MSSO	OC
08905	x		MSSR	RG
08906	x		FSNY	TE
08907	x	O	MSNC	CD
08908	xz		FSNL	NL
08909	x		MSSS	SF
08910	x		MSNU	CL
08911	x	D	MSNU	CL
08912	x		MSNU	CL
08913	x	D	MSNA	AN
08914	x		MSSB	BY
08915	x	F	MSNL	LO

08918	x	D	MSNA	AN
08919	x		FSNT	TI
08920	x	F	MSNB	BS
08921	x		MSNC	CD
08922	x	D	FSSM	ML
08923	x	F	MSSS	SF
08924	x	D	MSSR	RG
08925	x		MSNA	AN
08926	x		MSSW	WN
08927	x		MSSB	BY
08928	x	FR	MSNB	BS
08931	x		FSNH	HT
08932	x		FSWK	CF
08933	x*	0	NKJD	EH
08934	x		MSSW	WN
08935	x		MSSA	BR
08937	x	D	MSSL	LA
08938	xr	0	FSSM	ML
08939	x		MSNA	AN
08940	x		NKJH	SU
08941	x		MSSL	LA
08942	x		FSWK	CF
08944	x	D	MSSO	OC
08945	x		MSSL	LA
08946	x	D	MSSR	RG
08947	x		MSSO	OC
08948	x		MSSO	OC
08949	x		MSSA	BR
08950	x	F	FSNL	NL
08951	x	D	MSNA	AN
08952	x		FSSM	ML
08953	x	D	MSSL	LA
08954	x	F	MSSL	LA
08955	x		MSSL	LA
08956	x		MSSS	SF
08957	x		MSSS	SF
08958	x		MSSS	SF

Names:

08562 The Doncaster Postman
08578 Libert Dickinson
08631 Eagle C.U.R.C.
08633 The Sorter
08647 Crimpsall
08701 GATESHEAD TMD 1852 – 1991
08772 CAMULODUNUM
08869 The Canary
08888 Postman's Pride

Class 08/9. Fitted with cut-down cab and headlight for Cwmmawr branch.

08993	(08592)	x		FSWL	LE	ASHBURNHAM
08994	(08462)	a	FR	FSWL	LE	GWENDRAETH
08995	(08687)	a	FC	FSWL	LE	KIDWELLY

CLASS 09 BR SHUNTER 0–6–0

Built: 1959 – 62 by BR at Darlington or Horwich Works.
Engine: English Electric 6KT of 298 kW (400 hp) at 680 rpm.
Main Generator: English Electric 801.
Traction Motors: English Electric 506.
Max. Tractive Effort: 111 kN (25000 lbf).
Cont. Tractive Effort: 39 kN (8800 lbf) at 11.6 mph.
Power At Rail: 201 kW (269 hp).
Brake Force: 19 t.
Weight: 50 t.
Max. Speed: 27 mph.
Length over Buffers: 8.92 m.
Wheel Diameter: 1372 mm.
RA: 5.

Formerly numbered 3665 – 71, 3719 – 21, 4099 – 4114.

CLASS 09/0. Built as Class 09.

09001		FSWK	CF
09003		NKJH	SU
09004		NKJH	SU
09005	D	FSCK	KY
09006		NKJH	SU
09007		NKJH	SU

09008	D	FSNT	TI	09018		NKJH	SU
09009	D	NKJH	SU	09019	D	NKJH	SU
09010	D	NKJH	SU	09020		NKJH	SU
09011	D	NKJH	SU	09021		NKJH	SU
09012	D	NKJH	SU	09022		NKJH	SU
09013	D	FSNT	TI	09023		NKJH	SU
09014	D	FSCK	KY	09024	D	NKJH	SU
09015	D	FSWK	CF	09025		NKJH	SU
09016	D	NKJH	SU	09026	D	NKJH	SU

Names:

09008	Sheffield Childrens Hospital	09012	Dick Hardy
09009	Three Bridges C.E.D.	09026	William Pearson

CLASS 09/1. Converted from Class 08. 90 V electrical equipment.

09101	(08833)	D	MSSR	RG
09102	(08832)	D	MSNC	CD
09103	(08766)	D	FSNY	TE
09104	(08749)	D	FSCN	TO
09105	(08835)	D	FSWK	CF

CLASS 09/2. Converted from Class 08. 100 V electrical equipment.

09201	(08421)	D	FSCN	TO
09202	(08732)	D	FSSM	ML
09203	(08781)	D	FSWK	CF
09204	(08717)	D	FSNY	TE
09205	(08620)	D	FSSM	ML

CLASS 20 ENGLISH ELECTRIC TYPE 1 Bo – Bo

Built: 1957 – 68 by English Electric Company at Vulcan Foundry, Newton le Willows or Robert Stephenson & Hawthorn, Darlington. 20001 – 128 were originally built with disc indicators whilst 20129 – 228 were built with four character headcode panels.
Engine: English Electric 8SVT Mk. II of 746 kW (1000 hp) at 850 rpm.
Main Generator: English Electric 819/3C.
Traction Motors: English Electric 526/5D (20001 – 48) or 526/8D (others).
Max. Tractive Effort: 187 kN (42000 lbf).
Cont. Tractive Effort: 111 kN (25000 lbf) at 11 mph.
Power At Rail: 574 kW (770 hp).
Brake Force: 35 t.
Design Speed: 75 mph.
Max. Speed: 60 mph.
Train Brakes: Air & vacuum.
Multiple Working: Blue Star Coupling Code.
Length over Buffers: 14.25 m.
Wheel Diameter: 1092 mm.
Weight: 73.5 t.
RA: 5.

Formerly numbered in series 8007 – 8198, 8306 – 8315.

CLASS 20/0. BR-owned Locomotives.

20007	st	TAKX	TO (S)	20046		FMXX	TE (U)
20016	st	FCGN	TO	20055	st	FCXX	TO (U)
20032	s	TAKX	TO (S)	20057	st	FCGN	TO

20059 st	FR	FCGN	TO	20132 st	FR	CDJN	TO
20066		CDJN	TO	20135 st		FCXX	TO (U)
20071 st		FCXX	TO (U)	20137	FR	FMXX	TE (S)
20072 st		TAKX	TO (U)	20138	FR	CDJN	TO
20073 st		FCXX	TO (U)	20140 st		FCXX	TO (U)
20075 st		TAKX	TO (U)	20142 st		FCXX	TO (U)
20081 st		FCGN	TO	20151 st		FCXX	TO (U)
20082 st		FCXX	TO (U)	20154 st		FCGN	TO
20087 st		CDJN	TO	20165	FR	FMXX	TE (S)
20090 st	FR	CDJN	TO (U)	20168 st		FCGN	TO
20092		CDJX	TE (S)	20169 st		CDJX	TE (S)
20094 st		FMXX	TE (U)	20177 st		FCXX	TO (U)
20096		FMXX	TE (U)	20186 st		FCXX	TO (U)
20104 st	FR	TAKX	TO (U)	20187 st		TAKX	TO (U)
20106 st		TAKX	TO (U)	20190 st		TAKX	TE (U)
20117 st		TAKX	TE (U)	20195 s		FCXX	TO (S)
20118	FR	FMXX	TE (S)	20196 st		FCXX	TO (S)
20121 st		TAKX	TE (U)	20210 st		FCXX	TO (U)
20128 st		TAKX	TO (S)	20214 st		FMXX	TE (S)
20131 st		TAKX	TO (U)	20215 st	FR	TAKX	TO (S)

CLASS 20/9. Privately-owned by Hunslet – Barclay Ltd.

Used on summer weedkilling trains. Stored at Kilmarnock during the winter.
Non-standard Liveries: 20901 – 6 are in Hunslet – Barclay two-tone grey livery with red lettering.

20901 (20041)	t	0	XYPD	HB	NANCY
20902 (20060)		0	XYPD	HB	LORNA
20903 (20083)		0	XYPD	HB	ALISON
20904 (20101)		0	XYPD	HB	JANIS
20905 (20225)	t	0	XYPD	HB	IONA
20906 (20219)		0	XYPD	HB	Kilmarnock 400

CLASS 26 BRCW TYPE 2 Bo – Bo

Built: 1958 – 59 by the Birmingham Rly Carriage & Wagon Co., Smethwick.
Engine: Sulzer 6LDA28 of 870 kW (1160 hp) at 750rpm.
Main Generator: Crompton Parkinson CG391A1.
Traction Motors: Crompton Parkinson C171A1 (26/0), C171D3 (26/1).
Max. Tractive Effort: 187 kN (42000 lbf).
Cont. Tractive Effort: 133 kN (30000 lbf) at 11.25 mph.
Power At Rail: 671 kW (900 hp).
Brake Force: 35 t.
Design Speed: 80 mph.
Max. Speed: 60 mph.
Length over Buffers: 15.47 m.
Wheel Diameter: 1092 mm.
Weight: 75 t (26/0), 74.5 t (26/1).
RA: 5 or 6.
Train Brakes: Air & vacuum.
Multiple Working: Blue Star Coupling Code.
Communication Equipment: This class is in the process of being fitted with cab to shore radio-telephone.

Formerly numbered 5301 – 43 (except 26007 (5300) & 26028 (5320).

CLASS 26/0. RA6.

26001	s	G	RAJE	IS
26003	s	C	RAJE	IS
26005	s	C	RAJE	IS
26006	s	C	RAJE	IS

Eastfield

26007	s	G	RAJE	IS
26008		C	RAJE	IS

CLASS 26/1. RA5.

26025	C	RAJE	IS
26032	FR	RAJE	IS
26036	C	RAJE	IS
26037	FR	RAJE	IS
26043	C	RAJE	IS

CLASS 31 BRUSH TYPE 2 A1A – A1A

Built: 1957 – 62 by Brush Traction at Loughborough. 31102/5 – 7/10/25/34/44/418/50/61/544 retain two headcode lights. Others have roof-mounted headcode boxes. 31215 has headcode box one end only.
Engine: English Electric 12SVT of 1100 kW (1470 hp) at 850 rpm.
Main Generator: Brush TG160-48.
Traction Motors: Brush TM73-68.
Max. Tractive Effort: 160 kN (35900 lbf) (190 kN (42800 lbf)*).
Cont. Tractive Effort: 83 kN (18700 lbf) at 23.5 mph. (99 kN (22250 lbf) at 19.7 mph *.)
Power At Rail: 872 kW (1170 hp).
Brake Force: 49 t.
Design Speed: 90 (80*) mph.
Max. Speed: 60 mph (90 mph 31/4)
RA: 5 or 6.
Length over Buffers: 17.30 m.
Driving Wheel Diameter: 1092 mm.
Centre Wheel Diameter: 1003 mm.
Weight: 107 – 111 t.
ETH Index (Class 31/4): 66.
Train Brakes: Air & vacuum.
Multiple Working: Blue Star Coupling Code.
Communication Equipment: This class is in the process of being fitted with cab to shore radio-telephone.

Non standard liveries:

31101 is BR blue with a red band around the bottom of the cabs and a full height BR logo.
31413 is BR blue with yellow cabsides, a light blue stripe along the bottom of the body and a red band around the bottom of the cabs.

Formerly numbered 5518/20 – 5862 (not in order).

CLASS 31/1. Standard Design. RA5.

31101		0	IHFB	BS
31102		C	CEJB	BS
31105	*	C	CEJB	BS
31106	*	C	CEJB	BS
31107		C	CEJB	BS
31110		C	CEJB	BS
31112	*	C	CEJB	BS
31113		C	CEJB	BS
31116		C	IMJB	BS
31119		C	IMJB	BS
31125		C	CEJB	BS
31126		C	IMJB	BS
31128		FO	RDJW	BS
31130		FC	FCFN	TO
31132		FO	RDJW	BS
31134		C	IMJW	BS
31135		C	NKJS	SF
31142		C	IWJC	CD

31144	**C**	IWJC	CD	31224	**C**	NKJS	SF
31145	**C**	IMJW	BS	31229	**C**	RCJC	CD
31146 r	**C**	RDDJ	BS	31230 *	**FO**	RBJI	IM
31147 r	**C**	RDDJ	BS	31232	**C**	IWJC	CD
31149	**FR**	NKJW	SF	31233	**C**	RCJC	CD
31154	**C**	IWJC	CD	31234	**FO**	IMJW	BS
31155	**C**	RDJW	BS	31235	**C**	IWJC	CD
31158	**C**	RDDJ	BS	31237	**C**	RDJW	BS
31159	**C**	IWJC	CD	31238	**C**	RCJC	CD
31160	**F**	NKJW	SF	31242	**C**	RCJC	CD
31163	**C**	IWJC	CD	31247	**FR**	RBJW	IM
31164	**FO**	RDJW	BS	31248	**FO**	IMJW	BS
31165	**G**	NKJS	SF	31250	**C**	NKJS	SF
31166	**C**	RDDJ	BS	31252	**FO**	IMJW	BS
31171	**FO**	IMJW	BS	31255	**C**	RCJC	CD
31174	**C**	RDJB	BS	31263	**C**	NKJS	SF
31178	**C**	RDJB	BS	31268	**C**	NKJS	SF
31180	**FR**	NKJW	SF	31270	**FC**	RCJC	CD
31181	**C**	NKJS	SF	31271	**FA**	IHFB	BS
31184	**FO**	IEJW	IM	31272	**C**	RCJC	CD
31185	**C**	RDJB	BS	31273	**C**	RCJC	CD
31186	**C**	RDJS	SF	31275	**FC**	FCFN	TO
31187	**C**	RDJS	SF	31276	**FC**	IEJI	IM
31188	**C**	RCJC	CD	31282	**FR**	FIJW	IM
31190	**C**	NKJS	SF	31285	**C**	RCJC	CD
31191	**C**	NKJS	SF	31290	**C**	NKJW	SF
31196	**C**	NKJS	SF	31294	**FA**	IEJW	IM
31199	**FC**	FCFN	TO	31296	**FA**	FIJW	IM
31200	**FC**	FCFN	TO	31301	**FR**	RCJC	CD
31201	**FC**	FCFN	TO	31302	**FP**	FCFN	TO
31203	**C**	IWJC	CD	31304	**FC**	FCFN	TO
31205	**FR**	IEJW	IM	31306	**C**	RCJC	CD
31206	**C**	IWJC	CD	31308	**C**	RDJB	BS
31207	**C**	RCJC	CD	31312	**FC**	FCFN	TO
31209	**FA**	IMJW	BS	31317	**FO**	RDJW	BS
31215	**FO**	IEJW	IM	31319	**FC**	FCFN	TO
31217	**FC**	RCJC	CD	31324	**FC**	RCJC	CD
31219	**C**	RDJS	SF	31327	**FR**	NKJW	SF

Names:

31102 Cricklewood
31105 Bescot TMD
31106 The Blackcountryman
31107 John H Carless VC
31116 RAIL 1981 – 1991
31130 Calder Hall Power Station
31146 Brush Veteran
31165 Stratford Major Depot

CLASS 31/4. Equipped with Train Heating. RA6.

31403			IHFB	BS	
31405		**M**	CEJB	BS	Mappa Mundi
31407	(31507)	**M**	IHFB	BS	
31408			RCKC	CD	
31410		**RR**	RCKC	CD	Granada Telethon
31411	(31511)	**D**	RCKC	CD	

31413					Severn Valley Railway
31415			CEJB	BS	
31417		**D**	IHRB	BS	
31418			RCKC	CD	
31420	(31172)	**M**	IHRB	BS	
31421	(31140)	**RR**	RCKC	CD	
31422	(31522)	**M**	IHRB	BS	
31423	(31197)	**M**	IHRB	BS	Jerome K. Jerome
31427	(31194)		RCKC	CD	
31432	(31153)		RCKC	CD	
31434	(31258)		IHRB	BS	
31435	(31179)	**C**	IHFB	BS	
31438	(31139)		RCKC	CD	
31439	(31239)	**RR**	RCKC	CD	North Yorkshire Moors Railway
31442	(31251)		RCKC	CD	
31450	(31133)		IXXS	BS (U)	
31455	(31555)	**RR**	RCKC	CD	Our Eli
31457	(31169)	**D**	IHRB	BS	
31459	(31256)		IHFB	BS	
31460	(31266)		CEJB	BS	
31461	(31129)	**D**	IHFB	BS	
31462	(31315)	**D**	CEJB	BS	
31466	(31115)	**C**	IHFB	BS	
31467	(31216)		CEJB	BS	

CLASS 31/5. Dedicated for Civil Engineer's Department Use. Train Heating Equipment isolated. RA6.

31512	(31412)	**C**	IWJB	BS	
31514	(31414)	**C**	IWJB	BS	
31516	(31416)	**C**	IWJB	BS	
31519	(31419)	**C**	IWJB	BS	
31524	(31424)	**C**	IWJB	BS	
31526	(31426)	**C**	IWJB	BS	
31530	(31430)	**C**	IWJB	BS	Sister Dora
31531	(31431)	**C**	IEJI	IM	
31533	(31433)	**C**	IWJB	BS	
31537	(31437)	**C**	IWJB	BS	
31541	(31441)	**C**	IEJI	IM	
31544	(31444)	**C**	IEJI	IM	Keighley and Worth Valley Railway
31545	(31445)	**C**	IWJB	BS	
31546	(31446)	**C**	IWJB	BS	
31547	(31447)	**C**	IEJI	IM	
31548	(31448)	**C**	IWJB	BS	
31549	(31449)	**C**	IEJI	IM	
31551	(31451)	**C**	IWJB	BS	
31552	(31452)	**C**	IEJI	IM	
31553	(31453)	**C**	IEJI	IM	
31554	(31454)	**C**	IWJB	BS	
31556	(31456)	**C**	IEJI	IM	
31558	(31458)	**C**	IEJI	IM	
31563	(31463)	**C**	RBJI	IM	

31565 (31465)	**C**	RDJB	BS	
31568 (31468)	**C**	RDJB	BS	The Enginemen's Fund
31569 (31469)	**C**	RDJB	BS	

CLASS 33 BRCW TYPE 3 Bo – Bo

Built: 1960 – 62 by the Birmingham Railway Carriage & Wagon Company, Smethwick.
Engine: Sulzer 8LDA28 of 1160 kW (1550 hp) at 750 rpm.
Main Generator: Crompton Parkinson CG391B1.
Traction Motors: Crompton Parkinson C171C2.
Max. Tractive Effort: 200 kN (45000 lbf).
Cont. Tractive Effort: 116 kN (26000 lbf) at 17.5 mph.
Power At Rail: 906 kW (1215 hp).
Brake Force: 35 t.
Design Speed: 85 mph.
Max. Speed: 60 mph.
Train Heating: Electric (y isolated).
Length over Buffers: 15.47 m.
Wheel Diameter: 1092 mm.
Weight: 77.5 t (78.5 t Class 33/1).
RA: 6.
ETH Index: 48.
Train Brakes: Air & vacuum.
Multiple Working: Blue Star Coupling Code.
Communication Equipment: This class is in the process of being fitted with cab to shore radio-telephone.

Formerly numbered in series 6500 – 97 but not in order.

Class 33/0. Standard Design.

33002	y	**C**	NKJM	EH	Sea King
33008	y	**G**	NKJE	EH	Eastleigh
33012	e		NKJR	SL	
33019	e	**C**	NKJM	EH	Griffon
33020	e		NKJR	SL	
33021	e	**FA**	NKJR	SL	
33023	e		NKJR	SL	
33025	e	**C**	NKJE	EH	Sultan
33026	e	**C**	NKJM	EH	Seafire
33029	e		NKJR	SL	
33030	e	**N**	NKJE	EH	
33033	e	**FA**	NKJR	SL	
33035	y	**N**	NKJM	EH	
33040	e		NKJR	SL	
33042	ys	**FA**	NKJR	SL	
33046	y	**C**	NKJM	EH	Merlin
33047	ys	**C**	NKJM	EH	Spitfire
33048	es		NKJR	SL	
33050	e	**FA**	NKJR	SL	Isle of Grain
33051	e	**C**	NKJE	EH	Shakespeare Cliff
33052	e		NKJR	SL	Ashford
33053	e	**FA**	NKJR	SL	
33057	ys	**C**	NKJM	EH	Seagull
33063	ys	**FA**	NKJR	SL	
33064	e	**FA**	NKJR	SL	
33065	e	**C**	NKJM	EH	Sealion

Class 33/1. Fitted with Buckeye Couplings & SR Multiple Working Equipment for use with SR EMUs, TC stock & class 73.

Also fitted with flashing light adaptor for use on Weymouth Quay line.

33101	e	**D**	NKFE	EH	
33103	e	**C**	NKJE	EH	
33108	e	**C**	NKJE	EH	
33109	e	**D**	NKFE	EH	
33114	e	**N**	NWXB	EH	Ashford 150
33116	e	**D**	NKFE	EH	
33117	e		NKJR	SL	
33118	e	**C**	NKJE	EH	

Class 33/2. Built to Former Loading Gauge of Hastings Line.

33201	es	**C**	NKJM	SL	
33202	ys	**C**	NKJM	SL	The Burma Star
33204	es	**FD**	MDIB	SL	
33206	es	**FD**	MDIB	SL	
33207	ys	**FA**	MDIB	SL	Earl Mountbatten of Burma
33208	es	**C**	NKJM	SL	
33211	es	**FD**	MDIB	SL	

CLASS 37 ENGLISH ELECTRIC TYPE 3 Co – Co

Built: 1960 – 5 by English Electric Company at Vulcan Foundry, Newton le Willows or Robert Stephenson & Hawthorn, Darlington. 37003 – 116/350/1/9 with the exception of 37019*/031/047/053/065*/072*/073/074/075*/100* (* one end only) retain box-type route indicators, the remainder having central headcode panels/marker lamps.
Engine: English Electric 12CSVT of 1300 kW (1750 hp) at 850 rpm.
Main Generator: English Electric 822/10G.
Traction Motors: English Electric 538/A.
Max. Tractive Effort: 245 kN (55500 lbf).
Cont. Tractive Effort: 156 kN (35000 lbf) at 13.6 mph.
Power At Rail: 932 kW (1250 hp).
Length over Buffers: 18.75 m.
Brake Force: 50 t.
Wheel Diameter: 1092 mm.
Design Speed: 90 mph.
Weight: 103 – 108 t.
Max. Speed: 80 mph.
RA: 5 or 7.
Train Heating: Electric (Class 37/4 only). **ETH Index:** 38
Train Brakes: Air & vacuum.
Multiple Working: Blue Star Coupling Code.
Communication Equipment: This class is in the process of being fitted with cab to shore radio-telephone.
Formerly numbered 6600 – 8, 6700 – 6999 (not in order). 37271 – 4 are the second locos to carry these numbers. They were renumbered to avoid confusion with Class 37/3 locos.

Class 37/0. Unrefurbished Locos. Technical details as above. RA5.

37003	+	**C**	IEJI	IM
37004		**FM**	RAJV	IS
37009	+	**FD**	MDTT	TI

37010			**C**	IGJK	CF	
37012			**C**	IGJK	CF	
37013		+	**F**	MDTT	TI	
37015		+	**FD**	MDTT	TI	
37019		+	**FD**	MDTT	TI	
37023			**C**	NKJS	SF	Stratford
37025			**C**	RAJV	IS	
37026	(37320)	+	**FD**	MDTT	TI	Shapfell
37029		+	**FD**	MDYX	TI (U)	
37031		+	**FD**	MDTT	TI	
37032	(37353)	+	**FR**	MDYX	TI (U)	
37035			**C**	IGJK	CF	
37037	(37321)		**FM**	FMAK	CF	
37038			**C**	IGJK	CF	
37040			**FM**	FMAK	CF	
37042		+	**FM**	FMAK	CF	
37043	(37354)		**C**	RAJV	IS	
37045	(37355)	+	**F**	MDTT	TI	
37046			**C**	IGJK	CF	
37047		+	**FD**	MDTT	TI	
37048			**FM**	RAJV	IS	
37049			**C**	RBJI	IM	Imperial
37051			**FM**	RAJV	IS	
37053		+	**FD**	MDTT	TI	
37054			**C**	IGJK	CF	
37055		+	**FD**	MDTT	TI	
37057		+	**BR**	MDTT	TI	
37058		+	**C**	IEJI	IM	
37059		+	**FD**	IISA	IS	Port of Tilbury
37063		+	**FD**	MDTT	TI	
37065		+	**FD**	MDTT	TI	
37066		+	**C**	FIJI	IM	
37068	(37356)	+	**FD**	MDTT	TI	Grainflow
37069		+	**C**	RAJV	IS	
37070			**FD**	MDYX	TI	
37071		+	**C**	FIJW	IM	
37072		+	**D**	FPEK	CF	
37073		+	**FD**	MDTT	TI	Fort William/An Gearasdan
37074		+	**FD**	MDTT	TI	
37075		+	**F**	MDTT	TI	
37077			**FM**	FMAK	CF	
37078		+	**FM**	FMAK	CF	
37079	(37357)	+	**FD**	MDTT	TI	Medite
37080			**FP**	FPAG	IM	
37083		+	**C**	FIJI	IM	
37087			**C**	RAJV	IS	
37088	(37323)		**D**	RAJV	IS	Clydesdale
37092			**C**	IGJK	CF	
37095		+	**C**	IEJI	IM	
37097			**C**	IGJK	CF	
37098		+	**C**	IGJK	CF	
37099	(37324)		**FM**	FMAK	CF	Clydebridge

37100		+	**FM**	FPAG	IM	
37101		+	**FD**	MDTT	TI	
37104			**C**	IEJI	IM	
37106		+	**FM**	RAJV	IS	
37107		+	**FD**	MDTT	TI	
37108	(37325)	+	**F**	MDTT	TI	
37109			**FM**	FMAK	CF	
37110		+	**FD**	MDTT	TI	
37111	(37326)		**FM**	FPAG	IM	Glengarnock
37113		+	**FD**	IISA	IS	Radio Highland
37114		+	**FD**	MDTT	TI	Dunrobin Castle
37116		+	**BR**	MDTT	TI	
37128		+	**BR**	MDWT	TI	
37131		+	**FD**	MDTT	TI	
37133			**C**	IISA	IS	
37137	(37312)		**FM**	FMXX	CF	Clyde Iron
37138			**FM**	FMAK	CF	
37139		+	**FC**	FCPM	ML	
37140			**C**	NKJS	SF	
37141			**C**	REJK	CF	
37142			**C**	REJK	CF	
37144		r	**FA**	FPAG	IM	
37146			**C**	REJK	CF	
37152	(37310)		**I**	IISA	IS	
37153			**C**	RAJV	IS	
37154		+	**FD**	MDTT	TI	Johnson Stevens Agencies
37156	(37311)	r	**C**	RAJV	IS	British Steel Hunterston
37158			**C**	REJK	CF	
37162		+	**D**	FPFR	IM	
37165	(37374)	+	**C**	RAJV	IS	
37167		+	**FC**	RAJV	IS	
37170		r	**C**	IISA	IS	
37174			**C**	REJK	CF	
37175			**C**	IISA	IS	
37178		+	**FD**	MDTT	TI	
37184			**FP**	RAJV	IS	
37185		+	**FD**	MDTT	TI	
37188			**FP**	FPAG	IM	
37190	(37314)		**FM**	RFJX	CF (U)	
37191			**C**	REJK	CF	
37194		+	**FD**	IISA	IS	British International Freight Association
37196			**C**	RAJV	IS	
37197		+	**C**	REJK	CF	
37198		+	**C**	NKJE	EH	
37201			**FM**	RAJV	IS	
37202			**FM**	FPYI	IM	
37203			**FM**	FMAK	CF	
37207			**C**	REJK	CF	
37209			**BR**	MDYX	IS (U)	
37211			**FA**	FIJI	IM	
37212		+	**FC**	RAJV	IS	

37213		+	**FC**	FCBK	CF	
37214		+	**FA**	IISA	IS	
37215			**FP**	RFJX	CF	
37216		r +	**G**	RDJS	SF	Great Eastern
37217		+	**FC**	FIJI	IM	
37218		+	**FD**	MDTT	TI	
37219		r		NKJS	SF	
37220		+	**FP**	FPFR	IM	
37221			**I**	IISA	IS	
37222		+	**FC**	FCBK	CF	
37223		+	**FC**	FCBK	CF	
37225		+	**FD**	MDTT	TI	
37227		+	**FM**	FMXX	CF	
37229		+	**FC**	FCPM	ML	
37230		+	**C**	REJK	CF	
37232		r	**C**	RAJV	IS	The Institution of Railway Signal Engineers
37235		+	**F**	MDTT	TI	
37238		+	**FD**	MDTT	TI	
37239		+	**FC**	FPAG	IM	The Coal Merchants' Association of Scotland
37240		+	**C**	RAJV	IS	
37241			**FM**	FPEK	CF	
37242		+	**FD**	MDTT	TI	
37244		+	**FD**	MDTT	TI	
37245			**C**	NKJS	SF	
37248		+	**FM**	MDYX	TI (U)	
37250		+	**FM**	FMAK	CF	
37251		+	**I**	IISA	IS	The Northern Lights
37252			**FD**	MDYX	IS	
37254		+	**C**	REJK	CF	
37255		+	**FM**	RAJV	IS	
37258		+	**C**	REJK	CF	
37261		+	**FD**	MDTT	TI	Caithness
37262		+	**D**	IISA	IS	Dounreay
37263			**C**	REJK	CF	
37264			**C**	IGJK	CF	
37271	(37303)	+	**FD**	MDTT	TI	
37272	(37304)	+	**FD**	MDTT	TI	
37274	(37308)	+	**FC**	NKJE	EH	
37275		+	**FM**	RAJV	IS	
37278		+	**FC**	MDWT	TI	
37280		+	**FP**	FPEK	CF	
37285		+	**F**	IISA	IS	
37293		+	**FM**	FMAK	CF	
37294		+	**C**	RAJV	IS	
37298		+	**FD**	MDTT	TI	

Class 37/3. Unrefurbished locos fitted with regeared (CP7) bogies.
Details as Class 37/0 except:

Max. Tractive Effort: 250 kN (56180 lbf).
Cont. Tractive Effort: 184 kN (41250 lbf) at 11.4 mph.

37350	(37119)	+	**FP**	FPCI	IM	
37351	(37002)	+	**C**	RAJV	IS	
37358	(37091)		**F**	MDRT	TI	P & O Containers
37359	(37118)		**FP**	MDRT	TI	
37370	(37127)		**C**	NKJS	SF	
37371	(37147)	+	**FR**	FPEK	CF	
37372	(37159)		**C**	IGJK	CF	
37373	(37160)		**FR**	MDRT	TI	
37375	(37193)	+	**FC**	FCPM	ML	
37376	(37199)	+	**FC**	FCPM	ML	
37377	(37200)	+	**FR**	FPYI	IM	
37378	(37204)	+	**FD**	MDRT	TI	
37379	(37226)		**FR**	NKJE	EH	
37380	(37259)		**FC**	FCPM	ML	
37381	(37284)	+	**FM**	MDRT	TI	
37382	(37145)		**FP**	FPCI	IM	

Class 37/4. Refurbished locos fitted with train heating. Main generator replaced by alternator. Regeared (CP7) bogies. Details as class 37/0 except:

Main Alternator: Brush BA1005A.
Max. Tractive Effort: 256 kN (57440 lbf).
Cont. Tractive Effort: 184 kN (41250 lbf) at 11.4 mph.
Power At Rail: 935 kW (1254 hp).
All have twin fuel tanks.

37401	(37268)	r	**M**	MDRM	ML	Mary Queen of Scots
37402	(37274)	r	**M**	RAJV	IS	Oor Wullie
37403	(37307)	r	**FD**	MDRM	ML	Glendarroch
37404	(37286)	r	**M**	RAJV	IS	Ben Cruachan
37405	(37282)	r	**M**	MDRT	TI	Strathclyde Region
37406	(37295)	r	**M**	MDRM	ML	The Saltire Society
37407	(37305)	r	**M**	FPAG	IM	Loch Long
37408	(37289)		**BR**	FPAG	IM	Loch Rannoch
37409	(37270)	r	**M**	MDRM	ML	Loch Awe
37410	(37273)	r	**M**	MDRM	ML	Aluminium 100
37411	(37290)		**FD**	MDRL	LA	
37412	(37301)		**FD**	MDRL	LA	
37413	(37276)	r	**FD**	MDRL	LA	Loch Eil Outward Bound
37414	(37287)	r	**FA**	RCMC	CD	
37415	(37277)	r	**M**	MDRT	TI	
37416	(37302)	r	**M**	MDRT	TI	
37417	(37269)	r	**M**	MDRT	TI	Highland Region
37418	(37271)	r	**FP**	FPCI	IM	Pectinidae
37419	(37291)		**M**	MDRT	TI	
37420	(37297)	r	**M**	MDRT	TI	The Scottish Hosteller
37421	(37267)	r	**FP**	FPCI	IM	Strombidae
37422	(37266)	r	**FA**	FABI	IM	
37423	(37296)	r	**M**	MDRM	ML	Sir Murray Morrison 1873 – 1948 Pioneer of British Aluminium Industry
37424	(37279)	r	**M**	MDRM	ML	Isle of Mull
37425	(37292)	r	**FA**	FABI	IM	Sir Robert McAlpine/ Concrete Bob (opp. sides)

37426	(37299)	r	**M**	MDRT	TI	
37427	(37288)	r	**FA**	FALY	TE	Bont Y Bermo
37428	(37281)	r	**FP**	FPAG	IM	David Lloyd George
37429	(37300)	r	**FA**	RCMC	CD	Eisteddfod Genedlaethol
37430	(37265)	r	**M**	MDRM	ML	Cwmbrân
37431	(37272)	r	**M**	FPYI	IM	Bullidae

Class 37/5. Refurbished locos. Main generator replaced by alternator. Regeared (CP7) bogies. Details as class 37/4 except:

Max. Tractive Effort: 248 kN (55590 lbf).
All have twin fuel tanks.

37501	(37005)		**FM**	FIJI	IM	
37502	(37082)		**FM**	FPCI	IM	
37503	(37017)		**FM**	FPTY	TE	British Steel Shelton
37504	(37039)		**FM**	FPEK	CF	
37505	(37028)		**FP**	FPTY	TE	
37506	(37007)		**FM**	FMTY	TE	British Steel Skinningrove
37507	(37036)		**FM**	FPYX	IM	
37508	(37090)	s	**FM**	FMTY	TE	
37509	(37093)		**FM**	FALY	TE	
37510	(37112)		**I**	IISA	IS	
37511	(37103)		**FM**	FMTY	TE	Stockton Haulage
37512	(37022)		**FM**	FMTY	TE	Thornaby Demon
37513	(37056)		**FM**	FMTY	TE	
37514	(37115)	s	**FM**	FMTY	TE	
37515	(37064)	s	**FM**	FMTY	TE	
37516	(37086)	s	**FM**	FMTY	TE	
37517	(37018)	s	**FM**	FMYI	IM	
37518	(37076)		**FM**	FMTY	TE	
37519	(37027)		**FM**	FMYI	IM	
37520	(37041)		**FM**	FMAK	CF	
37521	(37117)		**FP**	FPEK	CF	
37667	(37151)	s	**FP**	FPEK	CF	
37668	(37257)	s	**FP**	FPEK	CF	
37669	(37129)		**FD**	MDRL	LA	
37670	(37182)		**FD**	MDRL	LA	
37671	(37247)		**FD**	MDRL	LA	Tre Pol and Pen
37672	(37189)	s	**FD**	MDRL	LA	Freight Transport Association
37673	(37132)		**FD**	MDRL	LA	
37674	(37169)		**FD**	MDRL	LA	
37675	(37164)	s	**FD**	MDRL	LA	William Cookworthy
37676	(37126)		**FA**	FABI	IM	
37677	(37121)		**FA**	FABI	IM	
37678	(37256)		**FA**	FABI	IM	
37679	(37123)		**FA**	FALY	TE	
37680	(37224)		**FA**	FABI	IM	
37682	(37236)		**FA**	FALY	TE	
37683	(37187)		**F**	FALY	TE	
37684	(37134)		**FA**	FABI	IM	Peak National Park
37685	(37234)		**FR**	FALY	TE	
37686	(37172)		**FA**	FABI	IM	

37687	(37181)		**FA**	FABI	IM	
37688	(37205)		**FA**	FABI	IM	Great Rocks
37689	(37195)	s	**FC**	FCBK	CF	
37690	(37171)		**FO**	FCPM	ML	
37691	(37179)	s	**FO**	FCPM	ML	
37692	(37122)	s	**FC**	FCPM	ML	
37693	(37210)	s	**FC**	FCPM	ML	Sir William Arrol
37694	(37192)	s	**FC**	FCPM	ML	The Lass O' Ballochmyle
37695	(37157)	s	**FC**	FCPM	ML	
37696	(37228)	s	**FC**	FCPM	ML	
37697	(37243)	s	**FC**	FCBK	CF	
37698	(37246)	s	**FC**	FCBK	CF	Coedbach
37699	(37253)		**FC**	FCBK	CF	

Class 37/7. Refurbished locos. Main generator replaced by alternator. Regeared (CP7) bogies. Ballast weights added.
Details as class 37/4 except:
Main Alternator: GEC G564AZ (37796 – 803) Brush BA1005A (others).
Max. Tractive Effort: 276 kN (62000 lbf).
Weight: 120 t. **RA:** 7.
All have twin fuel tanks.

37701	(37030)	s	**FC**	FCKK	CF	
37702	(37020)	s	**FC**	FCKK	CF	Taff Merthyr
37703	(37067)	s	**FC**	FCKK	CF	
37704	(37034)	s	**FC**	FCKK	CF	
37705	(37060)		**FP**	FPFR	IM	
37706	(37016)		**FP**	FPCI	IM	Conidae
37707	(37001)		**FP**	FPCI	IM	
37708	(37089)		**FP**	FPCI	IM	
37709	(37014)		**FP**	FPFR	IM	
37710	(37044)		**FM**	FPYI	IM	
37711	(37085)		**FM**	FMHK	CF	Tremorfa Steel Works
37712	(37102)		**F**	FMTY	TE	Teesside Steelmaster
37713	(37052)		**FM**	FMTY	TE	British Steel Workington
37714	(37024)		**FM**	FMTY	TE	Thornaby TMD
37715	(37021)		**FM**	FMTY	TE	
37716	(37094)		**FM**	FMTY	TE	British Steel Corby
37717	(37050)		**FM**	FMTY	TE	Stainless Pioneer
37718	(37084)		**FM**	FMTY	TE	Hartlepool Pipe Mill
37719	(37033)		**FP**	FPCI	IM	
37796	(37105)	s	**FC**	FCKK	CF	
37797	(37081)	s	**FC**	FCKK	CF	
37798	(37006)	s	**FC**	FCKK	CF	
37799	(37061)	s	**FC**	FCKK	CF	Sir Dyfed/County of Dyfed
37800	(37143)	s	**FC**	FCKK	CF	Glo Cymru
37801	(37173)	s	**FC**	FCKK	CF	Aberthaw/Aberddawan
37802	(37163)	s	**FC**	FCKK	CF	
37803	(37208)	s	**FC**	FCKK	CF	
37883	(37176)		**FM**	FMTY	TE	
37884	(37183)		**F**	FMTY	TE	Gartcosh
37885	(37177)		**FM**	FMTY	TE	
37886	(37180)		**FM**	FMHK	CF	

37887	(37120)	s	**FC**	FCKK	CF	Caerphilly Castle Castell Caerffili (opp. sides)
37888	(37135)		**FP**	FPFR	IM	Petrolea
37889	(37233)		**FC**	FCKK	CF	
37890	(37168)		**FP**	FPFR	IM	
37891	(37166)		**FP**	FPCI	IM	
37892	(37149)		**FP**	FPFR	IM	Ripple Lane
37893	(37237)		**FP**	FPFR	IM	
37894	(37124)	s	**FC**	FCKK	CF	
37895	(37283)	s	**FC**	FCKK	CF	
37896	(37231)	s	**FC**	FCKK	CF	
37897	(37155)	s	**FC**	FCKK	CF	
37898	(37186)	s	**FC**	FCKK	CF	
37899	(37161)	s	**FC**	FCKK	CF	County of West Glamorgan/ Sir Gorllewin Morgannwg

Class 37/9. Refurbished Locos. Fitted with manufacturers prototype power units and ballast weights. Main generator replaced by alternator. Details as class 37/0 except:
Engine: Mirrlees MB275T of 1340 kW (1800 hp) at 1000 rpm (37901 – 4), Ruston RK270T of 1340 kW (1800 hp) at 900 rpm (37905 – 6).
Main Alternator: Brush BA1005A (GEC G564, 37905/6).
Max. Tractive Effort: 279 kN (62680 lbf).
Cont. Tractive Effort: 184 kN (41250 lbf) at 11.4 mph.
Weight: 120 t. **RA:** 7.
All have twin fuel tanks.

37901	(37150)		**FM**	FMHK	CF	Mirrlees Pioneer
37902	(37148)		**FM**	FMXX	CF (U)	
37903	(37249)		**FM**	FMHK	CF	
37904	(37125)		**FM**	FMHK	CF	
37905	(37136)	s	**FM**	FMHK	CF	Vulcan Enterprise
37906	(37206)	s	**FM**	FMHK	CF	

CLASS 43 HST POWER CAR Bo – Bo

Built: 1976 – 82 by BREL Crewe Works. Formerly numbered as coaching stock but now classified as locomotives. Include luggage compartment.
Engine: Paxman Valenta 12RP200L of 1680 kW (2250 hp) at 1500 rpm. (Mirrlees MB190 of 1680 kW (2250 hp)*.
Main Alternator: Brush BA1001B.
Traction Motors: Brush TMH68 – 46 or GEC G417AZ (43124 – 151/180). Frame mounted.
Max. Tractive Effort: 80 kN (17980 lbf).
Cont. Tractive Effort: 46 kN (10340 lbf) at 64.5 mph.
Power At Rail: 1320 kW (1770 hp).
Brake Force:
Weight: 70 t.
Max. Speed: 125 mph.
Train Brakes: Air.
ETH: Non standard 3-phase system.
Length over Buffers: 17.79 m.
Wheel Diameter: 1020 mm.
RA: 5.
Multiple Working: With one other similar vehicle.
Communication Equipment: All equipped with driver – guard telephone and cab to shore radio-telephone.

§ Modified to be able to remotely control a class 91 locomotive and to be remotely controlled by a class 91 locomotive.

43002	I	IWRP	PM	Top of the Pops
43003	I	IWRP	PM	
43004	I	IWRP	PM	Swan Hunter
43005	I	IWRP	PM	
43006	I	IWRP	LA	
43007	I	IWRP	LA	
43008	I	IWRP	LA	
43009	I	IWRP	PM	
43010	I	IWRP	PM	TSW Today
43011	I	IWRP	PM	Reader 125
43012	I	IWRP	PM	
43013 §	I	ICCS	EC	
43014 §	I	ICCS	EC	
43015	I	IWRP	PM	
43016	I	IWRP	PM	Gwyl Gerddi Cymru 1992 Garden Festival Wales 1992
43017	I	IWRP	PM	
43018	I	IWRP	PM	
43019	I	IWRP	PM	Dinas Abertawe/City of Swansea
43020	I	IWRP	LA	
43021	I	IWRP	LA	
43022	I	IWRP	LA	
43023	I	IWRP	LA	County of Cornwall
43024	I	IWRP	LA	
43025	I	IWRP	LA	
43026	I	IWRP	LA	City of Westminster
43027	I	IWRP	LA	
43028	I	IWRP	LA	
43029	I	IWRP	LA	
43030	I	IWRP	PM	
43031	I	IWRP	PM	
43032	I	IWRP	PM	The Royal Regiment of Wales
43033	I	IWRP	PM	
43034	I	IWRP	PM	
43035	I	IWRP	PM	
43036	I	IWRP	PM	
43037	I	IWRP	PM	
43038	I	IECP	NL	National Railway Museum The First Ten Years 1975 – 1985
43039	I	IECP	NL	
43040	I	IWRP	PM	Granite City
43041	I	IWRP	PM	City of Discovery
43042	I	IWCP	LA	
43043	I	IMLP	NL	
43044	I	IMLP	NL	
43045	I	IMLP	NL	The Grammar School Doncaster AD 1350
43046	I	IMLP	NL	
43047	I	IMLP	NL	Rotherham Enterprise
43048	I	IMLP	NL	

43049		I	IMLP	NL	Neville Hill
43050		I	IMLP	NL	
43051		I	IMLP	NL	The Duke and Duchess of York
43052		I	IMLP	NL	City of Peterborough
43053		I	IMLP	NL	County of Humberside
43054		I	IMLP	NL	
43055		I	IMLP	NL	
43056		I	IMLP	NL	
43057		I	IMLP	NL	Bounds Green
43058		I	IMLP	NL	
43059		I	IMLP	NL	
43060		I	IMLP	NL	County of Leicestershire
43061		I	IMLP	NL	City of Lincoln
43062		I	ICCS	EC	
43063		I	ICCS	EC	
43064		I	IMLP	NL	City of York
43065	§	I	ICCS	EC	
43066		I	IMLP	NL	
43067	§	I	ICCS	EC	
43068	§	I	ICCS	EC	
43069		I	ICCS	EC	
43070		I	ICCS	EC	
43071		I	ICCS	EC	
43072		I	IMLP	NL	
43073		I	IMLP	NL	
43074		I	IMLP	NL	
43075		I	IMLP	NL	
43076		I	IMLP	NL	BBC East Midlands Today
43077		I	IMLP	NL	County of Nottingham
43078		I	ICCS	EC	
43079		I	ICCS	EC	
43080	§	I	ICCS	EC	
43081		I	IMLP	NL	
43082		I	IMLP	NL	
43083		I	IMLP	NL	
43084	§	I	ICCS	EC	County of Derbyshire
43085		I	IMLP	NL	City of Bradford
43086		I	ICCP	PM	
43087		I	ICCP	PM	
43088		I	ICCP	PM	
43089		I	IWRP	LA	
43090		I	ICCS	EC	
43091		I	ICCS	EC	
43092		I	ICCS	EC	
43093		I	ICCS	EC	York Festival '88
43094		I	ICCS	EC	
43095		I	IECP	NL	
43096		I	IECP	NL	The Queens Own Hussars
43097		I	ICCS	EC	
43098		I	ICCS	EC	
43099		I	ICCS	EC	
43100		I	ICCS	EC	Craigentinny

43101		I	IWRP	LA	
43102		I	IWRP	LA	
43103		I	IWRP	LA	John Wesley
43104		I	IECP	NL	
43105		I	IECP	NL	
43106		I	IECP	NL	Songs of Praise
43107		I	IECP	NL	
43108		I	IECP	NL	
43109		I	IECP	NL	Yorkshire Evening Press
43110		I	IECP	NL	Darlington
43111		I	IECP	NL	
43112		I	IECP	NL	
43113		I	IECP	NL	
43114		I	IECP	NL	National Garden Festival Gateshead 1990
43115		I	IECP	NL	Yorkshire Cricket Academy
43116		I	IECP	NL	City of Kingston Upon Hull
43117		I	IECP	NL	
43118		I	IECP	NL	Charles Wesley
43119		I	IECP	NL	
43120		I	IECP	NL	
43121		I	IECP	NL	West Yorkshire Metropolitan County
43122		I	IWRP	LA	South Yorkshire Metropolitan County
43123	§	I	ICCS	EC	
43124		I	ICCP	PM	
43125		I	IWRP	PM	
43126		I	IWRP	PM	City of Bristol
43127		I	IWRP	PM	
43128		I	IWRP	PM	
43129		I	IWRP	PM	
43130		I	ICCP	PM	Sulis Minerva
43131		I	IWRP	PM	
43132		I	ICCP	PM	Worshipful Company of Carmen
43133		I	IWRP	PM	
43134		I	IWRP	PM	County of Somerset
43135		I	IWRP	PM	
43136		I	IWRP	PM	
43137		I	IWRP	PM	
43138		I	ICCP	PM	
43139		I	IWRP	PM	
43140		I	IWRP	OO	
43141		I	IWCP	OO	
43142		I	IWCP	OO	
43143		I	IWRP	LA	
43144		I	IWCP	OO	
43145		I	IWCP	OO	
43146		I	IWCP	OO	
43147		I	IWCP	OO	The Red Cross
43148		I	IWRP	OO	
43149		I	ICCP	PM	B.B.C. Wales Today
43150		I	ICCP	PM	Bristol Evening Post
43151		I	IWRP	PM	
43152		I	IWRP	LA	St. Peters School York AD 627

43153		I	ICCP	LA	University of Durham
43154		I	ICCP	LA	
43155		I	ICCP	LA	B.B.C. Look North
43156		I	ICCP	LA	
43157		I	ICCP	LA	Yorkshire Evening Post
43158		I	ICCP	LA	
43159		I	ICCP	LA	
43160		I	ICCP	LA	Storm Force
43161		I	ICCP	LA	Reading Evening Post
43162		I	ICCP	LA	Borough of Stevenage
43163		I	IWRP	LA	
43164		I	IWRP	LA	
43165		I	IWRP	LA	
43166		I	IWRP	LA	
43167	*	I	IWRP	PM	
43168	*	I	IWRP	PM	
43169	*	I	ICCP	PM	The National Trust
43170	*	I	ICCP	PM	
43171		I	IWRP	LA	
43172		I	IWRP	LA	
43173		I	IWRP	LA	
43174		I	IWRP	LA	
43175		I	IWRP	LA	
43176		I	IWRP	LA	
43177		I	IWRP	LA	
43178		I	IWRP	LA	
43179		I	IWRP	LA	Pride of Laira
43180		I	ICCP	PM	
43181		I	IWRP	LA	
43182		I	IWRP	LA	
43183		I	IWRP	LA	
43184		I	IWRP	LA	
43185		I	IWRP	LA	Great Western
43186		I	IWRP	LA	Sir Francis Drake
43187		I	IWRP	LA	
43188		I	IWRP	LA	City of Plymouth
43189		I	IWRP	LA	
43190		I	IWRP	LA	
43191		I	IWRP	LA	Seahawk
43192		I	IWRP	LA	City of Truro
43193		I	IWRP	LA	
43194		I	ICCP	LA	
43195		I	ICCP	LA	
43196		I	ICCP	LA	The Newspaper Society Founded 1836
43197		I	ICCP	LA	
43198		I	ICCP	LA	

CLASS 47 BRUSH TYPE 4 Co–Co

Built: 1963–67 by Brush Traction, Loughborough or BR Crewe Works.
Engine: Sulzer 12LDA28C of 1920 kW (2580 hp) at 750 rpm.
Main Generator: Brush TG160-60 Mk2, TG 160-60 Mk4 or TM172-50 Mk1.

Traction Motors: Brush TM64-68 Mk1 or Mk1A (axle hung).
Max. Tractive Effort: 267 kN (60000 lbf).(245 kN (55000 lbf) 47401 – 18)
Cont. Tractive Effort: 133 kN (30000 lbf) at 26 mph.
Power At Rail: 1550 kW (2080 hp).
Brake Force: 61 t.
Design Speed: 95 mph.
Max. Speed: various.
Length over Buffers: 19.38 m.
Wheel Diameter: 1143 mm.
Weight: 120.5 – 125 t.
RA: 6 or 7.
Train Brakes: Air & vacuum.
Multiple Working: Not equipped (Blue Star Coupling Code*).
ETH Index (47/4 & 47/7): 66 (75§).
Communication Equipment: Cab to shore radio-telephone.

a Vacuum brake isolated.

Formerly numbered 1100 – 11, 1500 – 1999 not in order. 47299 was also previously 47216. 47300 was previously 47468.

Class 47/0. Built with train heating boiler. RA6. Max Speed 75 mph.

47004		**FA**	IGJW	OC	
47016		**FO**	RCLC	CD	
47019		**FO**	IGJW	OC	
47033	a+	**FD**	MDDT	TI	
47049		**FD**	MDAT	TI	
47050	a+	**FD**	MDCT	TI	
47051	a+	**FD**	MDCT	TI	
47052		**FD**	MDAT	TI	
47053	a+	**FD**	MDDT	TI	Cory Brothers 1842-1992
47060	a	**FD**	MDAT	TI	Halewood Silver Jubilee 1988
47063		**FA**	MDYX	TI (U)	
47079		**FD**	MDWT	TI	
47085	+	**F**	MDDT	TI	
47095	+	**FD**	MDYX	TI (U)	
47105			IGJW	OC	
47108			IGJW	OC	
47114		**FA**	MDAT	TI	
47121			IGJW	OC	
47125	+	**FD**	MDDT	TI	
47142		**FR**	MDWT	TI	The Sapper
47144		**FD**	MDAT	TI	
47145			MDWT	TI	
47146			MDAT	TI	
47147		**FD**	MDAT	TI	
47150		**FD**	MDAT	TI	
47152		**FD**	MDAT	TI	
47156		**FD**	MDAT	TI	
47157		**F**	MDWT	TI	
47186	a+	**FD**	MDDT	TI	
47187		**FD**	MDAT	TI	
47188		**FD**	MDAT	TI	
47190		**FP**	MDYX	TI (U)	
47193		**FP**	FPCI	IM	Lucinidae
47194	+	**FD**	MDDT	TI	
47196		**FP**	MDWT	TI	

47197		**FP**	FPCI	IM	
47200	a+	**FD**	MDCT	TI	
47201		**FD**	MDAT	TI	
47204		**FD**	MDAT	TI	
47205		**FD**	MDAT	TI	
47206		**FD**	MDAT	TI	
47207		**FD**	MDWT	TI	Bulmers of Hereford
47209	a+	**FD**	MDDT	TI	Herbert Austin
47210		**FA**	MDAT	TI	Blue Circle Cement
47211	+	**FD**	MDDT	TI	
47212	+	**FP**	FPYI	IM	
47213	+	**FD**	MDDT	TI	
47214		**FD**	MDWT	TI	Distillers MG
47217	+	**FD**	MDDT	TI	
47218	+	**FD**	MDDT	TI	United Transport Europe
47219	a+	**FD**	MDCT	TI	Arnold Kunzler
47220		**FO**	MDYX	TI (U)	
47221	+	**FP**	FPCI	IM	
47222	a+	**FD**	MDCT	TI	
47223	+	**FP**	FPCI	IM	British Petroleum
47224	+	**FP**	FPCI	IM	Arcidae
47225		**FD**	MDAT	TI	
47226	+	**FD**	MDDT	TI	
47227		**FR**	MDYX	TI (U)	
47228	+	**FD**	MDDT	TI	
47229	a+	**FD**	MDDT	TI	
47231		**FD**	MDWT	TI	The Silcock Express
47234	+	**FD**	MDDT	TI	
47236	a+	**FD**	MDCT	TI	
47237	a+	**FD**	MDCT	TI	
47238		**FD**	MDAT	TI	Bescot Yard
47241	a	**FD**	MDAT	TI	
47245	+	**FD**	MDDT	TI	
47249		**FR**	MDWT	TI	
47256		**FD**	MDWT	TI	
47258		**FD**	MDAT	TI	
47270			MDWT	TI	
47276	+	**FP**	FPCI	IM	
47277		**FP**	FPCI	IM	
47278		**FP**	FPYX	IM (U)	Vasidae
47279		**FD**	MDAT	TI	
47280	a+	**FD**	MDCT	TI	Pedigree
47281		**FD**	MDAT	TI	
47283		**FD**	MDWT	TI	Johnnie Walker
47284	+	**FD**	MDDT	TI	
47285	a+	**FD**	MDCT	TI	
47286	a+	**F**	MDDT	TI	
47287		**FD**	MDAT	TI	
47288		**FD**	MDAT	TI	
47289		**FD**	MDAT	TI	
47290	+	**FD**	MDDT	TI	
47291	a+	**FD**	MDDT	TI	The Port of Felixstowe

47292		**FD**	MDAT	TI	
47293		**FD**	MDAT	TI	
47294	+	**FP**	FPCI	IM	
47295	+	**FP**	FPFR	IM	
47296		**FD**	MDAT	TI	
47297	a+	**FD**	MDDT	TI	
47298		**FD**	MDAT	TI	Pegasus
47299	+	**FD**	MDDT	TI	

Class 47/3. Built without Train Heat. (except 47300). RA6. Max Speed 75 mph. All equipped with slow speed control.

47300		**C**	CEJC	CD	
47301		**FR**	MDAT	TI	
47302	a	**FR**	MDAT	TI	
47303	a	**F**	MDAT	TI	
47304	+	**FD**	MDDT	TI	
47305		**FP**	MDAT	TI	
47306	a+	**FD**	MDCT	TI	
47307	+	**FD**	MDDT	TI	
47308		**F**	MDWT	TI	
47309		**FD**	MDAT	TI	The Halewood Transmission
47310	a+	**FD**	MDCT	TI	Henry Ford
47312		**FD**	MDAT	TI	
47313	a+	**FD**	MDCT	TI	
47314	a+	**FD**	MDDT	TI	Transmark
47315		**C**	IGJO	OC	
47316	a+	**FD**	MDCT	TI	
47317		**FD**	MDWT	TI	Willesden Yard
47318		**FO**	IWJD	CD	
47319	+	**FP**	FCCI	IM	Norsk Hydro
47320		**FO**	MDYX	TI (U)	
47321		**FD**	MDWT	TI	
47322		**FR**	MDWT	TI	
47323	a+	**FD**	MDCT	TI	
47325		**FO**	MDYX	TI (U)	
47326	a+	**FD**	MDCT	TI	
47327		**FO**	FPYX	IM (U)	
47328	+	**FA**	MDDT	TI	
47329		**C**	IWJD	CD	
47330	+	**FD**	MDDT	TI	Amlwch Freighter/ Trên Nwyddau Amlwch (opp. sides)
47331		**C**	IEJW	IM	
47332		**C**	CEJC	CD	
47333		**C**	CEJC	CD	Civil Link
47334		**C**	NKJO	OC	
47335		**FD**	MDAT	TI	
47336	+	**FP**	FPYX	IM (U)	
47337		**FO**	MDAT	TI	
47338	a+	**FD**	MDDT	TI	Warrington Yard
47339		**FD**	MDAT	TI	
47340		**C**	RCLC	CD	
47341		**C**	CEJC	CD	

Trainload Construction

Trainload Coal

Trainload Metals

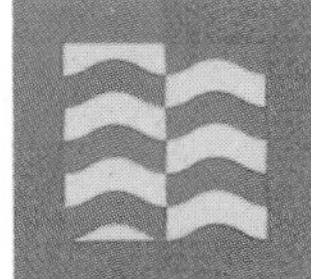

Trainload Petroleum

Railfreight Distribution

Trainload Freight and Railfreight Distribution sub-sector markings as used on omotives.

Class 03 No. 03079 at Sandown on 31st July 1992. *John Augustson*

▲ Departmental liveried Class 08 No. 08911 at Carlisle on 15th August 19
Kevin Con.

▼ Class 09 No. 09007 at Bournemouth Depot on 15th September 1992
Norman Barring.

Class 20s Nos. 20016 and 20081 both in plain blue livery leave Monks siding 25th August 1992 with a Parkside – Fiddlers Ferry merry-go-round (m.g.r.) al train. *Paul Greenland*

Class 20 No. 20901 'NANCY' leads the Chipmans weedkiller train through stleigh on 11th August 1992. *Brian Denton*

▲ BR green Class 26 No. 26001 'Eastfield' stands replendant outside Eastfi
TMD on 21st August 1992. *Colin J Marsc*

▼ Class 31 No. 31410 'Granada Telethon' in the new Regional Railways liv
is seen heading a fund raising train formed of the Manchester Pullman stc
into Morecambe on 19th July 1992. *Vincent Eastwo*

Class 31 No. 31164 in old Railfreight livery passes Stonybeck (north of Penrith) with a southbound engineers train on 5th July 1991.
Kevin Conkey

▲ Class 33 No. 33114 'Ashford 150' the only member of the class in Netwo
SouthEast livery leaves Basingstoke with the 11.15 Waterloo – Exeter on
August 1992. *John Augusts*

▼ Civil Engineers liveried class 33 No. 33202 'The Burma Star' is seen stabl
at Woking on 30th August 1992. *G W Morris*

Class 37s Nos. 37185 and 37107 both in Railfreight Distribution livery leave Felixstowe North Freightliner terminal on 14th May 1992 with a train for Leeds.
Michael J Collins

▲ The last Class 37/4 in revised blue livery, 37408 'Loch Rannoch' Inverness on 25th September 1992. *John Augusts*

▼ The 09.50 Glasgow Central – Penzance HST at Hest Bank on 16th May 1 with power cars 43013 and 43067 in charge. *Paul D Shann*

Class 47 No. 47196 in Trainload Petroleum livery is seen passing through ospel Oak with a westbound freightliner on 8th September 1992.

Kevin Conkey

Class 47 No. 47582 'County of Norfolk' in Parcels livery arriving at Ledbury ith the 13.40 Paddington – Hereford on 8th September 1991.

Hugh Ballantyne

▲ Class 50 No. 50033 'Glorious' in Network SouthEast livery is seen at C
Oak Common on 30th June 1990. *Kevin Conk*

▼ Class 56 No. 56032 'Sir De Morgannwg/County of South Glamorgan'
Trainload Metals livery passes Clay Cross on 28th August 1992 with the 13.
Wakefield – Cardiff Tidal metals train. *Paul Shann*

Class 58 No. 58002 'Daw Mill Colliery' in Trainload Coal livery at Ryecroft Walsall, on 24th July 1992 with merry-go-round (m.g.r.) empties for Littleton. *Paul Shannon*

Yeoman Class 59 No. 59002 'YEOMAN ENTERPRISE' is seen stabled at ɜstbury on 3rd September 1992. *Norman Preedy*

▲ Class 60s Nos. 60039 'Glastonbury Tor' in Trainload Construction livery a
60064 'Back Tor' in Trainload Petroleum livery head away from Sunderland Sou
Dock with Petrofina empties for Lindsey on 5th November 1991.

John Augusts

▼ Class 73 No. 73117 'University of Surrey' wearing old InterCity livery is se
on 10th April 1990 passing through Kensington Olympia with an engineers tra

Norman Barring

A West Coast Main Line service approaches Carlisle in the hands of Mainline ried 86101 'Sir William Stanier FRS' on 20th July 1991. *John Augustson*

Class 87 No. 87001 'Royal Scot' is seen stabled at Carlisle Citadel on 13th tember 1992. *Kevin Conkey*

▲ Belgian Railways liveried Class 90 No. 90128 'Vrachtverbinding' is pictu
resting between duties at Crewe on 30th August 1992.

John August

▼ Class 90 No. 90129 'Frachtverbindungen' in DB (German Federal Railw
'neurot' livery passing Slindon on 8th September 1992 with a Felixstowe – Basf
Hall freightliner.

Hugh Ballant

Former newspaper van No. 94052 in plain blue livery at Oxford on 4th June 2. *John Augustson*

Motorail van No. 96172 leaving Penrith on the rear of the 08.15 ton – Edinburgh on 23rd May 1992. *John Auguston*

4912

I2J (TSOE) OPEN STANDARD (END)

a. AI201. Mark 4. Air conditioned. 74S 2L. SIG bogies (BT41). ae. pa. ETH 6.

ote: 12232 was converted from the original 12405.

t No. 31047 Metro-Cammell 1989 onwards. 39.5 t.

2200	I	IECX	BN
2201	I	IECX	BN
2202	I	IECX	BN
2203	I	IECX	BN
2205	I	IECX	BN
2206	I	IECX	BN
2207	I	IECX	BN
2208	I	IECX	BN
2209	I	IECX	BN
2210	I	IECX	BN
2211	I	IECX	BN
2212	I	IECX	BN
2213	I	IECX	BN
2214	I	IECX	BN
2215	I	IECX	BN
2216	I	IECX	BN
12217	I	IECX	BN
12218	I	IECX	BN
12219	I	IECX	BN
12220	I	IECX	BN
12222	I	IECX	BN
12223	I	IECX	BN
12224	I	IECX	BN
12225	I	IECX	BN
12226	I	IECX	BN
12227	I	IECX	BN
12228	I	IECX	BN
12229	I	IECX	BN
12230	I	IECX	BN
12231	I	IECX	BN
12232	I	IECX	BN

L2J (TSOD) OPEN STANDARD (DISABLED ACCESS)

a. AL201. Mark 4. Air conditioned. 72S + wheelchair space 1L (suitable for disabled person). SIG bogies (BT41). ae. pa. p. ETH 6.

t No. 31048 Metro-Cammell 1989 onwards. 39.4 t.

2300	I	IECX	BN
2301	I	IECX	BN
2302	I	IECX	BN
2303	I	IECX	BN
2304	I	IECX	BN
2305	I	IECX	BN
2306	I	IECX	BN
2307	I	IECX	BN
2308	I	IECX	BN
2309	I	IECX	BN
2310	I	IECX	BN
2311	I	IECX	BN
2312	I	IECX	BN
2313	I	IECX	BN
2314	I	IECX	BN
2315	I	IECX	BN
12316	I	IECX	BN
12317	I	IECX	BN
12318	I	IECX	BN
12319	I	IECX	BN
12320	I	IECX	BN
12321	I	IECX	BN
12322	I	IECX	BN
12323	I	IECX	BN
12324	I	IECX	BN
12325	I	IECX	BN
12326	I	IECX	BN
12327	I	IECX	BN
12328	I	IECX	BN
12329	I	IECX	BN
12330	I	IECX	BN

AC2J (TSO) OPEN STANDARD

Dia. AC214. Mark 4. Air conditioned. 74S 2L. SIG bogies (BT41). ae. pa
ETH 6X.

Notes: 12405 is the second coach to carry that number. It was built from th
bodyshell originally intended for 12221. The original 12405 is now 12232
12490 – 12512 have now been cancelled.

Lot No. 31049 Metro-Cammell 1989 onwards. 39.9 t.

12400	I	IECX	BN
12401	I	IECX	BN
12402	I	IECX	BN
12403	I	IECX	BN
12404	I	IECX	BN
12405	I	IECX	BN
12406	I	IECX	BN
12407	I	IECX	BN
12408	I	IECX	BN
12409	I	IECX	BN
12410	I	IECX	BN
12411	I	IECX	BN
12412	I	IECX	BN
12413	I	IECX	BN
12414	I	IECX	BN
12415	I	IECX	BN
12416	I	IECX	BN
12417	I	IECX	BN
12418	I	IECX	BN
12419	I	IECX	BN
12420	I	IECX	BN
12421	I	IECX	BN
12422	I	IECX	BN
12423	I	IECX	BN
12424	I	IECX	BN
12425	I	IECX	BN
12426	I	IECX	BN
12427	I	IECX	BN
12428	I	IECX	BN
12429	I	IECX	BN
12430	I	IECX	BN
12431	I	IECX	BN
12432	I	IECX	BN
12433	I	IECX	BN
12434	I	IECX	BN
12435	I	IECX	BN
12436	I	IECX	BN
12437	I	IECX	BN
12438	I	IECX	BN
12439	I	IECX	BN
12440	I	IECX	BN
12441	I	IECX	BN
12442	I	IECX	BN
12443	I	IECX	BN
12444	I	IECX	BN
12445	I	IECX	BN
12446	I	IECX	BN
12447	I	IECX	BN
12448	I	IECX	BN
12449	I	IECX	BN
12450	I	IECX	BN
12451	I	IECX	BN
12452	I	IECX	BN
12453	I	IECX	BN
12454	I	IECX	BN
12455	I	IECX	BN
12456	I	IECX	BN
12457	I	IECX	BN
12458	I	IECX	BN
12459	I	IECX	BN
12460	I	IECX	BN
12461	I	IECX	BN
12462	I	IECX	BN
12463	I	IECX	BN
12464	I	IECX	BN
12465	I	IECX	BN
12466	I	IECX	BN
12467	I	IECX	BN
12468	I	IECX	BN
12469	I	IECX	BN
12470	I	IECX	BN
12471	I	IECX	BN
12472	I	IECX	BN
12473	I	IECX	BN
12474	I	IECX	BN
12475	I	IECX	BN
12476	I	IECX	BN
12477	I	IECX	BN
12478	I	IECX	BN
12479	I	IECX	BN
12480	I	IECX	BN
12481	I	IECX	BN
12482	I	IECX	BN
12483	I	IECX	BN

2484	**I**	IECX	BN
2485	**I**	IECX	BN
2486	**I**	IECX	BN
2487	**I**	IECX	BN
2488	**I**	IECX	BN
2489	**I**	IECX	BN
2513	**I**	IECX	BN
2514	**I**	IECX	BN
2515	**I**	IECX	BN
2516	**I**	IECX	BN
2517	**I**	IECX	BN
2518	**I**	IECX	BN
2519	**I**	IECX	BN
2520	**I**	IECX	BN
2521	**I**	IECX	BN
2522	**I**	IECX	BN
12523	**I**	IECX	BN
12524	**I**	IECX	BN
12525	**I**	IECX	BN
12526	**I**	IECX	BN
12527	**I**	IECX	BN
12528	**I**	IECX	BN
12529	**I**	IECX	BN
12530	**I**	IECX	BN
12531	**I**	IECX	BN
12532	**I**	IECX	BN
12533	**I**	IECX	BN
12534	**I**	IECX	BN
12535	**I**	IECX	BN
12536	**I**	IECX	BN
12537	**I**	IECX	BN
12538	**I**	IECX	BN

A11 (FK) CORRIDOR FIRST

ia. AA101. Mark 1. 42F 2L. ETH 3. d.

ote: 13233/6/7, 13303/14/6/26/35 are on loan to the Humberside Loco reservation Group at Hull Dairycoates (HU) and 13230 is on loan to the SRPS t Bo'ness.

3225 – 13237. Lot No. 30381 Ashford/Eastleigh 1959. B4 bogies. 33 t.
3303 – 13344. Lot No. 30667 Swindon 1962. Commonwealth bogies. 36 t.

3225	xk	**RR**	RDDY	DY
3227	xk	**RR**	RCLL	LL
3230	xk	**I**	ICHL	BO
3233	vk	**M**	ICHL	HU
3236	vk	**I**	ICHL	HU
3237	vk	**I**	ICHL	HU
3303	v	**M**	ICHL	HU
3306	v		ICHH	CL
3308	v	**N**	ICHH	CL
13314	vk	**M**	ICHL	HU
13316	v		ICHL	HU
13318	a pa	**I**	ICHV	BN
13326	v		ICHL	HU
13328	vf	**N**	NWRX	OM
13331	vf	**N**	NWRX	OM
13335	v		ICHL	HU
13341	vf	**I**	ICHV	BN
13344	vf		ICHH	CL

A1A (FK) CORRIDOR FIRST

ia. AA106. Mark 2A. Pressure ventilated. 42F 2L. B4 bogies. d. ETH 4.

3435 – 13462. Lot No. 30774 Derby 1968. 33 t.
3467 – 13475. Lot No. 30785 Derby 1968. 33 t.

3462/73 carried 19462/73 when previously declassified.

3435	v	**N**	NWRX	OM
3437	v	**N**	NWRX	OM
3444	v	**N**	NWRX	OM
3450	v	**N**	NWRX	OM
3459	a	**N**	NWXX	OM
13462	a	**N**	NWXX	OM
13467	a	**N**	NWXX	OM
13473	a	**N**	NWXX	OM
13475	v	**N**	NWRX	OM

AA1B (FK) CORRIDOR FIRST

Dia. AA107. Mark 2B. Pressure ventilated. 42F 2L. B4 bogies. ad. ETH 4.

13479/507 carried 19479/507 when previously declassified.

Lot No. 30789 Derby 1969. 33 t.

13479	N	NWXX	OM	13499	N	NWXX	EH
13482	N	NWXX	OM	13507	N	NWXX	EH
13493	N	NWXX	EH				

AA1C (FK) CORRIDOR FIRST

Dia. AA108. Mark 2C. Pressure ventilated. 42F 2L. B4 bogies. ad. pa. ETH 4

Lot No. 30797 Derby 1969 – 70. 33.5 t.

13525	N	NWXX	EH

AA1D (FK) CORRIDOR FIRST

Dia. AA109. Mark 2D. Air conditioned (Stones). 42F 2L. B4 bogies. ae. pa ETH 5. 13585 – 13607 require at least 800 V train heat supply.

Lot No. 30825 Derby 1971 – 2. 34.5 t.

13563		NSWZ	OM	13593	I	IXXB	ZN
13575	N	NWXX	OM	13595	I	IXXB	ZN
13581	I	IXXB	ZN	13596	I	IXXB	ZN
13582	I	ICHH	CL	13601	I	IXXB	BN
13583	I	IXXB	ZN	13603	I	IXXB	ZN
13585	I	ICHH	CL	13604	I	ICHV	BN
13592	I	IXXB	ZN	13607	I	ICHV	BN

SPECIAL NOTE: All BFKs were formerly numbered in the 14xxx series. Subtract 3000 from present number to obtain former number.

AB11 (BFK) CORRIDOR BRAKE FIRST

Dia. AB101. Mark 1. 24F 1L. vd. ETH 2.

17015. Lot No. 30668 Swindon 1961. Commonwealth bogies. 36 t.
17023. Lot No. 30718 Swindon 1963. Commonwealth bogies and metal window frames. 36 t.

17015 x	I	ICHV	BN	17023 x	I	ICHV	BN

AB1Z (BFK) CORRIDOR BRAKE FIRST

Dia. AB102. Mark 2. Pressure ventilated. 24F 1L. B4 bogies. d. ETH 4.

Lot No. 30756 Derby 1966 31.5 t.

17039 v	RR	RAIS	IS

AB1A (BFK) CORRIDOR BRAKE FIRST

Dia. AB103. Mark 2A. Pressure ventilated. 24F 1L. B4 bogies. d. ETH 4.

7056 – 17077. Lot No. 30775 Derby 1967 – 8. 32 t.
7079 – 17099. Lot No. 30786 Derby 1968. 32 t.

7056	a pt	**N**	NWXX	OM
7057	a pt	**N**	NWXX	OM
7058	a	**N**	NWXX	EH
7063	a pt	**N**	NWXX	OM
7064	v	**RR**	RAIS	IS
7068	v	**RR**	RAIS	IS
7069	a pt	**N**	NWXX	OM
7073	a pt	**N**	NWXX	OM
7076	a pt	**N**	NWXX	OM
7077	a	**N**	NWXX	OM
7079	a	**N**	NWXX	EH
17080	a pt	**N**	NWXX	OM
17081	a pt	**N**	NWXX	EH
17082	a pt	**N**	NWXX	OM
17086	a pt	**N**	NWXX	OM
17088	a pt	**N**	NWXX	OM
17089	v	**RR**	RAIS	IS
17090	v	**RR**	RAIS	IS
17091	v	**RR**	RAIS	IS
17096	a pt	**N**	NWXX	OM
17097	a pt	**N**	NWXX	OM
17099	v	**RR**	RAIS	IS

AB1C (BFK) CORRIDOR BRAKE FIRST

Dia. AB105. Mark 2C. Pressure ventilated. 24F 1L. B4 Bogies. ad. ETH 4.

Lot No. 30796 Derby 1969 – 70. 32.5 t.

7115	pt	**N**	NWXX	OM
7118		**RR**	RCLL	LL
7120	pt	**N**	NWXX	OM
7121	pt	**N**	NWXX	OM
17131	k pt		NXXZ	LA
17132	pt	**N**	NWXX	EH
17133	k pt	**N**	NWXX	EH

AB1D (BFK) CORRIDOR BRAKE FIRST

Dia. AB106. Mark 2D. Air conditioned (Stones equipment). 24F 1L. B4 Bogies. 17162 – 17172 require at least 800 V train heat supply. ae. pt. ETH 5.

MK – Stored at MoD Kineton.

Lot No. 30823 Derby 1971 – 2. 33.5 t.

17141	pg	**I**	ICHV	OM
17142	pg	**I**	IXXB	PC
17144		**I**	ICHD	LL
17146	pg	**I**	ICHX	CL
17147	pg	**I**	IWCL	OY
17148	pg	**I**	IXXT	MK
17151	pg	**I**	ICHD	LL
17153	pg	**I**	ICHV	OM
17155		**I**	IXXT	MK
17156		**I**	ICHD	LL
17158	pg	**I**	IXXB	ZN
17159	pg	**I**	ICHD	LL
17161	pg	**I**	IWCL	OY
17162	pg	**I**	IXXZ	ZH
17163		**I**	IXXT	MK
17164	pg	**I**	ICHX	BN
17165		**I**	ICHD	LL
17166	pg	**I**	IXXH	CL
17167	pg	**I**	ICHD	LL
17169	pg	**I**	ICHD	LL
17170	pg	**I**	ICHD	LL
17171	pg	**I**	ICHX	CL
17172	pg	**I**	ICHX	BN

AE1G (BFO) OPEN BRAKE FIRST

Dia. AE101. Mark 3B. Air conditioned. 36F 1L. BT10 bogies. ae. pg. ETH 5X. Fitted with hydraulic handbrake.

Lot No. 30990 Derby 1986. 35.81 t.

17173	I	IWCX	OY	17175	I	IWCX	OY
17174	I	IWCX	OY				

AB31 (BCK) CORRIDOR BRAKE COMPOSIT

Dia.AB301 (AB302*). Mark 1. As with the CKs there are two variants deper ding upon whether the standard class compartments have armrests. Each veh cle has two first class and three standard class compartments. 12F 18S 2L (12 24S 2L*). ETH 2.

21241 – 21246. Lot No. 30669 Swindon 1961 – 2. Commonwealth bogies 36 t.
21265 – 21274. Lot No. 30732 Derby 1964. Commonwealth bogies. 37 t.

21241	vd	E	ICHH	CL	21266	*ae	I	ICHV	BN
21242	vd	E	ICHH	CL	21268	*ae	I	ICHV	BN
21246	xd	I	ICHV	BN	21269	*ad	I	ICHV	BN
21265	*ae		ICHH	CL	21274	*ae	I	ICHV	BN

AB21 (BSK) CORRIDOR BRAKE STANDAR

Dia. AB201. Mark 1. Each vehicle has four compartments. 24S 1L. ETH 2. vd.

Lot No. 30573 Gloucester 1960. B4 bogies. 33 t.

35290	pt	N	NWRX	OM

The following lots of BSK all have metal window frames and melamine interic panelling:

35309 – 35317. Lot No. 30699 Wolverton 1962 – 3. Commonwealth bogies 37 t.
35452 – 35479. Lot No. 30721 Wolverton 1963. Commonwealth bogies. 37 t

f – Facelifted with fluorescent lighting.
g – Converted to ETH generator vehicle for Flying Scotsman Services. Still i BR stock. Carries No. '196'.

35309		N	NWRX	OM	35457			PHTX	HT
35317	pt	N	NWRX	OM	35465	f	I	ICHH	CL
35452	pt	N	RDDY	DY	35469	g	M	ICHL	BN
35453		RR	RDDY	DY	35479	pt	N	NWRX	OM
35455		N	NWRX	OM					

AB2A (BSK) CORRIDOR BRAKE STANDARD

Dia. AB204 (Mark 2A) or AB205 (Mark 2C). Pressure ventilated. Renumbere from BFK. 24S 1L. B4 bogies. d. ETH 4.

35500. Lot No. 30786 Derby 1968. 32 t.
35506 – 9/11. Lot No. 30796 Derby 1969 – 70. 32.5 t.
35510. Lot No. 30775 Derby 1968. 32 t.

35500	(17094)		N	RAIS	IS	35508	(17128)		RR	RCLL	LL
35505	( )					35509	(17138)	pt	RR	RCLL	LL
35506	(17122)	pt	RR	RCLL	LL	35510	(17075)	a	RR	RCLL	LL
35507	(17123)	pt	RR	RCLL	LL	35511	(17130)	pt	RR	RCLL	LL

2.2. HIGH SPEED TRAIN TRAILER CARS

HSTs run in formations of 7 or 8 trailer cars with a driving motor brake (pow car) at each end. All vehicles are classified mark 3. All trailer cars have BT1 bogies with disc brakes. Heating is by a three-phase supply and vehicles hav air conditioning. Max. Speed is 125 mph.

GN4G (TRB) TRAILER BUFFET FIRS

Dia. GN401. Converted from TRSB by fitting first class seats. Renumbered fro 404xx series by subtracting 200. pt. q. 23F.

40204 – 40228. Lot No. 30883 Derby 1976 – 7. 36.12 t.
40231 – 40233. Lot No. 30899 Derby 1978 – 9. 36.12 t.

40204		I	IWRR	PM
40205	p	I	IWRR	PM
40206		I	IWRR	PM
40207	p	I	IWRR	PM
40208	p	I	IWRR	PM
40209	p	I	IWRR	PM
40210	p	I	IWRR	PM
40211	p	I	ICCT	PM
40212		I	ICCT	PM
40213		I	IWRR	LA
40221	p	I	IWRR	PM
40228	p	I	IWRR	PM
40231	p	I	IWRR	LA
40232	p	I	ICCT	PM
40233		I	ICCT	PM

GK2G (TRSB) TRAILER BUFFET STANDARD

Dia. GK202. pt. Renumbered from 400xx series by adding 400. 35S.

40401 – 40427. Lot No. 30883 Derby 1976 – 7. 36.12 t.
40429 – 40437. Lot No. 30899 Derby 1978 – 9. 36.12 t.

40401	p	I	ICCE	EC
40402	pq	I	ICCE	EC
40403	pq	I	ICCT	LA
40414	pq	I	ICCT	PM
40415	pq	I	ICCT	LA
40416	pq	I	ICCE	EC
40417	pq	I	ICCT	LA
40418	pq	I	ICCT	LA
40419	pq	I	ICCE	EC
40420	pq	I	ICCE	EC
40422	pq	I	ICCE	EC
40423		I	ICCE	EC
40424	pq	I	ICCT	LA
40425	pq	I	ICCT	PM
40426	pq	I	ICCT	LA
40427	p	I	ICCE	EC
40429	pq	I	ICCE	EC
40430	pq	I	ICCE	EC
40434	pq	I	ICCT	LA
40435	pq	I	ICCE	EC
40436	q	I	ICCT	LA
40437	pq	I	ICCE	EC

GL1G (TRFK) TRAILER KITCHEN FIRST

Dia. GL101. pt. Reclassified from TRUK. Used in "Pullman" sets and a replacements for out of service TRFBs. pt. 24F.

* – Converted to lounge first seating 16F 1L. Dia. GM101.
Lot No. 30884 Derby 1976 – 7. 37 t.

40501		I	IMLX	NL
40505		I	IECD	NL
40511		I	IWRR	PM
40513	*	I	ICCT	PM

GK1G (TRFM) TRAILER MODULAR BUFFET FIRST

Dia. GK102. Converted to modular catering from 40719. pt. 17F.

Lot No. 30921 Derby 1978 – 9. 38.16 t.

40619	pq I	IMLR	NL

GK1G (TRFB) TRAILER BUFFET FIRST

Dia. GK101. These vehicles have larger kitchens than the 402xx and 404xx series vehicles, and are used in trains where full meal service is required. They have been renumbered from the 403xx series (in which the seats were unclassified) by adding 400 to previous number. pt. p. q. 17F.

40700 – 40721. Lot No. 30921 Derby 1978 – 9. 38.16 t.
40722 – 40735. Lot No. 30940 Derby 1979 – 80. 38.16 t.
40736 – 40753. Lot No. 30948 Derby 1980 – 1. 38.16 t.
40754 – 40757. Lot No. 30966 Derby 1982. 38.16 t.

40700	I	IMLR	NL
40701	I	IMLR	NL
40702	I	IMLR	NL
40703	I	IWRR	LA
40704	I	IECD	EC
40705	I	IECD	EC
40706	I	IECD	EC
40707	I	IWCW	LA
40708	I	IMLR	NL
40709	I	IWCW	LA
40710	I	IWRR	LA
40711	I	IECD	EC
40712	I	IWRR	LA
40713	I	IWRR	LA
40714	I	IECD	EC
40715	I	IWRR	PM
40716	I	IWRR	PM
40717	I	IWRR	PM
40718	I	IWRR	LA
40720	I	IECD	EC
40721	I	IWRR	LA
40722	I	IWRR	LA
40723	I	IWRR	LA
40724	I	IWRR	LA
40725	I	IWRR	LA
40726	I	IWRR	LA
40727	I	IWRR	LA
40728	I	IMLR	NL
40729	I	IMLR	NL
40730	I	IMLR	NL
40731	I	IWRR	LA
40732	I	IWRR	LA
40733	I	IWRR	LA
40734	I	IWRR	LA
40735	I	IECD	EC
40736	I	IWRR	LA
40737	I	IECD	EC
40738	I	IWCW	LA
40739	I	IWRR	PM
40740	I	IECD	EC
40741	I	IMLR	NL
40742	I	IWRR	LA
40743	I	IWRR	LA
40744	I	IWRR	PM
40745	I	IWRR	PM
40746	I	IMLR	NL
40747	I	IWRR	PM
40748	I	IECD	EC
40749	I	IMLR	NL
40750	I	IECD	EC
40751	I	IMLR	NL
40752	I	IWRR	PM
40753	I	IMLR	NL
40754	I	IMLR	NL
40755	I	IWRR	LA
40756	I	IMLR	NL
40757	I	IWRR	LA

GH1G (TF) TRAILER FIRS

Dia. GH102. pa. 48F 2L.

41003 – 41056. Lot No. 30881 Derby 1976 – 7. 33.66 t.
41057 – 41120. Lot No. 30896 Derby 1977 – 8. 33.66 t.
41121 – 41148. Lot No. 30938 Derby 1979 – 80. 33.66 t.
41149 – 41166. Lot No. 30947 Derby 1980. 33.66 t.
41167 – 41169. Lot No. 30963 Derby 1982. 33.66 t.
41170. Lot No. 30967 Derby 1982. Ex prototype vehicle. 33.66 t.

Note: 41170 was converted from 41001. 41178 is to be a prototype refurbishe vehicle and has been converted from 42011 which was damaged by fire.

41003	p	I	IWRR	PM
41004		I	IWRR	PM
41005	p	I	IWRR	PM
41006		I	IWRR	PM
41007	p	I	IWRR	PM
41008		I	IWRR	PM
41009	p	I	IWRR	PM
41010		I	IWRR	PM
41011	p	I	IWRR	PM
41012		I	IWRR	PM
41013	p	I	IWRR	PM
41014		I	IWRR	PM
41015	p	I	IWRR	PM
41016		I	IWRR	PM
41017	p	I	IWRR	PM
41018		I	IWRR	PM
41019	p	I	IWRR	PM
41020		I	IWRR	PM
41021	p	I	IWRR	PM
41022		I	IWRR	PM
41023	p	I	IWRR	LA
41024		I	IWRR	LA
41025	p	I	IWRR	LA
41026		I	IWRR	LA
41027	p	I	IWRR	LA
41028		I	IWRR	LA
41029	p	I	IWRR	LA
41030		I	IWRR	LA
41031	p	I	IWRR	LA
41032		I	IWRR	LA
41033	p	I	IWRR	LA
41034		I	IWRR	LA
41035	p	I	IWRR	LA
41036		I	IWRR	LA
41037	p	I	IWRR	LA
41038		I	IWRR	LA
41039		I	IECD	EC
41040		I	IECD	EC
41041	p	I	IMLR	NL
41042		I	IWRR	PM
41043		I	IECD	EC
41044		I	IECD	EC
41045		I	ICCT	LA
41046		I	IMLR	NL
41049		I	IWRR	PM
41050		I	IWRR	PM
41051		I	IWRR	LA
41052		I	IWRR	LA
41055		I	IWCW	LA
41056		I	IWCW	LA
41057		I	IMLR	NL
41058		I	IMLR	NL
41059		I	ICCE	EC
41060		I	IWRR	LA
41061		I	IMLR	NL
41062		I	IMLR	NL
41063		I	IMLR	NL
41064		I	IMLR	NL
41065		I	IWCW	LA
41066	p	I	IWRR	LA
41067		I	IMLR	NL
41068		I	IMLR	NL
41069		I	IMLR	NL
41070		I	IMLR	NL
41071		I	IMLR	NL
41072		I	IMLR	NL
41075		I	IMLR	NL
41076		I	IMLR	NL
41077		I	IMLR	NL
41078		I	IMLR	NL
41079		I	IMLR	NL
41080		I	IMLR	NL
41081		I	ICCE	EC
41082		I	IMLR	NL
41083		I	IMLR	NL
41084		I	IMLR	NL
41085		I	ICCE	EC
41086		I	ICCE	EC

1087		I	IECD	EC
1088		I	IECD	EC
1089		I	IWCW	LA
1090		I	IECD	EC
1091		I	IECD	EC
1092		I	IECD	EC
1093		I	IWCW	LA
1094		I	IWCW	LA
1095		I	ICCE	EC
1096		I	ICCE	EC
1097		I	IECD	EC
1098		I	IECD	EC
1099		I	IECD	EC
1100		I	IECD	EC
1101		I	IWRR	LA
1102		I	IWRR	LA
1103		I	IWRR	LA
1104		I	IWRR	LA
1105		I	IECD	EC
1106		I	IECD	EC
1107		I	ICCE	EC
1108		I	ICCT	LA
1109		I	ICCT	LA
1110		I	IWRR	PM
1111		I	IMLR	NL
1112		I	IMLR	NL
1113		I	IMLR	NL
1114		I	ICCE	EC
1115		I	IMLR	NL
1116		I	IWRR	LA
1117		I	IMLR	NL
1118		I	IECD	EC
1119		I	ICCE	EC
1120		I	IECD	EC
1121	p	I	IWRR	LA
1122		I	IWRR	LA
1123	p	I	IWRR	PM
1124		I	IWRR	PM
1125		I	IWRR	LA
1126	p	I	IWRR	LA
1127	p	I	IWRR	PM
1128		I	IWRR	PM
1129	p	I	IWRR	PM
41130		I	IWRR	PM
41131	p	I	IWRR	LA
41132		I	IWRR	LA
41133	p	I	IWRR	LA
41134		I	IWRR	LA
41135	p	I	IWRR	LA
41136		I	IWRR	PM
41137	p	I	IWRR	PM
41138		I	IWRR	PM
41139	p	I	IWRR	LA
41140		I	IWRR	LA
41141	p	I	IWRR	LA
41142		I	IWRR	LA
41143	p	I	IWRR	LA
41144		I	IWRR	LA
41145	p	I	IWRR	PM
41146		I	IWRR	PM
41147		I	ICCE	EC
41148		I	ICCE	EC
41149		I	ICCE	EC
41150		I	IECD	EC
41151		I	IECD	EC
41152		I	IECD	EC
41153		I	IMLR	NL
41154		I	IMLR	NL
41155		I	IMLR	NL
41156		I	IMLR	NL
41157		I	IWRR	LA
41158		I	IWRR	LA
41159		I	ICCT	PM
41160		I	ICCT	PM
41161		I	ICCT	PM
41162		I	ICCT	PM
41163		I	ICCT	PM
41164	p	I	IWRR	LA
41165		I	ICCT	LA
41166		I	ICCT	LA
41167		I	ICCT	LA
41168		I	ICCT	LA
41169		I	ICCT	LA
41170		I	IECD	EC
41178		I	IWRR	PM

H2G (TS) TRAILER STANDARD

ia. GH203. 76S 2L. pa.

2003 – 42090. Lot No. 30882 Derby 1976 – 7. 33.60 t.
2091 – 42250. Lot No. 30897 Derby 1977 – 9. 33.60 t.
2251 – 42305. Lot No. 30939 Derby 1979 – 80. 33.60 t.

42306 – 42322. Lot No. 30969 Derby 1982. 33.60 t.
42323 – 42341. Lot No. 30983 Derby 1984 – 5. 33.60 t.
42342. Lot No. 30949 Derby 1982. 33.47 t. Converted from TGS.
42343/5. Lot No. 30970 Derby 1982. 33.47 t. Converted from TGS.
42344. Lot No. 30964 Derby 1982. 33.47 t. Converted from TGS.
42346/7/50/1. Lot No. 30881 Derby 1976 – 7. 33.66 t. Converted from T
42348/9. Lot No. 30896 Derby 1977 – 8. 33.66 t. Converted from TF.
42353/5 – 7. Lot No. 30967 Derby 1982. Ex prototype vehicles. 33.66 t.
42352/4. Lot No. 30897 Derby 1977. Were TS from 1983 to 1992. 33.66

Notes: 42158 was also numbered 41177 for a time.
42342 – 5 were converted from TGS 44082/95/92/96 respectively.
42346 – 51 were converted from 41053/4, 41073/4, 41047/8 respectively
42352 – 57 were converted from 41176/1/5/2 – 4 respectively. They wer
originally 42142, 42001, 42114, 42000, 42002 and 41002 respectively.

42003	I	IWRR	PM
42004	I	IWRR	PM
42005	I	IWRR	PM
42006	I	IWRR	PM
42007	I	IWRR	PM
42008	I	IWRR	PM
42009	I	IWRR	PM
42010	I	IWRR	PM
42012	I	IWRR	PM
42013	I	IWRR	PM
42014	I	IWRR	PM
42015	I	IWRR	PM
42016	I	IWRR	PM
42017	I	IWRR	PM
42018	I	IWRR	PM
42019	I	IWRR	PM
42020	I	IWRR	PM
42021	I	IWRR	PM
42022	I	IWRR	PM
42023	I	IWRR	PM
42024	I	IWRR	PM
42025	I	IWRR	PM
42026	I	IWRR	PM
42027	I	IWRR	PM
42028	I	IWRR	PM
42029	I	IWRR	PM
42030	I	IWRR	PM
42031	I	IWRR	PM
42032	I	IWRR	PM
42033	I	IWRR	LA
42034	I	IWRR	LA
42035	I	IWRR	LA
42036	I	IWRR	LA
42037	I	IWRR	LA
42038	I	IWRR	LA
42039	I	IWRR	LA
42040	I	IWRR	LA
42041	I	IWRR	LA
42042	I	IWRR	LA
42043	I	IWRR	LA
42044	I	IWRR	LA
42045	I	IWRR	LA
42046	I	IWRR	LA
42047	I	IWRR	LA
42048	I	IWRR	LA
42049	I	IWRR	LA
42050	I	IWRR	LA
42051	I	IWRR	LA
42052	I	IWRR	LA
42053	I	IWRR	LA
42054	I	IWRR	LA
42055	I	IWRR	LA
42056	I	IWRR	LA
42057	I	IECD	EC
42058	I	IECD	EC
42059	I	IECD	EC
42060	I	IWRR	PM
42061	I	IWRR	PM
42062	I	IWCW	LA
42063	I	IECD	EC
42064	I	IECD	EC
42065	I	IECD	EC
42066	I	IWCW	LA
42067	I	IWCW	LA
42068	I	IWCW	LA
42069	I	IWRR	PM
42070	I	IWRR	PM
42071	I	IWRR	PM
42072	I	IWRR	PM
42073	I	IWRR	PM
42074	I	IWRR	PM
42075	I	IWRR	LA
42076	I	IWRR	LA
42077	I	IWRR	LA

2078	I	IWRR	LA
2079	I	IWRR	PM
2080	I	IWRR	PM
2081	I	IWCW	LA
2082	I	IWCW	LA
2083	I	IWCW	LA
2084	I	ICCT	PM
2085	I	ICCT	PM
2086	I	ICCT	PM
2087	I	ICCT	PM
2088	I	ICCT	PM
2089	I	IWRR	PM
2090	I	ICCT	PM
2091	I	ICCT	PM
2092	I	ICCT	PM
2093	I	ICCT	PM
2094	I	ICCT	PM
2095	I	ICCT	PM
2096	I	IWRR	LA
2097	I	IWRR	LA
2098	I	IWRR	LA
2099	I	IWRR	LA
2100	I	IMLR	NL
2101	I	IMLR	NL
2102	I	IMLR	NL
2103	I	ICCE	EC
2104	I	IECD	EC
2105	I	ICCT	LA
2106	I	IECD	EC
2107	I	IWCW	LA
2108	I	ICCT	LA
2109	I	ICCT	LA
2110	I	ICCT	LA
2111	I	IMLR	NL
2112	I	IMLR	NL
2113	I	IMLR	NL
2115	I	ICCE	EC
2116	I	ICCE	EC
2117	I	ICCE	EC
2118	I	IWRR	PM
2119	I	IMLR	NL
2120	I	IMLR	NL
2121	I	IMLR	NL
2122	I	IWRR	LA
2123	I	IMLR	NL
2124	I	IMLR	NL
2125	I	IMLR	NL
2126	I	IWCW	LA
2127	I	ICCE	EC
2128	I	ICCE	EC
2129	I	IWRR	LA
2130	I	ICCT	PM
42131	I	IMLR	NL
42132	I	IMLR	NL
42133	I	IMLR	NL
42134	I	IWRR	LA
42135	I	IMLR	NL
42136	I	IMLR	NL
42137	I	IMLR	NL
42138	I	IWRR	PM
42139	I	IMLR	NL
42140	I	IMLR	NL
42141	I	IMLR	NL
42143	I	IWRR	PM
42144	I	IWRR	PM
42145	I	IWRR	PM
42146	I	IECD	EC
42147	I	IMLR	NL
42148	I	IMLR	NL
42149	I	IMLR	NL
42150	I	IECD	EC
42151	I	IMLR	NL
42152	I	IMLR	NL
42153	I	IMLR	NL
42154	I	IECD	EC
42155	I	IMLR	NL
42156	I	IMLR	NL
42157	I	IMLR	NL
42158	I	IECD	EC
42159	I	IMLR	NL
42160	I	IMLR	NL
42161	I	IMLR	NL
42162	I	ICCE	EC
42163	I	IMLR	NL
42164	I	IMLR	NL
42165	I	IMLR	NL
42166	I	ICCE	EC
42167	I	ICCE	EC
42168	I	ICCE	EC
42169	I	ICCE	EC
42170	I	ICCE	EC
42171	I	IECD	EC
42172	I	IECD	EC
42173	I	ICCE	EC
42174	I	ICCE	EC
42175	I	ICCT	LA
42176	I	ICCT	LA
42177	I	ICCT	LA
42178	I	ICCE	EC
42179	I	IECD	EC
42180	I	IECD	EC
42181	I	IECD	EC
42182	I	IECD	EC
42183	I	IWCW	LA

42184	I	IWCW	LA
42185	I	IWCW	LA
42186	I	IECD	EC
42187	I	ICCE	EC
42188	I	ICCE	EC
42189	I	ICCE	EC
42190	I	IECD	EC
42191	I	IECD	EC
42192	I	IECD	EC
42193	I	IECD	EC
42194	I	IMLR	NL
42195	I	ICCE	EC
42196	I	IWRR	PM
42197	I	IWRR	PM
42198	I	IECD	EC
42199	I	IECD	EC
42200	I	IWRR	LA
42201	I	IWRR	LA
42202	I	IWRR	LA
42203	I	IWRR	LA
42204	I	IWRR	LA
42205	I	IMLR	NL
42206	I	IWRR	LA
42207	I	IWRR	LA
42208	I	IWRR	LA
42209	I	IWRR	LA
42210	I	IMLR	NL
42211	I	IECD	EC
42212	I	IECD	EC
42213	I	IECD	EC
42214	I	IECD	EC
42215	I	IECD	EC
42216	I	IWRR	LA
42217	I	ICCE	EC
42218	I	ICCE	EC
42219	I	IECD	EC
42220	I	IMLR	NL
42221	I	IWRR	LA
42222	I	ICCT	LA
42223	I	ICCT	LA
42224	I	ICCT	LA
42225	I	IMLR	NL
42226	I	IECD	EC
42227	I	IMLR	NL
42228	I	IMLR	NL
42229	I	IMLR	NL
42230	I	IMLR	NL
42231	I	ICCE	EC
42232	I	ICCE	EC
42233	I	ICCE	EC
42234	I	ICCE	EC
42235	I	IECD	EC
42236	I	IWRR	PM
42237	I	ICCE	EC
42238	I	ICCE	EC
42239	I	ICCE	EC
42240	I	IECD	EC
42241	I	IECD	EC
42242	I	IECD	EC
42243	I	IECD	EC
42244	I	IECD	EC
42245	I	IWRR	LA
42246	I	ICCE	EC
42247	I	ICCE	EC
42248	I	ICCE	EC
42249	I	ICCE	EC
42250	I	IWRR	LA
42251	I	IWRR	LA
42252	I	IWRR	LA
42253	I	IWRR	LA
42254	I	ICCE	EC
42255	I	IWRR	PM
42256	I	IWRR	PM
42257	I	IWRR	PM
42258	I	ICCE	EC
42259	I	IWRR	LA
42260	I	IWRR	LA
42261	I	IWRR	LA
42262	I	ICCE	EC
42263	I	IWRR	PM
42264	I	IWRR	LA
42265	I	IWRR	LA
42266	I	ICCE	EC
42267	I	IWRR	PM
42268	I	IWRR	PM
42269	I	IWRR	PM
42270	I	ICCE	EC
42271	I	IWRR	LA
42272	I	IWRR	LA
42273	I	IWRR	LA
42274	I	ICCE	EC
42275	I	IWRR	LA
42276	I	IWRR	LA
42277	I	IWRR	LA
42278	I	ICCE	EC
42279	I	IWRR	LA
42280	I	IWRR	LA
42281	I	IWRR	LA
42282	I	ICCE	EC
42283	I	IWRR	PM
42284	I	IWRR	PM
42285	I	IWRR	PM
42286	I	ICCT	PM
42287	I	IWRR	LA

42288	I	IWRR	LA
42289	I	IWRR	LA
42290	I	ICCT	PM
42291	I	IWRR	LA
42292	I	IWRR	LA
42293	I	IWRR	LA
42294	I	ICCT	PM
42295	I	IWRR	LA
42296	I	IWRR	LA
42297	I	IWRR	LA
42298	I	ICCT	PM
42299	I	IWRR	PM
42300	I	IWRR	PM
42301	I	IWRR	PM
42302	I	ICCT	PM
42303	I	ICCT	PM
42304	I	ICCT	PM
42305	I	ICCT	PM
42306	I	ICCT	LA
42307	I	ICCT	LA
42308	I	ICCT	LA
42309	I	ICCT	LA
42310	I	ICCT	LA
42311	I	ICCT	LA
42312	I	ICCT	LA
42313	I	ICCT	LA
42314	I	ICCT	LA
42315	I	ICCT	LA
42316	I	ICCT	LA
42317	I	ICCT	LA
42318	I	ICCT	LA
42319	I	ICCT	LA
42320	I	ICCT	LA
42321	I	ICCT	LA
42322	I	ICCT	LA
42323	I	IECD	EC
42324	I	IMLR	NL
42325	I	IWRR	PM
42326	I	ICCE	EC
42327	I	IMLR	NL
42328	I	IMLR	NL
42329	I	IMLR	NL
42330	I	ICCE	EC
42331	I	IMLR	NL
42332	I	IWRR	PM
42333	I	IWRR	PM
42334	I	ICCT	LA
42335	I	IMLR	NL
42336	I	ICCE	EC
42337	I	IMLR	NL
42338	I	ICCE	EC
42339	I	IMLR	NL
42340	I	IECD	EC
42341	I	IMLR	NL
42342	I	IWRR	LA
42343	I	IWRR	LA
42344	I	IWRR	LA
42345	I	IWRR	LA
42346	I	IWRR	PM
42347	I	IWRR	LA
42348	I	IWRR	LA
42349	I	IWRR	LA
42350	I	IWRR	LA
42351	I	IWRR	PM
42352	I	IMLR	NL
42353	I	ICCT	LA
42354	I	IECD	EC
42355	I	IWRR	LA
42356	I	IWRR	LA
42357	I	IWRR	LA

GJ2G (TGS) TRAILER GUARD'S STANDARD

Dia. GJ205. pg. 63S 1L + tip-up seat and wheelchair space.

44000. Lot No. 30953 Derby 1980. 33.47 t.
44001 – 44090. Lot No. 30949 Derby 1980 – 2. 33.47 t.
44091 – 44094. Lot No. 30964 Derby 1982. 33.47 t.
44095 – 44101. Lot No. 30970 Derby 1982. 33.47 t.

§ Fitted with side buffers and drophead buckeye couplings.

44000	I	ICCE	EC
44001	I	IWCW	LA
44002	I	IWRR	PM
44003	I	IWRR	PM
44004	I	IWRR	PM
44005	I	IWRR	PM
44006	I	IWRR	PM
44007	I	IWRR	PM
44008	I	IWRR	PM
44009	I	IWRR	PM
44010	I	IWRR	PM
44011	I	IWRR	LA

44012	I	IWRR	LA
44013	I	IWRR	LA
44014	I	IWRR	LA
44015	I	IWRR	LA
44016	I	IWRR	LA
44017	I	IWRR	LA
44018	I	IWRR	LA
44019	I	IECD	EC
44020	I	IWRR	PM
44021 §	I	ICCE	EC
44022	I	IWCW	LA
44023	I	IWRR	PM
44024	I	IWRR	PM
44025	I	IWRR	LA
44026	I	IWRR	PM
44027	I	IMLR	NL
44028	I	IWRR	LA
44029	I	IWRR	PM
44030	I	IWRR	LA
44031	I	IWRR	LA
44032	I	IWRR	PM
44033	I	IWRR	LA
44034	I	IWRR	LA
44035	I	IWRR	LA
44036	I	IWRR	PM
44037	I	IWRR	LA
44038	I	IWRR	LA
44039	I	IWRR	LA
44040	I	IWRR	PM
44041	I	IMLR	NL
44042	I	ICCE	EC
44043	I	IWCW	LA
44044	I	IMLR	NL
44045	I	IECD	EC
44046	I	IMLR	NL
44047	I	IMLR	NL
44048	I	IMLR	NL
44049	I	IWRR	PM
44050	I	IMLR	NL
44051	I	IMLR	NL
44052	I	IMLR	NL
44053	I	IMLR	NL
44054	I	IMLR	NL
44055	I	ICCE	EC
44056 §	I	IECD	EC
44057	I	ICCT	LA
44058 §	I	IECD	EC
44059 §	I	IWCW	LA
44060	I	ICCE	EC
44061	I	IECD	EC
44062	I	ICCE	EC
44063	I	IECD	EC
44064	I	IWRR	LA
44065	I	ICCT	PM
44066	I	IWRR	LA
44067	I	IECD	EC
44068	I	ICCT	PM
44069	I	ICCT	PM
44070	I	IMLR	NL
44071	I	IMLR	NL
44072	I	ICCT	PM
44073	I	IMLR	NL
44074	I	ICCE	EC
44075	I	ICCE	EC
44076	I	ICCT	PM
44077	I	IECD	EC
44078	I	ICCE	EC
44079	I	ICCE	EC
44080	I	IECD	EC
44081	I	ICCT	LA
44083	I	IMLR	NL
44084	I	ICCT	LA
44085	I	IMLR	NL
44086 §	I	IWRR	LA
44087	I	ICCT	LA
44088	I	ICCT	LA
44089	I	ICCT	LA
44090	I	ICCT	LA
44091	I	ICCT	LA
44093	I	IWRR	LA
44094	I	IECD	EC
44097 §	I	ICCE	EC
44098 §	I	IECD	EC
44099	I	IWRR	OO
44100	I	ICCE	EC
44101 §	I	ICCT	LA

GH2G (TCSD) TRAILER CONDUCTOR STANDARD

Dia. GH201. pg. To be converted from 44084. Guard's compartment to be converted to walk-through conductor's compartment with a disabled persons toilet also provided. The car will be marshalled adjacent to the buffet.

45084. Lot No. 30949 Derby 1982. 33.47 t.

45084

3. DIESEL MULTIPLE UNITS

This section contains details of all BR diesel multiple units. With this issue, we have changed the format of the section on first generation or 'heritage' units. Since these generally now operate in fixed formations, we have included columns for both set number and position in the set. We hope that you like our innovative approach.

NUMBERING

Diesel mechanical and diesel hydraulic multiple unit vehicles are numbered in the series 51000 – 59999. All vehicles numbered in the 53000 – 53999 series were originally numbered in the series 50000 – 50999, and were renumbered by having 3000 added to their original numbers. All vehicles in the series 54000 – 54504 were originally numbered in the series 56000 – 56504, and were renumbered by having 2000 subtracted from their original numbers.

Diesel electric multiple unit vehicles are numbered in the series 60108 – 60999. A number of vehicles which were numbered in the series 60000 – 60107 were renumbered during 1989 to avoid conficting with Class 60 locomotives. The previous numbers of the remaining vehicle is given in the text.

Regional prefix letters used to be carried preceeding the vehicle number, but these are now no longer used and many have been removed. The prefixes were: E – Eastern Region, M – London Midland Region, S – Southern Region, SC – Scottish Region. Prefixes are not shown in this book as they no longer officially form part of the vehicle number.

VEHICLE CODES

The codes used by the BR Operating Department to describe the various different types of diesel multiple unit vehicles and quoted in the class headings are as follows:

Diesel Mechanical & Diesel Hydraulic Units.

DMBC Driving Motor Brake Composite.
DMBS Driving Motor Brake Standard.
DMCL Driving Motor Composite with Lavatory.
DMS Driving Motor Standard.
DMSL Driving Motor Standard with Lavatory.
DTCL Driving Trailer Composite with Lavatory
DTS Driving Trailer Standard
DTSL Driving Trailer Standard with Lavatory.
MS Motor Standard.
MSL Motor Standard with Lavatory.
TC Trailer Composite.
TCL Trailer Composite with Lavatory.
TS Trailer Standard.
TSL Trailer Standard with Lavatory.

It should be noted that as all vehicles are of an open configuration the letter 'O' is omitted for all vehicles.

The letters (A) and (B) may be added to the above codes to differentiate between two cars of the same operating type which have differences between them. Note that a consistent system is used, rather than the official operator codes which are sometimes inconsistent.

A composite is a vehicle containing both First and Standard class accommodation, and vehicles are described as such even though most first class accommodation has now been declassified on most vehicles. This is done so as to differentiate between the different styles of seat provided in standard and erstwhile first class areas of a vehicle. At the time of writing only composite vehicles allocated to BY, OO and RG depots retained first class accommodation in use as such.

A brake vehicle is a vehicle containing seperate specific accommodation for the guard (as opposed to the use of spare driving cabs on second generation units).

Diesel Electric Units.

DMBSO Driving Motor Brake Standard (Open).
DTCsoL Driving Trailer Composite with Lavatory (Semi-Open).
DTSOL Driving Trailer Standard with Lavatory (Open).
DTSO Driving Trailer Standard (Open).
TCsoL Trailer Composite with Lavatory (Semi-Open).
TSO Trailer Standard (Open).
TSOL Trailer Standard with Lavatory (Open).

The notes as above apply regarding composite and brake vehicles. A semi-open composite vehicle has first class accommodation in compartments with a side corridor and standard class accommodation provided in an open saloon.

DIAGRAMS AND DESIGN CODES

For each type of vehicle, the official design code consists of a seven character code of two letters, four numbers and another letter, e.g. DP2010A. The first five characters of this are the diagram code and are given in the class heading or sub heading. These are explained as follows:

1st Letter

This is always 'D' for a diesel multiple unit vehicle.

2nd Letter

as follows for various vehicle types:

P Driving motor passenger vehicles without a brake compartment.
Q Driving motor passenger vehicles with a brake compartment.
R Non-Driving motor passenger vehicles.
S Driving trailer passenger vehicles.
T Trailer passenger vehicles without a brake compartment.
U Trailer passenger vehicles with a brake compartment.
X Parcels and Mails vehicles and single unit railcars.

1st Figure

This denotes the class of accommodation as follows:

2 Standard class accommodation (incl. declassified seats).
3 Composite accommodation.
5 No passenger accommodation.

2nd & 3rd Figures

These denote distinguish between the different designs of vehicle, each different design being allocated a unique two digit number.

Special Note

Where vehicles have been declassified the correct design code for a declassified vehicle is given, even though this may be at variance with official records which do not show the reality of the current position. A declassified composite is still referred to as a composite if it still retains the first class style seats in the erstwhile first class section of the vehicle. Its declassification is denoted by the fact that the first figure of the design code is a '2'.

GENERAL NOTES

LOT NUMBERS

Each batch of vehicles is allocated a Lot (or batch) number when ordered and these are quoted in class headings and sub headings.

BUILDERS

These are shown in class headings where the following abbreviations are used:

Alexander	Walter Alexander Ltd., Falkirk.
Barclay	Andrew Barclay Ltd., Kilmarnock.
BRCW	Birmingham Railway Carriage & Wagon Company Ltd.
Derby	BR Derby Carriage Works or British Rail Engineering Limited, Derby Carriage Works. (Became BREL Ltd. and is now ABB Derby.
Gloucester	Gloucester Railway Carriage & Wagon Company Ltd.
Leyland Bus	Leyland Bus Ltd., Workington.
Metro-Cammell	Metropolitan-Cammell Ltd.
Pressed Steel	Pressed Steel Ltd.
York	British Rail Engineering Ltd., York (Became BREL Ltd. and is now ABB York.

Where a dual BR works builder is shown (e.g. Ashford/Eastleigh) the first named built the underframe and the last named built the body and assembled the vehicle. For second generation vehicles, the first name is that of the main contractor with the second name being the underframe and final assembly subcontractor

ACCOMMODATION

This information is given in class headings and sub headings in the form nF nS nL, where n is the number of seats or lavatories and F, S & L denote first class seats, standard class seats and lavatories respectively. (e.g. 12F 54S 1L denotes 12 first class seats, 54 standard class seats and one lavatory). In declassified vehicles, the capacity is still shown in terms of first and standard class seats to differentiate between the two physically different seat types available, although all seats are officially standard class in such instances.

WEIGHTS

Approximate weights in working order are given in tons for all vehicle types in the class headings and sub headings as appropriate.

DIMENSIONS

The dimensions of each type of vehicle are given in metric units, with length followed by width. All lengths quoted are over buffers (1st generation vehicles) or couplings (2nd generation vehicles). All widths quoted are maxima.

ABBREVIATIONS

The following are used throughout this section:

DEMU	diesel electric multiple unit.
DHMU	diesel hydraulic multiple unit.
DMMU	diesel mechanical multiple unit.
DMU	diesel multiple unit (general term).
F	First class seats.
g	Gangwayed where other members of the class are not.
hp	horsepower.
kW	Kilowatts.
L	Lavatories.
m	metres.
mph	miles per hour.
r	Fitted with radio electronic token block apparatus.
S	Standard class seats.
t	tons.
w	Retains Tungsten lighting.
(S)	Stored servicable. (Not necessarily at allocated depot).
(U)	Stored unservicable. (Not necessarily at allocated depot).
	retaining original seats.
§	Fitted with headlight and radio electronic token block apparatus.

FIRST GENERATION DMUS

There are three basic types of first generation vehicle as referred to in the class headings as follows:

Standard. (known as 'low density' by BR). Exterior doors are located in entrance vestibules. Largely unidirectional 3 + 2 seating is provided in standard class, with 2 + 2 seating in first class. Where no specific type of vehicle is quoted in class headings the vehicle is of this type.

Suburban. (known as 'high density' by BR). Exterior doors to each seating bay. Back to back seating arranged 3 + 2 in standard class with 2 + 1 seating in first class. Built as non-gangwayed, but all now gangwayed.

Cross Country. Exterior doors are located in entrance vestibules. These were originally designed for longer distance services and have 2 + 2 seating in standard class, with 2 + 1 in first class.

STANDARD FEATURES.

Gangways:

Unless stated otherwise, all vehicles are gangwayed at non driving ends with British Standard gangways.

Transmission:

All motor vehicles have mechanical transmission consisting of a cardan shaft and freewheel to a four-speed epicylic gearbox with a further cardan shaft to the final drive, each engine driving the inner axle of one bogie.

Brakes:

All units are vacuum braked.

Doors:

All units are equipped with slam doors.

Lighting:

All cars are fitted with fluorescent lighting unless otherwise stated.

Couplings:

Screw couplings are used on all vehicles. All remaining first generation vehicles may be coupled together to work in multiple up to a maximum of 6 motor cars or 12 cars in total in a formation. First generation vehicles may not be coupled in multiple with second generation vehicles.

LAYOUT OF SECTION

In the lists which follow, the number is followed by any notes applicable to the vehicle, the livery code, the sector code, the depot code, the set number and the position within the set. Note: The second power car in a power twin is allotted position 3, whereas driving trailers are alloted position 2.

CLASS 119 GLOUCESTER CROSS COUNTRY

Engines: Two Leyland 1595 of 112 kW (150 hp).
Bogies: DD10.
Dimensions: 20.45 x 2.82 m.

DMBC. Dia. DQ302. Lot No. 30421 1959. 18F 16S. 37.5 t.

51060	w	**N**	NWXX	RG	575	1
51073	w	**N**	NWXX	RG	594	1
51074	w	**N**	NWXX	RG	595	1
51076	w	**N**	RDTS	TS	119 596	1
51079	w	**N**	NWXX	RG	588	1

DMSL. Dia. DP203. Lot No. 30422 1958 – 59. 68S 2L. 38.5 t.

51086	w	**N**	NWXX	RG	595	3
51088	w	**N**	NWXX	RG	575	3
51099	w	**N**	RDTS	TS	119 596	3
51104	w	**N**	NWXX	RG	594	3
51107	w	**N**	NWXX	RG	588	3

CLASS 116 DERBY SUBURBAN

Engines: Two Leyland 680/1 of 112 kW (150 hp).
Bogies: DD10.
Dimensions: 20.45 x 2.82 m.

DMBS. Dia. DQ230. Lot No. 30446 1958. 65S. 36.5 t.

51128		RDTS	TS	57	1
51129		RDTS	TS	56	1
51131		RDTS	TS	326	1
51134		RDTS	TS	392	1
51138		RDTS	TS	325	3
51140		RDTS	TS	319	1

DMS. Dia. DP220. Lot No. 30447 1958. 89S. 36.5 t.

51141		RFXX	TS	0	1
51142		RDTS	TS	322	3
51144		RDTS	TS	321	3
51146	w	RDTS	TS	402	4
51147		RDTS	TS	392	3
51149		RDTS	TS	319	3
51151		RDTS	TS	327	3

CLASS 101 METRO-CAMMELL

Engines: Two Leyland or AEC of 112 kW (150 hp).
Bogies: DD15.
Dimensions: 18.49 x 2.82 m.

DMBS. Dia. DQ202 (★DQ232). Lot No. 30467 1958 – 59. 52S (★49S with additional luggage rack). 32.5 t.

51175	§	**RR**	RDNC	NC	101 658	1
51177		**RR**	RCLO	LO	101 683	1
51179		**RR**	RCLO	LO	101 677	1
51184			RDTS	TS	57	3
51185		**S**	RDTS	TS	101 689	1
51187		**S**	RACK	CK	101 684	1
51188		**RR**	RAHA	HA	101 694	1
51189		**RR**	RCLO	LO	101 660	1
51190	★	**N**	RAHA	HA	830	1
51192		**RR**	RAHA	HA	101 693	1
51201		**RR**	RCLO	LO	101 663	1
51205		**RR**	RCLO	LO	101 676	1
51208		**N**	NWRX	OO	221	1
51210		**RR**	RCLO	LO	101 678	1
51211	★	**N**	NWRX	RG	831	1
51213	§	**RR**	RDNC	NC	101 659	1
51215		**N**	NWRX	RG	200	1
51218			RCLO	LO	242	1
51221		**N**	NWRX	RG	207	1
51222	§	**N**	RDNC	NC	101 225	1
51224		**RR**	RDTS	TS	101 679	1
51225		**N**	NWRX	RG	202	1
51226	★	**N**	RAHA	HA	832	1
51228		**RR**	RCLO	LO	101 681	1
51230	§	**RR**	RDNC	NC	101 656	1
51231		**S**	RACK	CK	101 686	1
51245			RCLO	LO	245	1
51246			RAHA	HA	829	1
51247		**S**	RACK	CK	101 687	1
51252	§		RDNC	NC	76	1
51253		**RR**	RAHA	HA	101 691	1

CLASS 118 — BRCW SUBURBAN

Engines: Two Leyland 680/1 of 112 kW (150 hp).
Bogies: DD10.
Dimensions: 20.45 x 2.82 m.

DMBS. Dia. DQ220. Lot No. 30543 1960. 65S. 36.5 t.

51314	w	RDTS	TS	317	1
51316		RDTS	TS	318	1

DMS. Dia. DP221. Lot No. 30545 1960. 89S. 36.5 t.

51329	w	RDTS	TS	317	3
51331		RDTS	TS	0	1

CLASS 117 — PRESSED STEEL SUBURBAN

Engines: Two Leyland 680/1 of 112 kW (150 hp).
Bogies: DD10.
Dimensions: 20.45 x 2.82 m.

Non-standard Livery: GWR chocolate & cream.

DMBS. Dia. DQ220. Lot No. 30546 1959 – 60. 65S. 36.5 t.

51332	N	NWRX	RG	400	1
51333	N	NWRX	RG	401	1
51334	RR	RDTS	TS	117 311	1
51335	N	NWRX	RG	402	1
51336	N	NWRX	OO	403	1
51339	RR	RDTS	TS	117 313	1
51340	N	NWRX	RG	405	1
51341	N	NWRX	RG	406	1
51342	N	NWRX	OO	407	1
51343	N	NWRX	RG	213	1
51344	N	NWRX	OO	409	1
51345	N	NWRX	RG	410	1
51346	N	NWRX	OO	411	1
51347	N	NWRX	OO	412	1
51349	N	NWRX	OO	413	1
51350	N	NGBX	BY	701	1
51351	N	NWRX	OO	415	1
51352	RR	RDTS	TS	117 314	1
51353	RR	RDTS	TS	117 301	1
51354	N	NWRX	RG	417	1
51355	N	NWXX	RG	418	1
51356	N	NGBX	BY	702	1
51358	N	NWRX	RG	420	1
51359	N	NWRX	OO	421	1
51360		RDTS	TS	302	1
51361	N	NWRX	RG	423	1
51362	N	NWRX	OO	424	1
51363	N	NWRX	RG	425	1
51364		RDTS	TS	303	1
51365		RDTS	TS	304	1
51366	N	NWRX	RG	428	1
51367	N	NWRX	RG	205	1
51368	0	RDTS	TS	117 305	1
51369	RR	RDTS	TS	117 306	1
51370		RDTS	TS	307	1
51371	RR	RDTS	TS	117 308	1
51372		RDTS	TS	309	1
51373	RR	RDTS	TS	117 310	1

DMS. Dia. DP221. Lot No. 30548 1959 – 60. 89S. 36.5 t.

51374	N	NWRX	RG	400	3
51375	N	NWRX	RG	401	3
51376	RR	RDTS	TS	117 311	3
51377	N	NWRX	RG	402	3
51378	N	NWRX	OO	403	3
51381	N	NWRX	RG	405	3
51382	RR	RDTS	TS	117 313	3
51383	N	NWRX	RG	406	3
51384	N	NWRX	OO	407	3

51385	**N**	NWRX	RG	408	3
51386	**N**	NWRX	OO	409	3
51387	**N**	NWRX	RG	410	3
51388	**N**	NWRX	OO	411	3
51389	**N**	NWRX	OO	412	3
51391	**N**	NWRX	OO	413	3
51392	**N**	NGBX	BY	701	3
51393	**N**	NWRX	OO	415	3
51394	**RR**	RDTS	TS	117 314	3
51395	**RR**	RDTS	TS	117 301	3
51396	**N**	NWRX	RG	417	3
51397	**N**	NWXX	RG	418	3
51398	**N**	NGBX	BY	702	3
51399	**N**	NWRX	RG	423	3
51400	**N**	NWRX	RG	420	3
51401	**N**	NWRX	RG	421	3
51402		RDTS	TS	302	3
51404	**N**	NWRX	OO	424	3
51405	**N**	NWRX	RG	425	3
51406		RDTS	TS	303	3
51407		RDTS	TS	304	3
51408	**N**	NWRX	RG	428	3
51409	**N**	NWRX	OO	429	3
51410	**O**	RDTS	TS	117 305	3
51411	**RR**	RDTS	TS	117 306	3
51412		RDTS	TS	307	3
51413	**RR**	RDTS	TS	117 308	3
51414		RDTS	TS	309	3
51415	**RR**	RDTS	TS	117 310	3

CLASS 101 — METRO-CAMMELL

Engines: Two Leyland or AEC of 112 kW (150 hp).
Bogies: DD15.
Dimensions: 18.49 x 2.82 m.

DMBS. Dia. DQ202 (★DQ232). Lot No. 30500 1959. 52S (★49S with additional luggage rack). 32.5 t.

51426 §	**RR**	RDNC	NC	101 653	1
51427		RCLO	LO	239	1
51428	**RR**	RCLO	LO	101 655	1
51429	**RR**	RCLO	LO	101 665	1
51431 ★	**S**	RDTS	TS	101 688	1
51432 ★	**N**	NWXX	RG	835	1
51434 ★	**N**	NWXX	RG	836	1
51435	**S**	RDTS	TS	101 690	1
51442	**RR**	RCLO	LO	101 664	1
51444 §	**N**	RDNC	NC	101 223	1
51445	**N**	NWRX	RG	224	1
51463	**RR**	RCLO	LO	101 661	1

DMCL. Dia. DP317 (DP210*). Lot No. 30501 1959. 12F 46S with additiona luggage racks 1L. 32.5t.

* Converted to DMSL seating 72S 1L.

51496 *	**RR**	RCLO	LO	101 677	3
51498	**N**	NWXX	RG	835	3
51499	**N**	RAHA	HA	832	3
51500 *	**S**	RACK	CK	101 686	3
51501 *	**S**	RDTS	TS	101 688	3
51503	**N**	NWXX	RG	836	3
51505 * §	**RR**	RDNC	NC	101 682	3
51506 * §	**RR**	RCLO	LO	101 681	3
51509 * §	**S**	RACK	CK	101 684	3
51511 *	**S**	RDTS	TS	101 689	3
51512 *	**S**	RACK	CK	101 687	3
51530 *		RELA	LA	870	3
51533 * §	**RR**	RDTS	TS	101 679	3

CLASS 108 DERBY 'LIGHTWEIGHT'

Engines: Two Leyland 680/1 or 680/13 of 112 kW (150 hp).
Bogies: DD7.
Dimensions: 18.49 x 2.79 m.

DMCL. Dia. DP311 or *DP226. Lot No. 30461 1959 – 60. 12F 52S 1L. 28.5 t.

51567			RCLO	LO	615	3
51568			RDTS	TS (S)	66	3
51572	w	**N**	NWRX	RG	490	3

CLASS 115 DERBY SUBURBAN

Engines: Two Leyland Albion of 149 kW (200 hp).
Bogies: DD13.
Dimensions: 20.45 x 2.82 m.
Note: All these cars are fitted with power sanding equipment.

DMBS. Dia. DQ233. Lot No. 30530 1960. 74S. 38.5 t.

51651	**N**	NGBX	BY	750	1
51652	**N**	NGBX	BY	752	3
51654	**N**	NGBX	BY	752	1
51661	**N**	NGBX	BY	754	1
51676	**N**	NNDX	BY	230	1

CLASS 101 METRO-CAMMELL

Engines: Two Leyland of 112 kW (150 hp).
Bogies: DD15.
Dimensions: 18.49 x 2.82 m.

DMBS. Dia. DQ202. Lot No. 30587 1959. 52S 1L. 32.5 t.

51800	§	**RR**	RDNC	NC	101 654	1

DMCL. Dia. DP210. Lot No. 30588 1959. 12F 53S 1L. 32.5 t.

* Converted to DMSL seating 72S 1L.

51803	★	**RR**	RCLO	LO	101 676	3
51808			RDTS	TS	38	3

CLASS 115 — DERBY SUBURBAN

Engines: Two Leyland Albion of 149 kW (200 hp).
Bogies: DD13.
Dimensions: 20.45 x 2.82 m.
Note: All BY allocated cars are fitted with power sanding equipment.

51851 – 51860. DMBS. Dia. DQ233. Lot No. 30595 1960. 74S. 38.5 t.
51862 – 51897. DMBS. Dia. DQ233. Lot No. 30598 1960. 74S. 38.5 t.

51851			RDTS	TS	402	1
51852			RDTS	TS	403	1
51853			RDTS	TS	404	1
51855		**N**	NGBX	BY	754	3
51859			RDTS	TS	321	1
51860			RDTS	TS	412	1
51862			RDTS	TS	410	1
51868			RDTS	TS	320	1
51869			RDTS	TS	323	1
51878		**N**	NGBX	BY	750	3
51880			RDTS	TS	414	1
51884			RDTS	TS (S)	0	1
51897			RDTS	TS	0	1

CLASS 108 — DERBY 'LIGHTWEIGHT'

Engines: Two Leyland 680/1 or 680/13 of 112 kW (150 hp).
Bogies: DD7.
Dimensions: 18.49 x 2.82 m.

DMBS. Dia. DQ213. Lot No. 30601 1960 – 61. 52S. 29.5 t.

51907			RCLO	LO	262	1
51909		**N**	NNDX	BY	231	1
51912	w	**N**	NGBX	BY	755	1
51914		**N**	NNDX	BY	232	1
51916	w	**N**	NGBX	BY	755	3
51919			RDTS	TS	940	1
51933			RCLO	LO	618	1
51942		**N**	NNDX	BY	233	1
51943			RDTS	TS	66	1
51947	w		RDTS	TS	64	1

DMCL. Dia. DP227. Lot No. 30660 1960 – 61. 12F 53S 1L. 28.5 t.

52044			RDTS	TS	39	3
52048			RDTS	TS	940	3
52054			RCLO	LO	618	3

CLASS 116 DERBY SUBURBAN

Engines: Two Leyland 680/1 of 112 kW (150 hp).
Bogies: DD10.
Dimensions: 20.45 x 2.82 m.

DMBS. Dia. DQ230. Lot No. 30211 1957. 65S. 36.5 t.

53053			RDTS	TS	39	1
53054	w		RDTS	TS	36	1
53055	w		RDTS	TS	324	1
53060	w		RDTS	TS	52	1
53071	w		RDTS	TS	54	1
53090			RDTS	TS	327	1

DMS. Dia. DP220. Lot No. 30213 1957. 89S. 36.5 t.

53101	w		RDTS	TS	324	3
53102			RDTS	TS	318	3
53106	w		RDTS	TS	403	4
53114	w		RDTS	TS	323	3
53116	w		RDTS	TS	412	4
53124			RDTS	TS	410	4
53132			RDTS	TS	0	1

CLASS 101 METRO-CAMMELL

Engines: Two Leyland or AEC of 112 kW (150 hp).
Bogies: DD15.
Dimensions: 18.49 x 2.82 m.

DMSL. Dia. DP214. Lot No. 30253 1956. 72S 1L. 32.5 t.

53160		**RR**	RCLO	LO	101 685	3
53163		**RR**	RELA	LA	101 680	3

DMBS. Dia. DQ202. Lot No. 30254 1957. 52S. 32.5 t.

53164		**RR**	RCLO	LO	101 685	1
53165			RCLO	LO	294	1

53168 – 53171. DMCL. Dia. DP214. Lot No. 30255 1957. 12F 53S 1L. 32.5 t.
53177 – 53193. DMCL. Dia. DP214. Lot No. 30256 1957. 12F 53S 1L. 32.5 t.

* Converted to DMSL seating 72S 1L.

53168			RDTS	TS	56	3
53170	*	**RR**	RAHA	HA	101 692	3
53171	*	**RR**	RAHA	HA	101 691	3
53177	*	**S**	RDTS	TS	101 690	3
53193	§		RDNC	NC	58	3

53198 – 53208. DMBS. Dia. DQ202. Lot No. 30259 1957. 52S. 32.5 t.
53211 – 53231. DMBS. Dia. DQ202. Lot No. 30261 1957. 52S. 32.5 t.

53198	§	**RR**	RDNC	NC	101 652	1
53200			RELA	LA	870	1

3201	§	RR	RDNC	NC	101 651	1
3202			RCLO	LO	241	1
3203			RCLO	LO	243	1
3204		RR	RELA	LA	101 680	1
3208	§		RDNC	NC	88	1
3211		RR	RCLO	LO	101 657	1
3216	§		RDNC	NC	58	1
3228		RR	RCLO	LO	101 662	1
3231			RCLO	LO	240	1

MCL. Dia. DP213. Lot No. 30263 1957. 12F 45S 1L. 32.5 t. 2+2 seating.

3245			RDTS	TS	36	3

MBS. Dia. DQ202. Lot No. 30266 1957. 52S. 32.5 t.

3253		RR	RAHA	HA	101 692	1
3256	§	RR	RDNC	NC	101 682	1

MCL. Dia. DP210 (★DP317). Lot No. 30267 1957. 12F 53S 1L. (★12F 46S with additional luggage racks 1L). 32.5 t.

Converted to DMSL seating 72S 1L.

3265	★	N	NWRX	RG	831	3
3266	*	RR	RAHA	HA	101 693	3
3267			RDTS	TS	54	3
3268	*	RR	RAHA	HA	101 694	3
3269	*	RR	RCLO	LO	101 683	3

3291. DMBS. Dia. DQ202. Lot No. 30270 1957. 52S. 32.5 t.
3305 – 53315. DMBS. Dia. DQ202 (★DQ232). Lot No. 30275 1958. 52S. ★49S with additional luggage rack) 32.5 t.

3291			RCLO	LO	244	1
3305			RAHA	HA	829	3
3308	★	N	NWXX	RG	838	1
3310	★	N	NWXX	RG	839	1
3311	★	N	NWXX	RG	840	1
3312	★	N	NWXX	RG	841	1
3314	★	N	NWXX	RG	842	1
3315			RAHA	HA	874	1

MCL. Dia. DP210 (★DP317). Lot No. 30276 1958. 12F 53S 1L (★12F 46S with additional luggage racks 1L) 32.5 t.

Converted to DMSL seating 72S 1L.

3321	*		RDTS	TS	52	3
3322	★	N	NWXX	RG	840	3
3326	★	N	NWXX	RG	839	3
3327	★	N	NWXX	RG	842	3
3330	*		RAHA	HA	874	3
3331	★	N	NWXX	RG	838	3
3332	★	N	NWXX	RG	841	3
3333	★	N	RAHA	HA	830	3

CLASS 104 BRCW

Engines: Two Leyland 680/1 of 112 kW (150 hp).
Bogies: DD14.
Dimensions: 18.49 x 2.82 m.

53477. DMBS. Dia. DQ205. Lot No. 30293 1957. 52S 1L. 31.5 t.
53540. DMBS. Dia. DQ205. Lot No. 30296 1958. 52S 1L. 31.5 t.

53477	**N**	NWRX	RG	408	1
53540	**N**	NWRX	OO	263	1

CLASS 108 DERBY 'LIGHTWEIGHT

Engines: Two Leyland 680/1 or 680/13 of 112 kW (150 hp).
Bogies: DD7.
Dimensions: 18.49 x 2.82 m.

53599. DMBS. Dia. DQ212. Lot No. 30406 1958. 52S. 29.5 t.
53627 – 53628. DMBS. Dia. DQ212. Lot No. 30407 1958 – 59. 52S. 29.5

53599	**N**	NWRX	RG	490	1
53627		RCLO	LO	615	1
53628	**N**	NWRX	RG	212	1

DMCL. Dia. DP219. Lot No. 30408 1958. 12F 50S 1L. 28.5 t. Luggage rac opposite toilet.

53632		RDTS	TS	64	3
53645		RDTS	TS	61	3

CLASS 101 METRO-CAMMEL

Engines: Two Leyland or AEC of 112 kW (150 hp).
Bogies: DD15.
Dimensions: 18.49 x 2.82 m.

DMSL. Dia. DP210. Lot No. 30271 1957. 72S 1L. 32.5 t.

53746	**RR**	RCLO	LO	101 678	3

CLASS 116 DERBY SUBURBA

Engines: Two Leyland 680/1 of 112 kW (150 hp).
Bogies: DD10.
Dimensions: 20.45 x 2.82 m.

DMBS. Dia. DQ230. Lot No. 30363 1957 – 58. 65S. 36.5 t.

53818		RDTS	TS	325	1
53822		RDTS	TS	61	1
53838	w	RDTS	TS	38	1
53863	w	RDTS	TS	322	1

DMS. Dia. DP220. Lot No. 30364 1957 – 58. 89S. 36.5 t.

53891		RDTS	TS	326	3

53897		RDTS	TS	0	1
53902		RDTS	TS	320	3
53916	w	RDTS	TS	0	1
53919		RDTS	TS	404	4
53921		RDTS	TS	414	4

CLASS 108 DERBY 'LIGHTWEIGHT'

Engines: Two Leyland 680/1 or 680/13 of 112 kW (150 hp).
Bogies: DD7.
Dimensions: 18.49 x 2.79 m.

DMBS. Dia. DQ212. Lot No. 30465 1959. 52S. 29.5 t.

53971		RCLO	LO	280	1
53980	w	RFXX	LO	0	1
53987	w	RFXX	LO	0	1

CLASS 101 METRO-CAMMELL

Bogies: DT11.
Dimensions: 18.49 x 2.82 m.

54050 – 54061. DTCL. Dia. DS302 (*DS206). Lot No. 30260 1957. 12F 53S 1L. 25.5 t.
54062 – 54091. DTCL. Dia. DS302 (*DS206). Lot No. 30262 1957. 12F 53S 1L. 25.5 t.

§ Converted to DTSL seating 72S 1L.

54050	*		RCLO	LO	294	2
54055	*	**RR**	RCLO	LO	101 662	2
54056	§*	**RR**	RDNC	NC	101 656	2
54060	*		RDNC	NC	88	2
54061	*	**RR**	RCLO	LO	101 664	2
54062	*	**RR**	RCLO	LO	101 655	2
54068	§	**N**	RDNC	NC	101 223	2
54081		**N**	NWRX	RG	200	2
54085	*	**RR**	RCLO	LO	101 657	2
54091	§*	**RR**	RDNC	NC	101 658	2

CLASS 108 DERBY 'LIGHTWEIGHT'

Bogies: DT8.
Dimensions: 18.49 x 2.79 m.

DTCL. Dia. DS310 or DS207. Lot No. 30409 1958. 12F 53S 1L. 21.5 t.

54194	**N**	NNDX	BY	233	2
54203		RCLO	LO	241	2
54208		RCLO	LO	245	2

CLASS 101 METRO-CAMMELL

Bogies: DT11.
Dimensions: 18.49 x 2.82 m.

DTCL. Dia. DS303. Lot No. 30340 1957. 12F 45S 1L. 25.5 t. 2+2 seating

54220	§	**N**	RDNC	NC	101 225	2

CLASS 108 DERBY 'LIGHTWEIGHT

Bogies: DT8.
Dimensions: 18.49 x 2.79 m. (DS310), 18.49 x 2.82 DS311).

54223 – 54270. DTCL. Dia. DS310 or DS207. Lot No. 30466 1959. 12F 53S 1L. 21.5 t.
54271 – 54279. DTCL. Dia. DS311 or DS2??. Lot No. 30499 1960. 12F 53S 1L. 22.5 t.

54223		**N**	NWRX	RG	213	2
54228		**N**	NNDX	BY	232	2
54256	w		RCLO	LO	243	2
54257		**N**	NNDX	BY	230	2
54270	w		RCLO	LO	244	2
54271	w	**N**	NNDX	BY	231	2
54279		**N**	NNDX	RG	212	2

CLASS 101 METRO-CAMMELL

Bogies: DT11.
Dimensions: 18.49 x 2.82 m.

DTCL. Dia. DS302 (*DS206). Lot No. 30468 1958. 12F 53S 1L. 25.5 t.

* Converted to DTSL seating 72S 1L.

54343	*	**RR**	RCLO	LO	101 660	2
54346	§*	**RR**	RDNC	NC	101 652	2
54347	*	**RR**	RCLO	LO	101 663	2
54352	§*	**RR**	RDNC	NC	101 659	2
54358	§*	**RR**	RDNC	NC	101 653	2
54362		**N**	NWRX	RG	224	2
54365	*	**RR**	RCLO	LO	101 661	2
54368	§		RDNC	NC	76	2
54372		**N**	NWRX	RG	202	2
54379	§*	**RR**	RDNC	NC	101 651	2
54380			RCLO	LO	239	2
54385		**N**	NWRX	RG	205	2
54388			RCLO	LO	240	2
54393	*	**RR**	RCLO	LO	101 665	2
54396		**N**	NWRX	RG	207	2
54399			RCLO	LO	242	2
54402		**N**	NWRX	OO	221	2
54408	§*	**RR**	RDNC	NC	101 654	2

CLASS 108 DERBY 'LIGHTWEIGHT'

ogies: DT8.
imensions: 18.49 x 2.82 m.

TCL. Dia. DS311. Lot No. 30602 1960. 12F 53S 1L. 22.5 t.

4490	*		RCLO	LO	262	2
4495	w	**N**	NWRX	OO	263	2
4504	w*		RCLO	LO	280	2

CLASS 122 GLOUCESTER SUBURBAN

ngines: Two AEC 220 of 112 kW (150 hp).
angways: Non gangwayed single cars with cabs at each end.
ogies: DD10.
imensions: 20.45 x 2.82 m.

MBS. Dia. DX202. Lot No. 30419 1958. 65S. 36.5 t.

5000	**RR**	RELA	LA	122 100	1
5003		RELA	LA	122 103	1
5006	**RR**	RELA	LA	122 106	1
5009	**RR**	RELA	LA	122 109	1
5012	**RR**	RELA	LA	122 112	1

CLASS 121 PRESSED STEEL SUBURBAN

ngines: Two Leyland 1595 of 112 kW (150 hp).
angways: Non gangwayed single cars with cabs at each end.
ogies: DD10.
imensions: 20.45 x 2.82 m.

MBS. Dia. DX201. Lot No. 30518 1960. 65S. 38.0 t.

5022	**N**	NWRX	OO	122	1
5023	**N**	NNDX	BY	123	1
5024	**N**	NWRX	OO	124	1
5025	**N**	NWRX	OO	125	1
5027	**N**	NWRX	OO	127	1
5028	**N**	NWRX	OO	128	1
5029	**N**	NWRX	OO	129	1
5030	**N**	NWRX	OO	130	1
5031	**N**	NNDX	BY	131	3

CLASS 116 DERBY SUBURBAN

ogies: DT9b.
imensions: 20.45 x 2.82 m.

S. Dia. DT209. Lot No. 30385 1957. 98S. 29.5 t.

9032	RDTS	TS	327	2

CLASS 101 METRO-CAMMEL

Bogies: DT11.
Dimensions: 18.49 x 2.82 m.

59072. TSL. Dia. DT202. Lot No. 30257 1957. 71S 1L. 25.5 t.
59091. TSL. Dia. DT228. Lot No. 30264 1957. ★58S plus additional luggag racks 1L. 25.5 t.
59110 – 59111. TSL. Dia. DT202 (★DT228). Lot No. 30269 1957 – 58. 71 1L (★58S plus additional luggage racks 1L). 25.5 t. Renumbered from 59101/ to avoid conflict with Class 59 locos.

59072		**N**	NWRX	RG	831	2
59091	★	**N**	NWXX	RG	841	2
59110	★	**N**	NWXX	RG	842	2
59111		**N**	RAHA	HA	830	2

TCL. Dia. DT220 or ★DT228. Lot No. 30277 1958. 12F 53S 1L (★58S 1L 25.5 t.

59115	★	**N**	NWRX	RG	408	2
59117	★	**N**	NWXX	RG	840	2
59118			RAHA	HA	829	2
59125	★	**N**	NWXX	RG	838	2

TS. Dia. DT202 (★DT228). Lot No. 30273 1957. 71S 1L. (★64S plus add tional luggage racks 1L). 25.5 t.

59302		**RR**	RAHA	HA	101 693	2
59303		**RR**	RAHA	HA	101 692	2
59306	★	**N**	NWXX	RG	839	2

CLASS 116 DERBY SUBURBAN

Bogies: DT9b.
Dimensions: 20.45 x 2.82 m.

TC. Dia. DT219. Lot No. 30365 1957 – 58. 20F 68S. 29.0 t.

59335	RDTS	TS	403	3

CLASS 119 GLOUCESTER CROSS-COUNTRY

Bogies: DT9.
Dimensions: 20.45 x 2.82 m.
Note: These vehicles were formerly trailer buffet seconds, but the buffets hav now been removed and converted into an additional luggage area.

TSL. Dia. DT216. Lot No. 30423 1958 – 59. 60S 2L. 31.5 t.

59416	**N**	RDTS	TS	319	2
59419	**N**	NWXX	RG	575	2
59430	**N**	NWXX	RG	595	2
59435	**N**	NWXX	RG	594	2
59437	**N**	NWXX	RG	588	2

CLASS 116 — DERBY SUBURBAN

ogies: DT9b.
imensions: 20.45 x 2.82 m.

C. Dia. DT219. Lot No. 30448 1957 – 58. 20F 68S. 29.0 t.

9446		RDTS	TS	412	3

CLASS 118 — BRCW SUBURBAN

ogies: DT9.
imensions: 20.45 x 2.82 m.

CL. Dia. DT230. Lot No. 30544 1960. 22F 48S 2L. 30.5 t.

9481	w	RDTS	TS	317	2
9483		RDTS	TS	318	2

CLASS 117 — PRESSED STEEL SUBURBAN

ogies: DT9.
imensions: 20.45 x 2.82 m.

CL. Dia. DT305 (*DT230). Lot No. 30547 1959 – 60. 22F 48S 2L. 30.5 t.

on-standard Livery: GWR chocolate & cream.

Converted to TSL seating 78S 1L.

9484		N	NWRX	RG	400	2
9485		N	NWRX	RG	401	2
9486	*	RR	RDTS	TS	117 310	2
9487		N	NWRX	RG	402	2
9488		N	NWRX	OO	403	2
9489		RR	RDTS	TS	117 314	2
9490	*		RDTS	TS	309	2
9491		N	NWRX	RG	405	2
9492	*	RR	RDTS	TS	117 313	2
9493		N	NWRX	RG	406	2
9494		N	NWRX	OO	407	2
9495		N	NWRX	RG	429	2
9496		N	NWRX	OO	409	2
9497		N	NWRX	RG	410	2
9498		N	NWRX	OO	411	2
9499		N	NWRX	OO	412	2
9500	*	RR	RDTS	TS	117 311	2
9501		N	NWRX	OO	413	2
9503		N	NWRX	OO	415	2
9505	*	RR	RDTS	TS	117 301	2
9506		N	NWRX	RG	417	2
9507		N	NWXX	RG	418	2
9508		N	NWXX	RG	0	1
9509	*	RR	RDTS	TS	117 308	2
9510		N	NWRX	RG	420	2

59511		N	NWRX	OO	421	2
59512	*		RDTS	TS	302	2
59513		N	NWRX	RG	423	2
59514		N	NWRX	OO	424	2
59515		N	NWRX	RG	425	2
59516	*		RDTS	TS	303	2
59517	*		RDTS	TS	304	2
59518		N	NWRX	RG	428	2
59520	*	O	RDTS	TS	117 305	2
59521	*	RR	RDTS	TS	117 306	2
59522	*		RDTS	TS	307	2

CLASS 101 METRO-CAMMELL

Bogies: DT11.
Dimensions: 18.49 x 2.82 m.

TSL. Dia. DT228. Lot No. 30502 1959. 72S 1L (★58S 1L). 25.5 t.

59530	★	N	NWXX	RG	835	2
59536		RR	RAHA	HA	101 691	2
59539		RR	RAHA	HA	101 694	2
59540	★	N	NWXX	RG	836	2

TSL. Dia. DT228. Lot No. 30510 1959. 58S 1L. 25.5 t.

59570		N	RAHA	HA	832	2

CLASS 127 DERBY SUBURBAN

Bogies: DT9.
Dimensions: 20.45 x 2.82 m.

TSL. Dia. DT226. Lot No. 30522 1959. 86S 2L. 30.5 t.

59591	RDTS	TS	412	2
59592	RDTS	TS	323	2
59600	RDTS	TS	321	2
59602	RDTS	TS	410	2
59603	RDTS	TS	324	2
59604	RDTS	TS	404	2
59607	RDTS	TS	403	2
59609	RDTS	TS	326	2
59611	RDTS	TS	325	2
59614	RDTS	TS	402	2

TS. Dia. DT229. Lot No. 30523 1959. 96S. 29.5 t.

59641	RDTS	TS	414	2

CLASS 115 DERBY SUBURBAN

Bogies: DT9.
Dimensions: 20.45 x 2.82 m.

59658. TS. Dia. DT229. Lot No. 30531 1960. 96S. 29.5 t.
59713. TS. Dia. DT229. Lot No. 30596 1960. 96S. 29.5 t.
59734 – 59735. TS. Dia. DT229. Lot No. 30599 1960. 96S. 29.5 t.

59658		RDTS	TS	402	3
59713		RDTS	TS	410	3
59734	N	RDTS	TS	414	3
59735	N	RDTS	TS	404	3

TCL. Dia. DT227. Lot No. 30600 1960. 30F 38S 2L. 30.5 t.

59745	RDTS	TS	0	1
59751	RDTS	TS	320	2
59753	RDTS	TS	322	2

3.2. FORMATIONS OF "HERITAGE" DMUS

This section details formations of first generation DMUs. It should be noted that formations do vary from time to time.

NETWORK SOUTHEAST

These are generally kept in fixed formations. Certain units are being withdrawn and replaced with Class 165 and 166 'Network Turbos'.

CLASS 121 SINGLE CARS ("BUBBLE CARS")

122	OO	NWRX	55022
123	BY	NNDX	55023
124	OO	NWRX	55024
125	OO	NWRX	55025
127	OO	NWRX	55027
128	OO	NWRX	55028
129	OO	NWRX	55029
130	OO	NWRX	55030
131	BY	NNDX	55031

POWER CAR/DRIVING TRAILER TWINS

200	RG	NWRX	51215	54081	(101/101)
202	RG	NWRX	51225	54372	(101/101)
205	RG	NWRX	51367	54385	(117/101)
207	RG	NWRX	51221	54396	(101/101)
212	RG	NWRX	53628	54279	(108/108)
213	RG	NWRX	51343	54223	(117/108)
221	OO	NWRX	51208	54402	(101/101)
224	RG	NWRX	51445	54362	(101/101)
230	BY	NNDX	51676	54257	(115/108)
231	BY	NNDX	51909	54271	(108/108)
232	BY	NNDX	51914	54228	(108/108)
233	BY	NNDX	51942	54194	(108/108)
263	OO	NWRX	53540	54495	(104/108)

CLASS 117 2 or 3-CAR UNITS

§ Class 101 car.
* Class 104 car.

400	RG	NWRX	51332	59484	51374
401	RG	NWRX	51333	59485	51375
402	RG	NWRX	51335	59487	51377
403	OO	NWRX	51336	59488	51378
405	RG	NWRX	51340	59491	51381
406	RG	NWRX	51341	59493	51383

07	OO	NWRX	51342	59494	51384
08	RG	NWRX	53477§	59115*	51385
09	OO	NWRX	51344	59496	51386
10	RG	NWRX	51345	59497	51387
11	OO	NWRX	51346	59498	51388
12	OO	NWRX	51347	59499	51389
13	OO	NWRX	51349	59501	51391
15	OO	NWRX	51351	59503	51393
17	RG	NWRX	51354	59506	51396
18	RG	NWXX	51355	59507	51397
20	RG	NWRX	51358	59510	51400
21	OO	NWRX	51359	59511	51401
23	RG	NWRX	51361	59513	51399
24	OO	NWRX	51362	59514	51404
25	RG	NWRX	51363	59515	51405
28	RG	NWRX	51366	59518	51408
29	RG	NWRX		59495	51409

LASS 104/108 2-CAR POWER TWIN

90	RG	NWRX	53599		51572

LASS 119 3-CAR UNITS

75	RG	NWXX	51060	59419	51088
88	RG	NWXX	51079	59437	51107
94	RG	NWXX	51073	59435	51104
95	RG	NWXX	51074	59430	51086

LASS 117 POWER TWINS

01	BY	NGBX	51350		51392
02	BY	NGBX	51356		51398

LASS 115 POWER TWINS

50	BY	NGBX	51651		51878
52	BY	NGBX	51654		51652
54	BY	NGBX	51661		51855
55	BY	NGBX	51912		51916

LASS 101 THREE CAR UNITS

31	RG	NWRX	51211	59072	53265
35	RG	NWXX	51432	59530	51498
36	RG	NWXX	51434	59540	51503
38	RG	NWXX	53308	59125	53331
39	RG	NWXX	53310	59306	53326
40	RG	NWXX	53311	59117	53322
41	RG	NWXX	53312	59091	53332
42	RG	NWXX	53314	59110	53327

PARE CAR

9508 RG NWXX

REGIONAL RAILWAYS

Regional Railways' units have in the past often not been kept in fixed form tions, but this situation has now changed and fixed formations are now usual kept, with the exception of the Tyseley suburban units which change regular These units are, however subject to early withdrawal.

UNREFURBISHED CLASS 116/101 (108*) POWER TWINS

036	TS	RDTS	53054	53245
038	TS	RDTS	53838	51808
039	TS	RDTS	53053	52044*
052	TS	RDTS	53060	53321
054	TS	RDTS	53071	53267
056	TS	RDTS	51129	53168
057	TS	RDTS	51128	51184
061	TS	RDTS	53822	53645

UNREFURBISHED CLASS 108 POWER TWINS

064	TS	RDTS	51947	53632
066	TS	RDTS	51943	51568
615	LO	RCLO	53627	51567
618	LO	RCLO	51933	52054

UNREFURBISHED CLASS 101 POWER TWINS AND 3-CAR UNITS

058	NC	RDNC	53216		53193
829	HA	RAHA	51246	59118	53305
830	HA	RAHA	51190	59111	53333
832	HA	RAHA	51226	59570	51499
870	LA	RELA	53200		51530
874	HA	RAHA	53315		53330
940	TS	RDTS	51919		52048

UNREFURBISHED CLASS 101 (108*) POWER CAR/DRIVING TRAILER TWIN

076	NC	RDNC	51252	54368
088	NC	RDNC	53208	54060
239	LO	RCLO	51427	54380
240	LO	RCLO	53231	54388
241	LO	RCLO	53202	54203*
242	LO	RCLO	51218	54399
243	LO	RCLO	53203	54256*
244	LO	RCLO	53291	54270*
245	LO	RCLO	51245	54208*
262	LO	RCLO	51907*	54490*
280	LO	RCLO	53971*	54504*
294	LO	RCLO	53165	54050

MISCELLANEOUS 3 & 4-CAR SUBURBAN UNITS

317	TS	RDTS	51314	59481	51329
318	TS	RDTS	51316	59483	53102
319	TS	RDTS	51140	59416	51149
320	TS	RDTS	51868	59751	53902
321	TS	RDTS	51859	59600	51144
322	TS	RDTS	53863	59753	51142
323	TS	RDTS	51869	59592	53114
324	TS	RDTS	53055	59603	53101
325	TS	RDTS	53818	59611	51138
326	TS	RDTS	51131	59609	53891
327	TS	RDTS	53090	59032	51151

392	TS	RDTS	51134		51147	
402	TS	RDTS	51851	59614	59658	51146
403	TS	RDTS	51852	59607	59335	53106
404	TS	RDTS	51853	59604	59735	53919
410	TS	RDTS	51862	59602	59713	53124
412	TS	RDTS	51860	59591	59446	53116
414	TS	RDTS	51880	59641	59734	53921

REFURBISHED CLASS 101 POWER CAR/DRIVING TRAILER TWINS

101 223	NC	RDNC	51444	54068
101 225	NC	RDNC	51222	54220
101 651	NC	RDNC	53201	54379
101 652	NC	RDNC	53198	54346
101 653	NC	RDNC	51426	54358
101 654	NC	RDNC	51800	54408
101 655	LO	RCLO	51428	54062
101 656	NC	RDNC	51230	54056
101 657	LO	RCLO	53211	54085
101 658	NC	RDNC	51175	54091
101 659	NC	RDNC	51213	54352
101 660	LO	RCLO	51189	54343
101 661	LO	RCLO	51463	54365
101 662	LO	RCLO	53228	54055
101 663	LO	RCLO	51201	54347
01 664	LO	RCLO	51442	54061
01 665	LO	RCLO	51429	54393

REFURBISHED CLASS 101 POWER TWINS AND 3-CAR UNITS

101 676	LO	RCLO	51205		51803
101 677	LO	RCLO	51179		51496
101 678	LO	RCLO	51210		53746
101 679	TS	RDTS	51224		51533
101 680	LA	RELA	53204		53163
101 681	LO	RCLO	51228		51506
101 682	NC	RDNC	53256		51505
101 683	LO	RCLO	51177		53269
101 684	CK	RACK	51187		51509
101 685	LO	RCLO	53164		53160
101 686	CK	RACK	51231		51500
101 687	CK	RACK	51247		51512
101 688	TS	RDTS	51431		51501
101 689	TS	RDTS	51185		51511
101 690	TS	RDTS	51435		53177
101 691	HA	RAHA	51253	59536	53171
101 692	HA	RAHA	53253	59303	53170
101 693	HA	RAHA	51192	59302	53266
101 694	HA	RAHA	51188	59539	53268

CLASS 117 3-CAR UNITS

117 301	TS	RDTS	51353	59505	51395
302	TS	RDTS	51360	59512	51402
303	TS	RDTS	51364	59516	51406
304	TS	RDTS	51365	59517	51407
117 305	TS	RDTS	51368	59520	51410
117 306	TS	RDTS	51369	59521	51411
307	TS	RDTS	51370	59522	51412
117 308	TS	RDTS	51371	59509	51413
309	TS	RDTS	51372	59490	51414
117 310	TS	RDTS	51373	59486	51415
117 311	TS	RDTS	51334	59500	51376
117 313	TS	RDTS	51339	59492	51382
117 314	TS	RDTS	51352	59489	51394

CLASS 119 2-CAR UNIT

119 596	TS	RDTS	51076		51099

CLASS 122 SINGLE CARS ("BUBBLE CARS")

122 100	LA	RELA	55000
122 103	LA	RELA	55003
122 106	LA	RELA	55006
122 109	LA	RELA	55009
122 112	LA	RELA	55012

SPARE CARS

51141	TS	RFXX
51331	TS	RDTS
51884	TS	RDTS
51897	TS	RDTS
53132	TS	RDTS
53897	TS	RDTS
53916	TS	RDTS
53980	LO	RFXX
53987	LO	RFXX
59745	TS	RDTS

3.3. SECOND GENERATION DMUS

There are five basic types of second generation vehicle as referred to in the clas headings as follows:

- **Railbus** (known as 'Pacers' on BR). Folding power operated exterior doors Bus-type 3+2 (2+2 on class 141) largely unidirectional seating. Limited lug gage space. Four wheel chassis. 75 mph.
- **Sprinter.** Sliding power operated exterior double doors to large entranc vestibules. High backed 3+2 seating. Limited luggage space. 75 mph.
- **Super Sprinter.** Sliding/sliding plug power-operated exterior doors. High back ed 2+2 largely unidirectional seating with some tables. 75 mph.
- **Express.** Sliding plug power-operated exterior doors. Air conditioned. Hig backed 2+2 half-facing and half-unidirectional seating with some tables. 9 mph.
- **Network Turbo.** Sliding power operated exterior double doors to large en trance vestibules. 3+2 seating. Limited luggage space. 90 mph.

Public Address System: All vehicles are equipped with public address, wit transmission equipment for driving vehicles.

Transmission: All vehicles unless otherwise stated are fitted with Voith T211 hydraulic transmission and a Gmeinder final drive.

Gangways: Unless stated otherwise, all vehicles have flexible diaphragn gangways.

Couplings: Unless otherwise stated all vehicles are fitted with BSI automati couplings at their outer ends. Railbus types are fitted with bar couplings at thei inner ends, but all other types have BSI couplings at their inner ends unless other wise stated.

Brakes: All vehicles have air brakes.

CLASS 141 LEYLAND BUS/BREL RAILBUS

DMS – DMSL. Built from Leyland National bus parts on four-wheeled underframes.

Engine: One Leyland TL11 152 kW (205 hp) (v Cummins LTA 10R).
Transmission: Mechanical. Self Changing Gears. (v Hydraulic. Voith T211r).
Gangways: Within unit only.
Doors: Folding.
Dimensions: 15.45 x 2.50 m.
Seats: 2 + 2 bus style.
Maximum Speed: 75 mph.

DMS. Dia. DP228 Lot No. 30977 Derby 1984. Modified by Barclay 1988 – 89. 50S. 26.0 t.
DMSL. Dia. DP229 Lot No. 30978 1984. Modified by Barclay 1988 – 89.44S 1L. 26.5 t.

141 101		Y	RBNL	NL	55521 55541
141 102		Y	RBNL	NL	55502 55522
141 103		Y	RBNL	NL	55503 55523
141 105		Y	RBNL	NL	55505 55525
141 106		Y	RBNL	NL	55506 55526
141 107		Y	RBNL	NL	55507 55527
141 108		Y	RBNL	NL	55508 55528
141 109		Y	RBNL	NL	55509 55529
141 110		Y	RBNL	NL	55510 55530
141 111		Y	RBNL	NL	55511 55531
141 112		Y	RBNL	NL	55512 55532
141 113	v	Y	RBNL	NL	55513 55533
141 114		Y	RBNL	NL	55514 55534
141 115		Y	RBNL	NL	55515 55535
141 116		Y	RBNL	NL	55516 55536
141 117		Y	RBNL	NL	55517 55537
141 118		Y	RBNL	NL	55518 55538
141 119		Y	RBNL	NL	55519 55539
141 120		Y	RBNL	NL	55520 55540

CLASS 142 LEYLAND BUS/BREL RAILBUS

DMS – DMSL. Development of Class 141 with wider body and improved appearance.

Engine: One Leyland TL11 152 kW (205 hp).
Transmission: Hydraulic. Voith T211r.
Gangways: Within unit only.
Doors: Folding.
Dimensions: 15.55 x 2.80 m.
Seats: 2 + 3 bus style.
Maximum Speed: 75 mph.

142 001 – 142 044

Non-Standard Livery: Chocolate & Cream.

55542 – 55591. DMS. Dia. DP234 Lot No. 31003 Derby 1985 – 6. 62S. 24.5 t.
55592 – 55641. DMSL. Dia. DP235 Lot No. 31004 Derby 1985 – 6. 59S 1L. 25.0 t.
55701 – 55746. DMS. Dia. DP234 Lot No. 31013 Derby 1986 – 7. 62S. 24.5 t.
55747 – 55792. DMSL. Dia. DP235 Lot No. 31014 Derby 1986 – 7. 59S 1L. 25.0 t.

142 001	**G**	RCNH	NH	55542	55592
142 002	**G**	RCNH	NH	55543	55593
142 003	**G**	RCNH	NH	55544	55594
142 004	**G**	RCNH	NH	55545	55595
142 005	**G**	RCNH	NH	55546	55596
142 006	**G**	RCNH	NH	55547	55597
142 007	**G**	RCNH	NH	55548	55598
142 008	**G**	RCNH	NH	55549	55599
142 009	**G**	RCNH	NH	55550	55600
142 010	**G**	RCNH	NH	55551	55601
142 011	**G**	RCNH	NH	55552	55602
142 012	**G**	RCNH	NH	55553	55603
142 013	**G**	RCNH	NH	55554	55604
142 014	**G**	RCNH	NH	55555	55605
142 015	**0**	RBHT	HT	55556	55606
142 016	**0**	RBHT	HT	55557	55607
142 017	**0**	RBHT	HT	55558	55608
142 018	**0**	RBHT	HT	55559	55609
142 019	**T**	RBHT	HT	55560	55610
142 020	**T**	RBHT	HT	55561	55611
142 021	**T**	RBHT	HT	55562	55612
142 022	**T**	RBHT	HT	55563	55613
142 023	**RR**	RCNH	NH	55564	55614
142 024	**0**	RBHT	HT	55565	55615
142 025	**0**	RBHT	HT	55566	55616
142 026	**0**	RBHT	HT	55567	55617
142 027	**0**	RCNH	NH	55568	55618
142 028	**PR**	RCNH	NH	55569	55619
142 029	**PR**	RCNH	NH	55570	55620
142 030	**PR**	RCNH	NH	55571	55621
142 031	**PR**	RCNH	NH	55572	55622
142 032	**PR**	RCNH	NH	55573	55623
142 033	**PR**	RCNH	NH	55574	55624
142 034	**PR**	RCNH	NH	55575	55625
142 035	**PR**	RCNH	NH	55576	55626
142 036	**PR**	RCNH	NH	55577	55627
142 037	**PR**	RCNH	NH	55578	55628
142 038	**PR**	RCNH	NH	55579	55629
142 039	**PR**	RCNH	NH	55580	55630
142 040	**PR**	RCNH	NH	55581	55631
142 041	**PR**	RCNH	NH	55582	55632
142 042	**PR**	RCNH	NH	55583	55633
142 043	**PR**	RCNH	NH	55584	55634
142 044	**PR**	RCNH	NH	55585	55635

142 045	**PR**	RCNH	NH	55586	55636
142 046	**PR**	RCNH	NH	55587	55637
142 047	**PR**	RCNH	NH	55588	55752
142 048	**PR**	RCNH	NH	55589	55639
142 049	**PR**	RCNH	NH	55590	55640
142 050	**PR**	RBHT	HT	55591	55641
142 051	**PR**	RCNH	NH	55701	55747
142 052	**PR**	RCNH	NH	55702	55748
142 053	**PR**	RCNH	NH	55703	55749
142 054	**PR**	RCNH	NH	55704	55750
142 055	**PR**	RCNH	NH	55705	55751
142 056	**PR**	RCNH	NH	55706	55638
142 057	**PR**	RCNH	NH	55707	55753
142 058	**PR**	RCNH	NH	55708	55754
142 060	**PR**	RCNH	NH	55710	55756
142 061	**PR**	RCNH	NH	55711	55757
142 062	**PR**	RBNH	NH	55712	55758
142 063	**PR**	RBNH	NH	55713	55759
142 064	**PR**	RCNH	NH	55714	55760
142 065	**PR**	RBHT	HT	55715	55761
142 066	**PR**	RBHT	HT	55716	55762
142 067	**PR**	RBNH	NH	55717	55763
142 068	**PR**	RBNL	NL	55718	55764
142 069	**PR**	RCNH	NH	55719	55765
142 070	**PR**	RBNL	NL	55720	55766
142 071	**PR**	RBHT	HT	55721	55767
142 072	**PR**	RBNL	NL	55722	55768
142 073	**PR**	RBNL	NL	55723	55769
142 074	**PR**	RBNL	NL	55724	55770
142 075	**PR**	RBNL	NL	55725	55771
142 076	**PR**	RBNL	NL	55726	55772
142 077	**PR**	RBNL	NL	55727	55773
142 078	**PR**	RBNL	NL	55728	55774
142 079	**PR**	RBNL	NL	55729	55775
142 080	**PR**	RBNL	NL	55730	55776
142 081	**PR**	RBNL	NL	55731	55777
142 082	**PR**	RBNL	NL	55732	55778
142 083	**PR**	RBNL	NL	55733	55779
142 084	**PR**	RBNL	NL	55734	55780
142 085	**PR**	RBNL	NL	55735	55781
142 086	**PR**	RBNL	NL	55736	55782
142 087	**PR**	RBNL	NL	55737	55783
142 088	**PR**	RBNL	NL	55738	55784
142 089	**PR**	RBNL	NL	55739	55785
142 090	**PR**	RBNL	NL	55740	55786
142 091	**PR**	RBNL	NL	55741	55787
142 092	**PR**	RBNL	NL	55742	55788
142 093	**PR**	RBNL	NL	55743	55789
142 094	**PR**	RBNL	NL	55744	55790
142 095	**PR**	RBNL	NL	55745	55791
142 096	**PR**	RBNL	NL	55746	55792

CLASS 143 ALEXANDER/BARCLAY RAILBUS

DMS – DMSL. Similar design to Class 142, but bodies built by W. Alexande with Barclay underframes.

Engine: One Leyland TL11 152 kW (205 hp).
Transmission: Hydraulic. Voith T211r.
Gangways: Within unit only.
Doors: Folding.
Dimensions: 15.55 x 2.70 m.
Seats: 2 + 3 bus style.
Maximum Speed: 75 mph.

DMS. Dia. DP236 Lot No. 31005 Andrew Barclay 1985 – 6. 62S. 24.5 t.
DMSL. Dia. DP237 Lot No. 31006 Andrew Barclay 1985 – 6. 60S 1L. 25.0 t

143 601	**RR**	RECF	CF	55642	55667
143 602	**RR**	RECF	CF	55651	55668
143 603	**RR**	RECF	CF	55658	55669
143 604	**RR**	RECF	CF	55645	55670
143 605	**RR**	RECF	CF	55646	55671
143 606	**RR**	RECF	CF	55647	55672
143 607	**RR**	RECF	CF	55648	55673
143 608	**RR**	RECF	CF	55649	55674
143 609	**RR**	RECF	CF	55650	55675
143 610	**RR**	RECF	CF	55643	55676
143 611	**RR**	RECF	CF	55652	55677
143 612	**RR**	RECF	CF	55653	55678
143 613	**RR**	RECF	CF	55654	55679
143 614	**RR**	RECF	CF	55655	55680
143 615	**RR**	RECF	CF	55656	55681
143 616	**RR**	RECF	CF	55657	55682
143 617	**RR**	RECF	CF	55644	55683
143 618	**RR**	RECF	CF	55659	55684
143 619	**RR**	RECF	CF	55660	55685
143 620	**RR**	RECF	CF	55661	55686
143 621	**RR**	RECF	CF	55662	55687
143 622	**RR**	RECF	CF	55663	55688
143 623	**RR**	RECF	CF	55664	55689
143 624	**RR**	RECF	CF	55665	55690
143 625	**RR**	RECF	CF	55666	55691

CLASS 144 ALEXANDER/BREL RAILBUS

DMS – DMSL or DMS – MS – DMSL. Similar design to Class 143, but under frames built by BREL as subcontractor to W. Alexander.

Engine: One Leyland TL11 152 kW (205 hp).
Transmission: Hydraulic. Voith T211r.
Gangways: Within unit only.
Doors: Folding.
Dimensions: 15.25 x 2.70 m.

Seats: 2 + 3 bus style.
Maximum Speed: 75 mph.

DMS. Dia. DP240 Lot No. 31015 Derby 1986 – 7. 62S and wheelchair space. 24.2 t.
MS. Dia. DR205 Lot No. Derby 31037 1987. 73S. 22.6 t.
DMSL. Dia. DP241 Lot No. Derby 31016 1986 – 7. 60S 1L. 25.0 t.

144 001	**Y**	RBNL	NL	55801		55824
144 002	**Y**	RBNL	NL	55802		55825
144 003	**Y**	RBNL	NL	55803		55826
144 004	**Y**	RBNL	NL	55804		55827
144 005	**Y**	RBNL	NL	55805		55828
144 006	**Y**	RBNL	NL	55806		55829
144 007	**Y**	RBNL	NL	55807		55830
144 008	**Y**	RBNL	NL	55808		55831
144 009	**Y**	RBNL	NL	55809		55832
144 010	**Y**	RBNL	NL	55810		55833
144 011	**Y**	RBNL	NL	55811		55834
144 012	**Y**	RBNL	NL	55812		55835
144 013	**Y**	RBNL	NL	55813		55836
144 014	**Y**	RBNL	NL	55814	55850	55837
144 015	**Y**	RBNL	NL	55815	55851	55838
144 016	**Y**	RBNL	NL	55816	55852	55839
144 017	**Y**	RBNL	NL	55817	55853	55840
144 018	**Y**	RBNL	NL	55818	55854	55841
144 019	**Y**	RBNL	NL	55819	55855	55842
144 020	**Y**	RBNL	NL	55820	55856	55843
144 021	**Y**	RBNL	NL	55821	55857	55844
144 022	**Y**	RBNL	NL	55822	55858	55845
144 023	**Y**	RBNL	NL	55823	55859	55846

CLASS 150/0 BREL PROTOTYPE SPRINTER

DMSL – MS – DMS. Prototype Sprinter.

Engine: One Cummins NT855R5 of 210 kW (285 hp).
Bogies: One BX8P and one BX8T.
Couplings: BSI at outer end of driving vehicles, bar non-driving ends.
Transmission: Hydraulic. Voith T211r with Gmeinder final drive.
Gangways: Within unit only.
Doors: Sliding.
Seats: Various types now fitted. (2 + 2*)
Dimensions: 20.06 x 2.82 m (outer cars), 20.18 x 2.82 m (inner car).
Maximum Speed: 75 mph.

DMSL. Dia. DP230. Lot No. 30984 York 1984. 76S 1L (58S 1L*). 35.8 t.
MS. Dia. DR202. Lot No. 30986 York 1984. 84S (72S*). 34.4 t.
DMS. Dia. DP231. Lot No. 30985 York 1984. 79S (60S*). 35.6 t.

Note: 150 002 was converted to 154 002 at RTC Derby in 1986. It has now been converted back to a Class 150.

150 001	r	**P**	RDTS	TS	55200	55400	55300
150 002	r	**CE**	RDTS	TS	55201	55401	55301

CLASS 150/1 BREL SPRINTER

DMSL – DMS or DMSL – DMSL (Class 150/2) – DMS or DMSL – DMS (Class 150/2) – DMS.

Engine: One Cummins NT855R5 of 210 kW (285 hp).
Bogies: One BP38 and one BT38.
Gangways: Within unit only.
Doors: Sliding.
Seats: 2 + 3 facing. (★ Reseated with part unidirectional and part facing seating).
Dimensions: 20.06 x 2.82 m.
Maximum Speed: 75 mph.

DMSL. Dia. DP238. Lot No. 31011 York 1985 – 6. 68S 1L (72S 1L★). 36.5 t.
DMS. Dia. DP239. Lot No. 31012 York 1985 – 6. 70S (★76S). 38.45 t.

Note: The centre cars of three-car units are Class 150/2 vehicles. For details see next Class.

150 101	★	**CE**	RDTS	TS	52101		57101
150 102	★	**CE**	RDTS	TS	52102		57102
150 103	★	**CE**	RDTS	TS	52103		57103
150 104	★	**CE**	RDTS	TS	52104		57104
150 105	★	**CE**	RDTS	TS	52105		57105
150 106	★	**CE**	RDTS	TS	52106		57106
150 107	★	**CE**	RDTS	TS	52107		57107
150 108	★	**CE**	RDTS	TS	52108	57226	57108
150 109	★	**CE**	RDTS	TS	52109	52220	57109
150 110	★	**CE**	RDTS	TS	52110	57220	57110
150 111	★	**CE**	RDTS	TS	52111	57206	57111
150 112	★	**CE**	RDTS	TS	52112	52204	57112
150 113	★	**CE**	RDTS	TS	52113	52226	57113
150 114	★	**CE**	RDTS	TS	52114	57204	57114
150 115	r★	**CE**	RDTS	TS	52115	52206	57115
150 116	r★	**CE**	RDTS	TS	52116	52202	57116
150 117	r★	**CE**	RDTS	TS	52117	57209	57117
150 118	r★	**CE**	RDTS	TS	52118	57212	57118
150 119	r★	**CE**	RDTS	TS	52119		57119
150 120	r★	**CE**	RDTS	TS	52120		57120
150 121	r★	**CE**	RDTS	TS	52121		57121
150 122	r★	**CE**	RDTS	TS	52122		57122
150 123	r★	**CE**	RDTS	TS	52123		57123
150 124	r★	**CE**	RDTS	TS	52124		57124
150 125	r★	**CE**	RDTS	TS	52125		57125
150 126	r★	**CE**	RDTS	TS	52126		57126
150 127	r★	**CE**	RDTS	TS	52127		57127
150 128	r★	**CE**	RDTS	TS	52128		57128
150 129	r★	**CE**	RDTS	TS	52129		57129
150 130	r★	**CE**	RDTS	TS	52130	57202	57130
150 131	r★	**CE**	RDTS	TS	52131		57131
150 132	r★	**CE**	RDTS	TS	52132		57132
150 133	r	**GM**	RCNH	NH	52133	52218	57133
150 134	r	**GM**	RCNH	NH	52134	57218	57134

150 135	r	**GM**	RCNH	NH	52135	52222	57135
150 136	r	**GM**	RCNH	NH	52136	57222	57136
150 137	r	**GM**	RCNH	NH	52137	52224	57137
150 138	r	**GM**	RCNH	NH	52138	57224	57138
150 139	r	**GM**	RCNH	NH	52139		57139
150 140	r	**GM**	RCNH	NH	52140		57140
150 141	r	**GM**	RCNH	NH	52141		57141
150 142	r	**GM**	RCNH	NH	52142		57142
150 143	r	**P**	RCNH	NH	52143		57143
150 144	r	**P**	RCNH	NH	52144		57144
150 145	r	**P**	RCNH	NH	52145		57145
150 146	r	**RR**	RCNH	NH	52146		57146
150 147	r	**P**	RCNH	NH	52147		57147
150 148	r	**P**	RCNH	NH	52148		57148
150 149	r	**P**	RCNH	NH	52149		57149
150 150	r	**P**	RCNH	NH	52150		57150

CLASS 150/2 BREL SPRINTER

DMSL – DMS.

Engine: One Cummins NT855R5 of 210 kW (285 hp).
Bogies: One BP38 and one BT38.
Gangways: Throughout.
Doors: Sliding.
Seats: 2 + 3 mainly unidirectional.
Dimensions: 20.06 x 2.82 m.
Maximum Speed: 75 mph.

DMSL. Dia. DP242. Lot No. 31017 York 1986 – 87. 70S 1L. 35.8 t.
DMS. Dia. DP243. Lot No. 31018 York 1986 – 7. 73S and luggage space. 34.90 t.

150 201	**RN**	RCNH	NH	52201	57201
150 203	**RN**	RCNH	NH	52203	57203
150 205	**P**	RCNH	NH	52205	57205
150 207	**RN**	RCNH	NH	52207	57207
150 208	**P**	RAHA	HA	52208	57208
150 210	**CE**	RDTS	TS	52210	57210
150 211	**RN**	RCNH	NH	52211	57211
150 213	**RN**	RCNH	NH	52213	57213
150 214	**CE**	RDTS	TS	52214	57214
150 215	**GM**	RCNH	NH	52215	57215
150 216	**CE**	RDTS	TS	52216	57216
150 217	**GM**	RCNH	NH	52217	57217
150 219	**P**	RELA	LA	52219	57219
150 221	**P**	RELA	LA	52221	57221
150 223	**GM**	RCNH	NH	52223	57223
150 225	**GM**	RCNH	NH	52225	57225
150 227	**P**	RDTS	TS	52227	57227
150 228	**P**	RAHA	HA	52228	57228
150 229	**RR**	RDTS	TS	52229	57229
150 230	**P**	RELA	LA	52230	57230

150 231	**P**	RDTS	TS	52231	57231
150 232	**P**	RELA	LA	52232	57232
150 233	**P**	RELA	LA	52233	57233
150 234	**P**	RELA	LA	52234	57234
150 235	**P**	RDTS	TS	52235	57235
150 236	**P**	RELA	LA	52236	57236
150 237	**P**	RDTS	TS	52237	57237
150 238	**P**	RELA	LA	52238	57238
150 239	**P**	RELA	LA	52239	57239
150 240	**P**	RELA	LA	52240	57240
150 241	**P**	RELA	LA	52241	57241
150 242	**P**	RELA	LA	52242	57242
150 243	**P**	RECF	CF	52243	57243
150 244	**P**	RECF	CF	52244	57244
150 245	**P**	RAHA	HA	52245	57245
150 246	**P**	RECF	CF	52246	57246
150 247	**P**	RELA	LA	52247	57247
150 248	**P**	RELA	LA	52248	57248
150 249	**P**	RELA	LA	52249	57249
150 250	**P**	RAHA	HA	52250	57250
150 251	**P**	RECF	CF	52251	57251
150 252	**P**	RAHA	HA	52252	57252
150 253	**P**	RELA	LA	52253	57253
150 254	**P**	RECF	CF	52254	57254
150 255	**P**	RAHA	HA	52255	57255
150 256	**P**	RAHA	HA	52256	57256
150 257	**P**	RAHA	HA	52257	57257
150 258	**P**	RAHA	HA	52258	57258
150 259	**P**	RAHA	HA	52259	57259
150 260	**P**	RAHA	HA	52260	57260
150 261	**P**	RECF	CF	52261	57261
150 262	**P**	RAHA	HA	52262	57262
150 263	**P**	RECF	CF	52263	57263
150 264	**P**	RAHA	HA	52264	57264
150 265	**P**	RECF	CF	52265	57265
150 266	**P**	RECF	CF	52266	57266
150 267	**P**	RECF	CF	52267	57267
150 268	**P**	RECF	CF	52268	57268
150 269	**P**	RECF	CF	52269	57269
150 270	**P**	RECF	CF	52270	57270
150 271	**P**	RECF	CF	52271	57271
150 272	**P**	RECF	CF	52272	57272
150 273	**P**	RECF	CF	52273	57273
150 274	**P**	RECF	CF	52274	57274
150 275	**P**	RECF	CF	52275	57275
150 276	**P**	RECF	CF	52276	57276
150 277	**P**	RECF	CF	52277	57277
150 278	**P**	RECF	CF	52278	57278
150 279	**P**	RECF	CF	52279	57279
150 280	**P**	RECF	CF	52280	57280
150 281	**P**	RECF	CF	52281	57281
150 282	**P**	RECF	CF	52282	57282

150 283	**P**	RAHA	HA	52283 57283
150 284	**P**	RAHA	HA	52284 57284
150 285	**P**	RAHA	HA	52285 57285

CLASS 153 LEYLAND BUS SUPER SPRINTER

DMSL. Converted by Hunslet-Barclay, Kilmarnock from Class 155 two-car units.

Engine: One Cummins NT855R5 of 213 kW (285 hp).
Bogies: One P3-10 and one BT38.
Gangways: Throughout.
Doors: Sliding plug.
Seats: 2 + 2 facing/unidirectional with wheelchair space.
Dimensions: 23.21 x 2.70 m.
Maximum Speed: 75 mph.

DMSL. Dia. DX203. Lot No. 31026 1987 – 8. 72S 1L (disabled persons toilet) + 3 tip-up seats. 38.8 t.

Note: Cars numbered in the 573XX series are being renumbered so that the last two digits correspond with the set number.

153 301	**RR**	RBHT	HT	52301
153 302	**RR**	RECF	CF	52302
153 303	**RR**	RECF	CF	52303
153 304	**RR**	RDTS	TS	52304
153 305	**RR**	RECF	CF	52305
153 306	**RR**	RDTS	TS	52306
153 307	**RR**	RDTS	TS	52307
153 308	**RR**	RECF	CF	52308
153 309	**RR**	RDTS	TS	52309
153 310	**RR**	RCNH	NH	52310
153 311	**RR**	RDTS	TS	52311
153 312	**RR**	RECF	CF	52312
153 313	**RR**	RCNH	NH	52313
153 314	**RR**	RDTS	TS	52314
153 315	**RR**	RDTS	TS	52315
153 316	**RR**	RCNH	NH	52316
153 317	**RR**	RBHT	HT	52317
153 318	**RR**	RELA	LA	52318
153 319	**RR**	RBHT	HT	52319
153 320	**RR**	RDTS	TS	52320
153 321	**RR**	RDTS	TS	52321
153 322	**RR**	RDTS	TS	52322
153 323	**RR**	RDTS	TS	52323
153 324	**RR**	RCNH	NH	52324
153 325	**RR**	RDNC	NC	52325
153 326	**RR**	RDTS	TS	52326
153 327	**RR**	RELA	LA	52327
153 328	**RR**	RDTS	TS	52328
153 329	**RR**	RDTS	TS	52329
153 330	**RR**	RCNH	NH	52330
153 331	**RR**	RBHT	HT	52331

153 332	**RR**	RCNH	NH	52332
153 333	**RR**	RDTS	TS	52333
153 334	**RR**	RDTS	TS	52334
153 335	**RR**	RDTS	TS	52335
153 351	**RR**	RBHT	HT	57301
153 352	**RR**	RBHT	HT	57302
153 353	**RR**	RECF	CF	57303
153 354	**RR**	RCNH	NH	57304
153 355	**RR**	RELA	LA	57305
153 356	**RR**	RDTS	TS	57356
153 357	**RR**	RDTS	TS	57307
153 358	**RR**	RBHT	HT	57308
153 359	**RR**	RCNH	NH	57309
153 360	**RR**	RCNH	NH	57310
153 361	**RR**	RCNH	NH	57311
153 362	**RR**	RELA	LA	57312
153 363	**RR**	RCNH	NH	57363
153 364	**RR**	RDTS	TS	57314
153 365	**RR**	RDTS	TS	57365
153 366	**RR**	RDTS	TS	57366
153 367	**RR**	RCNH	NH	57317
153 368	**RR**	RECF	CF	57318
153 369	**RR**	RCNH	NH	57319
153 370	**RR**	RELA	LA	57370
153 371	**RR**	RDTS	TS	57321
153 372	**RR**	RECF	CF	57322
155 373	**RR**	RECF	CF	57323
153 374	**RR**	RELA	LA	57374
153 375	**RR**	RDTS	TS	57325
153 376	**RR**	RDTS	TS	57326
153 377	**RR**	RELA	LA	57327
153 378	**RR**	RDTS	TS	57328
153 379	**RR**	RDTS	TS	57329
153 380	**RR**	RELA	LA	57380
153 381	**RR**	RDTS	TS	57331
153 382	**RR**	RELA	LA	57332
153 383	**RR**	RDNC	NC	57383
153 384	**RR**	RDTS	TS	57334
153 385	**RR**	RDTS	TS	57385

CLASS 155 LEYLAND BUS SUPER SPRINTER

DMSL – DMS.

Engine: One Cummins NT855R5 of 213 kW (285 hp).
Bogies: One P3-10 and one BT38.
Gangways: Throughout.
Doors: Sliding plug.
Seats: 2 + 2 facing/unidirectional with wheelchair space in DMSL.
Dimensions: 23.21 x 2.70 m.
Maximum Speed: 75 mph.

DMSL. Dia. DP248. Lot No. 31057 1988. 80S 1L (disabled persons toilet). 39.0 t.
DMS. Dia. DP249. Lot No. 31058 1988. 80S and parcels area. 38.7 t.

155 341	**Y**	RBNL	NL	52341 57341
155 342	**Y**	RBNL	NL	52342 57342
155 343	**Y**	RBNL	NL	52343 57343
155 344	**Y**	RBNL	NL	52344 57344
155 345	**Y**	RBNL	NL	52345 57345
155 346	**Y**	RBNL	NL	52346 57346
155 347	**Y**	RBNL	NL	52347 57347

CLASS 156 METRO-CAMMELL SUPER SPRINTER

DMSL – DMS.

Engine: One Cummins NT855R5 of 210 kW (285 hp).
Bogies: One P3-10 and one BT38.
Gangways: Throughout.
Doors: Sliding.
Seats: 2 + 2 facing/unidirectional with wheelchair space in DMSL.
Dimensions: 23.03 x 2.73 m.
Maximum Speed: 75 mph.

DMSL. Dia. DP244. Lot No. 31028 1988 – 9. 74S (72S★) 1L (disabled persons toilet). 36.1 t.
DMS. Dia. DP245. Lot No. 31029 1987 – 9. 35.5 t. 76S (74S★) + parcels area.

156 401	r	**P**	RDNC	NC	52401 57401
156 402	r	**P**	RDNC	NC	52402 57402
156 403	r	**P**	RDTS	TS	52403 57403
156 404	r	**P**	RDNC	NC	52404 57404
156 405	r	**P**	RDNC	NC	52405 57405
156 406	r	**P**	RDNC	NC	52406 57406
156 407	r	**P**	RDNC	NC	52407 57407
156 408	r	**P**	RDNC	NC	52408 57408
156 409		**P**	RDDY	DY	52409 57409
156 410		**P**	RDDY	DY	52410 57410
156 411		**P**	RDDY	DY	52411 57411
156 412		**P**	RDDY	DY	52412 57412
156 413		**P**	RDDY	DY	52413 57413
156 414		**P**	RDDY	DY	52414 57414
156 415		**P**	RDDY	DY	52415 57415
156 416		**P**	RDDY	DY	52416 57416
156 417		**P**	RDDY	DY	52417 57417
156 418		**P**	RDDY	DY	52418 57418
156 419		**P**	RDDY	DY	52419 57419
156 420		**P**	RDDY	DY	52420 57420
156 421		**P**	RDDY	DY	52421 57421
156 422		**P**	RDDY	DY	52422 57422
156 423		**P**	RDDY	DY	52423 57423
156 424		**P**	RCNH	NH	52424 57424
156 425		**P**	RCNH	NH	52425 57425
156 426		**P**	RCNH	NH	52426 57426

156 427	P	RCNH	NH	52427	57427
156 428	P	RCNH	NH	52428	57428
156 429	P	RCNH	NH	52429	57429
156 430	P	RACK	CK	52430	57430
156 431	P	RACK	CK	52431	57431
156 432	P	RACK	CK	52432	57432
156 433	P	RACK	CK	52433	57433
156 434	P	RACK	CK	52434	57434
156 435	P	RAHA	HA	52435	57435
156 436	P	RACK	CK	52436	57436
156 437	P	RACK	CK	52437	57437
156 438	P	RBHT	HT	52438	57438
156 439	P	RACK	CK	52439	57439
156 440	P	RCNH	NH	52440	57440
156 441	P	RCNH	NH	52441	57441
156 442	P	RACK	CK	52442	57442
156 443	P	RBHT	HT	52443	57443
156 444	P	RBHT	HT	52444	57444
156 445	r★ P	RACK	CK	52445	57445
156 446	r★ P	RAIS	IS	52446	57446
156 447	r★ P	RAHA	HA	52447	57447
156 448	P	RBHT	HT	52448	57448
156 449	r★ P	RACK	CK	52449	57449
156 450	r★ P	RACK	CK	52450	57450
156 451	P	RBHT	HT	52451	57451
156 452	P	RCNH	NH	52452	57452
156 453	r★ P	RACK	CK	52453	57453
156 454	P	RBNL	NL	52454	57454
156 455	P	RCNH	NH	52455	57455
156 456	r★ P	RAHA	HA	52456	57456
156 457	r★ P	RAIS	IS	52457	57457
156 458	r★ P	RAIS	IS	52458	57458
156 459	P	RCNH	NH	52459	57459
156 460	P	RCNH	NH	52460	57460
156 461	P	RCNH	NH	52461	57461
156 462	P	RDTS	TS	52462	57462
156 463	P	RBHT	HT	52463	57463
156 464	P	RCNH	NH	52464	57464
156 465	r★ P	RACK	CK	52465	57465
156 466	P	RCNH	NH	52466	57466
156 467	P	RDTS	TS	52467	57467
156 468	P	RDTS	TS	52468	57468
156 469	P	RBHT	HT	52469	57469
156 470	P	RBNL	NL	52470	57470
156 471	P	RBNL	NL	52471	57471
156 472	P	RBNL	NL	52472	57472
156 473	P	RBNL	NL	52473	57473
156 474	r★ P	RAIS	IS	52474	57474
156 475	P	RBNL	NL	52475	57475
156 476	P	RAHA	HA	52476	57476
156 477	r★ P	RAIS	IS	52477	57477
156 478	r★ P	RAIS	IS	52478	57478

156 479	**P**	RBNL	NL	52479 57479
156 480	**P**	RBNL	NL	52480 57480
156 481	**P**	RBNL	NL	52481 57481
156 482	**P**	RBNL	NL	52482 57482
156 483	**P**	RBNL	NL	52483 57483
156 484	**P**	RBNL	NL	52484 57484
156 485	r★ **P**	RAHA	HA	52485 57485
156 486	**P**	RBNL	NL	52486 57486
156 487	**P**	RBNL	NL	52487 57487
156 488	**P**	RBNL	NL	52488 57488
156 489	**P**	RBNL	NL	52489 57489
156 490	**P**	RBNL	NL	52490 57490
156 491	**P**	RBNL	NL	52491 57491
156 492	r★ **P**	RACK	CK	52492 57492
156 493	r★ **P**	RAHA	HA	52493 57493
156 494	r★ **P**	RAHA	HA	52494 57494
156 495	r★ **P**	RAHA	HA	52495 57495
156 496	r★ **P**	RACK	CK	52496 57496
156 497	**P**	RBNL	NL	52497 57497
156 498	**P**	RBNL	NL	52498 57498
156 499	r★ **P**	RAIS	IS	52499 57499
156 500	r★ **P**	RAHA	HA	52500 57500
156 501	**S**	RACK	CK	52501 57501
156 502	**S**	RACK	CK	52502 57502
156 503	**S**	RACK	CK	52503 57503
156 504	**S**	RAHA	HA	52504 57504
156 505	**S**	RAHA	HA	52505 57505
156 506	**S**	RACK	CK	52506 57506
156 507	**S**	RACK	CK	52507 57507
156 508	**S**	RACK	CK	52508 57508
156 509	**S**	RACK	CK	52509 57509
156 510	**S**	RACK	CK	52510 57510
156 511	**S**	RACK	CK	52511 57511
156 512	**S**	RACK	CK	52512 57512
156 513	**S**	RACK	CK	52513 57513
156 514	**S**	RACK	CK	52514 57514

CLASS 158/0 BREL EXPRESS

DMSL (B) – DMSL (A) or DMCL – DMSL* or DMSL (B) – MSL – DMSL (A).

Engine: One Cummins NTA855R of 260 kW (350 hp) One Perkins 2006-TWH of 260 kW (350 hp)★ or 300 kW (400 hp)§.
Bogies: One BREL P4 and one BREL T4 per car.
Gangways: Throughout.
Doors: Sliding plug.
Seats: 2 + 2 facing/unidirectional (first & standard classes).
Dimensions: 23.21 x 2.70 m.
Maximum Speed: 90 mph.

DMSL (B).. Dia. DP252. Lot No. 31051 Derby 1990 – 2. 68S + wheelchair space 1L (disabled persons toilet). Public telephone and trolley space. 38.5 t.

158 701 – 158 746

DMCL.. Dia. DP252. Lot No. 31051 Derby 1989 – 90. 15F 51S + wheelchai space 1L (disabled persons toilet). Public telephone and trolley space. 38.5 t
MSL. Dia. DR207. Lot No. 31050 Derby 1991. t. 70S 2L.
DMSL (A). Dia. DP251. Lot No. 31052 Derby 1990 – 92. 70S 1L and parcels area. 37.8 t.

158 701	*	**RE**	RAHA	HA	52701	57701
158 702	*	**RE**	RAHA	HA	52702	57702
158 703	*	**RE**	RAHA	HA	52703	57703
158 704	*	**RE**	RAHA	HA	52704	57704
158 705	*	**RE**	RAHA	HA	52705	57705
158 706	*	**RE**	RAHA	HA	52706	57706
158 707	*	**RE**	RAHA	HA	52707	57707
158 708	*	**RE**	RAHA	HA	52708	57708
158 709	*	**RE**	RAHA	HA	52709	57709
158 710	*	**RE**	RAHA	HA	52710	57710
158 711	*	**RE**	RAHA	HA	52711	57711
158 712	*	**RE**	RAHA	HA	52712	57712
158 713	*	**RE**	RAHA	HA	52713	57713
158 714	*	**RE**	RAHA	HA	52714	57714
158 715	*	**RE**	RAHA	HA	52715	57715
158 716	*	**RE**	RAHA	HA	52716	57716
158 717	*	**RE**	RAHA	HA	52717	57717
158 718	*	**RE**	RAHA	HA	52718	57718
158 719	*	**RE**	RAHA	HA	52719	57719
158 720	*	**RE**	RAHA	HA	52720	57720
158 721	*	**RE**	RAHA	HA	52721	57721
158 722	*	**RE**	RAHA	HA	52722	57722
158 723	*	**RE**	RAHA	HA	52723	57723
158 724	*	**RE**	RAHA	HA	52724	57724
158 725	*	**RE**	RAHA	HA	52725	57725
158 726	*	**RE**	RAHA	HA	52726	57726
158 727	*	**RE**	RAHA	HA	52727	57727
158 728	*	**RE**	RAHA	HA	52728	57728
158 729	*	**RE**	RAHA	HA	52729	57729
158 730	*	**RE**	RAHA	HA	52730	57730
158 731	*	**RE**	RAHA	HA	52731	57731
158 732	*	**RE**	RAHA	HA	52732	57732
158 733	*	**RE**	RAHA	HA	52733	57733
158 734		**RE**	RAHA	HA	52734	57734
158 735		**RE**	RAHA	HA	52735	57735
158 736		**RE**	RAHA	HA	52736	57736
158 737		**RE**	RAHA	HA	52737	57737
158 738		**RE**	RAHA	HA	52738	57738
158 739		**RE**	RAHA	HA	52739	57739
158 740		**RE**	RAHA	HA	52740	57740
158 741		**RE**	RAHA	HA	52741	57741
158 742		**RE**	RAHA	HA	52742	57742
158 743		**RE**	RAHA	HA	52743	57743
158 744		**RE**	RAHA	HA	52744	57744
158 745		**RE**	RAHA	HA	52745	57745
158 746		**RE**	RAHA	HA	52746	57746

158 747		**RE**	RBNL	NL	52747		57747
158 748		**RE**	RBNL	NL	52748		57748
158 749		**RE**	RBNL	NL	52749		57749
158 750		**RE**	RBNL	NL	52750		57750
158 751		**RE**	RBNL	NL	52751		57751
158 752		**RE**	RBNL	NL	52752		57752
158 753		**RE**	RBNL	NL	52753		57753
158 754		**RE**	RBNL	NL	52754		57754
158 755		**RE**	RBNL	NL	52755		57755
158 756		**RE**	RBNL	NL	52756		57756
158 757		**RE**	RBNL	NL	52757		57757
158 758		**RE**	RBNL	NL	52758		57758
158 759		**RE**	RBNL	NL	52759		57759
158 760		**RE**	RBNL	NL	52760		57760
158 761		**RE**	RBNL	NL	52761		57761
158 762		**RE**	RBNL	NL	52762		57762
158 763		**RE**	RBNL	NL	52763		57763
158 764		**RE**	RBNL	NL	52764		57764
158 765		**RE**	RBNL	NL	52765		57765
158 766		**RE**	RBNL	NL	52766		57766
158 767		**RE**	RBNL	NL	52767		57767
158 768		**RE**	RBNL	NL	52768		57768
158 769		**RE**	RBNL	NL	52769		57769
158 770		**RE**	RBNL	NL	52770		57770
158 771		**RE**	RBHT	HT	52771		57771
158 772		**RE**	RBNL	NL	52772		57772
58 773		**RE**	RBHT	HT	52773		57773
58 774		**RE**	RBHT	HT	52774		57774
58 775		**RE**	RBHT	HT	52775		57775
58 776		**RE**	RBHT	HT	52776		57776
58 777		**RE**	RBHT	HT	52777		57777
58 778		**RE**	RBHT	HT	52778		57778
58 779		**RE**	RBHT	HT	52779		57779
58 780	r	**RE**	RDNC	NC	52780		57780
58 781	r	**RE**	RDNC	NC	52781		57781
58 782	r	**RE**	RDNC	NC	52782		57782
58 783	r	**RE**	RDNC	NC	52783		57783
58 784	r	**RE**	RDNC	NC	52784		57784
58 785	r	**RE**	RDNC	NC	52785		57785
58 786	r	**RE**	RDNC	NC	52786		57786
58 787	r	**RE**	RDNC	NC	52787		57787
58 788	r	**RE**	RDNC	NC	52788		57788
58 789	r	**RE**	RDNC	NC	52789		57789
58 790	r	**RE**	RDNC	NC	52790		57790
58 791	r	**RE**	RDNC	NC	52791		57791
58 792	r	**RE**	RDNC	NC	52792		57792
58 793	r	**RE**	RDNC	NC	52793		57793
58 794	r	**RE**	RDNC	NC	52794		57794
58 795	r	**RE**	RDNC	NC	52795		57795
58 796	r	**RE**	RDNC	NC	52796		57796
58 797	r	**RE**	RDNC	NC	52797		57797
58 798		**RE**	RBHT	HT	52798	58715	57798

158 799	**RE**	RBHT	HT	52799	58716	57799
158 800	**RE**	RBHT	HT	52800	58717	57800
158 801	**RE**	RBHT	HT	52801	58701	57801
158 802	**RE**	RBHT	HT	52802	58702	57802
158 803	**RE**	RBHT	HT	52803	58703	57803
158 804	**RE**	RBHT	HT	52804	58704	57804
158 805	**RE**	RBHT	HT	52805	58705	57805
158 806	**RE**	RBHT	HT	52806	58706	57806
158 807	**RE**	RBHT	HT	52807	58707	57807
158 808	**RE**	RBHT	HT	52808	58708	57808
158 809	**RE**	RBHT	HT	52809	58709	57809
158 810	**RE**	RBHT	HT	52810	58710	57810
158 811	**RE**	RBHT	HT	52811	58711	57811
158 812	**RE**	RBHT	HT	52812	58712	57812
158 813	**RE**	RBHT	HT	52813	58713	57813
158 814	**RE**	RBHT	HT	52814	58714	57814
158 815	★ **RE**	RECF	CF	52815		57815
158 816	★ **RE**	RECF	CF	52816		57816
158 817	★ **RE**	RECF	CF	52817		57817
158 818	★ **RE**	RECF	CF	52818		57818
158 819	★ **RE**	RECF	CF	52819		57819
158 820	★ **RE**	RECF	CF	52820		57820
158 821	★ **RE**	RECF	CF	52821		57821
158 822	★ **RE**	RECF	CF	52822		57822
158 823	★ **RE**	RECF	CF	52823		57823
158 824	★ **RE**	RECF	CF	52824		57824
158 825	★ **RE**	RECF	CF	52825		57825
158 826	★ **RE**	RECF	CF	52826		57826
158 827	★ **RE**	RECF	CF	52827		57827
158 828	★ **RE**	RECF	CF	52828		57828
158 829	★ **RE**	RECF	CF	52829		57829
158 830	★ **RE**	RECF	CF	52830		57830
158 831	★ **RE**	RECF	CF	52831		57831
158 832	★ **RE**	RECF	CF	52832		57832
158 833	★ **RE**	RECF	CF	52833		57833
158 834	★ **RE**	RECF	CF	52834		57834
158 835	★ **RE**	RECF	CF	52835		57835
158 836	★ **RE**	RECF	CF	52836		57836
158 837	★ **RE**	RECF	CF	52837		57837
158 838	★ **RE**	RECF	CF	52838		57838
158 839	★ **RE**	RECF	CF	52839		57839
158 840	★ **RE**	RECF	CF	52840		57840
158 841	★ **RE**	RECF	CF	52841		57841
158 842	★r **RE**	RDNC	NC	52842		57842
158 843	★r **RE**	RDNC	NC	52843		57843
158 844	★r **RE**	RDNC	NC	52844		57844
158 845	★r **RE**	RDNC	NC	52845		57845
158 846	★r **RE**	RDNC	NC	52846		57846
158 847	★r **RE**	RDNC	NC	52847		57847
158 848	★r **RE**	RDNC	NC	52848		57848
158 849	★r **RE**	RDNC	NC	52849		57849
158 850	★r **RE**	RDNC	NC	52850		57850

58 851	★r **RE**	RDNC	NC	52851	57851
58 852	★r **RE**	RDNC	NC	52852	57852
58 853	★r **RE**	RDNC	NC	52853	57853
58 854	★r **RE**	RDNC	NC	52854	57854
58 855	★r **RE**	RDNC	NC	52855	57855
58 856	★r **RE**	RDNC	NC	52856	57856
58 857	★r **RE**	RDNC	NC	52857	57857
58 858	★r **RE**	RDNC	NC	52858	57858
58 859	★r **RE**	RDNC	NC	52859	57859
58 860	★r **RE**	RDNC	NC	52860	57860
58 861	★r **RE**	RDNC	NC	52861	57861
58 862	§r **RE**	RDNC	NC	52862	57862
58 863	§ **RE**	RECF	CF	52863	57864
58 864	§ **RE**	RECF	CF	52864	57864
58 865	§ **RE**	RECF	CF	52865	57865
58 866	§ **RE**	RECF	CF	52866	57866
58 867	§ **RE**	RECF	CF	52867	57867
58 868	§ **RE**	RECF	CF	52868	57868
58 869	§ **RE**	RECF	CF	52869	57869
58 870	§ **RE**	RECF	CF	52870	57870
58 871	§ **RE**	RECF	CF	52871	57871
58 872	§ **RE**	RECF	CF	52872	57872

LASS 158/9 BREL EXPRESS

MSL – DMS. Units leased by West Yorkshire PTE. Details as for Class 158/0 xcept for seating layout and toilets.

MSL.. Dia. DP252. Lot No. 31051 Derby 1990 – 2. 70S + wheelchair space – (disabled persons toilet). Public telephone and trolley space. 38.1 t.
MS. Dia. DP251. Lot No. 31052 Derby 1990 – 92. 72S and parcels area. 7.8 t.

58 901	**Y**	RBNL	NL	52901	57901
58 902	**Y**	RBNL	NL	52902	57902
58 903	**Y**	RBNL	NL	52903	57903
58 904	**Y**	RBNL	NL	52904	57904
58 905	**Y**	RBNL	NL	52905	57905
58 906	**Y**	RBNL	NL	52906	57906
58 907	**Y**	RBNL	NL	52907	57907
58 908	**Y**	RBNL	NL	52908	57908
58 909	**Y**	RBNL	NL	52909	57909
58 910	**Y**	RBNL	NL	52910	57910

LASS 159 BREL EXPRESS

MCL – TSL – DMSL. Built as Class 158 by BREL. Under conversion to Class 59 by Rosyth Dockyard.

ngine: One Perkins 2006-TWH of 300 kW (400 hp).
ogies: One BREL P4 and one BREL T4 per car.
angways: Throughout.
oors: Sliding plug.

159 001 – 159 022

Seats: 2 + 2 facing/unidirectional (standard class), 2 + 1 facing (first class).
Dimensions: 23.21 x 2.82 m.
Maximum Speed: 90 mph.

DMCL.. Dia. DP252. Lot No. 31051 Derby 1992. 24F 35S 1L (disabled per-sons toilet). 38.5 t.
MSL. Dia. DR207. Lot No. 31050 Derby 1992. t. 70S 2L.
DMSL. Dia. DP251. Lot No. 31052 Derby 1992. 70S 1L and parcels area 37.8 t.

159 001	**N**	NWXX	SA	52873	58718	57873
159 002	**N**	NWXX	SA	52874	58719	57874
159 003	**N**	NWXX	SA	52875	58720	57875
159 004	**N**	NWXX	SA	52876	58721	57876
159 005	**N**	NWXX	SA	52877	58722	57877
159 006	**N**	NWXX	SA	52878	58723	57878
159 007	**N**	NWXX	SA	52879	58724	57879
159 008	**N**	NWXX	SA	52880	58725	57880
159 009	**N**	NWXX	SA	52881	58726	57881
159 010	**N**	NWXX	SA	52882	58727	57882
159 011	**N**	NWXX	SA	52883	58728	57883
159 012	**N**	NWXX	SA	52884	58729	57884
159 013	**N**	NWXX	SA	52885	58730	57885
159 014	**N**	NWXX	SA	52886	58731	57886
159 015	**N**	NWXX	SA	52887	58732	57887
159 016	**N**	NWXX	SA	52888	58733	57888
159 017	**N**	NWXX	SA	52889	58734	57889
159 018	**N**	NWXX	SA	52890	58735	57890
159 019	**N**	NWXX	SA	52891	58736	57891
159 020	**N**	NWXX	SA	52892	58737	57892
159 021	**N**	NWXX	SA	52893	58738	57893
159 022	**N**	NWXX	SA	52894	58739	57894

CLASS 165/0 BREL NETWORK TURBO

DMCL – DMS or DMC – MS – DMS. Network SouthEast Units for Chiltern Line (Marylebone) services

Engine: One Perkins 2006-TWH of 260 kW (350 hp).
Bogies: One BREL P3 and one BREL T3 per car.
Transmission: Hydraulic. Voith T211r with Gmeinder final drive.
Gangways: Within unit only.
Doors: Sliding plug.
Seats: 2 + 3.
Dimensions: 23.50 x 2.85 t.
Maximum Speed: 75 mph.

58801 – 58822. 58873 – 58878. DMCL. Dia. DP319. Lot No. 31087 York 1990. 16F 72S 1L. 37.0 t.
58823 – 58833. DMCL. Dia. DP320. Lot No. 31089 York 1991 – 1992. 24F 60S 1L. 37.0 t.
MS. Dia. DR208. Lot No. 31090 York 1991 – 1992. 106S. 37.0 t.
DMS. Dia. DP253. Lot No. 31088 York 1991 – 1992. 98S. 37.0 t.

65 001	**N**	NMYX	AL	58801		58834
65 002	**N**	NMYX	AL	58802		58835
65 003	**N**	NMYX	AL	58803		58836
65 004	**N**	NMYX	AL	58804		58837
65 005	**N**	NMYX	AL	58805		58838
65 006	**N**	NMYX	AL	58806		58839
65 007	**N**	NMYX	AL	58807		58840
65 008	**N**	NMYX	AL	58808		58841
65 009	**N**	NMYX	AL	58809		58842
65 010	**N**	NMYX	AL	58810		58843
65 011	**N**	NMYX	AL	58811		58844
65 012	**N**	NMYX	AL	58812		58845
65 013	**N**	NMYX	AL	58813		58846
65 014	**N**	NMYX	AL	58814		58847
65 015	**N**	NMYX	AL	58815		58848
65 016	**N**	NMYX	AL	58816		58849
65 017	**N**	NMYX	AL	58817		58850
65 018	**N**	NMYX	AL	58818		58851
65 019	**N**	NMYX	AL	58819		58852
65 020	**N**	NMYX	AL	58820		58853
65 021	**N**	NMYX	AL	58821		58854
65 022	**N**	NMYX	AL	58822		58855
65 023	**N**	NMYX	AL	58873		58867
65 024	**N**	NMYX	AL	58874		58868
65 025	**N**	NMYX	AL	58875		58869
65 026	**N**	NMYX	AL	58876		58870
65 027	**N**	NMYX	AL	58877		58871
65 028	**N**	NMYX	AL	58878		58872
65 029	**N**	NMYX	AL	58823	55404	58856
65 030	**N**	NMYX	AL	58824	55405	58857
65 031	**N**	NMYX	AL	58825	55406	58858
65 032	**N**	NMYX	AL	58826	55407	58859
65 033	**N**	NMYX	AL	58827	55408	58860
65 034	**N**	NMYX	AL	58828	55409	58861
65 035	**N**	NMYX	AL	58829	55410	58862
65 036	**N**	NMYX	AL	58830	55411	58863
65 037	**N**	NMYX	AL	58831	55412	58864
65 038	**N**	NMYX	AL	58832	55413	58865
65 039	**N**	NMYX	AL	58833	55414	58866

LASS 165/1 BREL NETWORK TURBO

MCL – DMS or DMCL – MS – DMS. Network SouthEast Units for Thames Line addington) services

gine: One Perkins 2006-TWH of 260 kW (350 hp).
gies: One BREL P3 and one BREL T3 per car.
ansmission: Hydraulic. Voith T211r with Gmeinder final drive.
ngways: Within unit only.
ors: Sliding plug.
ats: 2 + 3.
mensions: 23.50 x 2.85 t.

165 101 – 165 137

Maximum Speed: 90 mph.

58953 – 58969. DMCL. Dia. DP320. Lot No. 31098 York 1992. 24F 60S 1L. 37.0 t.
58879 – 58898. DMCL. Dia. DP319. Lot No. 31096 York 1992. 16F 72S 1L. 37.0 t.
MS. Dia. DR208. Lot No. 31099 York 1992. 106S. 37.0 t.
DMS. Dia. DP253. Lot No. 31097 York 1992. 98S. 37.0 t.

165 101	N	NWRX	RG	58916	55415	58953
165 102	N	NWRX	RG	58917	55416	58954
165 103	N	NWRX	RG	58918	55417	58955
165 104	N	NWRX	RG	58919	55418	58956
165 105	N	NWRX	RG	58920	55419	58957
165 106	N	NWRX	RG	58921	55420	58958
165 107	N	NWRX	RG	58922	55421	58959
165 108	N	NWRX	RG	58923	55422	58960
165 109	N	NWRX	RG	58924	55423	58961
165 110	N	NWRX	RG	58925	55424	58962
165 111	N	NWRX	RG	58926	55425	58963
165 112	N	NWRX	RG	58927	55426	58964
165 113	N	NWRX	RG	58928	55427	58965
165 114	N	NWRX	RG	58929	55428	58966
165 115	N	NWRX	RG	58930	55429	58967
165 116	N	NWRX	RG	58931	55430	58968
165 117	N	NWRX	RG	58932	55431	58969
165 118	N	NWRX	RG	58879		58933
165 119	N	NWRX	RG	58880		58934
165 120	N	NWRX	RG	58881		58935
165 121	N	NWRX	RG	58882		58936
165 122	N	NWRX	RG	58883		58937
165 123	N	NWRX	RG	58884		58938
165 124	N	NWRX	RG	58885		58939
165 125	N	NWRX	RG	58886		58940
165 126	N	NWRX	RG	58887		58941
165 127	N	NWRX	RG	58888		58942
165 128	N	NWRX	RG	58889		58943
165 129	N	NWRX	RG	58890		58944
165 130	N	NWRX	RG	58891		58945
165 131	N	NWRX	RG	58892		58946
165 132	N	NWRX	RG	58893		58947
165 133	N	NWRX	RG	58894		58948
165 134	N	NWRX	RG	58895		58949
165 135	N	NWRX	RG	58896		58950
165 136	N	NWRX	RG	58897		58951
165 137	N	NWRX	RG	58898		58952

Class 101 2-car unit No. 101678 in Regional Railways livery forming the 14.25 Llandudno – Blaenau Ffestiniog approaches Llandudno Junction on 17th August 1992. *Chris Morrison*

▲ Class 104/121 hybrid 2-car unit No. L263 (53540/54289) forms the 1
Slough – Paddington at West Ealing on 27th July 1992. *Brian De*

▼ Class 108 2-car unit No. 039 in blue and grey livery forms a Derby – Skeg
service at Attenborough on 22nd July 1992. *Brian De*

-car Class 116 unit T324 arrives at Leamington Spa with the 08.55 from ingham Snow Hill on 20th April 1991. *Hugh Ballantyne*

-car Class 117 unit 117313 climbs Hatton Bank with a Leamington – Tyseley working on 2nd June 1992. *Chris Morrison*

ɜubble Car' Class 121 No. 55031 at West Ealing on a Paddington to Green-
service on 6th August 1992. *Hugh Ballantyne*

ʼest Yorkshire PTE liveried Class 141 No. 141109 leaving Castleford on 2nd
ıst 1990 with the 07.54 Leeds – Goole. *Hugh Ballantyne*

:lass 142 No. 142071 arriving at Bolton with the 15.45 Hazel Grove – Wigan gate on 2nd May 1992. *Hugh Ballantyne*

:hocolate and cream liveried Class 142 No. 142519 passing Gateshead with nderland – Newcastle service on 3rd October 1990. *Hugh Ballantyne*

▲ Class 143 No. 143602 in Regional Railways livery leaving Hartlepool or
April 1992 with the 11.45 Hexham – Middlesborough. *John Augus*

▼ 3-car West Yorkshire PTE Class 144 No. 144018 at Skipton on 13th
1992 with the 15.16 service to Bradford. *Hugh Ballan*

Centro liveried Class 150/1 No. 150116 passing Hatton on a Leamington – Birmingham Snow Hill service on 7th December 1991. *Chris Morrison*

Class 150/1 No. 150136 in the new Greater Manchester PTE livery pauses eyland on 15th August 1992 with the 08.20 Stockport – Blackpool North. *M. Hilbert*

▲ Provincial liveried Class 150/2 No. 150282 heads towards Porth wit
Treherbert bound service on 11th January 1992. *Nic Joyn*

▼ Class 153 No. 153301 approaching Durham on 14th May 1992 with
16.31 service from Newcastle. *John August*

Class 155 No. 155342 leaving Preston with a Leeds train on 25th August 2. *Norman Barrington*

Strathclyde PTE liveried Class 156 No. 156512 leaves Carlisle on 10th July '2 with the 15.48 Glasgow Central – Newcastle. *Kevin Conkey*

Class 158 No. 158723 in Provincial express livery pauses at Dunkfield whilst
he rear of a Edinburgh – Inverness service on 9th July 1992. Note the special
vploughs fitted to all Scottish 158s. *Norman Barrington*

Class 158 No. 158907 leaves York with the 15.08 Newcastle – Liverpool Lime
t on 20th May 1992. *John Augustson*

Network-SouthEast liveried Class 158 No. 158874 passing Port Creek whilst forming a Portsmouth – Salisbury crew

'Network Turbo' Class 165/1 No. 165108 leaving Oxford on 6th August 1992 as the 09.20 to Paddington.
Hugh Ballantyne

▲ Class 205 DEMU No. 205029 has recently been restored to southern railv
green. It is seen at Basingstoke on 10th September 1992 with a service to Salisb
Norman Barring

▼ Network-SouthEast liveried Class 207 No. 207001 at Clapham Junctior
10th September 1992 with the Kensington Olympia shuttle.
Norman Barring

CLASS 166 ABB NETWORK EXPRESS TURBO

DMCL – MS – DMCL. Network SouthEast Units for Paddington – Oxford/Newbury services. Air conditioned. Under constuction.

Engine: One Perkins 2006-TWH of 260 kW (350 hp).
Bogies: One BREL P3 and one BREL T3 per car.
Transmission: Hydraulic. Voith T211r with Gmeinder final drive.
Gangways: Within unit only.
Doors: Sliding plug.
Seats: 2+3.
Dimensions: 23.50 x 2.85 t.
Maximum Speed: 90 mph.

DMCL. Dia. DP321. Lot No. 31116 York 1992 – 3. 16F 72S 1L. . t.
MS. Dia. DR209. Lot No. 31117 York 1992 – 3. 96S. . t.

166 001	N	NWRX	58101	58601	58122
166 002	N	NWRX	58102	58602	58123
166 003	N	NWRX	58103	58603	58124
166 004	N	NWRX	58104	58604	58125
166 005	N	NWRX	58105	58605	58126
166 006	N	NWRX	58106	58606	58127
166 007	N	NWRX	58107	58607	58128
166 008	N	NWRX	58108	58608	58129
166 009	N	NWRX	58109	58609	58130
166 010	N	NWRX	58110	58610	58131
166 011	N	NWRX	58111	58611	58132
166 012	N	NWRX	58112	58612	58133
166 013	N	NWRX	58113	58613	58134
166 014	N	NWRX	58114	58614	58135
166 015	N	NWRX	58115	58615	58136
166 016	N	NWRX	58116	58616	58137
166 017	N	NWRX	58117	58617	58138
166 018	N	NWRX	58118	58618	58139
166 019	N	NWRX	58119	58619	58140
166 020			58120	58610	58141
166 021			58121	58621	58142

3.4. DIESEL ELECTRIC MULTIPLE UNITS

All SR diesel-electric multiple unit power cars have above-floor-mounted engine and all vehicles are equipped with buckeye couplings and were built at Eastleig with frames laid at Ashford.

CLASS 205 3H

DMBSO – TSOL – DTCsoL. Buckeye couplings.

Engine: English Electric 4SRKT engines of 450 kW (600 hp).
Transmission: Two EE 507 traction motors on the inner bogie.
Gangways: Non-gangwayed.
Dimensions: 20.28 x 2.82 m.
Maximum Speed: 75 mph.

60108 – 117/154. DMBSO. Dia DB203. Lot No. 30332 1957. 52S. 56 t.
60120. DMBSO. Dia DB203. Lot No. 30398 1957. 52S. 56 t.
60122 – 124. DMBSO. Dia DB203. Lot No. 30540 1958 – 59. 52S. 56 t.
60145 – 151. DMBSO. Dia DB204. Lot No. 30671 1960 – 62. 42S. 56 t.
60650 – 670. TSO. Dia DH203. Lot No. 30542 1958 – 59. 104S. 30 t.
60672 – 678. TSO. Dia DH203. Lot No. 30672 1960 – 62. 104S. 30 t.
60800 – 817. DTCsoL. Dia DE302. Lot No. 30333 1956 – 57. 19F 50S 2L
60822 – 824. DTCsoL. Dia DE302. Lot No. 30541 1958 – 59. 19F 50S 2L
60826 – 832. DTCsoL. Dia DE303. Lot No. 30673 1960 – 62. 13F 62S 2L. 32

§ – One compartment converted to luggage compartment. 13F 50S 2L. Dia. DE301.

60154 was renumbered from 60100.

205 001	(1101)	§	**N**	NSLX	SU	60154	60650	60800
205 008	(1108)		**N**	NSLX	SU	60120	60651	60814
205 009	(1109)		**N**	NSLX	SU	60108	60658	60808
205 012	(1112)		**N**	NSLX	SU	60111	60661	60811
205 015	(1115)		**N**	NSLX	SU	60114	60664	60801
205 016	(1116)		**N**	NSLX	SU	60115	60665	60815
205 018	(1118)		**N**	NSLX	SU	60117	60667	60817
205 023	(1123)		**N**	NSLX	SU	60122	60668	60822
205 024	(1124)	§	**N**	NSLX	SU	60123	60669	60823
205 025	(1125)	§	**N**	NSLX	SU	60124	60670	60824
205 027	(1127)		**N**	NSLX	SU	60145	60672	60826
205 028	(1128)		**N**	NSLX	SU	60146	60673	60827
205 029	(1129)		**SG**	NWXX	EH	60147	60674	60828
205 031	(1131)			NSLX	SU	60149	60676	60830
205 032	(1132)		**N**	NWXX	EH	60150	60677	60831
205 033	(1133)		**N**	NWXX	EH	60151	60678	60832

CLASS 205/1 3H

DMBSO – TSO – DTSOL. Refurbished 1980. Fluorescent lighting. PA.

Engine: English Electric 4SRKT engines of 450 kW (600 hp).
Transmission: Two EE 507 traction motors on the inner bogie.
Gangways: Within unit only.

imensions: 20.28 x 2.82 m.
laximum Speed: 75 mph.

MBSO. Dia DB203. Lot No. 30332 1957. 39S. 57 t.
SO. Dia DH203. Lot No. 30542 1959. 98S. 30 t.
TSOL. Dia DE204. Lot No. 30333 1957. 76S 2L. 32 t.

05 101	(1111)	**N**	NKCX	SU	60110	60660	60810

LASS 207/0 3D

MBSO – TCsoL – DTSO. Buckeye couplings.

ngine: English Electric 4SRKT engines of 450 kW (600 hp).
ransmission: Two EE 507 traction motors on the inner bogie.
angways: Non-gangwayed.
imensions: 20.34 x 2.74 m. (DMBSO), 20.32 x 2.74 m. (DTS), 20.34 x 2.74 ı. (TCsoL).
laximum Speed: 75 mph.

MBSO. Dia DB205. Lot No. 30625 1962. 42S. 56 t.
CsoL. Dia DH301. Lot No. 30626 1962. 24F 42S 1L. 31 t.
TSO. Dia DE201. Lot No. 30627 1962. 76S. 32 t.

07 001	(1301)	**N**	NWXX	EH	60126	60600	60900
07 010	(1310)	**N**	NWXX	EH	60135	60609	60909
07 013	(1313)	**N**	NWXX	EH	60138	60612	60912
07 017	(1317)	**N**	NWXX	EH	60142	60616	60916

LASS 207/1 2D

MBSO – DTSO. Buckeye couplings.

ngine: English Electric 4SRKT engines of 450 kW (600 hp).
ransmission: Two EE 507 traction motors on the inner bogie.
angways: Fitted with gangways within unit.
imensions: 20.34 x 2.74 m. (DMBSO), 20.32 x 2.74 m. (DTS).
laximum Speed: 75 mph.

MBSO. Dia DB205. Lot No. 30625 1962. 40S. 56 t.
TSO. Dia DE201. Lot No. 30627 1962. 75S. 32 t.

07 101	(1304)	**N**	NKCX	SU	60129	60903
07 102	(1305)	**N**	NKCX	SU	60130	60904
07 103	(1302)	**N**	NKCX	SU	60127	60901

3.5. DEPARTMENTAL DMUs

For information in this section we wish to thank Roger Butcher and Peter Hall.

Various vehicles.

RDB 975010	(79900)	ZA	LaboratoryCoach 19 (Iris).
TDB 975023	(55001)	LO	Route learning car.
TDB 975025	(60755)	SL	NSE inspection saloon.
ADB 975042	(55019)	BY	Route learning and Sandite car. (L119)
TDB 975540	(55016)	TS	Route learning car. (T008).
DB 977391	(51433)	ZA	Ultrasonic test train car.
DB 977392	(53167)	ZA	Ultrasonic test train car.
TDB 977466	(54286)	LA	Sandite vehicle.
TDB 977486	(54285)	TS	Sandite vehicle. T006
RDB 977645	(60450)	ZA	Laboratory Coach.
ADB 977649	(60200)	ZA	Held for further use.
ADB 977650	(60201)	ZA	Held for further use.
RDB 977693	(53222)	ZA	Laboratory Coach 19 (Iris 2).
RDB 977694	(53338)	ZA	Laboratory Coach.19 (Iris 2).
ADB 977696	(60522)	EH	Sandite vehicle.
ADB 977722	(55020)	OO	Route learning & Sandite vehicle. L120.
ADB 977723	(55021)	BY	Route learning & Sandite vehicle. L121.

Test Units.

ZA	977769 (53036)	977770 (54027)
ZA	977775 (55929)	977776 (54904)

Sandite Units.

T003	TS	977826 (55033)	977827 (53886)	
T004	TS	977828 (55034)	977829 (53093)	
T005	TS	977824 (55026)	977825 (53881)	
T007	TS	977752 (51306)	977753 (51321)	
T009	TS	977842 (55032)	977843 (51153)	
901	LO	977744 (51906)	977839 (53642)	
902	LO	977746 (53929)	977748 (53950)	
903	LO	977750 (53959)	977768 (51911)	
904	LO	977765 (51938)	977766 (53944)	
905	HT	977806 (51937)	977807 (52053)	
906	HT	977808 (51903)	977809 (53958)	
907	HT	977810 (51901)	977811 (53956)	
908	LO	977812 (51945)	977813 (52060)	
909	LO	977814 (53926)	977815 (52059)	
910	HT	977836 (53941)	977838 (53981)	
921	CF	977816 (53982)	977817 (52061)	
922	CF	977818 (53939)	977819 (52046)	
923	CF	977820 (53629)	977821 (52058)	
924	CF	977822 (51563)	977823 (51561)	
925	LA	977840 (51932)	977841 (52047)	
931	HA	977832 (52005)	977833 (52025)	Carries 001
932	HA	977830 (51990)	977831 (52030)	Carries 002
933	HA	977834 (51993)	977835 (52012)	Carries 003

1066	SU	977376 (60002)	977379 (60504)	977377 (60003)
1067	SU	977698 (60152)	977697 (60523)	977699 (60153)

New Build:

RDB 999507	ZA	Wickham self propelled laboratory.
DB 999600	ZA	Civil Engineer's track recording unit.
DB 999601	ZA	Civil Engineer's track recording unit.

4. ELECTRIC MULTIPLE UNITS

GENERAL

BR design electric multiple unit vehicles are numbered in the series 61000 – 78999. SR vehicles carry numbers in the SR 14000 – 15999 number series, and there is one unit kept for special duties with vehicles numbered in the LNER 6xxxx number series. Isle of Wight and Waterloo & City line vehicles are numbered in a separate series.

Regional prefix letters used to be carried preceeding the vehicle number, but these are now no longer used and many have been removed. The prefixes were: E – Eastern Region, M – London Midland Region, S – Southern Region, SC – Scottish Region. Prefixes are not shown in this book as they no longer officially form part of the vehicle number. In addition, SR number series vehicles used to carry the suffix S.

In this section, stock is generally listed in order of the unit or set number. The set number is stated first, followed by any notes applicable to the particular set. These are followed by codes for livery, sector and depot respectively. Finally the numbers of the individual cars in the set are given, in order. Please note that reformations can and do occur.

NOTES

nless stated otherwise, all multiple unit vehicles are of BR design, or designed y contractors for BR and have buckeye couplings and tread brakes. Seating 3+2 in standard class open vehicles, 2+2 in first class open vehicles, 12 a non-corridor standard class compartment, 8 to a corridor standard class ompartment and 6 to a corridor first class compartment. In express stock, open andards have 2+2 seating and open firsts have 2+1 seating.

ABBREVIATIONS

he following abbreviations are used in this book:

perator Codes:

ach vehicle is referred to by an operator code as follows:

Motor
M Driving Motor
DM Battery Driving Motor
Trailer
T Driving Trailer
DT Battery Driving Trailer
Brake, i.e. vehicle with luggage space and guards compartment.

First
Standard
Composite
Unclassified
B Buffet Car
handbrake fitted.
SM Buffet Standard (Modular)
MV Parcels and Mails Van
V Luggage Van
Open vehicle
Side corridor with lavatory
o Semi-open vehicle.
Open or semi-open Vehicle with lavatory
ILS Motor Luggage Standard (an MBS minus the guards equipment)

he letters (A) and (B) may be added to the above codes to differentiate betveen two cars of the same operating type which have differences between nem. Note that a consistent system is used, rather than the official operator odes which are sometimes inconsistent.

lotes:

1) Compartment Stock (non-corrridor) has no suffix.
2) Semi-open composites generally have the first class accommodation in comartments and the standard class in open saloons.
3) Unless stated otherwise, it is assumed that motor vehicles are fitted with antographs. If the pantograph is on a trailer, then the trailer has the prefix 'P', .g. PTSO – Pantograph trailer open standard.

Builder Codes:

ABB	ABB Transportation Ltd.
AEI	Associated Electrical Industries Ltd.
BRCW	The Birmingham Railway Carriage & Wagon Co. Ltd.
BTH	The British Thomson Houston Co. Ltd.
CP	Crompton-Parkinson Ltd.
EE	The English Electric Co. Ltd.
GEC	The General Electric Company Ltd.
Gloucester	The Gloucester Railway Carriage and Wagon Co. Ltd.
Hunslet	Hunslet Transportation Projects Ltd.
Metro-Cammell	The Metropolitan Cammell Railway Carriage and Wagon Co. Ltd.

Other Abbreviations:

(S)	Stored Serviceable
(U)	Stored Unserviceable
LNER	London & North Eastern Railway
SR	Southern Railway

DIAGRAMS AND DESIGN CODES

For each type of vehicle, the official design code consists of a seven character code of two letters, four numbers and another letter, e.g. EC2040B. The first five characters of this are the diagram code and are given in the class heading or sub heading. These are explained as follows:

1st Letter

This is always 'E' for an electric multiple unit vehicle.

2nd Letter

as follows for various vehicle types:

A Driving motor passenger vehicles.
B Driving motor passenger vehicles with a brake compartment.
C Non-Driving motor passenger vehicles.
D Non-Driving trailer passenger vehicles with a brake compartment.
E Driving Trailer passenger vehicles.
F Battery Driving Trailer passenger vehicles.
G Driving Trailer passenger vehicles with a brake compartment.
H Trailer passenger vehicles.
I Battery Driving Motor passenger vehicles.
J Trailer passenger vehicles with a brake compartment.
N Trailer passenger vehicles with a buffet compartment.
O Battery Driving Trailer passenger vehicles with a brake compartment.
P Trailer passenger vehicles with a handbrake.
X Driving Motor Luggage Vans.
Y Non-driving Motor Luggage Van.

1st Figure

1 First class accommodation.
2 Standard class accommodation (incl. declassified seats).
3 Composite accommodation.
5 No passenger accommodation.

.1. 25 kV a.c. OVERHEAD EMUs.

ote: All units are 25 kV overhead only except where stated otherwise.

LASS 302

DTCOL – MBSO – TSOL – DTSO or BDTCOL – MBSO – DTSO. All remaining nits refurbished with new seats, fluorescent lighting and pa.
angways: Within unit.
raction Motors: Four EE536A 143.5 kW.
imensions: 19.50 x 2.82 m (outer cars), 19.36 x 2.82 m (inner cars).
aximum Speed: 75 mph.

5084 – 75205. BDTCOL. Lot No. 30436. York/Doncaster 1958 – 59. Dia. F303. 24F 52S 1L. 39.5 t. B5 bogies.
5311 – 75358. BDTCOL. Lot No. 30440. York/Doncaster 1959. Dia. EF303. 4F 52S 1L. 39.5 t. B5 bogies.
1060 – 61091. MBSO. Lot No. 30434. York 1958 – 59. Dia. ED216. 76S. 5.3 t. Gresley Bogies.
1122 – 61226. MBSO. Lot No. 30438. York 1960. Dia. ED216. 76S. 55.3 t. resley Bogies.
0060 – 70091. TSOL. Lot No. 30437. York/Doncaster 1958 – 59. Dia. EH223. 6S 1L. 34.4 t. B4 bogies.
0122 – 70226. TSOL. Lot No. 30441. York 1959 – 61. Dia. EH223. 86S 1L. 4.4 t. B4 bogies.
5033 – 75079. DTSO. Lot No. 30435. York 1958 – 59. Dia. EE219. 88S. 3.4 t. B4 or B5 bogies.
5236 – 75283. DTSO. Lot No. 30439. York 1959 – 60. Dia. EE219. 88S. 3.4 t. B4 or B5 bogies.

★ Temporarily running as Class 305/2.

02 201			**N**	NTSX	EM	75085	61060	70060	75033
02 202			**N**	NTSX	EM	75086	61061	70061	75034
02 203	(302 263)		**N**	NTSX	EM	75311	61122	70122	75236
02 204			**N**	NTSX	EM	75088	61063	70063	75036
02 205			**N**	NTSX	EM	75089	61064	70064	75037
02 206		★	**N**	NTSX	EM		61065		
02 207	(302 310)		**N**	NTSX	EM	75358	61226	70226	75283
02 209			**N**	NTSX	EM	75093	61068	70068	75041
02 210			**N**	NTSX	EM	75094	61069	70069	75042
02 211			**N**	NTSX	EM	75095	61070	70070	75043
02 212			**N**	NTSX	EM	75096	61071	70071	75044
02 213			**N**	NTSX	EM	75097	61072	70072	75060
02 214	(302 304)		**N**	NTSX	EM	75352	61220	70220	75277
02 215			**N**	NTSX	EM	75099	61074	70074	75062
02 216			**N**	NTSX	EM	75100	61075	70075	75063
02 217		★	**N**	NTSX	EM		61076		
02 218			**N**	NTSX	EM	75191	61077	70077	75065
02 219			**N**	NTSX	EM	75192	61078	70078	75066
02 220		★	**N**	NTSX	EM		61079		
02 221			**N**	NTSX	EM	75194	61080	70080	75068

302 222			**N**	NNEX	EM	75195	61081	70081	75069
302 223	(302 293)		**N**	NTSX	EM	75341	61209	70209	75266
302 224			**N**	NTSX	EM	75197	61083	70083	75071
302 225			**N**	NTSX	EM	75198	61084	70084	75072
302 226		★	**N**	NTSX	EM		61085		
302 227	(302 277)		**N**	NNEX	EM	75325	61193	70193	75250
302 228			**N**	NNEX	EM	75201	61087	70087	75075
302 229			**N**	NNEX	EM	75202	61088	70088	75076
302 230	(302 232)		**N**	NNEX	EM	75205	61091	70091	75079
Spare			**N**	NNEX	EM (S)		61224		

Class 302/9. Parcels Units. BDTPMV – MPMV – DTPMV.

68100/3. BDTPMV. Dia. EF501. Lot No. 30435. York 1959.
68101 – 2. BDTPMV. Dia. EF501. Lot No. 30439. York 1959.
68020 – 1. MPMV. Dia. ED501. Lot No. 30434. York 1959.
68022 – 3. MPMV. Dia. ED501. Lot No. 30438. York 1960.
68207/10. DTPMV. Dia. EE501. Lot No. 30435. York 1959.
68208 – 9. DTPMV. Dia. EE501. Lot No. 30439. York 1959.

302 990	**P**	RPMA	IL	68100	68020	68207
302 991	**P**	RPMA	IL	68101	68021	68208
302 992	**P**	RPMA	IL	68102	68022	68209
302 993	**P**	RPMA	IL	68103	68023	68210

Former numbers of converted vehicles:

68020 (61090)	68023 (61222)	68102 (75218)	68208 (75217)
68021 (61067)	68100 (75084)	68103 (75078)	68209 (75219)
68022 (61227)	68101 (75221)	68207 (75082)	68210 (75074)

CLASS 303

DTSO – MBSO – BDTSO. Sliding doors.
Bogies: Gresley.
Gangways: None Gangwayed within units only (r).
Traction Motors: Four MV 155 kW.
Dimensions: 19.50 x 2.82 m (outer cars), 19.36 x 2.82 m (inner cars).
Maximum Speed: 75 mph.

Class 303/0. Unrefurbished sets.

DTSO. Dia. EE206. 83S. 34.4 t.
MBSO. Dia. ED201. 70S. 56.4 t.
BDTSO. Dia. EF202. 83S. 38.4 t.

Class 303/1. Refurbished with 2 + 2 seating and hopper-type window vents. Denoted by 'r'

DTSO. Dia. EE241. 56S. 34.4 t.
MBSO. Dia. ED220. 48S. 56.4 t.
BDTSO. Dia. EF217. 56S. 38.4 t.

75566 – 75599. DTSO. Lot No. 30579 Pressed Steel 1959 – 60.
75747 – 75801. DTSO. Lot No. 30629 Pressed Steel 1960 – 61.
61481 – 61514. MBSO. Lot No. 30580 Pressed Steel 1959 – 60.
61813 – 61867. MBSO. Lot No. 30630 Pressed Steel 1960 – 61.

75601 – 75634. BDTSO. Lot No. 30581 Pressed Steel 1959 – 60.
75803 – 75857. BDTSO. Lot No. 30631 Pressed Steel 1960 – 61.

303 001	r	**S**	RAGW	GW	75566	61481	75601
303 003	r	**S**	RAGW	GW	75568	61483	75603
303 004	r	**S**	RAGW	GW	75569	61484	75604
303 006	r	**S**	RAGW	GW	75571	61486	75606
303 008	r	**S**	RAGW	GW	75573	61488	75608
303 009	r	**S**	RAGW	GW	75574	61489	75609
303 010	r	**S**	RAGW	GW	75575	61490	75610
303 011	r	**S**	RAGW	GW	75576	61491	75611
303 012	r	**S**	RAGW	GW	75577	61492	75612
303 013	r	**S**	RAGW	GW	75578	61493	75613
303 014	r	**S**	RAGW	GW	75579	61494	75614
303 016	r	**S**	RAGW	GW	75750	61496	75616
303 019	r	**S**	RAGW	GW	75584	61499	75619
303 020	r	**S**	RAGW	GW	75585	61500	75620
303 021	r	**S**	RAGW	GW	75586	61501	75621
303 023	r	**S**	RAGW	GW	75588	61503	75623
303 024	r	**S**	RAGW	GW	75589	61504	75624
303 025	r	**S**	RAGW	GW	75590	61505	75625
303 027	r	**S**	RAGW	GW	75592	61507	75627
303 028	r	**S**	RAGW	GW	75600	61508	75635
303 032	r	**S**	RAGW	GW	75597	61512	75632
303 034	r	**S**	RAGW	GW	75599	61514	75634
303 038	r	**S**	RAGW	GW	75748	61814	75804
303 040	r	**S**	RAGW	GW	75581	61816	75806
303 043	r	**S**	RAGW	GW	75572	61819	75809
303 045	r	**S**	RAGW	GW	75755	61821	75811
303 046	r	**S**	RAGW	GW	75756	61822	75812
303 047	r	**S**	RAGW	GW	75757	61823	75813
303 048		**0**	RAGW	GW	75752	61824	75808
303 054	r	**S**	RAGW	GW	75764	61830	75820
303 055	r	**S**	RAGW	GW	75765	61831	75821
303 056	r	**S**	RAGW	GW	75766	61832	75822
303 058	r	**S**	RAGW	GW	75768	61834	75824
303 061	r	**S**	RAGW	GW	75771	61837	75827
303 065	r	**S**	RAGW	GW	75775	61841	75831
303 070	r	**S**	RAGW	GW	75780	61846	75836
303 073		**S**	RAGW	GW	75783	61849	75839
303 077	r	**S**	RAGW	GW	75787	61853	75843
303 079	r	**S**	RAGW	GW	75789	61855	75845
303 080	r	**S**	RAGW	GW	75790	61856	75846
303 083	r	**S**	RAGW	GW	75793	61859	75849
303 085	r	**S**	RAGW	GW	75795	61861	75851
303 087	r	**S**	RAGW	GW	75797	61863	75853
303 088	r	**S**	RAGW	GW	75798	61864	75854
303 089	r	**S**	RAGW	GW	75799	61865	75855
303 090	r	**S**	RAGW	GW	75800	61866	75856
303 091	r	**S**	RAGW	GW	75801	61867	75857
Spare	r	**S**	RFXX	GW (S)		61813	75803

Note: 75752 carries "75758" and 75808 carries "75814"

CLASS 304

BDTSOL – MBSO – DTBSO. Originally 4 cars.
Bogies: Gresley.
Gangways: None.
Traction Motors: Four BTH 155 kW.
Maximum Speed: 75 mph.
Dimensions: 19.53 x 2.82 m (outer cars), 19.36 x 2.82 m (inner cars).

Class 304/1. These cars have pairs of narrow windows instead of wide windows and the MBSOs were formerly MBS and were refurbished with new seats etc.

BDTSOL. Dia. EF203. Lot No. 30429 Wolverton 1960. 80S 2L. 36.8 t.
MBSO. Dia. ED215. Lot No. 30428 Wolverton 1960. 72S. 54.5 t.
DTBSO. Dia. EG202. Lot No. 30430 Wolverton 1960. 82S. 32.5 t.

304 002	RDLG	LG	75046	61046	75646
304 003	RCLG	LG	75047	61047	75647
304 004	RDLG	LG	75048	61048	75648
304 005	RCLG	LG	75049	61049	75649
304 006	RDLG	LG	75050	61050	75650
304 008	RCLG	LG	75052	61052	75652
304 009	RDLG	LG	75053	61053	75653
304 010	RCLG	LG	75054	61054	75654
304 013	RDLG	LG	75057	61057	75657
304 014	RCLG	LG	75058	61058	75658
304 015	RCLG	LG	75059	61059	75659

Class 304/2. Standard design with wide windows.

75681 – 75698. BDTSOL. Dia. EF204. Lot No. 30610 Wolverton 1960 – 61 80S 2L. 36.8 t.
75868 – 75875. BDTSOL. Dia. EF204. Lot No. 30645 Wolverton 1961. 80S 2L. 36.8 t.
61629 – 61646. MBSO. Dia. ED203. Lot No. 30607 Wolverton 1960 – 61. 72S 54.5 t.
61873 – 61880. MBSO. Dia. ED203. Lot No. 30642 Wolverton 1961. 72S 54.5 t.
75661 – 75678. DTBSO. Dia. EG203. Lot No. 30608 Wolverton 1960 – 61 82S. 32.5 t.
75858 – 75865. DTBSO. Dia. EG203. Lot No. 30643 Wolverton 1961. 82S 32.5 t.

304 017		RDLG	LG	75681	61629	75661
304 019	**RR**	RCLG	LG	75683	61631	75663
304 021		RCLG	LG	75685	61633	75665
304 024		RDLG	LG	75688	61636	75668
304 027		RCLG	LG	75691	61639	75671
304 029		RCLG	LG	75693	61641	75673
304 030		RDLG	LG	75694	61642	75674
304 032		RDLG	LG	75696	61644	75676
304 033		RDLG	LG	75697	61645	75677
304 034		RCLG	LG	75698	61646	75678
304 036	**RR**	RCLG	LG	75868	61873	75858

304 037	RR	RCLG	LG	75869	61874	75859
304 040	RR	RCLG	LG	75872	61877	75862
304 042		RCLG	LG	75874	61879	75864
304 043		RCLG	LG	75875	61880	75865

CLASS 305/1

BDTSO – MBSO – DTSO. All facelifted with fluorescent lighting and PA.
Bogies: Gresley.
Gangways: None.
Traction Motors: Four GEC WT380 of 153 kW.
Dimensions: 19.53 x 2.82 m (outer cars), 19.34 x 2.82 m (inner cars).
Maximum Speed: 75 mph.

BDTSO. Dia. EF205. Lot No. 30570 York 1960. 34.9 t. 92S.
MBSO. Dia. ED204. Lot No. 30571 York 1960. 56.4 t. 84S.
DTSO. Dia. EE209. Lot No. 30572 York 1960. 31.5 t. 92S.

305 401		N	NNEX	EM	75462	61429	75514
305 403	(305 445)	N	NNEX	EM	75506	61473	75558
305 410		N	NNEX	EM	75471	61438	75523
305 412			NNEX	EM	75473	61440	75525
305 416		N	NNEX	EM	75477	61444	75529
305 417			NNEX	EM	75476	61445	75530
305 420			NNEX	EM	75481	61448	75533

CLASS 305/2

BDTCOL – MBSO – TSOL – DTSO. All facelifted with fluorescent lighting, new seats and PA.
Bogies: Gresley.
Gangways: Originally non-gangwayed, but now gangwayed within unit.
Traction Motors: Four GEC WT380 of 153 kW.
Dimensions: 19.53 x 2.82 m (outer cars), 19.36 x 2.82 m (inner cars).
Maximum Speed: 75 mph.

BDTCOL. Dia. EF304. Lot No. 30566 York/Doncaster 1960.24F 52S 1L. 36.5 t.
MBSO. Dia. ED216. Lot No. 30567 York/Doncaster 1960. 76S. 56.5 t.
TSOL. Dia. EH223. Lot No. 30568 York/Doncaster 1960. 86S 1L. 31.5 t.
DTSO. Dia. EE220. Lot No. 30569 York/Doncaster 1960. 88S. 32.7 t.

305 501	RR	RAGW	GW	75424	61410	70356	75443
305 502	RR	RAGW	GW	75425	61421	70357	75444
305 503	RR	RCLG	LG	75426	61412		75445
305 504	RR	RCLG	LG	75427	61413		75446
305 506	RR	RCLG	LG	75429	61415		75448
305 507	RR	RCLG	LG	75430	61416		75449
305 508	RR	RAGW	GW	75431	61417	70363	75450
305 509	RR	RCLG	LG	75432	61418		75451
305 510	RR	RCLG	LG	75433	61419		75452
305 511	RR	RCLG	LG	75434	61420		75453
305 513	RR	RCLG	LG	75436	61422		75455
305 514	N	RFXX	BP (S)	75437	61423		75456
305 515	RR	RCLG	LG	75438	61424		75457

305 516	**RR** RCLG	LG	75439	61425		75458
305 517	**RR** RAGW	GW	75440	61426	70372	75459
305 518	**RR** RCLG	LG	75441	61427		75460
305 519	**RR** RAGW	GW	75442	61428	70374	75461

Spare TSOL (DTSO*)

70358	70360	70362	70365	70368	70370	70373	75447*
70359	70361	70364	70366	70369	70371		

CLASS 305/3

BDTSO – MBSO – TCsoL – DTSO. New batch formed by strengthening clas[s] 305/1 with Class 302 TCsoL (which have since been removed). All facelifte[d] with fluorescent lighting, new seats and PA.
Bogies: Gresley.
Gangways: None.
Traction Motors: Four GEC WT380 of 153 kW.
Dimensions: 19.53 x 2.82 m (outer cars), 19.36 x 2.82 m (inner cars).
Maximum Speed: 75 mph.

BDTSO. Dia. EF205. Lot No. 30570 York 1960. 34.9 t. 92S.
MBSO. Dia. ED204. Lot No. 30571 York 1960. 56.4 t. 84S.
DTSO. Dia. EE209. Lot No. 30572 York 1960. 31.5 t. 92S.

305 521	(305 403)	**N**	RFXX		75464	61431	75516
305 525	(305 419)	**N**	NNEX	EM	75480	61447	75532
305 526	(305 422)	**N**	RFXX		75483	61450	75535
305 527	(305 446)	**N**	NNEX	EM	75507	61474	75559
305 528	(305 451)	**N**	NNEX	EM	75512	61479	75564
Spare		**N**	NNEX	EM		61433	

CLASS 305/2

BDTCOL – MBSO – TSOL – DTSO. These sets are Class 302 units temporaril[y] reformed with power cars from Class 305/1. All facelifted with fluorescen[t] lighting, new seats and PA.
Gangways: None.
Traction Motors: Four GEC WT380 of 153 kW.
Dimensions: 19.36 x 2.82 m.
Maximum Speed: 75 mph.

75090 – 75199. BDTCOL. Lot No. 30436. York/Doncaster 1958 – 59. Dia. EF303. 24F 52S 1L. 39.5 t. B5 bogies.
75356. BDTCOL. Lot No. 30440. York/Doncaster 1959. Dia. EF303. 24F 52S 1L. 39.5 t. B5 bogies.
MBSO. Dia. ED204. Lot No. 30571 York 1960. 56.4 t. 84S.
70065 – 70088. TSOL. Lot No. 30437. York/Doncaster 1958 – 59. Dia. EH223. 86S 1L. 34.4 t. B4 bogies.
70224. TSOL. Lot No. 30441. York 1959 – 61. Dia. EH223. 86S 1L. 34.4 t. B4 bogies.
75038 – 75073. DTSO. Lot No. 30435. York 1958 – 59. Dia. EE219. 88S. 33.4 t. B4 or B5 bogies.
75281. DTSO. Lot No. 30439. York 1959 – 60. Dia. EE219. 88S. 33.4 t. B4 or B5 bogies.

305 594	(302 226)	**N**	NNEX	EM	75199 61430 70088 75073
305 595	(302 220)	**N**	NNEX	EM	75193 61446 70079 75067
305 596	(302 208)	**N**	NNEX	EM	75356 61480 70224 75281
305 598	(302 217)	**N**	NNEX	EM	75190 61435 70076 75064
305 599	(302 206)	**N**	NNEX	EM	75090 61434 70065 75038

CLASS 306

DMSO – TBSO – DTSO. Converted 1960 – 1 from 1500 V d.c. Kept for special workings. LNER design. Sliding doors. Screw couplings.
Bogies: LNER bogies.
Gangways: None.
Traction Motors: Four Crompton Parkinson of 155 kW.
Dimensions: 18.41 x 2.90 m (DMSO), 16.78 x 2.90 m (TBSO), 16.87 x 2.90 m (DTSO).
Maximum Speed: 65 mph.
Non-standard Livery: Original BR multiple unit green.

DMSO. Dia. EA217. Lot No. 363 Metro-Cammell. 1949. 51.7 t. 62S.
TBSO. Dia. EJ201. Lot No. 364 1949. Metro-Cammell. 26.4 t. 46S.
DTSO. Dia. EE211. Lot No. 365 1949. BRCW. 27.9 t. 60S.

306 017	**0**	NGEX	IL	65217 65417 65617

CLASS 307

BDTBSO – MSO – TSO – DTCOL. 25 kV a.c. overhead. Converted 1960 – 1 from 1500 V d.c. All refurbished with new seats, fluorescent lighting, PA.
Bogies: Gresley (MSO), B4 (TSO and DTCO) B5 (BDTBSO).
Gangways: Originally non-gangwayed, but now gangwayed within unit.
Traction Motors: Four GEC WT344 of 130 kW.
Dimensions: 19.50 x 2.83 m.
Maximum Speed: 75 mph.

BDTBSO. Dia. EO202. Lot No. 30205 Ashford/Eastleigh 1954 – 6. 66S. 43 t.
MSO. Dia. EC204. Lot No. 30203 Ashford/Eastleigh 1954 – 6. 86S. 47.5 t.
TSOL. Dia. EH222. Lot No. 30204 Ashford/Eastleigh 1954 – 6. 86S 1L. 31 t.
DTCOL. Dia. EE307. Lot No. 30206 Afd./Elh 1954 – 6. 24F 52S 1L. 33 t.

MK Stored at MoD Kineton (near Fenny Compton).

307 102	**N**	PPMB	MK (S)	75002 61002 70002 75102
307 103		PPMB	MK (S)	75003 61003 70003 75103
307 104		PPMB	MK (S)	75004 61004 70004 75104
307 105	**Y**	PPMB	MK (S)	75030 61005 70005 75122
307 107		PPMB	MK (S)	75007 61007 70007 75107
307 108		PPMB	MK (S)	75008 61008 70008 75108
307 109		PPMB	MK (S)	75009 61009 70009 75109
307 110		PPMB	MK (S)	75010 61010 70010 75110
307 111	**Y**	PPMB	MK (S)	75011 61011 70011 75111
307 112		PPMB	MK (S)	75012 61012 70012 75112
307 113		PPMB	MK (S)	75013 61013 70013 75113
307 114		PPMB	MK (S)	75014 61014 70014 75114
307 115		PPMB	MK (S)	75015 61015 70015 75115
307 116		PPMB	MK (S)	75016 61016 70018 75116

307 117	N	PPMB	MK (S)	75017 61017 70017 75117
307 119		PPMB	MK (S)	75019 61019 70019 75119
307 120	Y	PPMB	MK (S)	75005 61020 70030 75105
307 122	Y	PPMB	MK (S)	75022 61022 70022 75120
307 123		PPMB	MK (S)	75023 61023 70023 75123
307 124	N	PPMB	MK (S)	75024 61024 70024 75124
307 125		PPMB	MK (S)	75025 61025 70025 75125
307 126	N	PPMB	MK (S)	75026 61026 70026 75126
307 127		PPMB	MK (S)	75027 61027 70027 75127
307 128		PPMB	MK (S)	75028 61028 70028 75128
307 129		PPMB	MK (S)	75029 61029 70029 75129
307 130	Y	PPMB	MK (S)	75020 61030 70020 75130
307 131		PPMB	MK (S)	75031 61031 70031 75131
307 132	N	PPMB	MK (S)	75032 61032 70032 75132

CLASS 308

BDTCOL – MBSO – TSOL – DTSO. Refurbished with new seats, fluorescent lighting and pa.
Bogies: Gresley.
Gangways: Originally non-gangwayed, but now gangwayed within unit.
Traction Motors: Four English Electric 536A of 143.5 kW.
Dimensions: 19.36 x 2.82 m (outer cars), 19.35 x 2.82 m (inner cars).
Maximum Speed: 75 mph.

75878 – 75886. BDTCOL. Dia. EF304. Lot No. 30652 Yk 1961. 24F 52S 1L. 36.3 t.
75896 – 75919. BDTCOL. Dia. EF304. Lot No. 30656 Yk 1961. 24F 52S 1L. 36.3 t.
75435. BDTCOL. Dia. EF304. Lot No. 30566 York/Doncaster 1960. 24F 52S 1L. 36.5 t. Class 305/1 car.

61883 – 61891. MBSO. Dia. ED216. Lot No. 30653 York 1961. 76S. 55.0 t.
61892 – 61915. MBSO. Dia. ED216. Lot No. 30657 York 1961. 76S. 55.0 t.
70367. TSOL. Dia. EH223. Lot No. 30568 York/Doncaster 1960. 86S 1L. 31.4 t.
70611 – 70619. TSOL. Dia. EH223. Lot No. 30654 York 1961. 86S 1L. 31.4 t.
70620 – 70643. TSOL. Dia. EH223. Lot No. 30658 York 1961. 86S 1L. 31.4 t.
75887 – 75895. DTSO. Dia. EE220. Lot No. 30655 York 1961. 88S. 33 t.
75929 – 75952. DTSO. Dia. EE220. Lot No. 30659 York 1961. 88S. 33 t.

308 133		N	NTSX	EM	75878 61883 70611 75887
308 134		N	NTSX	EM	75879 61884 70612 75888
308 136		N	NTSX	EM	75881 61886 70614 75890
308 137		N	NTSX	EM	75882 61887 70615 75891
308 138		N	NTSX	EM	75883 61888 70367 75892
308 139		N	NTSX	EM	75884 61889 70617 75893
308 140		N	NTSX	EM	75885 61890 70618 75894
308 141		N	NTSX	EM	75886 61891 70619 75895
308 142		N	NTSX	EM	75896 61892 70620 75929
308 143		N	NTSX	EM	75897 61893 70621 75930
308 144	*	N	NTSX	EM	75435 61894 70622 75931
308 145		N	NTSX	EM	75899 61895 70623 75932
308 146		N	NTSX	EM	75900 61896 70624 75933

308 147	**N**	NTSX	EM	75901 61897 70625 75934
308 148	**N**	NTSX	EM	75902 61898 70626 75935
308 149	**N**	NTSX	EM	75903 61899 70627 75936
308 150	**N**	NTSX	EM	75904 61900 70628 75937
308 151	**N**	NTSX	EM	75905 61901 70629 75938
308 152	**N**	NTSX	EM	75913 61902 70630 75939
308 153	**N**	NTSX	EM	75907 61903 70631 75940
308 154	**N**	NTSX	EM	75908 61904 70632 75941
308 155	**N**	NTSX	EM	75909 61905 70633 75942
308 156	**N**	NTSX	EM	75880 61906 70613 75889
308 157	**N**	NTSX	EM	75911 61907 70635 75944
308 158	**N**	NTSX	EM	75912 61908 70636 75945
308 159	**N**	NTSX	EM	75906 61909 70637 75946
308 160	**N**	NTSX	EM	75914 61910 70638 75947
308 161	**N**	NTSX	EM	75915 61911 70639 75948
308 162	**N**	NTSX	EM	75916 61912 70640 75949
308 163	**N**	NTSX	EM	75917 61913 70641 75950
308 164	**N**	NTSX	EM	75918 61914 70642 75951
308 165	**N**	NTSX	EM	75919 61915 70643 75952

CLASS 309/1 ESSEX EXPRESS STOCK

DMBSO(T) – TSOL – TCsoL – BDTSOL. Built 1962 – 3 as 2 car units. Made up to four cars by the conversion of loco-hauled stock in 1973/80 – 1. All now refurbished with fluorescent lighting, hopper ventilators, new seating, PA.
Bogies: Commonwealth.
Gangways: Throughout.
Traction Motors: Four GEC of 210 kW.
Dimensions: 19.76 x 2.82 m (outer cars), 19.67 x 2.82 m (inner cars).
Maximum Speed: 100 mph.

DMBSO(T). Dia. EB206. Lot No. 30684 York 1962 – 63. 44S. 60 t.
71107 – 71110. TSOL. Dia. EH227. Lot No. 30871 Wolverton 1973 – 74. 64S 2L. 35 t.
71569 – 71572. TSOL. Dia. EH227. Lot No. 30954 Wolverton 1978 – 81. 64S 2L. 35 t.
71111 – 71114. TCsoL. Dia. EH309. Lot No. 30872 Wolverton 1973 – 74. 24F 28S 1L. 36 t.
71573 – 71576. TCsoL. Dia. EH309. Lot No. 30954 Wolverton 1978 – 81. 24F 28S 1L. 36 t.
BDTSOL. Dia. EF213. Lot No. 30683 York 1960 – 62. 60S 1L. 40 t.
BDTSOL. Dia. EF213. Lot No. 30683 York 1960 – 62. 60S 1L. 40 t.

Note: 61940/2 are DMBSO and seat 52S.

309 601	**N**	NGEX	CC	61940 71569 71573 75984
309 602	**N**	NGEX	CC	61941 71570 71574 75985
309 603	**N**	NGEX	CC	61942 71571 71575 75986
309 604	**N**	NGEX	CC	61943 71572 71576 75987
309 605	**N**	NGEX	CC	61944 71108 71113 75988
309 606	**N**	NGEX	CC	61945 71109 71112 75989
309 607	**N**	NGEX	CC	61946 71107 71111 75990
309 608	**N**	NGEX	CC	61947 71110 71114 75991

CLASS 309/2 ESSEX EXPRESS STOCK

BDTCsoL – MBSOL(T) – TSO – DTSOL. Built 1962 – 3 as 2 car units. Units 309 611 – 309 618 formerly contained griddle cars, but these were withdrawn and their place has been taken by the conversion of loco-hauled TSOs on refurbishment. All refurbished with fluorescent lighting, hopper ventilators, new seating, PA.
Bogies: Commonwealth.
Gangways: Throughout.
Traction Motors: Four GEC of 210 kW.
Dimensions: 19.76 x 2.82 m (outer cars), 19.67 x 2.82 m (inner cars).
Maximum Speed: 100 mph.

75638 – 44. BDTCsoL. Dia. EF301. Lot No. 30679 York 1962. 18F 32S 2L 40 t.
75963 – 67. BDTCsoL. Dia. EF213. Lot No. 30675 York 1962. 18F 32S 2L 40 t.
61926 – 31. MBSO(T). Dia. ED209. Lot No. 30676 York 1962. 44S 2L. 58 t
61933 – 39. MBSO(T). Dia. ED209. Lot No. 30680 York 1962. 44S 2L. 58 t
70254 – 59. TSO. Dia. EH229. Lot No. 30677 York 1962. 68S 35 t.
71755 – 61. TSO. Dia. EH228. Lot No. 31001 Wolverton 1984 – 87. 68S. 35 t
75970 – 75. DTSOL. Dia. EF213. Lot No. 30678 York 1962. 56S 2L 37 t.
75977 – 83. DTSOL. Dia. EF213. Lot No. 30682 York 1962 – 1963. 56S 2L 37 t.

61933/29/30/31 are MBSO and seat 48S 2L.

309 612		**N**	NGEX	CC	75638	61933	71755	75977
309 613	p	**N**	NGEX	CC	75639	61934	71756	75978
309 616	p	**N**	NGEX	CC	75642	61937	71759	75981
309 617	p	**N**	NGEX	CC	75643	61938	71760	75974
309 618	p	**N**	NGEX	CC	75966	61939	71761	75983
309 623		**N**	NGEX	CC	75641	61927	71758	75980
309 624		**N**	NGEX	CC	75965	61928	70256	75972
309 626		**N**	NGEX	CC	75967	61930	70258	75982
309 627		**N**	NGEX	CC	75644	61931	70259	75975

Former numbers of converted hauled stock:

71107 (26203)	71113 (16244)	71573 (16264)	71756 (5068)
71108 (26189)	71114 (16252)	71574 (16257)	71758 (5058)
71109 (26196)	71569 (5047)	71575 (16242)	71759 (5062)
71110 (26204)	71570 (5050)	71576 (16259)	71760 (5056)
71111 (16246)	71571 (5059)	71755 (5051)	71761 (5066)
71112 (16249)	71572 (5061)		

CLASS 310

Disc brakes. All facelifted. with new panels and PA.
Bogies: B4.
Gangways: Within unit.
Traction Motors: Four EE546 of 201.5 kW.

Dimensions: 19.86 x 2.82 m (outer cars), 19.93 x 2.82 m (inner cars).
Maximum Speed: 75 mph.

BDTSOL. Dia. EF211. Lot No. 30745 Derby 1965 – 67. 80S 2L. 37.3 t.
76228. BDTSOL. Formerly a DTCOL to Lot 39748. Dia. EF210. Seats 68S 2L.
76998. BDTSOL. Rebuilt from TSO 70756 to Lot 30747. Dia. EF214. Seats 75S 2L.
MBSO. Dia. ED219. Lot No. 30746 Derby 1965 – 67. 68S. 57.2 t.
TSO. Dia. EH232. Lot No. 30747 Derby 1965 – 67. 98S. 31.7 t.
DTCOL (310/0). Dia. EE306. Lot No. 30748 Derby 1965 – 67. 25F 43S 2L. 34.4 t.
DTSOL (310/1). Dia. EE237. Lot No. 30748 Derby 1965 – 67. 75S 2L. 34.4 t.

Class 310/0. BDTSOL – MBSO – TSO – DTCOL.

310 046	N	NTSX	EM	76130	62071	70731	76180
310 047	N	NTSX	EM	76131	62072	70732	76181
310 049	N	NTSX	EM	76133	62074	70734	76183
310 050	N	NTSX	EM	76134	62075	70735	76184
310 051	N	NTSX	EM	76135	62076	70736	76185
310 052	N	NTSX	EM	76136	62077	70737	76186
310 056	N	NTSX	EM	76140	62081	70741	76190
310 057	N	NTSX	EM	76141	62082	70742	76191
310 058	N	NTSX	EM	76142	62083	70743	76192
310 059	N	NTSX	EM	76143	62084	70744	76205
310 060	N	NTSX	EM	76144	62085	70745	76194
310 061	N	NTSX	EM	76145	62086	70746	76195
310 064	N	NTSX	EM	76148	62089	70749	76198
310 065	N	NTSX	EM	76149	62090	70750	76199
310 066	N	NTSX	EM	76228	62091	70751	76200
310 067	N	NTSX	EM	76151	62092	70752	76201
310 068	N	NTSX	EM	76152	62093	70753	76202
310 069	N	NTSX	EM	76153	62094	70754	76203
310 070	N	NTSX	EM	76154	62095	70755	76204
310 074	N	NTSX	EM	76158	62099	70759	76208
310 075	N	NTSX	EM	76159	62100	70760	76209
310 077	N	NTSX	EM	76161	62102	70762	76211
310 079	N	NTSX	EM	76163	62104	70764	76222
310 080	N	NTSX	EM	76164	62105	70765	76214
310 081	N	NTSX	EM	76165	62106	70766	76215
310 082	N	NTSX	EM	76166	62107	70767	76216
310 083	N	NTSX	EM	76167	62108	70768	76217
310 084	N	NTSX	EM	76168	62109	70769	76218
310 085	N	NTSX	EM	76169	62110	70770	76219
310 086	N	NTSX	EM	76170	62111	70771	76220
310 087	N	NTSX	EM	76171	62112	70772	76221
310 088	N	NTSX	EM	76172	62113	70773	76213
310 089	N	NTSX	EM	76173	62114	70774	76223
310 091	N	NTSX	EM	76175	62116	70776	76225
310 092	N	NTSX	EM	76176	62117	70777	76226
310 093	N	NTSX	EM	76177	62118	70778	76227
310 094	N	NTSX	EM	76998	62119	70780	76193
310 095	N	NTSX	EM	76179	62120	70779	76229

Class 310/1. BDTSOL – MBSO – TSO – DTSOL.

310 101	(310 073)	**PM**	RDBY	BY	76157	62098	70758	76207
310 102	(310 055)	**PM**	RDBY	BY	76139	62080	70740	76189
310 103	(310 076)	**PM**	RDBY	BY	76160	62101	70761	76210
310 104	(310 078)	**PM**	RDBY	BY	76162	62103	70763	76212
310 105	(310 090)	**PM**	RDBY	BY	76174	62115	70775	76224
310 106	(310 072)	**PM**	RDBY	BY	76156	62097	70757	76206
310 107	(310 062)	**PM**	RDBY	BY	76146	62087	70747	76196
310 108	(310 048)	**PM**	RDBY	BY	76132	62073	70733	76182
310 109	(310 053)	**PM**	RDBY	BY	76137	62078	70738	76187
310 110	(310 054)	**PM**	RDBY	BY	76138	62079	70739	76188
310 111	(310 063)	**PM**	RDBY	BY	76147	62088	70748	76197

CLASS 311

DTSO – MBSO – BDTSO. Sliding doors.
Bogies: Gresley.
Gangways: Non-gangwayed.
Traction Motors: Four AEI 165 kW.
Dimensions: 19.50 x 2.82 m (outer cars), 19.36 x 2.82 m (inner cars).
Maximum Speed: 75 mph.

DTSO. Dia. EE214. Lot No. 30767 Cravens 1967. 83S. 34.4 t.
MBSO. Dia. ED211. Lot No. 30768 Cravens 1967. 70S. 56.4 t.
BDTSO. Dia. EF212. Lot No. 30769 Cravens 1967. 83S. 38.4 t.

311 103	RAGW	GW	76414	62174	76433
311 104	RAGW	GW	76415	62175	76434

CLASS 312

BDTSOL – MBSO – TSO – DTCOL. Disc brakes PA.
Bogies: B4.
Gangways: Within unit.
Traction Motors: Four EE546 of 201.5 kW.
Dimensions: 19.86 x 2.82 m (outer cars), 19.93 x 2.82 m (inner cars).
Maximum Speed: 90 mph.

Class 312/0. Standard design.

76994 – 97 BDTSOL. Dia. EF213. Lot No. 30891 York 1976. 84S 1L. 34.9 t.
62657 – 60 MBSO. Dia. ED214. Lot No. 30892 York 1976. 68S. 56 t.
71277 – 80 TSO. Dia. EH209. Lot No. 30893 York 1976. 98S. 30.5 t.
78045 – 48 DTCOL. Dia. EE305. Lot No. 30894 York 1976. 25F 47S 2L.
76949 – 74 BDTSOL. Dia. EF213. Lot No. 30863 York 1977 – 78. 84S 1L. 34.9 t.
62484 – 509 MBSO. Dia. ED212. Lot No. 30864 York 1977 – 78. 68S. 56 t.

71168 – 93 TSO. Dia. EH209. Lot No. 30865 York 1977 – 78. 98S. 30.5 t.
78000 – 25 DTCOL. Dia. EE305. Lot No. 30866 York 1977 – 78. 25F 47S 2L.

Notes: 312 727 – 730 were formerly numbered 312 201 – 204.

312 701	**N**	NGEX	CC	76949	62484	71168	78000
312 702	**N**	NGEX	CC	76950	62485	71169	78001
312 703	**N**	NGEX	CC	76951	62486	71170	78002
312 704	**N**	NGEX	CC	76952	62487	71171	78003
312 705	**N**	NGEX	CC	76953	62488	71172	78004
312 706	**N**	NGEX	CC	76954	62489	71173	78005
312 707	**N**	NGEX	CC	76972	62490	71174	78024
312 708	**N**	NGEX	CC	76956	62491	71175	78007
312 709	**N**	NGEX	CC	76957	62492	71176	78008
312 710	**N**	NGEX	CC	76958	62493	71177	78009
312 711	**N**	NGEX	CC	76959	62494	71178	78010
312 712	**N**	NGEX	CC	76960	62495	71179	78011
312 713	**N**	NGEX	CC	76961	62496	71180	78012
312 714	**N**	NGEX	CC	76962	62497	71181	78013
312 715	**N**	NGEX	CC	76963	62498	71182	78014
312 716	**N**	NGEX	CC	76964	62499	71183	78015
312 717	**N**	NGEX	CC	76965	62500	71184	78016
312 718	**N**	NGEX	CC	76966	62501	71185	78017
312 719	**N**	NGEX	CC	76967	62502	71186	78018
312 720	**N**	NGEX	CC	76968	62503	71187	78019
312 721	**N**	NGEX	CC	76969	62504	71188	78020
312 722	**N**	NGEX	CC	76970	62505	71189	78021
312 723	**N**	NGEX	CC	76971	62506	71190	78022
312 724	**N**	NGEX	CC	76955	62507	71191	78023
312 725	**N**	NGEX	CC	76973	62508	71192	78006
312 726	**N**	NGEX	CC	76974	62509	71193	78025
312 727	**N**	NGEX	CC	76994	62657	71277	78045
312 728	**N**	NGEX	CC	76995	62658	71278	78046
312 729	**N**	NGEX	CC	76996	62659	71279	78047
312 730	**N**	NGEX	CC	76997	62660	71280	78048

Class 312/1. Can also operate on 6.25 kV a.c. overhead.

BDTSOL. Dia. EF213. Lot No. 30867 York 1975 – 76. 84S 2L. 34.9 t.
MBSO. Dia. ED213. Lot No. 30868 York 1975 – 76. 68S. 56 t.
TSO. Dia. EH209. Lot No. 30869 York 1975 – 76. 98S. 30.5 t.
DTCOL. Dia. EE305. Lot No. 30870 York 1975 – 76. 25F 47S 2L.

312 781	**N**	NGEX	CC	76975	62510	71194	78026
312 782	**N**	NGEX	CC	76976	62511	71195	78027
312 783	**N**	NGEX	CC	76977	62512	71196	78028
312 784	**N**	NGEX	CC	76978	62513	71197	78029
312 785	**N**	NGEX	CC	76979	62514	71198	78030
312 786	**N**	NTSX	EM	76980	62515	71199	78031
312 787	**N**	NTSX	EM	76981	62516	71200	78032
312 788	**N**	NTSX	EM	76982	62517	71201	78033
312 789	**N**	NTSX	EM	76983	62518	71202	78034
312 790	**N**	NTSX	EM	76984	62519	71203	78035
312 791	**N**	NTSX	EM	76985	62520	71204	78036

312 792	**N**	NTSX	EM	76986 62521 71205 78037
312 793	**N**	NTSX	EM	76987 62522 71206 78038
312 794	**N**	NTSX	EM	76988 62523 71207 78039
312 795	**N**	NTSX	EM	76989 62524 71208 78040
312 796	**N**	NTSX	EM	76990 62525 71209 78041
312 797	**N**	NTSX	EM	76991 62526 71210 78042
312 798	**N**	NTSX	EM	76992 62527 71211 78043
312 799	**N**	NTSX	EM	76993 62528 71212 78044

CLASS 313

DMSO – PTSO – BDMSO. Tightlock couplers. Sliding doors. Disc and rheostatic brakes. PA. Cab to shore radio.
System: 25 kV a.c. overhead/750 V d.c. third rail.
Bogies: BX1.
Gangways: Within unit. End doors.
Traction Motors: Four GEC G310AZ of 82.125 kW.
Dimensions: 19.80 x 2.82 m (outer cars), 19.92 x 2.82 m (inner cars).
Maximum Speed: 75 mph.

DMSO (A). Dia. EA204. Lot No. 30879 York 1976 – 77. 74S. 36.4 t.
PTSO. Dia. EH210. Lot No. 30880 York 1976 – 77. 84S. 30.5 t.
DMSO (B). Dia. EI201. Lot No. 30885 York 1976 – 77. 74S. 37.6 t.

* – Extra shoegear for Euston – Watford line services. Class 313/1.

313 001	*	**N**	NNLX	BY	62529 71213 62593
313 002	*	**N**	NNLX	BY	62530 71214 62594
313 003	*	**N**	NNLX	BY	62531 71215 62595
313 004	*	**N**	NNLX	BY	62532 71216 62596
313 005	*	**N**	NNLX	BY	62533 71217 62597
313 006	*	**N**	NNLX	BY	62534 71218 62598
313 007	*	**N**	NNLX	BY	62535 71219 62599
313 008	*	**N**	NNLX	BY	62536 71220 62600
313 009	*	**N**	NNLX	BY	62537 71221 62601
313 010	*	**N**	NNLX	BY	62538 71222 62602
313 011	*	**N**	NNLX	BY	62539 71223 62603
313 012	*	**N**	NNLX	BY	62540 71224 62604
313 013	*	**N**	NNLX	BY	62541 71225 62605
313 014	*	**N**	NNLX	BY	62542 71226 62606
313 015	*	**N**	NNLX	BY	62543 71227 62607
313 016	*	**N**	NNLX	BY	62544 71228 62608
313 017	*	**N**	NNLX	BY	62545 71229 62609
313 018	*	**N**	NGNX	HE	62546 71230 62610
313 019	*	**N**	NGNX	HE	62547 71231 62611
313 020	*	**N**	NGNX	HE	62548 71232 62612
313 021	*	**N**	NNLX	BY	62549 71233 62613
313 022	*	**N**	NNLX	BY	62550 71234 62614
313 023	*	**N**	NGNX	HE	62551 71235 62615
313 024		**N**	NGNX	HE	62552 71236 62616
313 025		**N**	NGNX	HE	62553 71237 62617
313 026		**N**	NGNX	HE	62554 71238 62618
313 027		**N**	NGNX	HE	62555 71239 62619

313 028	**N**	NGNX	HE	62556 71240 62620
313 029	**N**	NGNX	HE	62557 71241 62621
313 030	**N**	NGNX	HE	62558 71242 62622
313 031	**N**	NGNX	HE	62559 71243 62623
313 032	**N**	NGNX	HE	62560 71244 62624
313 033	**N**	NGNX	HE	62561 71245 62625
313 034	**N**	NGNX	HE	62562 71246 62626
313 035	**N**	NGNX	HE	62563 71247 62627
313 036	**N**	NGNX	HE	62564 71248 62628
313 037	**N**	NGNX	HE	62565 71249 62629
313 038	**N**	NGNX	HE	62566 71250 62630
313 039	**N**	NGNX	HE	62567 71251 62631
313 040	**N**	NGNX	HE	62568 71252 62632
313 041	**N**	NGNX	HE	62569 71253 62633
313 042	**N**	NGNX	HE	62570 71254 62634
313 043	**N**	NGNX	HE	62571 71255 62635
313 044	**N**	NGNX	HE	62572 71256 62636
313 045	**N**	NGNX	HE	62573 71257 62637
313 046	**N**	NGNX	HE	62574 71258 62638
313 047	**N**	NGNX	HE	62575 71259 62639
313 048	**N**	NGNX	HE	62576 71260 62640
313 049	**N**	NGNX	HE	62577 71261 62641
313 050	**N**	NGNX	HE	62578 71262 62642
313 051	**N**	NGNX	HE	62579 71263 62643
313 052	**N**	NGNX	HE	62580 71264 62644
313 053	**N**	NGNX	HE	62581 71265 62645
313 054	**N**	NGNX	HE	62582 71266 62646
313 055	**N**	NGNX	HE	62583 71267 62647
313 056	**N**	NGNX	HE	62584 71268 62648
313 057	**N**	NGNX	HE	62585 71269 62649
313 058	**N**	NGNX	HE	62586 71270 62650
313 059	**N**	NGNX	HE	62587 71271 62651
313 060	**N**	NGNX	HE	62588 71272 62652
313 061	**N**	NGNX	HE	62589 71273 62653
313 062	**N**	NGNX	HE	62590 71274 62654
313 063	**N**	NGNX	HE	62591 71275 62655
313 064	**N**	NGNX	HE	62592 71276 62656

CLASS 314

DMSO – PTSO – DMSO. Thyristor control. Tightlock couplers. Sliding doors. Disc and rheostatic brakes. PA. Cab to shore radio.
Bogies: BX1.
Gangways: Within unit. End doors.
Traction Motors: Four GEC G310AZ (Brush TM61-53*) of 82.125 kW.
Dimensions: 19.80 x 2.82 m (outer cars), 19.92 x 2.82 m (inner cars).
Maximum Speed: 75 mph.

DMSO. Dia. EA206. Lot No. 30912 York 1979. 68S. 34.5 t.
PTSO. Dia. EH211. Lot No. 30913 York 1979. 76S. 33.0 t.

314 201	*	**S**	RAGW	GW	64583 71450 64584
314 202	*	**S**	RAGW	GW	64585 71451 64586

314 204	*	**S**	RAGW	GW	64589 71453 64590
314 205	*	**S**	RAGW	GW	64591 71454 64592
314 206	*	**S**	RAGW	GW	64593 71455 64594
314 207		**S**	RAGW	GW	64595 71456 64596
314 208		**S**	RAGW	GW	64597 71457 64598
314 209		**S**	RAGW	GW	64599 71458 64600
314 210		**S**	RAGW	GW	64601 71459 64602
314 211		**S**	RAGW	GW	64603 71460 64604
314 212		**S**	RAGW	GW	64605 71461 64606
314 213		**S**	RAGW	GW	64607 71462 64608
314 214		**S**	RAGW	GW	64609 71463 64610
314 215		**S**	RAGW	GW	64611 71464 64612
314 216		**S**	RAGW	GW	64613 71465 64614
Spare	*	**S**	RAGW	GW (S)	64587 71452

CLASS 315

DMSO – TSO – PTSO – DMSO. Thyristor control. Tightlock couplers. Sliding doors. Disc and rheostatic brakes. PA.
Bogies: BX1.
Gangways: Within unit. End doors.
Traction Motors: Four Brush TM61-53 (GEC G310AZ*) of 82.125 kW.
Dimensions: 19.80 x 2.82 m (outer cars), 19.92 x 2.82 m (inner cars).
Maximum Speed: 75 mph.

64461 – 64582. DMSO. Dia. EA207. Lot No. 30902 York 1980 – 81. 74S. 35 t.
71281 – 71341. TSO. Dia. EH216. Lot No. 30904 York 1980 – 81. 86S. 25.5 t.
71389 – 71449. PTSO. Dia. EH217. Lot No. 30903 York 1980 – 81. 84S. 32 t.

315 801	**N**	NGEX	IL	64461 71281 71389 64462
315 802	**N**	NGEX	IL	64463 71282 71390 64464
315 803	**N**	NGEX	IL	64465 71283 71391 64466
315 804	**N**	NGEX	IL	64467 71284 71392 64468
315 805	**N**	NGEX	IL	64469 71285 71393 64470
315 806	**N**	NGEX	IL	64471 71286 71394 64472
315 807	**N**	NGEX	IL	64473 71287 71395 64474
315 808	**N**	NGEX	IL	64475 71288 71396 64476
315 809	**N**	NGEX	IL	64477 71289 71397 64478
315 810	**N**	NGEX	IL	64479 71290 71398 64480
315 811	**N**	NGEX	IL	64481 71291 71399 64482
315 812	**N**	NGEX	IL	64483 71292 71400 64484
315 813	**N**	NGEX	IL	64485 71293 71401 64486
315 814	**N**	NGEX	IL	64487 71294 71402 64488
315 815	**N**	NGEX	IL	64489 71295 71403 64490
315 816	**N**	NGEX	IL	64491 71296 71404 64492
315 817	**N**	NGEX	IL	64493 71297 71405 64494
315 818	**N**	NGEX	IL	64495 71298 71406 64496
315 819	**N**	NGEX	IL	64497 71299 71407 64498
315 820	**N**	NGEX	IL	64499 71300 71408 64500
315 821	**N**	NGEX	IL	64501 71301 71409 64502
315 822	**N**	NGEX	IL	64503 71302 71410 64504
315 823	**N**	NGEX	IL	64505 71303 71411 64506

315 824		**N**	NGEX	IL	64507	71304	71412	64508
315 825		**N**	NGEX	IL	64509	71305	71413	64510
315 826		**N**	NGEX	IL	64511	71306	71414	64512
315 827		**N**	NGEX	IL	64513	71307	71415	64514
315 828		**N**	NGEX	IL	64515	71308	71416	64516
315 829		**N**	NGEX	IL	64517	71309	71417	64518
315 830		**N**	NGEX	IL	64519	71310	71418	64520
315 831		**N**	NGEX	IL	64521	71311	71419	64522
315 832		**N**	NGEX	IL	64523	71312	71420	64524
315 833		**N**	NGEX	IL	64525	71313	71421	64526
315 834		**N**	NGEX	IL	64527	71314	71422	64528
315 835		**N**	NGEX	IL	64529	71315	71423	64530
315 836		**N**	NGEX	IL	64531	71316	71424	64532
315 837		**N**	NGEX	IL	64533	71317	71425	64534
315 838		**N**	NGEX	IL	64535	71318	71426	64536
315 839		**N**	NGEX	IL	64537	71319	71427	64538
315 840		**N**	NGEX	IL	64539	71320	71428	64540
315 841		**N**	NGEX	IL	64541	71321	71429	64542
315 842	*	**N**	NGEX	IL	64543	71322	71430	64544
315 843	*	**N**	NGEX	IL	64545	71323	71431	64546
315 844	*	**N**	NGEX	IL	64547	71324	71432	64548
315 845	*	**N**	NGEX	IL	64549	71325	71433	64550
315 846	*	**N**	NGEX	IL	64551	71326	71434	64552
315 847	*	**N**	NGEX	IL	64553	71327	71435	64554
315 848	*	**N**	NNEX	IL	64555	71328	71436	64556
315 849	*	**N**	NNEX	IL	64557	71329	71437	64558
315 850	*	**N**	NNEX	IL	64559	71330	71438	64560
315 851	*	**N**	NNEX	IL	64561	71331	71439	64562
315 852	*	**N**	NNEX	IL	64563	71332	71440	64564
315 853	*	**N**	NNEX	IL	64565	71333	71441	64566
315 854	*	**N**	NNEX	IL	64567	71334	71442	64568
315 855	*	**N**	NNEX	IL	64569	71335	71443	64570
315 856	*	**N**	NNEX	IL	64571	71336	71444	64572
315 857	*	**N**	NNEX	IL	64573	71337	71445	64574
315 858	*	**N**	NNEX	IL	64575	71338	71446	64576
315 859	*	**N**	NNEX	IL	64577	71339	71447	64578
315 860	*	**N**	NNEX	IL	64579	71340	71448	64580
315 861	*	**N**	NNEX	IL	64581	71341	71449	64582

CLASS 317

DTSO – MSO – TCOL – DTSO. Thyristor control. Tightlock couplers. Sliding doors. Disc brakes. PA.
Bogies: BP20 (MSO), BT13 (others).
Gangways: Throughout.
Traction Motors: Four GEC G315BZ of 247.5 kW.
Dimensions: 19.83 x 2.82 m (outer cars), 19.92 x 2.82 m (inner cars).
Maximum Speed: 100 mph.

Class 317/1. Pressure ventilated.

DTSO(A) Dia. EE216. Lot No. 30955 York 1981 – 82. 74S. 29.44 t.
MSO. Dia. EC202. Lot No. 30958 York 1981 – 82. 79S. 49.76 t.

TCOL. Dia. EH307. Lot No. 30957 Derby 1981 – 82. 22F 46S 2L. 28.80 t. Controlled emission toilets (but decommisioned).
DTSO(B) Dia. EE235 (EE232★). Lot No. 30956 York 1981 – 82. 70S. (71S★). 29.28 t.

317 301		N	NNEX	HE	77024	62661	71577	77048
317 302		N	NNEX	HE	77001	62662	71578	77049
317 303		N	NNEX	HE	77002	62663	71579	77050
317 304		N	NNEX	HE	77003	62664	71580	77051
317 305		N	NNEX	HE	77004	62665	71581	77052
317 306		N	NNEX	HE	77005	62666	71582	77053
317 307		N	NNEX	HE	77006	62667	71583	77054
317 308		N	NNEX	HE	77007	62668	71584	77055
317 309		N	NNEX	HE	77008	62669	71585	77056
317 310		N	NNEX	HE	77009	62670	71586	77057
317 311		N	NNEX	HE	77010	62671	71587	77058
317 312		N	NNEX	HE	77011	62672	71588	77059
317 313		N	NNEX	HE	77012	62673	71589	77060
317 314		N	NNEX	HE	77013	62674	71590	77061
317 315		N	NNEX	HE	77014	62675	71591	77062
317 316		N	NNEX	HE	77015	62676	71592	77063
317 317		N	NNEX	HE	77016	62677	71593	77064
317 318		N	NNEX	HE	77017	62678	71594	77065
317 319		N	NNEX	HE	77018	62679	71595	77066
317 320		N	NNEX	HE	77019	62680	71596	77067
317 321		N	NNEX	HE	77020	62681	71597	77068
317 322		N	NNEX	HE	77021	62682	71598	77069
317 323		N	NNEX	HE	77022	62683	71599	77070
317 324		N	NGNX	HE	77023	62684	71600	77071
317 325		N	NGNX	HE	77000	62685	71601	77072
317 326		N	NGNX	HE	77025	62686	71602	77073
317 327		N	NGNX	HE	77026	62687	71603	77074
317 328		N	NGNX	HE	77027	62688	71604	77075
317 329		N	NGNX	HE	77028	62689	71605	77076
317 330		N	NGNX	HE	77029	62690	71606	77077
317 331		N	NGNX	HE	77030	62691	71607	77078
317 332		N	NGNX	HE	77031	62692	71608	77079
317 333		N	NGNX	HE	77032	62693	71609	77080
317 334		N	NGNX	HE	77033	62694	71610	77081
317 335		N	NGNX	HE	77034	62695	71611	77082
317 336		N	NGNX	HE	77035	62696	71612	77083
317 337	★	N	NGNX	HE	77036	62697	71613	77084
317 338	★	N	NGNX	HE	77037	62698	71614	77085
317 339	★	N	NGNX	HE	77038	62699	71615	77086
317 340	★	N	NGNX	HE	77039	62700	71616	77087
317 341	★	N	NGNX	HE	77040	62701	71617	77088
317 342	★	N	NGNX	HE	77041	62702	71618	77089
317 343	★	N	NGNX	HE	77042	62703	71619	77090
317 344	★	N	NGNX	HE	77043	62704	71620	77091
317 345	★	N	NGNX	HE	77044	62705	71621	77092
317 346	★	N	NGNX	HE	77045	62706	71622	77093
317 347	★	N	NGNX	HE	77046	62707	71623	77094
317 348	★	N	NGNX	HE	77047	62708	71624	77095

Class 317/2. Convection heating.

77200 – 19. DTSO(A). Dia. EE224. Lot No. 30994 York 1985 – 86. 74S. 29.31 t.
77280 – 83. DTSO(A). Dia. EE224. Lot No. 31007 York 1987. 74S. 29.31 t.
62846 – 65. MSO. Dia. EC205. Lot No. 30996 York 1985 – 86. 79S. 50.08 t.
62886 – 89. MSO. Dia. EC205. Lot No. 31009 York 1987. 79S. 50.08 t.
71734 – 53. TCOL. Dia. EH308. Lot No. 30997 Yk 1985 – 86. 22F 46S 2L. 28.28 t.
71762 – 65. TCOL. Dia. EH308. Lot No. 31010 York 1987. 22F 46S 2L. 28.28 t.
77220 – 39. DTSO(B). Dia. EE225. Lot No. 30995 York 1985 – 86. 29.28 t. 71S.
77284 – 87. DTSO(B). Dia. EE225. Lot No. 31008 York 1987. 29.28 t. 71S.

317 349	**N**	NGNX	HE	77200	62846	71734	77220
317 350	**N**	NGNX	HE	77201	62847	71735	77221
317 351	**N**	NGNX	HE	77202	62848	71736	77222
317 352	**N**	NGNX	HE	77203	62849	71739	77223
317 353	**N**	NGNX	HE	77204	62850	71738	77224
317 354	**N**	NGNX	HE	77205	62851	71737	77225
317 355	**N**	NGNX	HE	77206	62852	71740	77226
317 356	**N**	NGNX	HE	77207	62853	71742	77227
317 357	**N**	NGNX	HE	77208	62854	71741	77228
317 358	**N**	NGNX	HE	77209	62855	71743	77229
317 359	**N**	NGNX	HE	77210	62856	71744	77230
317 360	**N**	NGNX	HE	77211	62857	71745	77231
317 361	**N**	NGNX	HE	77212	62858	71746	77232
317 362	**N**	NGNX	HE	77213	62859	71747	77233
317 363	**N**	NGNX	HE	77214	62860	71748	77234
317 364	**N**	NGNX	HE	77215	62861	71749	77235
317 365	**N**	NNEX	HE	77216	62862	71750	77236
317 366	**N**	NNEX	HE	77217	62863	71752	77237
317 367	**N**	NNEX	HE	77218	62864	71751	77238
317 368	**N**	NNEX	HE	77219	62865	71753	77239
317 369	**N**	NNEX	HE	77280	62886	71762	77284
317 370	**N**	NNEX	HE	77281	62887	71763	77285
317 371	**N**	NNEX	HE	77282	62888	71764	77286
317 372	**N**	NNEX	HE	77283	62889	71765	77287

Name: TCOL No. 71746 of set 317 361 is named 'Kings Lynn Festival'.

CLASS 318

DTSOL – MSO – DTSO. Thyristor control. Tightlock couplers. Sliding doors. Disc brakes. PA. Cab to shore radio.
Bogies: BP20 (MSO), BT13 (others).
Gangways: Throughout.
Traction Motors: Four Brush TM 2141 of 268 kW.
Dimensions: 19.83 x 2.82 m (outer cars), 19.92 x 2.82 m (inner cars).
Maximum Speed: 90 mph.

77240 – 59. DTSOL. Dia. EE227. Lot No. 30999 York 1985 – 86. 66S 1L. 30.01 t.
77288. DTSOL. Dia. EE227. Lot No. 31020 York 1986 – 87. 66S 1L. 30.01 t.

62866 – 85. MSO. Dia. EC207. Lot No. 30998 York 1985 – 86. 79S. 50.90 t.
62890. MSO. Dia. EC207. Lot No. 31019 York 1987. 79S. 50.90 t.
77260 – 79. DTSO. Dia. EE228. Lot No. 31000 York 1985 – 86. 71S. 26.60 t.
77289. DTSO. Dia. EE228. Lot No. 31021 York 1987. 71S. 26.60 t.

318 250	**S**	RAGW	GW	77260	62866	77240
318 251	**S**	RAGW	GW	77261	62867	77241
318 252	**S**	RAGW	GW	77262	62868	77242
318 253	**S**	RAGW	GW	77263	62869	77243
318 254	**S**	RAGW	GW	77264	62870	77244
318 255	**S**	RAGW	GW	77265	62871	77245
318 256	**S**	RAGW	GW	77266	62872	77246
318 257	**S**	RAGW	GW	77267	62873	77247
318 258	**S**	RAGW	GW	77268	62874	77248
318 259	**S**	RAGW	GW	77269	62875	77249
318 260	**S**	RAGW	GW	77270	62876	77250
318 261	**S**	RAGW	GW	77271	62877	77251
318 262	**S**	RAGW	GW	77272	62878	77252
318 263	**S**	RAGW	GW	77273	62879	77253
318 264	**S**	RAGW	GW	77274	62880	77254
318 265	**S**	RAGW	GW	77275	62881	77255
318 266	**S**	RAGW	GW	77276	62882	77256
318 267	**S**	RAGW	GW	77277	62883	77257
318 268	**S**	RAGW	GW	77278	62884	77258
318 269	**S**	RAGW	GW	77279	62885	77259
318 270	**S**	RAGW	GW	77289	62890	77288

Name: DTSOL No. 77240 of set 318 250 is named 'GEOFF SHAW'.

CLASS 319

Thyristor control. Tightlock couplers. Sliding doors. Disc brakes. PA. Cab to shore radio.
System: 25 kV a.c. overhead/750 V d.c. third rail.
Bogies: P7-4 (MSO), T3-7 (others).
Gangways: Within unit. End doors.
Traction Motors: Four GEC G315BZ of 247.5 kW.
Dimensions: 19.83 x 2.82 m (outer cars), 19.92 x 2.82 m (inner cars).
Maximum Speed: 100 mph.

Class 319/0. DTSO – MSO – TSOL – DTSO.

77291 – 381. DTSO. Dia. EE233. Lot No. 31022 (odd nos.) York 1987 – 8. 82S. 30 t.
77431 – 457. DTSO. Dia. EE233. Lot No. 31038 (odd nos.) York 1988. 82S. 30 t.
62891 – 936. MSO. Dia. EC209. Lot No. 31023 York 1987 – 8. 82S. 51 t.
62961 – 974. MSO. Dia. EC209. Lot No. 31039 York 1988. 82S. 51 t.
71772 – 817. TSOL. Dia. EH234. Lot No. 31024 York 1987 – 8. 77S 2L. 51 t.
71866 – 879. TSOL. Dia. EH234. Lot No. 31040 York 1988. 77S 2L. 51 t.
77290 – 380. DTSO. Dia. EE234. Lot No. 31025 (even nos.) York 1987 – 8. 78S. 30 t.
77430 – 456. DTSO. Dia. EE234. Lot No. 31041 (even nos.) York 1988. 78S. 30 t.

319 001	N	NSLX	SU	77291	62891	71772	77290
319 002	N	NSLX	SU	77293	62892	71773	77292
319 003	N	NSLX	SU	77295	62893	71774	77294
319 004	N	NSLX	SU	77297	62894	71775	77296
319 005	N	NSLX	SU	77299	62895	71776	77298
319 006	N	NSLX	SU	77301	62896	71777	77300
319 007	N	NSLX	SU	77303	62897	71778	77302
319 008	N	NSLX	SU	77305	62898	71779	77304
319 009	N	NSLX	SU	77307	62899	71780	77306
319 010	N	NSLX	SU	77309	62900	71781	77308
319 011	N	NSLX	SU	77311	62901	71782	77310
319 012	N	NSLX	SU	77313	62902	71783	77312
319 013	N	NSLX	SU	77315	62903	71784	77314
319 014	N	NSLX	SU	77317	62904	71785	77316
319 015	N	NSLX	SU	77319	62905	71786	77318
319 016	N	NSLX	SU	77321	62906	71787	77320
319 017	N	NSLX	SU	77323	62907	71788	77322
319 018	N	NMLX	SU	77325	62908	71789	77324
319 019	N	NMLX	SU	77327	62909	71790	77326
319 020	N	NMLX	SU	77329	62910	71791	77328
319 021	N	NMLX	SU	77331	62911	71792	77330
319 022	N	NMLX	SU	77333	62912	71793	77332
319 023	N	NMLX	SU	77335	62913	71794	77334
319 024	N	NMLX	SU	77337	62914	71795	77336
319 025	N	NMLX	SU	77339	62915	71796	77338
319 026	N	NMLX	SU	77341	62916	71797	77340
319 027	N	NMLX	SU	77343	62917	71798	77342
319 028	N	NMLX	SU	77345	62918	71799	77344
319 029	N	NMLX	SU	77347	62919	71800	77346
319 030	N	NMLX	SU	77349	62920	71801	77348
319 031	N	NMLX	SU	77351	62921	71802	77350
319 032	N	NMLX	SU	77353	62922	71803	77352
319 033	N	NMLX	SU	77355	62923	71804	77354
319 034	N	NMLX	SU	77357	62924	71805	77356
319 035	N	NMLX	SU	77359	62925	71806	77358
319 036	N	NMLX	SU	77361	62926	71807	77360
319 037	N	NMLX	SU	77363	62927	71808	77362
319 038	N	NMLX	SU	77365	62928	71809	77364
319 039	N	NMLX	SU	77367	62929	71810	77366
319 040	N	NMLX	SU	77369	62930	71811	77368
319 041	N	NMLX	SU	77371	62931	71812	77370
319 042	N	NMLX	SU	77373	62932	71813	77372
319 043	N	NMLX	SU	77375	62933	71814	77374
319 044	N	NMLX	SU	77377	62934	71815	77376
319 045	N	NMLX	SU	77379	62935	71816	77378
319 046	N	NMLX	SU	77381	62936	71817	77380
319 047	N	NMLX	SU	77431	62961	71866	77430
319 048	N	NMLX	SU	77433	62962	71867	77432
319 049	N	NMLX	SU	77435	62963	71868	77434
319 050	N	NMLX	SU	77437	62964	71869	77436
319 051	N	NMLX	SU	77439	62965	71870	77438
319 052	N	NMLX	SU	77441	62966	71871	77440

319 053	**N**	NMLX	SU	77443	62967	71872	77442
319 054	**N**	NMLX	SU	77445	62968	71873	77444
319 055	**N**	NMLX	SU	77447	62969	71874	77446
319 056	**N**	NMLX	SU	77449	62970	71875	77448
319 057	**N**	NMLX	SU	77451	62971	71876	77450
319 058	**N**	NMLX	SU	77453	62972	71877	77452
319 059	**N**	NMLX	SU	77455	62973	71878	77454
319 060	**N**	NMLX	SU	77457	62974	71879	77456

Class 319/1. DTCO – MSO – TSOL – DTSO.

DTCO. Dia. EE310. Lot No. 31063 York 1990. 16F 54S. 29 t.
MSO. Dia. EC214. Lot No. 31064 York 1990. 79S. 50.6 t.
TSOL. Dia. EH238. Lot No. 31065 York 1990. 74S 2L. 31 t.
DTSO. Dia. EE240. Lot No. 31066 York 1990. 78S. 29.7 t.

319 161	**N**	NMLX	SU	77459	63043	71929	77458
319 162	**N**	NMLX	SU	77461	63044	71930	77460
319 163	**N**	NMLX	SU	77463	63045	71931	77462
319 164	**N**	NMLX	SU	77465	63046	71932	77464
319 165	**N**	NMLX	SU	77467	63047	71933	77466
319 166	**N**	NMLX	SU	77469	63048	71934	77468
319 167	**N**	NMLX	SU	77471	63049	71935	77470
319 168	**N**	NMLX	SU	77473	63050	71936	77472
319 169	**N**	NMLX	SU	77475	63051	71937	77474
319 170	**N**	NMLX	SU	77477	63052	71938	77476
319 171	**N**	NMLX	SU	77479	63053	71939	77478
319 172	**N**	NMLX	SU	77481	63054	71940	77480
319 173	**N**	NMLX	SU	77483	63055	71941	77482
319 174	**N**	NMLX	SU	77485	63056	71942	77484
319 175	**N**	NMLX	SU	77487	63057	71943	77486
319 176	**N**	NMLX	SU	77489	63058	71944	77488
319 177	**N**	NMLX	SU	77491	63059	71945	77490
319 178	**N**	NMLX	SU	77493	63060	71946	77492
319 179	**N**	NMLX	SU	77495	63061	71947	77494
319 180	**N**	NMLX	SU	77497	63062	71948	77496
319 181	**N**	NMLX	SU	77973	63093	71979	77974
319 182	**N**	NMLX	SU	77975	63094	71980	77976
319 183	**N**	NMLX	SU	77977	63095	71981	77978
319 184	**N**	NMLX	SU	77979	63096	71982	77980
319 185	**N**	NMLX	SU	77981	63097	71983	77982
319 186	**N**	NMLX	SU	77983	63098	71984	77984

CLASS 320

DTSO – MSO – DTSO. Thyristor control. Tightlock couplers. Sliding doors. Dis brakes. PA.
Bogies: P7-4 (MSO), T3-7 (others).
Gangways: Within unit.
Traction Motors: Brush TM2141B of 268 kW.
Dimensions: 19.83 x 2.82 m (outer cars), 19.92 x 2.82 m (inner car).
Maximum Speed: 75 mph.

DTSO (A). Dia. EE238. Lot No. 31060 York 1990. 77S. 30.7 t.

ISO. Dia. EC212. Lot No. 31062 York 1990. 77S. 52.1 t.
TSO (B). Dia. EE239. Lot No. 31061 York 1990. 76S 31.7 t.

20 301	**S**	RAGW	GW	77899	63021	77921
20 302	**S**	RAGW	GW	77900	63022	77922
20 303	**S**	RAGW	GW	77901	63023	77923
20 304	**S**	RAGW	GW	77902	63024	77924
20 305	**S**	RAGW	GW	77903	63025	77925
20 306	**S**	RAGW	GW	77904	63026	77926
20 307	**S**	RAGW	GW	77905	63027	77927
20 308	**S**	RAGW	GW	77906	63028	77928
20 309	**S**	RAGW	GW	77907	63029	77929
20 310	**S**	RAGW	GW	77908	63030	77930
20 311	**S**	RAGW	GW	77909	63031	77931
20 312	**S**	RAGW	GW	77910	63032	77932
20 313	**S**	RAGW	GW	77911	63033	77933
20 314	**S**	RAGW	GW	77912	63034	77934
20 315	**S**	RAGW	GW	77913	63035	77935
20 316	**S**	RAGW	GW	77914	63036	77936
20 317	**S**	RAGW	GW	77915	63037	77937
20 318	**S**	RAGW	GW	77916	63038	77938
20 319	**S**	RAGW	GW	77917	63039	77939
20 320	**S**	RAGW	GW	77918	63040	77940
20 321	**S**	RAGW	GW	77919	63041	77941
20 322	**S**	RAGW	GW	77920	63042	77942

LASS 321

TCO (DTSO on Class 321/9) – MSO – TSOL – DTSO. Thyristor control. ightlock couplers. Sliding doors. Disc brakes. PA.
ogies: P7-4 (MSO), T3-7 (others).
angways: Within unit.
raction Motors: Brush TM2141B (268 kW).
imensions: 19.83 x 2.82 m (outer cars), 19.92 x 2.82 m (inner cars).
laximum Speed: 100 mph.

lote: Lot numbers and diagrams were officially changed on 09/02/90.

lass 321/3. Units built for Liverpool Street workings.

TCO. Dia. EE308. Lot No. 31053 York 1988 – 90. 12F 56S. 29.3 t.
ISO. Dia. EC210. Lot No. 31054 York 1988 – 90. 79S. 51.5 t.
SOL. Dia. EH235. Lot No. 31055 York 1988 – 90. 74S 2L. 28 t.
TSO. Dia. EE236. Lot No. 31056 York 1988 – 90. 78S. 29.1 t.

321 301	**N**	NGEX	IL	78049	62975	71880	77853
321 302	**N**	NGEX	IL	78050	62976	71881	77854
321 303	**N**	NGEX	IL	78051	62977	71882	77855
321 304	**N**	NGEX	IL	78052	62978	71883	77856
321 305	**N**	NGEX	IL	78053	62979	71884	77857
321 306	**N**	NGEX	IL	78054	62980	71885	77858
321 307	**N**	NGEX	IL	78055	62981	71886	77859
321 308	**N**	NGEX	IL	78056	62982	71887	77860
321 309	**N**	NGEX	IL	78057	62983	71888	77861
321 310	**N**	NGEX	IL	78058	62984	71889	77862

321 311	**N**	NGEX	IL	78059	62985	71890	77863
321 312	**N**	NGEX	IL	78060	62986	71891	77864
321 313	**N**	NGEX	IL	78061	62987	71892	77865
321 314	**N**	NGEX	IL	78062	62988	71893	77866
321 315	**N**	NGEX	IL	78063	62989	71894	77867
321 316	**N**	NGEX	IL	78064	62990	71895	77868
321 317	**N**	NGEX	IL	78065	62991	71896	77869
321 318	**N**	NGEX	IL	78066	62992	71897	77870
321 319	**N**	NGEX	IL	78067	62993	71898	77871
321 320	**N**	NGEX	IL	78068	62994	71899	77872
321 321	**N**	NGEX	IL	78069	62995	71900	77873
321 322	**N**	NGEX	IL	78070	62996	71901	77874
321 323	**N**	NGEX	IL	78071	62997	71902	77875
321 324	**N**	NGEX	IL	78072	62998	71903	77876
321 325	**N**	NGEX	IL	78073	62999	71904	77877
321 326	**N**	NGEX	IL	78074	63000	71905	77878
321 327	**N**	NGEX	IL	78075	63001	71906	77879
321 328	**N**	NGEX	IL	78076	63002	71907	77880
321 329	**N**	NGEX	IL	78077	63003	71908	77881
321 330	**N**	NGEX	IL	78078	63004	71909	77882
321 331	**N**	NGEX	IL	78079	63005	71910	77883
321 332	**N**	NGEX	IL	78080	63006	71911	77884
321 333	**N**	NGEX	IL	78081	63007	71912	77885
321 334	**N**	NGEX	IL	78082	63008	71913	77886
321 335	**N**	NGEX	IL	78083	63009	71914	77887
321 336	**N**	NGEX	IL	78084	63010	71915	77888
321 337	**N**	NGEX	IL	78085	63011	71916	77889
321 338	**N**	NGEX	IL	78086	63012	71917	77890
321 339	**N**	NGEX	IL	78087	63013	71918	77891
321 340	**N**	NGEX	IL	78088	63014	71919	77892
321 341	**N**	NGEX	IL	78089	63015	71920	77893
321 342	**N**	NGEX	IL	78090	63016	71921	77894
321 343	**N**	NGEX	IL	78091	63017	71922	77895
321 344	**N**	NGEX	IL	78092	63018	71923	77896
321 345	**N**	NGEX	IL	78093	63019	71924	77897
321 346	**N**	NGEX	IL	78094	63020	71925	77898
321 347	**N**	NGEX	IL	78131	63105	71991	78280
321 348	**N**	NGEX	IL	78132	63106	71992	78281
321 349	**N**	NGEX	IL	78133	63107	71993	78282
321 350	**N**	NGEX	IL	78134	63108	71994	78283
321 351	**N**	NGEX	IL	78135	63109	71995	78284
321 352	**N**	NGEX	IL	78136	63110	71996	78285
321 353	**N**	NGEX	IL	78137	63111	71997	78286
321 354	**N**	NGEX	IL	78138	63112	71998	78287
321 355	**N**	NGEX	IL	78139	63113	71999	78288
321 356	**N**	NGEX	IL	78140	63114	72000	78289
321 357	**N**	NGEX	IL	78141	63115	72001	78290
321 358	**N**	NGEX	IL	78142	63116	72002	78291
321 359	**N**	NGEX	IL	78143	63117	72003	78292
321 360	**N**	NGEX	IL	78144	63118	72004	78293
321 361	**N**	NGEX	IL	78145	63119	72005	78294
321 362	**N**	NGEX	IL	78146	63120	72006	78295

21 363	**N**	NGEX	IL	78147 63121 72007 78296
21 364	**N**	NGEX	IL	78148 63122 72008 78297
21 365	**N**	NGEX	IL	78149 63123 72009 78298
21 366	**N**	NGEX	IL	78150 63124 72010 78299

ame: DTSOL No. 71891 of set 321 312 is named 'Southend-on-Sea'.

ass 321/4. Units built for WCML workings.

TCO. Dia. EE309. Lot No. 31067 York 1989 – 90. 28F 40S. 29.3 t.
SO. Dia. EC210. Lot No. 31068 York 1989 – 90. 79S. 51.5 t.
SOL. Dia. EH235. Lot No. 31069 York 1989 – 90. 74S 2L. 28 t.
TSO. Dia. EE236. Lot No. 31070 York 1989 – 90. 78S. 29.1 t.

21 401	**N**	NNWX	BY	78095 63063 71949 77943
21 402	**N**	NNWX	BY	78096 63064 71950 77944
21 403	**N**	NNWX	BY	78097 63065 71951 77945
21 404	**N**	NNWX	BY	78098 63066 71952 77946
21 405	**N**	NNWX	BY	78099 63067 71953 77947
21 406	**N**	NNWX	BY	78100 63068 71954 77948
21 407	**N**	NNWX	BY	78101 63069 71955 77949
21 408	**N**	NNWX	BY	78102 63070 71956 77950
21 409	**N**	NNWX	BY	78103 63071 71957 77951
21 410	**N**	NNWX	BY	78104 63072 71958 77952
21 411	**N**	NNWX	BY	78105 63073 71959 77953
21 412	**N**	NNWX	BY	78106 63074 71960 77954
21 413	**N**	NNWX	BY	78107 63075 71961 77955
21 414	**N**	NNWX	BY	78108 63076 71962 77956
21 415	**N**	NNWX	BY	78109 63077 71963 77957
21 416	**N**	NNWX	BY	78110 63078 71964 77958
21 417	**N**	NNWX	BY	78111 63079 71965 77959
21 418	**N**	NNWX	BY	78112 63080 71966 77960
21 419	**N**	NNWX	BY	78113 63081 71967 77961
21 420	**N**	NNWX	BY	78114 63082 71968 77962
21 421	**N**	NNWX	BY	78115 63083 71969 77963
21 422	**N**	NNWX	BY	78116 63084 71970 77964
21 423	**N**	NNWX	BY	78117 63085 71971 77965
21 424	**N**	NNWX	BY	78118 63086 71972 77966
21 425	**N**	NNWX	BY	78119 63087 71973 77967
21 426	**N**	NNWX	BY	78120 63088 71974 77968
21 427	**N**	NNWX	BY	78121 63089 71975 77969
21 428	**N**	NNWX	BY	78122 63090 71976 77970
21 429	**N**	NNWX	BY	78123 63091 71977 77971
21 430	**N**	NNWX	BY	78124 63092 71978 77972
21 431	**N**	NNWX	BY	78151 63125 72011 78300
21 432	**N**	NNWX	BY	78152 63126 72012 78301
21 433	**N**	NNWX	BY	78153 63127 72013 78302
21 434	**N**	NNWX	BY	78154 63128 72014 78303
21 435	**N**	NNWX	BY	78155 63129 72015 78304
21 436	**N**	NNWX	BY	78156 63130 72016 78305
21 437	**N**	NNWX	BY	78157 63131 72017 78306
21 438	**N**	NNWX	BY	78158 63132 72018 78307
21 439	**N**	NNWX	BY	78159 63133 72019 78308
21 440	**N**	NNWX	BY	78160 63134 72020 78309

321 441	N	NNEX	IL	78161	63135	72021	78310
321 442	N	NNEX	IL	78162	63136	72022	78311
321 443	N	NNEX	IL	78125	63099	71985	78274
321 444	N	NNEX	IL	78126	63100	71986	78275
321 445	N	NNEX	IL	78127	63101	71987	78276
321 446	N	NNEX	IL	78128	63102	71988	78277
321 447	N	NNEX	IL	78129	63103	71989	78278
321 448	N	NNEX	IL	78130	63104	71990	78279

Class 321/9. West Yorkshire PTE Units. DTSO(A) – MSO – TSOL – DTSO(B

DTSO (A). Dia. EE277. Lot No. 31108 York 1991. 78S. 29.3 t.
MSO. Dia. EC216. Lot No. 31109 York 1991. 79S. 51.5 t.
TSOL. Dia. EH240. Lot No. 31110 York 1991. 74S 2L. 28 t.
DTSO (B). Dia. EE277. Lot No. 31111 York 1991. 78S. 29.1 t.

321 901	Y	RBNL	NL	77990	63153	72128	77993
321 902	Y	RBNL	NL	77991	63154	72129	77994
321 903	Y	RBNL	NL	77992	63155	72130	77995

CLASS 322 STANSTED EXPRESS STOC

DTCO – MSO – TSOL – DTSO. Units dedicated for use on Stansted Airport se vices. Thyristor control. Tightlock couplers. Sliding doors. Disc brakes. PA
Bogies: P7-4 (MSO), T3-7 (others).
Gangways: Within unit.
Traction Motors: Brush TM2141B (268 kW).
Dimensions: 19.83 x 2.82 m (outer cars), 19.92 x 2.82 m (inner cars).
Maximum Speed: 100 mph.
Non-Standard Livery: Light grey with broad green band and narrow white a dark grey bands. White at cantrail level and on outer ends of end cars. 'Stanst Express' lettering.

DTCO. Dia. EE313. Lot No. 31094 York 1990. 35F 22S. 30.43 t.
MSO. Dia. EC215. Lot No. 31092 York 1990. 70S. 52.27 t.
TSOL. Dia. EH239. Lot No. 31093 York 1990. 60S 2L. 29.51 t.
DTSO. Dia. EE242. Lot No. 31091 York 1990. 65S. 29.77 t.

322 481	0	NNEX	IL	78163	63137	72023	77985
322 482	0	NNEX	IL	78164	63138	72024	77986
322 483	0	NNEX	IL	78165	63139	72025	77987
322 484	0	NNEX	IL	78166	63140	72026	77988
322 485	0	NNEX	IL	78167	63141	72027	77989

CLASS 323

DMSO(A) – TSOL – DMSO(B). New units under construction for West Midlan PTE and Greater Manchester PTE areas. Aluminium alloy bodies. Thyristor co trol. Tightlock couplers. Sliding doors. Disc brakes. PA.
Bogies:
Gangways: Within unit.
Traction Motors:
Dimensions:
Maximum Speed: 75 mph.

MSO(A). Dia. EA272. Lot No. 31112 Hunslet 1992 – 3. 98S (82S*). . t.
SOL. Dia. EH296. Lot No. 31113 Hunslet 1992 – 3. 88S 1L. (80S 1L*). . t.
MSO(B). Dia. EA272. Lot No. 31114 Hunslet 1992 – 3. 98S (82S*). . t.

23 201	**CE**	RDBY	64001	72201	65001
23 202	**CE**	RDBY	64002	72202	65002
23 203	**CE**	RDBY	64003	72203	65003
23 204	**CE**	RDBY	64004	72204	65004
23 205	**CE**	RDBY	64005	72205	65005
23 206	**CE**	RDBY	64006	72206	65006
23 207	**CE**	RDBY	64007	72207	65007
23 208	**CE**	RDBY	64008	72208	65008
23 209	**CE**	RDBY	64009	72209	65009
23 210	**CE**	RDBY	64010	72210	65010
23 211	**CE**	RDBY	64011	72211	65011
23 212	**CE**	RDBY	64012	72212	65012
23 213	**CE**	RDBY	64013	72213	65013
23 214	**CE**	RDBY	64014	72214	65014
23 215	**CE**	RDBY	64015	72215	65015
23 216	**CE**	RDBY	64016	72216	65016
23 217	**CE**	RDBY	64017	72217	65017
23 218	**CE**	RDBY	64018	72218	65018
23 219	**CE**	RDBY	64019	72219	65019
23 220	**CE**	RDBY	64020	72220	65020
23 221	**CE**	RDBY	64021	72221	65021
23 222	**CE**	RDBY	64022	72222	65022
23 223	* **GM**	RCLG	64023	72223	65023
23 224	* **GM**	RCLG	64024	72224	65024
23 225	* **GM**	RCLG	64025	72225	65025
23 226	**GM**	RCLG	64026	72226	65026
23 227	**GM**	RCLG	64027	72227	65027
23 228	**GM**	RCLG	64028	72228	65028
23 229	**GM**	RCLG	64029	72229	65029
23 230	**GM**	RCLG	64030	72230	65030
23 231	**GM**	RCLG	64031	72231	65031
23 232	**GM**	RCLG	64032	72232	65032
23 233	**GM**	RCLG	64033	72233	65033
23 234	**GM**	RCLG	64034	72234	65034
23 235	**GM**	RCLG	64035	72235	65035
23 236	**GM**	RCLG	64036	72236	65036
23 237	**GM**	RCLG	64037	72237	65037
23 238	**GM**	RCLG	64038	72238	65038
23 239	**GM**	RCLG	64039	72239	65039

4.2. SOUTHERN REGION 750 V d.c. EMUs

These classes are all allocated to the Southern Region and operate on the thi rail system at 750 – 850 V d.c. Except where stated otherwise, all multiple unit can run in multiple with one another. Buffet cars have electric cooking. In add tion to the class number, the old SR designations e.g. 2 Hap are quoted togeth with the year of introduction of their type of control gear. Whilst outer coup ings are buckeyes on all units, 1951 and 1957-type suburban units have cent buffers and three link couplings within a unit.

CLASS 438 — 4 T

DTSO – TFK – TBSK – DTSO or DTSO – TBSK – DTSO. Converted from loc hauled stock. Unpowered units which worked push & pull with class 431/2 tra tor units and class 33/1 and 73 locos. Express stock. Two units remain an have regained their original numbers for use on charter and special service

Electrical Equipment: 1966-type.
Bogies: B5 (SR) bogies.
Gangways: Throughout.
Dimensions: 19.66 x 2.82 m.
Maximum Speed: 90 mph.

DTSO. Dia. EE266. Lot No. 30764 York 1966 – 67. 64S. 32 t.
TCK. Dia. EH363. Lot No. 30766 York 1966 – 67. 42F 2L. 33.5 t.
TBSK. Dia. EJ260. Lot No. 30765 York 1966 – 67. 32S 1L. 35.5 t.

Renumbered from 8010/8017. Formerly class 491.

410	(8010)	pa	**B**	NSSX	BM	76288	70859	70812	7628
417	(8017)	pa	**B**	NSSX	BM	76302	70860	70826	7630
Spare		pa	**N**	NKCX	RE	76275			
Spare			**N**	NSSX	BM (S)	76327			

Former numbers of vehicles converted from hauled stock:

70812 (34987)	70860 (13019)	76288 (4391)	76302 (4382)
70826 (34980)	76275 (3929)	76301 (4375)	76327 (4018)
70859 (13040)	76287 (4379)		

CLASS 421 — 4 Cig (PHASE 2

DTCsoL (A) – MBSO – TSO – DTCsoL (B). Express stock. All facelifted with ne trim, fluorescent lighting in saloons, PA.

Note: The following details apply to all Class 421 (phase 2) sets.

Diagram Numbers: EE369, ED264, EH287, EE369.
Electrical Equipment: 1963-type.
Bogies: Two Mk. 6 motor bogies (MBSO). B5 (SR) bogies (trailer cars).
Gangways: Throughout.
Traction Motors: Four EE507 of 185 kW.
Dimensions: 19.75 x 2.82 m.
Maximum Speed: 90 mph.

6561 – 76570. DTCsoL(A). Lot No. 30802 York 1970. 18F 36S 2L. 35.5 t.
6581 – 76610. DTCsoL(A). Lot No. 30806 York 1970. 18F 36S 2L. 35.5 t.
6717 – 76787. DTCsoL(A). Lot No. 30814 York 1970 – 72. 18F 36S 2L. 5.5 t.
6859. DTCsoL(A). Lot No. 30827 York 1972. 18F 36S 2L. 35.5 t.
2277 – 62286. MBSO. Lot No. 30804 York 1970. 56S. 49t.
2287 – 62316. MBSO. Lot No. 30808 York 1970. 56S. 49t.
2355 – 62425. MBSO. Lot No. 30816 York 1970. 56S. 49t.
2430. MBSO. Lot No. 30829 York 1972. 56S. 49t.
0967 – 70996. TSO. Lot No. 30809 York 1970 – 71. 72S. 31.5t.
1035 – 71105. TSO. Lot No. 30817 York 1970. 72S. 31.5t.
1106. TSO. Lot No. 30830 York 1972. 72S. 31.5t.
1926 – 71928. TSO. Lot No. 30805 York 1970. 72S. 31.5t.
6571 – 76580. DTCsoL(B). Lot No. 30802 York 1970. 24F 28S 2L. 35 t.
6611 – 76640. DTCsoL(B). Lot No. 30807 York 1970. 24F 28S 2L. 35 t.
6788 – 76858. DTCsoL(B). Lot No. 30815 York 1970 – 72. 24F 28S 2L. 35 t.
6859. DTCsoL(B). Lot No. 30828 York 1972. 18F 36S 2L. 35 t.

lass 421/5. 'Greyhound' Units.

itted with an additional stage of field weakening to improve the maximum attainable speed.

301	(1814)	**N**	NSSX	EH	76595	62301	70981	76625
302	(1815)	**N**	NSSX	EH	76584	62290	70970	76614
303	(1816)	**N**	NSSX	EH	76581	62287	70967	76611
304	(1817)	**N**	NSSX	EH	76583	62289	70969	76613
305	(1818)	**N**	NSSX	EH	76717	62355	71035	76788
306	(1819)	**N**	NSSX	EH	76723	62361	71041	76794
307	(1820)	**N**	NSSX	EH	76586	62292	70972	76616
308	(1821)	**N**	NSSX	EH	76627	62298	70978	76622
309	(1822)	**N**	NSSX	EH	76594	62300	70980	76624
310	(1823)	**N**	NSSX	EH	76567	62283	71926	76577
311	(1824)	**N**	NSSX	EH	76561	62277	71927	76571
312	(1825)	**N**	NSSX	EH	76562	62278	71928	76572
313	(1252)	**N**	NSSX	EH	76596	62302	70982	76626
314	(1244)	**N**	NSSX	EH	76588	62294	70974	76618
315	(1264)	**N**	NSSX	EH	76608	62314	70994	76638
316	(1241)	**N**	NSSX	EH	76585	62291	70971	76615
317	(1253)	**N**	NSSX	EH	76597	62303	70983	76592
318	(1849)	**N**	NSSX	EH	76590	62296	70976	76620
319	(1852)	**N**	NSSX	EH	76591	62297	70977	76621
320	(1836)	**N**	NSSX	EH	76593	62299	70979	76623
321	(1844)	**N**	NSSX	EH	76589	62295	70975	76619
322	(1838)	**N**	NSSX	EH	76587	62293	70973	76617

ormer numbers of converted buffet cars:

1926 (69315)	71927 (69330)	71928 (69331)

lote: No new Lot Nos were issued for the above conversions.

CLASS 411/4* & 411/5 REFURBISHED 4 Cep

DMSO (A) – TBCK – TSOL – DMSO (B). Kent Coast Express Stock. Refurbished and renumbered from the 71/72xx series. Fitted with hopper ventilators, Inter-City 70 seats, fluorescent lighting and PA.

Electrical Equipment: 1957-type (*1951-type).
Bogies: One Mk. 4 (Mk 3B§) motor bogie (DMSO). Commonwealth trailer bogies.
Gangways: Throughout.
Traction Motors: Two EE507 of 185 kW.
Dimensions: 19.75 x 2.82 m.
Maximum Speed: 90 mph.

★ – 70345 is a TBFK with one compartment declassified. It is from the original refurbished unit (1500), has a different interior colour scheme and does not have hopper ventilators.

61305 has four seats at inner vestibule end replaced by luggage racks.

DMSO (A). Dia. EA263. 64S. 44.15 t.
TBCK. Dia. EJ361. 24F 6S 2L. 36.17 t.
TSOL. Dia. EH282. 64S 2L. 33.78 t.
DMSO (B). Dia. EA264. 64S. 43.54 t.

Lot numbers are as follows, all cars being built at Ashford/Eastleigh:

61033 – 61040. 30108 1956.
61041 – 61044. 30111 1956.
61229 – 61240. 30449 1958.
61304 – 61409. 30454 1958 – 59.
61694 – 61811. 30619 1960 – 61.
61868 – 61870. 30638 1960 – 61.
61948 – 61961. 30708 1963.
70033 – 70036. 30109 1956.
70037 – 70040. 30110 1956.
70041 – 70042. 30112 1956.
70043 – 70044. 30639 1961.
70229 – 70234. 30450 1958.
70235 – 70240. 30451 1958.
70241. 30640 1961.
70260 – 70302. 30455 1958 – 59.
70303 – 70355. 30456 1958 – 59.
70503 – 70551. 30620 1960 – 61.
70552 – 70610. 30621 1960 – 61.
70653 – 70659. 30709 1963.
70660 – 70666. 30710 1963.

1501	*	**N**	NKCX	RE	61041	70041	70034	61042
1502	*	**N**	NKCX	RE	61040	70040	70036	61039
1503	*	**N**	NKCX	RE	61033	70037	70033	61034
1504	*	**N**	NKCX	RE	61043	70042	71712	61037
1505	*	**N**	NKCX	RE	61044	70039	70035	61038
1506		**N**	NKCX	RE (U)	61314	70325	70282	61348
1507		**N**	NKCX	RE	61363	70332	70289	61362
1508		**N**	NKCX	RE	61305	70303	70260	61304
1509		**N**	NKCX	RE	61335	70318	70275	61334
1510		**N**	NKCX	RE	61365	70333	70290	61364
1511		**N**	NKCX	RE	61367	70334	70291	61366
1512		**N**	NKCX	RE	61321	70311	70268	61320
1513		**N**	NKCX	RE	61796	70321	70278	61340
1514		**N**	NKCX	RE	61327	70314	70271	61326
1515		**N**	NKCX	RE	61345	70323	70280	61344
1516		**N**	NKCX	RE	61319	70310	70267	61318
1517		**N**	NKCX	RE	61317	70309	70266	61316

1518		N	NKCX	RE	61333	70317	70274	61332
1519		N	NKCX	RE	61403	70352	70516	61402
1520		N	NKCX	RE	61343	70327	70284	61380
1521		N	NKCX	RE	61353	70324	70281	61352
1522		N	NKCX	RE	61347	70341	70665	61346
1523		N	NKCX	RE	61383	70342	70299	61382
1524		N	NKCX	RE	61309	70305	70262	61308
1525		N	NKCX	RE	61235	70238	70232	61236
1526		N	NKCX	RE	61239	70240	70234	61240
1527		N	NKCX	RE	61237	70239	70233	61238
1528		N	NKCX	RE	61379	70340	70297	61378
1529		N	NKCX	RE	61355	70328	70285	61354
1530		N	NKCX	RE	61331	70316	70273	61330
1531		N	NKCX	RE	61233	70237	70231	61234
1532		N	NKCX	RE	61391	70346	71626	61390
1533		N	NKCX	RE	61393	70347	71627	61385
1534		N	NKCX	RE	61405	70353	71628	61404
1535		N	NKCX	RE	61397	70349	71629	61396
1536		N	NKCX	RE	61399	70350	71631	61398
1537		N	NKCX	RE	61229	70235	70229	61230
1538		N	NKCX	RE	61307	70304	70261	61306
1539		N	NKCX	RE	61401	70351	71632	61400
1540		N	NKCX	RE	61870	70343	70300	61384
1541		N	NKCX	RE	61409	70355	71633	61408
1542		N	NKCX	RE	61395	70348	71634	61394
1543		N	NKCX	RE	61323	70312	70269	61322
1544		N	NKCX	RE	61315	70308	70265	61349
1545		N	NKCX	RE	61359	70330	70287	61358
1546		N	NKCX	RE	61357	70329	70286	61356
1547	★	N	NKCX	RE	61329	70345	70272	61328
1548		N	NKCX	RE	61375	70338	70295	61374
1549		N	NKCX	RE	61339	70320	70277	61338
1550		N	NKCX	RE	61313	70307	70264	61312
1551		N	NKCX	RE	61325	70313	70270	61324
1552		N	NKCX	RE	61373	70337	70294	61372
1553		N	NKCX	RE	61351	70306	70263	61350
1554		N	NKCX	RE	61369	70335	70292	61368
1555		N	NKCX	RE	61311	70326	70283	61310
1556		N	NKCX	RE	61371	70336	70293	61370
1557		N	NKCX	RE	61337	70331	70288	61360
1558		N	NKCX	RE	61361	70319	70276	61336
1559		N	NKCX	RE	61377	70339	70296	61376
1560		N	NKCX	RE	61387	70344	70301	61386
1561		N	NKCX	RE	61231	70604	70230	61232
1562		N	NKCX	RE	61407	70236	70241	61406
1563	§	N	NKCX	RE	61740	70575	70526	61741
1564	§	N	NKCX	RE	61788	70599	70550	61789
1565	§	N	NKCX	RE	61762	70586	71711	61763
1566	§	N	NKCX	RE	61722	70566	70517	61723
1567	§	N	NKCX	RE	61786	70598	70549	61787
1568	§	N	NKCX	RE	61766	70588	70539	61767
1569	§	N	NKCX	RE	61782	70596	70547	61783

1570	§	N	NKCX	RE	61738	70574	70525	61739
1571	§	N	NKCX	RE	61806	70608	71636	61807
1572	§	N	NKCX	RE	61734	70572	70523	61735
1573	§	N	NKCX	RE	61726	70568	70519	61727
1574	§	N	NKCX	RE	61792	70601	71635	61793
1575	§	N	NKCX	RE	61768	70583	70540	61769
1576	§	N	NKCX	RE	61770	70590	70541	61771
1577	§	N	NKCX	RE	61718	70564	70515	61719
1578	§	N	NKCX	RE	61700	70555	70506	61701
1579	§	N	NKCX	RE	61772	70591	70542	61773
1580	§	N	NKCX	RE	61756	70589	70534	61757
1581	§	N	NKCX	RE	61784	70597	70548	61785
1582	§	N	NKCX	RE	61748	70603	71630	61797
1583	§	N	NKCX	RE	61746	70578	70529	61747
1584	§	N	NKCX	RE	61752	70581	70532	61753
1585	§	N	NKCX	RE	61710	70560	70511	61711
1586	§	N	NKCX	RE	61714	70562	70513	61715
1587	§	N	NKCX	RE	61764	70587	71625	61765
1588	§	N	NKCX	RE	61720	70044	70520	61721
1589	§	J	NKCX	RE	61742	70576	70527	61743
1590	§	N	NKCX	RE	61696	70553	70504	61697
1591	§	N	NKCX	RE	61790	70600	70551	61791
1592	§	N	NKCX	RE	61778	70594	70545	61779
1593	§	N	NKCX	RE	61730	70570	70521	61731
1594	§	N	NKCX	RE	61754	70582	70533	61755
1595	§	N	NKCX	RE	61704	70557	70508	61705
1596	§	N	NKCX	RE	61716	70563	70514	61717
1597	§	N	NKCX	RE	61708	70559	70510	61709
1598	§	N	NKCX	RE	61780	70595	70546	61781
1599	§	N	NKCX	RE	61706	70558	70509	61707
1600	§	N	NKCX	RE	61724	70567	70518	61725
1601	§	N	NKCX	RE	61776	70593	70544	61777
1602	§	N	NKCX	RE	61958	70565	70279	61959
1603	§	N	NKCX	RE	61728	70569	70298	61729
1604	§	N	NKCX	RE	61732	70571	70522	61733
1605	§	N	NKCX	RE	61712	70561	70512	61713
1606	§	N	NKCX	RE	61694	70552	70503	61695
1607	§	N	NKCX	RE	61698	70554	70505	61699
1608	§	N	NKCX	RE	61960	70659	70666	61961
1609	§	N	NKCX	RE	61744	70577	70528	61745
1610	§	N	NKCX	RE	61750	70580	70531	61751
1611	§	N	NKCX	RE	61758	70584	70537	61759
1612	§	N	NKCX	RE	61794	70602	70535	61795
1613	§	N	NKCX	RE	61760	70585	70536	61761
1614	§	N	NKCX	RE	61702	70556	70507	61703
1615	§	N	NKCX	RE	61956	70657	70664	61957
1616	§	N	NKCX	RE	61950	70654	70543	61951
1617	§	N	NKCX	RE	61800	70605	70661	61801
1618	§	N	NKCX	RE	61868	70043	70663	61869
1619	§	N	NKCX	RE	61952	70655	70662	61953
1620	§	N	NKCX	RE	61948	70653	70660	61949
1621	§	N	NKCX	RE	61810	70610	70524	61811

ormer numbers of converted hauled stock:

1625 (4381)	71629 (3992)	71633 (4072)	71636 (4065)
1626 (3916)	71630 (3988)	71634 (4059)	71711 (3994)
1627 (3921)	71631 (4436)	71635 (3990)	71712 (4062)
1628 (3844)	71632 (4063)		

LASS 421/3 & 421/6 — 4 Cig (PHASE 1)

TCsoL – MBSO – TSO – DTCsoL. Express stock. Fitted with electric parking rake. Facelifted with new trim, fluorescent lighting in saloons, PA.

iagram Numbers: EE369, ED264, EH287, EE369.
ectrical Equipment: 1963-type.
ogies: Two Mk. 4 motor bogies (MBSO). B5 (SR) bogies (trailer cars).
angways: Throughout.
raction Motors: Four EE507 of 185 kW.
imensions: 19.75 x 2.82 m.
laximum Speed: 90 mph.

TCsoL(A). Dia. EE364. Lot No. 30741 York 1964 – 65. 18F 36S 2L. 35.5 t.
IBSO. Dia. ED260. Lot No. 30742 York 1964 – 65. 56S. 49 t.
SO. Dia. EH275. Lot No. 30730 York 1964 – 65. 72S. 31.5 t.
TCsoL(B). Dia. EE363. Lot No. 30740 York 1964 – 65. 24F 28S 2L.

Units reformed from Class 422 to enable all Class 422 power cars to have lk. 6 motor bogies. Phase 1 units with phase 2 TSOs.

701	(7312)	**N**	NSXX	BI	76087	62028	70706	76033
702	(7326)	**N**	NSXX	BI	76101	62042	70720	76047
703	(7322)	**N**	NSXX	BI	76097	62038	70716	76043
704	(7317)	**N**	NSXX	BI	76092	62033	70711	76038
705	(7301)	**N**	NSXX	BI	76076	62017	70695	76022
706	(7319)	**N**	NSXX	BI	76094	62035	70713	76040
707	(7309)	**N**	NSXX	BI	76084	62025	70703	76030
708	(7335)	**N**	NSXX	BI	76110	62051	70729	76056
709	(7328)	**N**	NSXX	BI	76103	62044	70722	76049
710	(7303)	**N**	NSXX	BI	76078	62019	70697	76024
711	(7033)	**N**	NSXX	BI	76114	62055	71766	76060
712	(7304)	**N**	NSXX	BI	76079	62020	70698	76025
713	(7047)	**N**	NSXX	BI	76128	62069	71767	76074
714	(7302)	**N**	NSXX	BI	76077	62018	70696	76023
715	(7307)	**N**	NSXX	BI	76082	62023	70701	76028
716	(7325)	**N**	NSXX	BI	76100	62041	71768	76046
717	(7308)	**N**	NSXX	BI	76083	62024	70702	76029
718	(7306)	**N**	NSXX	BI	76081	62022	70700	76027
719	(7035)	**N**	NSXX	BI	76116	62057	70719	76062
720	(7038)	**N**	NSXX	BI	76098	62039	71769	76044
721	(7315)	**N**	NSXX	BI	76090	62031	70709	76036
722	(7331)	**N**	NSXX	BI	76106	62047	70725	76052
723	(7332)	**N**	NSXX	BI	76107	62048	70726	76053
724	(7039)	**N**	NSXX	BI	76120	62061	71770	76066
725	(7313)	**N**	NSXX	BI	76088	62029	70707	76034
726	(7334)	**N**	NSXX	BI	76109	62050	70728	76055

1727	(7336)		N	NSXX	BI	76111	62052	70730	7605
1728	(7324)		N	NSXX	BI	76099	62040	70718	7604
1729	(7329)		N	NSXX	BI	76104	62045	70723	7605
1730	(7330)		N	NSXX	BI	76105	62046	70724	7611
1731	(7320)		N	NSXX	BI	76095	62036	70714	7604
1732	(7321)		N	NSXX	BI	76096	62037	70715	7604
1733	(1757)	*	N	NSXX	BI	76122	62063	71047	7606
1734	(1751)	*	N	NSXX	BI	76063	62054	71044	7605
1735	(1754)	*	N	NSXX	BI	76117	62058	71050	7605
1736	(1753)	*	N	NSXX	BI	76124	62065	71052	7607
1737	(1755)	*	N	NSXX	BI	76121	62062	71058	7606
1738	(1752)	*	N	NSXX	BI	76129	62064	71046	7606
1739	(1759)	*	N	NSXX	BI	76123	62070	71066	7607
1740	(1762)	*	N	NSXX	BI	76126	62067	71097	7607
1741	(1114)		N	NSXX	BI	76089	62030	70708	7603
1742	(1111)		N	NSXX	BI	76086	62027	70705	7603
1743	(1756)	*	N	NSXX	BI	76118	62059	71065	7606
1744	(1758)	*	N	NSXX	BI	76127	62068	71064	7607
1745	(1110)		N	NSXX	BI	76085	62026	70704	7603
1746	(1116)		N	NSXX	BI	76091	62032	70710	7603
1747	(1118)		N	NSXX	BI	76026	62034	70712	7609
1748	(1760)	*	N	NSXX	BI	76115	62056	71067	7606
1749	(1761)	*	N	NSXX	BI	76112	62053	71068	7605
1750	(1105)		N	NSXX	BI	76080	62021	70699	7603
1751	(1100)		N	NSXX	BI	76125	62066	71051	7607
1752	(1123)		N	NSXX	BI	76119	62060	70717	7606
1753	(1127)		N	NSXX	BI	76102	62043	70721	7604

Former numbers of converted buffet cars:

71766 (69303) | 71767 (69314) | 71768 (69317) | 71769 (69305) | 71770 (69308)

CLASS 421 — 4 Cig (PHASE 2

DTCsoL – MBSO – TSO – DTCsoL. Express stock. Facelifted with new trin
fluorescent lighting in saloons, PA. For details see earlier.

Class 421/4. Standard Facelifted Units.

1801	(7427)	N	NSXX	BI	76777	62415	71095	7684
1803	(7430)	N	NSXX	BI	76780	62418	71098	7685
1804	(7428)	N	NSXX	BI	76778	62416	71096	7684
1805	(7432)	N	NSXX	BI	76782	62420	71100	7685
1806	(7433)	N	NKCX	RE	76783	62421	71101	7685
1807	(7434)	N	NKCX	RE	76784	62422	71102	7685
1808	(7435)	N	NKCX	RE	76785	62423	71103	7685
1809	(7436)	N	NKCX	RE	76786	62424	71104	7685
1810	(7437)	N	NKCX	RE	76787	62425	71105	7685
1811	(7431)	N	NKCX	RE	76781	62419	71099	7685
1812	(7407)	N	NKCX	RE	76757	62395	71075	7682
1813	(7438)	N	NKCX	RE	76859	62430	71106	7686
1831	(1254)	N	NSXX	BI	76598	62304	70984	7662
1832	(1269)	N	NSXX	BI	76719	62357	71037	7679

833	(1238)	N	NSXX	BI	76582	62288	70968	76612
834	(1258)	N	NSXX	BI	76566	62282	70988	76576
835	(1257)	N	NSXX	BI	76601	62307	70987	76631
837	(1272)	N	NSSX	EH	76722	62360	71040	76793
839	(1263)	N	NKCX	RE	76607	62313	70993	76637
840	(1274)	N	NKCX	RE	76724	62362	71042	76795
841	(1259)	N	NKCX	RE	76603	62309	70989	76633
842	(1275)	N	NKCX	RE	76725	62363	71043	76796
843	(1281)	N	NKCX	RE	76731	62369	71049	76802
845	(1255)	N	NSXX	BI	76599	62305	70985	76629
846	(1287)	N	NSSX	EH	76737	62375	71055	76808
847	(1256)	N	NSSX	EH	76600	62306	70986	76630
848	(1261)	N	NSSX	EH	76605	62311	70991	76635
850	(1268)	N	NSSX	EH	76718	62356	71036	76789
851	(1271)	N	NSSX	EH	76721	62359	71039	76792
853	(1262)	N	NSXX	BI	76606	62312	70992	76636
854	(1288)	N	NSXX	BI	76738	62376	71056	76809
855	(1270)	N	NSXX	BI	76720	62358	71038	76791
856	(1289)	N	NSXX	BI	76739	62377	71057	76810
857	(1266)	N	NSXX	BI	76610	62316	70996	76640
858	(1260)	N	NSXX	BI	76604	62310	70990	76634
859	(1277)	N	NSXX	BI	76727	62365	71045	76798
860	(1202)	N	NSXX	BI	76752	62390	71070	76823
861	(1285)	N	NSXX	BI	76735	62373	71053	76806
862	(1286)	N	NSXX	BI	76736	62374	71054	76807
863	(1292)	N	NSXX	BI	76742	62380	71060	76813
864	(1291)	N	NSXX	BI	76741	62379	71059	76812
865	(1295)	N	NSXX	BI	76745	62383	71063	76639
866	(1293)	N	NSXX	BI	76743	62381	71061	76814
867	(1294)	N	NSXX	BI	76744	62382	71062	76815
868	(1201)	N	NSXX	BI	76751	62389	71069	76822
869	(1203)	N	NSXX	BI	76753	62391	71071	76804
870	(1221)	N	NSSX	EH	76108	62409	71089	76842
871	(1206)	N	NSSX	EH	76756	62394	71074	76827
872	(1208)	N	NSSX	EH	76771	62396	71076	76829
873	(1209)	N	NSSX	EH	76759	62397	71077	76830
874	(1205)	N	NSXX	BI	76755	62393	71073	76826
875	(1204)	N	NSXX	BI	76754	62392	71072	76825
876	(1211)	N	NSSX	EH	76761	62399	71079	76832
877	(1213)	N	NSSX	EH	76763	62401	71081	76834
878	(1218)	N	NSSX	EH	76768	62406	71086	76839
879	(1210)	N	NSSX	EH	76760	62398	71078	76831
880	(1220)	N	NSSX	EH	76770	62408	71088	76841
881	(1212)	N	NSSX	EH	76762	62400	71080	76833
882	(1215)	N	NSSX	EH	76765	62403	71083	76836
883	(1214)	N	NSSX	EH	76764	62402	71082	76835
884	(1217)	N	NSSX	EH	76767	62405	71085	76838
885	(1219)	N	NSSX	EH	76769	62407	71087	76840
886	(1222)	N	NSSX	EH	76772	62410	71090	76843
887	(1216)	N	NSSX	EH	76766	62404	71084	76837
8	(1223)	N	NSSX	EH	76773	62411	71091	76844
8	(1224)	N	NSSX	EH	76774	62412	71092	76845

18	(1225)		N	NSSX	EH	76775 62413 71093 7684
18	(1226)		N	NSSX	EH	76776 62414 71094 7684

CLASS 422/2 — 4 Big (PHASE 2

DTCsoL (A) – MBSO – TSRB – DTCsoL (B). Express stock.

Diagram Numbers: EE369, ED264, EN260, EE369.
Electrical Equipment: 1963-type.
Bogies: Two Mk. 6 motor bogies (MBSO). B5 (SR) bogies (trailer cars).
Gangways: Throughout.
Traction Motors: Four EE507 of 185 kW.
Dimensions: 19.75 x 2.82 m.
Maximum Speed: 90 mph.

69332 – 69339. TSRB. Lot No. 30805 York 1970. 40S. 35 t.

2203	(7051)		N	NSXX	BI	76563 62279 69332 7657
2204	(7052)		N	NSXX	BI	76564 62280 69336 7657
2205	(7053)		N	NSXX	BI	76565 62281 69339 7657
2206	(7054)		N	NSXX	BI	76602 62308 69338 7663
2208	(7056)		N	NSXX	BI	76568 62284 69334 7657
2209	(7057)		N	NSXX	BI	76569 62285 69335 7657
2210	(7058)		N	NSXX	BI	76570 62286 69337 7658

CLASS 422/3 — Facelifted 4 Big (PHASE 2/1

DTCsoL (A) – MBSO – TSRB – DTCsoL (B). Express stock. Units reformed from Class 421 to ensure that all Class 422 power cars have Mk. 6 motor bogies Phase 2 units with phase 1 TSRBs (except for 69333 which is a phase 2 TSRB)

Diagram Numbers: EE369, ED264, EN260, EE369.
Electrical Equipment: 1963-type.
Bogies: Two Mk. 6 motor bogies (MBSO). B5 (SR) bogies (trailer cars).
Gangways: Throughout.
Traction Motors: Four EE507 of 185 kW.
Dimensions: 19.75 x 2.82 m.
Maximum Speed: 90 mph.

69301 – 69318. TSRB. Lot No. 30744 York 1966. 40S. 35 t.
69333. TSRB. Lot No. 30805 York 1970. 40S. 35 t.

n Buffet not facelifted.

2251	(1276)		N	NSXX	BI	76726 62364 69302 7679
2252	(1278)		N	NSXX	BI	76728 62366 69312 7679
2253	(1284)		N	NSXX	BI	76734 62372 69313 7680
2254	(1282)		N	NSXX	BI	76732 62370 69306 7680
2255	(1290)		N	NSXX	BI	76740 62378 69310 7681
2256	(1297)		N	NSXX	BI	76747 62385 69307 7681
2257	(1279)		N	NSXX	BI	76729 62367 69311 7680
2258	(1296)		N	NSXX	BI	76746 62384 69316 7681
2259	(1298)		N	NSXX	BI	76748 62386 69318 7681
2260	(1299)		N	NSXX	BI	76749 62387 69304 7682
2261	(1300)		N	NSXX	BI	76750 62388 69301 7682
2262	(1802)	n	N	NSXX	BI	76779 62417 69333 7685

CLASS 412 REFURBISHED 4 Bep

DMSO (A) – TBCK – TRB – DMSO (B). Kent Coast Express Stock. Refurbished and renumbered from the 70xx series. Fitted with hopper ventilators, Inter-City 70 seats, fluorescent lighting and PA.

Electrical Equipment: 1957-type.
Bogies: One Mk 3B motor bogie (DMSO). Commonwealth trailer bogies.
Rebogied with Mk 6 motor bogies and B5(SR) trailer bogies.
Rebogied with B5(SR) trailer bogies.
Gangways: Throughout.
Traction Motors: Four EE507 of 185 kW.
Dimensions: 19.75 x 2.82 m.
Maximum Speed: 90 mph.

DMSO (A). Dia. EA263. 64S. 44.15 t.
TBCK. Dia. EJ361. 24F 6S 2L. 36.17 t.
TRSB. Dia. EN261. 24S 1L + 9 longitudinal buffet chairs. 35.5 t.
DMSO (B). Dia. EA264. 64S. 43.54 t.
Lot numbers are as follows, all cars being built at Ashford/Eastleigh:

61736 – 61809. 30619 1960 – 61.
61954 – 61955. 30708 1963.
69341 – 69347. 30622 1961.
70354. 30456 1959.
70573 – 70609. 30621 1960 – 61.
70656. 30709 1963.

2301	(7019)	**N**	NSSX	EH	61804	70607	69341	61805
2302	(7194)	**N**	NSSX	EH	61774	70592	69342	61775
2303	(7208)	**N**	NSSX	EH	61954	70656	69347	61955
2304	(7175)	**N**	NSSX	EH	61736	70573	69344	61737
2305		**N**	NSSX	EH	61798	70354	69345	61799
2306	(7021)	**N**	NSSX	EH	61808	70609	69346	61809
2307	(7018)	**N**	NSSX	EH	61802	70606	69343	61803

Former numbers of converted buffet cars:

69341 (69014)
69342 (69019)
69343 (69018)
69344 (69012)
69345 (69013)
69346 (69016)
69347 (69015)

CLASS 442 WESSEX EXPRESS STOCK

DTFsoL – TSOL(A) – MBRSM – TSOL(B) – DTSOL. New express stock for Waterloo – Bournemouth – Weymouth service. Air conditioned (heat pump system). Power-operated sliding plug doors. PA. Can be hauled and heated by any BR ETH fitted locomotive. Multiple working with class 33/1 and 73 locomotives.

Electrical Equipment: 1986-type.
Bogies: Mk 6 motor bogies (MBRSM). T4 trailer bogies.
Gangways: Throughout.
Traction Motors: Four EE546 of 300 kW recovered from class 432.
Dimensions: 23.00 x 2.74 m (inner cars), 23.15 x 2.74 m (outer cars).
Maximum Speed: 100 mph.

DTFsoL. Dia. EE160. Lot No. 31030 Derby 1988 – 89. 50F 1L. (36 in six compartments and 14 2 + 2 in one saloon). Public Telephone. 39.06 t.
TSOL (A). Dia. EH288. Lot No. 31032 Derby 1988 – 89. 80S 2L. 35.26 t.

MBRSM. Dia. ED265. Lot No. 31034 Derby 1988 – 89. 14S. 54.10 t.
TSOL (B). Dia. EH289. Lot No. 31033 Derby 1988 – 89. 76S 2L + wheelchai space. + 2 tip-up seats. 35.36 t.
DTSOL. Dia. EE273. Lot No. 31031 Derby 1988 – 89. 78S 1L. 39.06 t.

2401	**N**	NSSX	BM	77382	71818	62937	71842	77406
2402	**N**	NSSX	BM	77383	71819	62938	71843	77407
2403	**N**	NSSX	BM	77384	71820	62941	71844	77408
2404	**N**	NSSX	BM	77385	71821	62939	71845	77409
2405	**N**	NSSX	BM	77386	71822	62944	71846	77410
2406	**N**	NSSX	BM	77389	71823	62942	71847	77411
2407	**N**	NSSX	BM	77388	71824	62943	71848	77412
2408	**N**	NSSX	BM	77387	71825	62945	71849	77413
2409	**N**	NSSX	BM	77390	71826	62946	71850	77414
2410	**N**	NSSX	BM	77391	71827	62948	71851	77415
2411	**N**	NSSX	BM	77392	71828	62940	71858	77422
2412	**N**	NSSX	BM	77393	71829	62947	71853	77417
2413	**N**	NSSX	BM	77394	71830	62949	71854	77418
2414	**N**	NSSX	BM	77395	71831	62950	71855	77419
2415	**N**	NSSX	BM	77396	71832	62951	71856	77420
2416	**N**	NSSX	BM	77397	71833	62952	71857	77421
2417	**N**	NSSX	BM	77398	71834	62953	71852	77416
2418	**N**	NSSX	BM	77399	71835	62954	71859	77423
2419	**N**	NSSX	BM	77400	71836	62955	71860	77424
2420	**N**	NSSX	BM	77401	71837	62956	71861	77425
2421	**N**	NSSX	BM	77402	71838	62957	71862	77426
2422	**N**	NSSX	BM	77403	71839	62958	71863	77427
2423	**N**	NSSX	BM	77404	71840	62959	71864	77428
2424	**N**	NSSX	BM	77405	71841	62960	71865	77429

Names:

62937 BEAULIEU
62938 COUNTY OF HAMPSHIRE
62941 THE NEW FOREST
62942 VICTORY
62943 THOMAS HARDY
62944 CITY OF PORTSMOUTH
62945 COUNTY OF DORSET
62951 MARY ROSE
62955 BBC SOUTH TODAY
62959 COUNTY OF SURREY

CLASS 423 — 4 Ve

DTCsoL – MBSO – TSO – DTCsoL. Outer suburban stock.

Electrical Equipment: 1963-type.
Bogies: Two Mk. 4 motor bogies (MBSO). B5 (SR) bogies (trailer cars).
Gangways: Throughout.
Traction Motors: Four EE507 of 185 kW.
Dimensions: 19.75 x 2.82 m.
Maximum Speed: 90 mph.

62121 – 40. MBSO. Dia. ED261. Lot No. 30760 Derby 1967. 58S. 49 t.
62182 – 216. MBSO. Dia. ED261. Lot No. 30773 York 1967 – 68. 58S. 49 t
62217 – 66. MBSO. Dia. ED263. Lot No. 30794 York 1968 – 69. 58S. 49 t
62267 – 76. MBSO. Dia. ED263. Lot No. 30800 York 1970. 58S. 49 t.
62317 – 54. MBSO. Dia. ED263. Lot No. 30813 York 1970 – 73. 58S. 49 t

62435 – 75. MBSO. Dia. ED263. Lot No. 30851 York 1973 – 74. 58S. 49 t.
70781 – 800. TSO. Dia. EH276. Lot No. 30759 Derby 1967. 98S. 31.5 t.
70872 – 906. TSO. Dia. EH276. Lot No. 30772 York 1967 – 68. 98S. 31.5 t.
70907 – 56. TSO. Dia. EH283. Lot No. 30793 York 1968 – 69. 98S. 31.5 t.
70957 – 66. TSO. Dia. EH283. Lot No. 30801 York 1970. 98S. 31.5 t.
70997 – 71034. TSO. Dia. EH283. Lot No. 30812 York 1970 – 73. 98S. 31.5 t.
71115 – 55. TSO. Dia. EH283. Lot No. 30852 York 1973 – 74. 98S. 31.5 t.
76230 – 69. DTCsoL. Dia. EE365. Lot No. 30758 York 1967. 18F 46S 1L. 35 t.
76333 – 402. DTCsoL. Dia. EE365. Lot No. 30771 Yk 1967 – 68. 18F 46S 1L. 35 t.
76441 – 540. DTCsoL. Dia. EE367. Lot No. 30792 Yk 1968 – 69. 18F 46S 1L. 35 t.
76541 – 60. DTCsoL. Dia. EE367. Lot No. 30799 York 1970. 18F 46S 1L. 35 t.
76641 – 716. DTCsoL. Dia. EE367. Lot No. 30811 Yk 1970 – 73. 18F 46S 1L. 35 t.
76861 – 942. DTCsoL. Dia. EE368. Lot No. 30853 Yk 1973 – 74. 18F 46S 1L. 35 t.

* Fitted with fluorescent lighting and PA.

Renumbered from 7700 – 7894 respectively with the last three digits unchanged.

3001	*	**N**	NSBX	WD	76230	62121	70781	76231
3002	*	**N**	NSBX	WD	76233	62122	70782	76232
3003	*	**N**	NSBX	WD	76234	62123	70783	76235
3006	*	**N**	NSBX	WD	76241	62126	70786	76240
3007	*	**N**	NSBX	WD	76243	62127	70787	76242
3008	*	**N**	NSBX	WD	76244	62128	70788	76245
3009	*	**N**	NSBX	WD	76246	62129	70789	76247
3010	*	**N**	NSBX	WD	76369	62130	70790	76249
3012	*	**N**	NSBX	WD	76252	62132	70792	76253
3013	*	**N**	NSBX	WD	76255	62133	70793	76254
3014	*	**N**	NSBX	WD	76257	62134	70794	76248
3015	*	**N**	NSBX	WD	76258	62135	70795	76259
3016	*	**N**	NSBX	WD	76261	62339	70796	76260
3017	*	**N**	NSBX	WD	76262	62137	70797	76263
3018	*	**N**	NSBX	WD	76265	62138	70875	76264
3019	*	**N**	NSBX	WD	76267	62349	70799	76266
3020	*	**N**	NSBX	WD	76269	62140	70800	76268
3026	*	**N**	NSBX	WD	76344	62187	70877	76343
3030	*	**N**	NSBX	WD	76352	62191	70881	76351
3032	*	**N**	NSBX	WD	76356	62193	70883	76355
3034	*	**N**	NSBX	WD	76360	62195	70885	76359
3035	*	**N**	NSBX	WD	76362	62196	70890	76361
3037	*	**N**	NSBX	WD	76366	62198	70888	76365
3046	*	**N**	NSBX	WD	76384	62207	70897	76383
3075	*	**N**	NSBX	WD	76480	62236	70926	76479
3078	*	**N**	NSBX	WD	76486	62239	70929	76485
3080	*	**N**	NSXX	BI	76490	62241	70931	76489
3092		**N**	NSXX	BI	76514	62253	70943	76513
3093		**N**	NSXX	BI	76516	62254	70944	76515

3134		**N**	NSXX	BI	76677	62249	71015	76678
3139	*	**N**	NSXX	BI	76687	62340	71020	76688
3147	*	**N**	NSXX	BI	76703	62348	71028	76704
3149	*	**N**	NSXX	BI	76707	62350	71030	76708
3152	*	**N**	NSXX	BI	76465	62353	71033	76714
3153	*	**N**	NSBX	WD	76715	62354	71034	76716
3154	*	**N**	NSBX	WD	76861	62435	71115	76862
3155	*	**N**	NSBX	WD	76863	62238	71116	76864
3156	*	**N**	NSBX	WD	76865	62437	71117	76873
3157	*	**N**	NSBX	WD	76867	62438	71118	76868
3158	*	**N**	NSBX	WD	76869	62439	71119	76870
3159	*	**N**	NSBX	WD	76871	62440	71120	76872
3160	*	**N**	NSBX	WD	76866	62441	71121	76874
3161	*	**N**	NKCX	RE	76875	62442	71122	76876
3162	*	**N**	NKCX	RE	76877	62443	71123	76878
3163		**N**	NKCX	RE	76879	62444	71124	76880
3164		**N**	NKCX	RE	76881	62445	71125	76882
3165	*	**N**	NKCX	RE	76883	62446	71126	76884
3166	*	**N**	NKCX	RE	76885	62447	71127	76886
3167	*	**N**	NKCX	RE	76887	62448	71128	76888
3169		**N**	NKCX	RE	76891	62450	71130	76892
3170	*	**N**	NKCX	RE	76893	62451	71131	76894
3171	*	**N**	NKCX	RE	76895	62452	71132	76896
3172	*	**N**	NKCX	RE	76897	62453	71133	76898
3173	*	**N**	NKCX	RE	76899	62454	71134	76900
3175	*	**N**	NKCX	RE	76903	62456	71136	76904
3176	*	**N**	NKCX	RE	76905	62457	71137	76906
3177	*	**N**	NKCX	RE	76907	62458	71138	76908
3178	*	**N**	NKCX	RE	76909	62463	71139	76910
3179		**N**	NKCX	RE	76911	62460	71140	76912
3180	*	**N**	NKCX	RE	76913	62461	71141	76914
3181		**N**	NKCX	RE	76915	62462	71142	76916
3182	*	**N**	NKCX	RE	76917	62459	71143	76918
3183	*	**N**	NKCX	RE	76919	62464	71144	76920
3184		**N**	NKCX	RE	76921	62465	71145	76922
3185		**N**	NKCX	RE	76923	62466	71146	76924
3186		**N**	NKCX	RE	76925	62467	71147	76926
3187	*	**N**	NKCX	RE	76927	62468	71148	76928
3188	*	**N**	NKCX	RE	76929	62469	71149	76930
3189	*	**N**	NKCX	RE	76931	62470	71150	76932
3190	*	**N**	NKCX	RE	76933	62471	71151	76934
3191		**N**	NKCX	RE	76935	62472	71152	76936
3192		**N**	NKCX	RE	76937	62473	71153	76938
3193		**N**	NKCX	RE	76939	62474	71154	76940
3194		**N**	NKCX	RE	76941	62475	71155	76942

CLASS 413/2 — 4 Cap

DTCsoL – MBSO – MLSO – DTSsoL. Formed 1982 by the combination of pairs of class 414 (2 Hap) units. Driving equipment removed from motor cars, plus one set of guard's equipment. Driving trailers all declassified.

Electrical Equipment: 1951-type.
Bogies: Mk. 4.
Gangways: Non-gangwayed.
Traction Motors: Two EE507 of 185 kW.
Dimensions: 19.49 x 2.82 m.
Maximum Speed: 90 mph.

All built at Eastleigh on frames laid at Ashford.

65393 – 65396. MBSO/MLSO. Dia. EB269. Lot No. 30314 1957. 84S. 42 t.
65398 – 65401. MBSO/MLSO. Dia. EB269. Lot No. 30319 1957. 84S. 42 t.
65404 – 65429. MBSO/MLSO. Dia. EB269. Lot No. 30388 1958. 84S. 42 t.
77115 – 77118. DTCsoL. Dia. EE221. Lot No. 30316 1957. 19F 50S 2L. 32.5 t.
77123. DTCsoL. Dia. EE221. Lot No. 30320 1957. 19F 50S 2L. 32.5 t.
77126 – 77150. DTCsoL. Dia. EE221. Lot No. 30389 1958. 19F 50S 2L. 32.5 t.

3201	**N**	NKSX	SG	77120	65398	65401	77123
3202	**N**	NKSX	SG	77118	65396	65412	77134
3203	**N**	NKSX	SG	77117	65395	65424	77146
3204	**N**	NKSX	SG	77132	65410	65420	77142
3205	**N**	NKSX	SG	77135	65413	65422	77144
3207	**N**	NKSX	SG	77126	65404	65428	77150
3208	**N**	NKSX	SG	77147	65425	65429	77537
3211	**N**	NKSX	SG	77115	65393	65427	77149

CLASS 413/3 4 Cap

DTCsoL – MBSO – MLSO – DTCsoL. Formed 1982 by the combination of pairs of class 414 (2 Hap) units. Driving equipment removed from motor cars, plus one set of guard's equipment. Driving trailers all declassified.

Electrical Equipment: 1957-type.
Bogies: Mk. 4.
Gangways: Non-gangwayed.
Traction Motors: Two EE507 of 185 kW.
Dimensions: 19.49 x 2.82 m.
Maximum Speed: 90 mph.

MBSO/MLSO. Dia. EB270. Lot No. 30452 Ashford/Eastleigh 1958 – 59. 84S. 42 t.
DTCsoL. Dia. EE222. Lot No. 30453 Ashford/Eastleigh 1958 – 59. 19F 50S 2L. 32.5 t.

3301	**N**	NKSX	SG	75373	61253	61255	75375
3302	**N**	NKSX	SG	75361	61241	61244	75364
3303	**N**	NKSX	SG	75370	61250	61252	75372
3304	**N**	NKSX	SG	75402	61282	61283	75403
3305	**N**	NKSX	SG	75399	61279	61302	75422
3306	**N**	NKSX	SG	75374	61254	61256	75376
3307	**N**	NKSX	SG	75378	61258	61271	75391
3311	**N**	NKSX	SG	75411	61291	61297	75417

New batch formed with the motor cars as outer vehicles. MBSO – 2DTCsoL – MBSO.

3321	N	NKSX	SG	61268	75388	75398	61278
3322	N	NKSX	SG	61262	75382	75415	61295
3323	N	NKSX	SG	61273	75393	75420	61300
3324	N	NKSX	SG	61270	75390	75423	61303
3325	N	NKSX	SG	61261	75381	75418	61298

CLASS 423/1 Facelifted 4 Vep.

DTCsoL – MBSO – TSO – DTCsoL. For details see 3000 series. Facelifted with fluorescent lighting, PA. The MBSO has been modified to seat 76S. Diagram numbers now EE373, ED266, EH291, EE373 respectively.

3404	(3441)	N	NSBX	WD	76378	62261	70894	76236
3405	(3005)	N	NSBX	WD	76239	62271	70785	76238
3411	(3011)	N	NSBX	WD	76251	62342	70791	76250
3421	(3168)	N	NKCX	RE	76889	62449	71129	76890
3422	(3040)	N	NKCX	RE	76372	62201	70891	76371
3423	(3061)	N	NKCX	RE	76452	62222	70912	76451
3424	(3031)	N	NKCX	RE	76354	62185	70882	76353
3425	(3023)	N	NSBX	WD	76338	62192	70874	76358
3426	(3047)	N	NSBX	WD	76386	62208	70898	76385
3427	(3041)	N	NSBX	WD	76374	62184	70892	76373
3428	(3062)	N	NSBX	WD	76454	62223	70913	76453
3429	(3021)	N	NSBX	WD	76334	62202	70872	76333
3430	(3028)	N	NSBX	WD	76348	62189	70879	76347
3431	(3064)	N	NSBX	WD	76458	62182	70915	76457
3432	(3054)	N	NSBX	WD	76400	62225	70905	76399
3433	(3057)	N	NSBX	WD	76444	62215	70908	76443
3434	(3066)	N	NSBX	WD	76462	62218	70917	76461
3435	(3025)	N	NSXX	BI	76342	62228	70876	76341
3436	(3029)	N	NSXX	BI	76350	62190	70880	76349
3437	(3027)	N	NSXX	BI	76346	62186	70878	76345
3438	(3100)	N	NSXX	BI	76530	62262	70951	76529
3439	(3055)	N	NSXX	BI	76402	62227	70906	76401
3440	(3102)	N	NSXX	BI	76534	62188	70953	76533
3442	(3081)	N	NSXX	BI	76492	62216	70932	76491
3443	(3082)	N	NSXX	BI	76494	62263	70933	76493
3444	(3038)	N	NSXX	BI	76368	62204	70889	76367
3445	(3060)	N	NKCX	RE	76450	62242	70911	76449
3446	(3101)	N	NKCX	RE	76532	62243	70952	76531
3447	(3044)	N	NKCX	RE	76380	62199	70895	76379
3448	(3042)	N	NKCX	RE	76376	62221	70886	76375
3449	(3022)	N	NKCX	RE	76336	62205	70873	76335
3450	(3060)	N	NKCX	RE	76460	62203	70916	76459
3451	(3079)	N	NKCX	RE	76488	62240	70930	76487
3452		N	NKCX	RE	76340	62183	71021	76690
3453	(3045)	N	NKCX	RE	76382	62226	70896	76381
3454		N	NKCX	RE	76390	62200	70798	76389
3455	(3048)	N	NSBX	WD	76388	62206	70899	76387
3456	(3063)	N	NSBX	WD	76456	62210	70914	76455
3457	(3050)	N	NSBX	WD	76392	62197	70901	76391
3458	(3051)	N	NSBX	WD	76394	62209	70902	76393

3459	(3052)	N	NSBX	WD	76396	62224	70903	76395
3460	(3105)	N	NSXX	BI	76540	62211	70956	76539
3461	(3104)	N	NSXX	BI	76538	62212	70955	76537
3462	(3103)	N	NSXX	BI	76536	62213	70954	76535
3463	(3053)	N	NSXX	BI	76398	62266	70904	76397
3464	(3056)	N	NSXX	BI	76442	62265	70907	76441
3465	(3106)	N	NSXX	BI	76542	62264	70957	76541
3466	(3067)	N	NSBX	WD	76464	62214	70918	76463
3467	(3058)	N	NSBX	WD	76446	62217	70909	76445
3468	(3059)	N	NSBX	WD	76448	62267	70910	76447
3469	(3108)	N	NSBX	WD	76546	62219	70959	76545
3470	(3083)	N	NSBX	WD	76496	62220	70934	76495
3471	(3084)	N	NKCX	RE	76498	62269	70935	76497
3472	(3085)	N	NKCX	RE	76500	62244	70936	76499
3473	(3086)	N	NKCX	RE	76502	62245	70937	76339
3474	(3087)	N	NKCX	RE	76504	62246	70938	76503
3475	(3111)	N	NKCX	RE	76552	62270	70962	76551
3476	(3109)	N	NSXX	BI	76548	62247	70960	76547
3477	(3110)	N	NSXX	BI	76550	62248	70961	76549
3478	(3122)	N	NSXX	BI	76653	62125	71003	76654
3479	(3123)	N	NSBX	WD	76655	62272	71004	76656
3480	(3072)	N	NSBX	WD	76474	62323	70923	76473
3481	(3119)	N	NSBX	WD	76648	62324	70900	76647
3482	(3124)	N	NSBX	WD	76657	62320	71005	76658
3483	(3126)	N	NSBX	WD	76661	62233	71007	76662
3484	(3073)	N	NSBX	WD	76476	62325	70924	76475
3485	(3089)	N	NSBX	WD	76508	62327	70940	76507
3486	(3074)	N	NSBX	WD	76478	62234	70925	76477
3487	(3090)	N	NSBX	WD	76510	62250	70941	76509
3488	(3127)	N	NSBX	WD	76663	62235	71008	76664
3489	(3128)	N	NSBX	WD	76665	62251	71009	76666
3490	(3143)	N	NSBX	WD	76695	62328	71024	76696
3491	(3076)	N	NKCX	RE	76337	62436	70927	76481
3492	(3129)	N	NKCX	RE	76667	62344	71010	76668
3493	(3130)	N	NKCX	RE	76669	62237	71011	76670
3494	(3133)	N	NKCX	RE	76675	62330	71014	76676
3495	(3145)	N	NKCX	RE	76699	62331	71026	76700
3496	(3132)	N	NKCX	RE	76673	62334	71013	76674
3497	(3131)	N	NKCX	RE	76671	62346	71012	76672
3498	(3146)	N	NKCX	RE	76701	62333	71027	76702
3499	(3174)	N	NKCX	RE	76901	62347	71135	76902
3500	(3070)	N	NKCX	RE	76470	62455	70921	76469
3501	(3091)	N	NSXX	BI	76512	62332	70942	76511
3502	(3150)	N	NSXX	BI	76709	62252	71031	76710
3503	(3136)	N	NSXX	BI	76681	62231	71017	76682
3504	(3151)	N	NSXX	BI	76711	62351	71032	76712
3505	(3071)	N	NSXX	BI	76472	62352	70922	76471
3506	(3112)	N	NSXX	BI	76554	62317	70963	76553
3507	(3114)	N	NSXX	BI	76558	62232	70965	76557
3508	(3117)	N	NSBX	WD	76643	62273	70998	76644
3509	(3115)	N	NSBX	WD	76560	62275	70966	76559
3510	(3116)	N	NSBX	WD	76641	62318	70997	76642

3511	(3118)	N	NSBX	WD	76645	62276	70999	76646
3512	(3135)	N	NSXX	BI	76679	62337	71016	76680
3513	(3141)	N	NSXX	BI	76691	62336	71022	76692
3514	(3137)	N	NSXX	BI	76683	62136	71018	76684
3515	(3107)	N	NSXX	BI	76544	62319	70958	76543
3516	(3142)	N	NSBX	WD	76693	62268	71023	76694
3517	(3138)	N	NSXX	BI	76685	62338	71019	76686
3518	(3140)	N	NSXX	BI	76689	62343	70887	76363
3519	(3113)	N	NSBX	WD	76556	62274	70964	76555
3520	(3144)	N	NSBX	WD	76697	62131	71025	76698
3521	(3077)	N	NSBX	WD	76484	62345	70928	76483
3522	(3148)	N	NSXX	BI	76705	62341	71029	76706
3523	(3121)	N	NSBX	WD	76651	62139	71002	76652
3524	(3068)	N	NSBX	WD	76466	62322	70919	76370
3525	(3096)	N	NSXX	BI	76522	62229	70947	76521
3526	(3097)	N	NSXX	BI	76524	62255	70948	76523
3527	(3095)	N	NSXX	BI	76520	62326	70946	76519
3528	(3094)	N	NSXX	BI	76518	62258	70945	76517
3529	(3125)	N	NSBX	WD	76659	62257	71006	76660
3530	(3069)	N	NSBX	WD	76468	62256	70920	76467
3531	(3120)	N	NSBX	WD	76649	62230	71001	76650
3532	(3099)	N	NSXX	BI	76528	62321	70950	76527
3533	(3098)	N	NSXX	BI	76364	62260	70949	76525
3534	(3088)	N	NSXX	BI	76506	62259	70939	76505
3535								
3536								
3537								
3538								
3539								
3540								
3541								
3542								
3543								
3544								
3545								
3546								
3547								
3548								
3549								
3550								
3551								
3552								
Spare						62335		

CLASS 414/3 — 2 Hap

DMBSO – DTCsoL.

Electrical Equipment: 1957-type.
Bogies: Mk. 4.
Gangways: Non-gangwayed.
Traction Motors: Two EE507 of 185 kW.

Dimensions: 19.49 x 2.82 m.
Maximum Speed: 90 mph.

DMBSO. Dia. EB270. Lot No. 30452 Ashford/Eastleigh 1959. 84S. 42 t.
DTCsoL. Dia. EE362. Lot No. 30453 Ashford/Eastleigh 1959. 19F 60S 1L. 32.5 t.

4308	**N**	NKCX	RE	61275 75395
4309	**N**	NKCX	RE	61276 75396
4311	**N**	NKCX	RE	61287 75407
4313	**N**	NKCX	RE	61290 75410
4314	**N**	NKCX	RE	61294 75414

CLASS 405 — 1936 type 4 Sub

DMBSO – TS – TSO – DMBSO. This unit is kept for special workings and is not compatible electrically with other SR EMUs. It has automatic air brakes, but no electro-pneumatic brakes.

Electrical Equipment: 1936-type.
Bogies: Central 43'' motor bogies and SR standard trailer bogies.
Gangways: Non-gangwayed.
Traction Motors: Two EE507 of 185 kW.
Dimensions: 19.05 x 2.82 m. (outer cars), 18.90 x 2.82 m (inner cars).
Maximum Speed: 75 mph.

DMBSO. Dia. EB265. Lot No. 3638 Eastleigh 1951. 82S. 42 t.
TS. Dia. EH262. Lot No. 3351 Eastleigh 1947. 120S. 27 t.
TSO. Dia. EH266. Lot No. 3384 Eastleigh 1948. 102S. 26 t.

4732	**SG**	NSXX	BI	12795 10239 12354 12796

CLASS 415/1 — SR DESIGN 4 EPB

DMBSO – 2TSO – DMBSO. Originally formed with a TS and a TSO, but all except 5001 now have 2TSO.

Electrical Equipment: 1951-type.
Bogies: Central 40'' motor bogies and SR standard trailer bogies.
Gangways: Non-gangwayed.
Traction Motors: Two EE507 of 185 kW.
Dimensions: 19.05 x 2.82 m. (outer cars), 18.90 x 2.82 m (inner cars).
Maximum Speed: 75 mph (90 mph e).

Built to various SR lots as shown, all at Lancing/Eastleigh.

★ Converted from class 405 (4 Sub) TS.

14001 – 14002. DMBSO. Dia. EB266. Lot No. 3638 1952. 82S. 40 t.
14039 – 14040. DMBSO. Dia. EB266. Lot No. 3756 1953. 82S. 40 t.
14069 – 14208. DMBSO. Dia. EB266. Lot No. 3757 1953 – 4. 82S. 40 t.
14231 – 14308. DMBSO. Dia. EB266. Lot No. 4016 1954 – 5. 82S. 40 t.
14313 – 14405. DMBSO. Dia. EB266. Lot No. 4099 1955 – 6. 82S. 40 t.
14417 – 14418. DMBSO. Dia. EB266. Lot No. 4172 1956. 82S. 40 t.
14439 – 14510. DMBSO. Dia. EB266. Lot No. 4173 1956 – 7. 82S. 40 t.
15101 – 15113. TSO. Dia. EH270. Lot No. 3638 1951 – 2. 102S. 27 t.

15118 – 15122. TSO. Dia. EH270. Lot No. 3756 1953. 102S. 27 t.
15135 – 15158. TSO. Dia. EH270. Lot No. 3757 1953 – 4. 102S. 27 t.
15207. TS. Dia. EH268. Lot No. 4016 1954 – 55. 120S. 28 t.
15234 – 15277/279 – 282. TSO. Dia. EH270. Lot No. 4016 1954 – 5. 102S. 27 t.
15335 – 15382. TSO. Dia. EH270. Lot No. 4099 1955 – 6. 102S. 27 t.
15395 – 15401. TSO. Dia. EH270. Lot No. 4172 1956. 102S. 27 t.
15405 – 15443. TSO. Dia. EH270. Lot No. 4173 1956 – 7. 102S. 27 t.
65300/65310. DMBSO. Dia. EB269. Lot No. 30114 Ashford/Eastleigh 1954. 84S. 42 t. BR design DMBSOs (ex class 416/2).

5001		**SG**	NKSX	SG	14001	15207	15101	14002
5124			NKSX	SG (U)	14248	15248	15252	14247
5131			NKSX	SG	14261	15412	15259	14262
5138			NKSX	SG	14275	15423	15266	14276
5145			NKSX	SG	14290	15158	15273	14289
5153			NKSX	SG	14305	15256	15281	14306
5154			NKSX	SG	14308	15279	15282	14307
5157			NKSX	SG	14313	15381	15335	14314
5159			NKSX	SG	14317	15105	15337	14318
5160			NKSX	SG	14319	15268	15338	14320
5176			NKSX	SG	14352	15396	15354	14351
5177			NKSX	SG	14354	15257	15355	14353
5185			NKSX	SG (U)	14369	15277	15363	14370
5190			NKSX	SG	14380	15361	15368	14379
5194			NKSX	SG	14388	15275	15372	14387
5195			NKSX	SG	14389	15239	15373	14390
5196			NKSX	SG	14392	15399	15374	14391
5209			NKSX	SG (U)	14039	15395	15397	14417
5220			NKSX	SG	14439	15349	15408	14260
5232			NKSX	SG	14464	15422	15420	14463
5240			NKSX	SG	14103	15425	15428	14480
5243			NKSX	SG	14405	15375	15356	14485
5248			NKSX	SG	14492	15443	15436	14510
5261			NKSX	SG	65300	15154	15413	65310
5266	(5020)		NKSX	SG (U)	14418	15234	15382	14040
5268	(5035)		NKSX	SG	14069	15113	15135	14070
5269	(5039)		NKSX	SG (U)	14078	15118	15139	14094
5270	(5040)		NKSX	SG	14080	15122	15140	14079
5275	(5049)		NKSX	SG	14098	15271	15149	14097
5277	(5052)		NKSX	SG	14104	15103	15152	14495
5279			NKSX	SG	14257	15429	15380	14258
5280			NKSX	SG	14232	15421	15410	14231

CLASS 415/4 FACELIFTED SR DESIGN 4 EPB

DMBSO – 2TSO – DMBSO. Facelifted with new trim, fluorescent lighting, PA.

Electrical Equipment: 1951-type.
Bogies: Central 40'' motor bogies and SR standard trailer bogies.
Gangways: Non-gangwayed.
Traction Motors: Two EE507 of 185 kW.
Dimensions: 19.05 x 2.82 m. (outer cars), 18.90 x 2.82 m (inner cars).

Maximum Speed: 75 mph. (90 mph e).

Built to various SR lots as shown, all at Lancing/Eastleigh.

★ Converted from class 405 (4 Sub) TS. Vehicles in the 154xx series were converted on facelifting.
§ Converted from class 415 TS.

14003 – 14030. DMBSO. Dia. EB277. Lot No. 3638 1952. 82S. 40 t.
14037 – 14066. DMBSO. Dia. EB277. Lot No. 3756 1953. 82S. 40 t.
14072 – 14206. DMBSO. Dia. EB277. Lot No. 3757 1953 – 4. 82S. 40 t.
14211 – 14304. DMBSO. Dia. EB277. Lot No. 4016 1954 – 5. 82S. 40 t.
14315 – 14410. DMBSO. Dia. EB277. Lot No. 4099 1955 – 6. 82S. 40 t.
14411 – 14430. DMBSO. Dia. EB277. Lot No. 4172 1956. 82S. 40 t.
14431 – 14520. DMBSO. Dia. EB277. Lot No. 4173 1956 – 7. 82S. 40 t.
14521 – 14570. DMBSO. Dia. EB278. Lot No. 4281 1957. 82S. 40 t. Former class 418/0 vehicle or 416/3 vehicles.

15001/10. 15466/67/71. TSO★. Dia. EH270. Lot No. 1094 1946. 102S. 27 t.
15002/19/23/27/30/39 – 42/48/50. 15450. TSO★. Lot No. 3351 1947. 102S. 27 t.
15009/11/20/29/37/44/51/52/56 – 58/61 – 62/65/66/68 – 71/73/75 – 78. TSO★. Lot No. 3463 1948. 102S. 27 t.
15012/54. TSO★. Lot No. 3386 1948. 102S. 27 t.
15033/34/36/45 – 47/53/55/59/60/67. TSO★. Lot No. 3231 1947. 102S. 27 t.
15104 – 15115. TSO. Lot No. 3638 1951 – 2. 102S. 27 t.
15119 – 15128. TSO. Lot No. 3756 1953. 102S. 27 t.
15136 – 15182. TSO§. Lot No. 3757 1953 – 4. 102S. 27 t.
15185 – 15227/231 – 265. TSO§. Lot No. 4016 1954 – 5. 102S. 27 t.
15285 – 15383. TSO§. Lot No. 4099 1955 – 6. 102S. 27 t.
15386 – 15403. TSO§. Lot No. 4172 1956. 102S. 27 t.
15404 – 15448. TSO. Lot No. 4173 1956 – 7. 102S. 27 t.
15449/65/79/80. TSO★. Lot No. 3384 1948. 102S. 27 t.
15451. TSO★. Lot No. 3617 1948. 102S. 27 t.
15452/59/61/64/69. TSO★. Lot No. 3504 1949. 102S. 27 t.
15453/63. TSO★. Lot No. 3385 1948. 102S. 27 t.
15454/56 – 58/60/62/68/70/76/78. TSO★. Lot No. 3464 1949. 102S. 27 t.
15481. TSO★. Lot No. 3505 1950. 102S. 27 t.

e – Express gear ratio.

5401	e	**N**	NKSX	SG	14556	15449	15450	14521
5402			NKSX	SG	14449	15464	15465	14407
5403		**N**	NKSX	SG	14286	15174	15221	14285
5404			NKSX	SG	14435	15036	15406	14436
5405		**N**	NKSX	SG	14470	15053	15216	14469
5407		**N**	NKSX	SG	14428	15392	15060	14427
5408		**N**	NKSX	SG	14297	15227	15313	14298
5409		**N**	NKSX	SG	14494	15065	15047	14206
5410	e	**N**	NKSX	SG	14540	15386	15304	14528
5411		**N**	NKSX	SG	14475	15056	15192	14476
5412			NKSX	SG	14415	15451	15452	14304
5413		**N**	NKSX	SG	14396	15326	15191	14395

5414		**N**	NSLX	SU (U)	14441	15039	15182	14442
5415		**N**	NSLX	SU (U)	14465	15040	15051	14466
5419		**N**	NKSX	SG	14473	15055	15058	14474
5421		**N**	NKSX	SG	14500	15068	15073	14499
5422		**N**	NKSX	SG	14467	15209	15050	14468
5423		**N**	NKSX	SG	14511	15074	15212	14512
5424		**N**	NKSX	SG	14447	15042	15052	14448
5425	e	**N**	NSLX	SU (U)	14538	15453	15454	14570
5426		**N**	NKSX	SG	14517	15077	15066	14518
5427		**N**	NKSX	SG	14453	15045	15046	14454
5428		**N**	NKSX	SG	14430	15393	15061	14429
5429		**N**	NKSX	SG (U)	14410	15333	15383	14409
5430		**N**	NKSX	SG	14496	15438	15437	14509
5431		**N**	NKSX	SG	14423	15390	15400	14424
5432		**N**	NKSX	SG	14486	15044	15447	14416
5433		**N**	NKSX	SG	14472	15054	15424	14471
5434		**N**	NKSX	SG	14498	15067	15455	14497
5435		**N**	NKSX	SG	14491	15403	15431	14267
5436		**N**	NKSX	SG	14534	15456	15457	14543
5437		**N**	NKSX	SG	14411	15384	15394	14412
5438		**N**	NKSX	SG	14530	15459	15458	14547
5441		**N**	NKSX	SG	14397	15327	15377	14398
5442		**N**	NKSX	SG	14537	15460	15461	14554
5443		**N**	NKSX	SG	14504	15070	15440	14503
5444		**N**	NKSX	SG	14535	15463	15462	14553
5445		**N**	NKSX	SG	14527	15020	15351	14529
5446		**N**	NKSX	SG	14531	15466	15467	14541
5447		**N**	NKSX	SG	14532	15468	15469	14550
5448		**N**	NKSX	SG	14539	15470	15471	14548
5449			NKSX	SG	14438	15291	15407	14437
5452	e	**N**	NKSX	SG	14536	15477	15476	14563
5453	e		NKSX	SG	14545	15479	15478	14525
5454	e	**N**	NKSX	SG	14555	15481	15480	14524
5455		**N**	NKSX	SG	14062	15023	15027	14054
5456		**N**	NKSX	SG	14482	15059	15001	14481
5457		**N**	NKSX	SG	14502	15069	15439	14501
5458		**N**	NKSX	SG	14431	15034	15404	14432
5459		**N**	NKSX	SG	14505	15071	15441	14506
5460		**N**	NKSX	SG	14515	15076	15446	14516
5461		**N**	NKSX	SG	14519	15078	15448	14520
5462		**N**	NKSX	SG	14021	15011	15111	14022
5463		**N**	NKSX	SG	14037	15019	15119	14038
5464		**N**	NKSX	SG	14081	15166	15159	14082
5465			NKSX	SG	14236	15196	15208	14350
5466			NKSX	SG	14004	15002	15220	14003
5467		**N**	NKSX	SG	14006	15062	15177	14005
5470			NKSX	SG	14315	15286	15215	14316
5471		**N**	NKSX	SG	14255	15206	15231	14256
5472			NKSX	SG	14508	15295	15169	14458
5473			NKSX	SG	14493	15029	15170	14058
5474			NKSX	SG	14065	15033	15224	14066
5475			NKSX	SG	14019	15010	15048	14020

5477		NKSX	SG	14013	15180	15233	14057
5478		NKSX	SG	14059	15030	15167	14060
5479		NKSX	SG	14322	15289	15317	14321
5481		NKSX	SG	14330	15293	15226	14329
5482		NKSX	SG	14017	15009	15297	14018
5483		NKSX	SG	14052	15175	15329	14051
5485	**N**	NKSX	SG	14105	15178	15185	14106
5486	**N***	NKSX	SG	14211	15161	15125	14072
5487	**N**	NKSX	SG	14361	15309	15359	14362
5488	**N**	NKSX	SG	14386	15321	15371	14385
5489	**N**	NKSX	SG	14024	15012	15112	14023
5490	**N**	NKSX	SG	14056	15433	15128	14205
5491	**N**	NKSX	SG	14029	15136	15115	14030
5492	**N**	NKSX	SG	14223	15246	15240	14224
5493	**N**	NKSX	SG	14028	15237	15114	14027
5494	**N**	NKSX	SG	14073	15236	15137	14074
5495	**N**	NKSX	SG	14095	15265	15148	14096
5496	**N**	NKSX	SG	14400	15336	15378	14399
5497	**N**	NKSX	SG	14246	15104	15251	14245

Old numbers of cars converted from class 405:

	0	1	2	3	4	5	6	7	8	9
5000–9		10398	10345	10333	10203	11454	10253	10228	10335	10201
5010–9	10391	10174	10169	10189	10184	10277	10251	10292	10238	10332
5020–9	10177	10254	10175	10309	10266	10456	10298	10281	10272	10202
5030–9	10278	10192	10280	10460	10470	10229	10459	10222	11451	10246
5040–9	10285	10322	10283	10275	10224	10452	10466	10468	10299	10176
5050–9	10260	10211	10223	10471	10167	10451	10190	10193	10188	10450
5060–9	10467	10226	10178	10194	10469	10212	10186	10453	10183	10225
5070–9	10180	10191	10179	10185	10168	10187	10227	10204	10182	10195
5080–4	11456	10208	10207	10395	11485					
5450–9	10337	8980	12361	12360	10139	12404	10133	10143	10132	12381
5460–9	10125	12393	10131	12359	12389	12355	10444	10448	10128	12390
5470–9	10124	10439	12391	10137	10446	10445	10129	12402	10141	12353
5480–1	12358	12398								
5449:	10480									

CLASSES 415/6 & 415/7 — BR DESIGN 4 EPB

DMBSO(A) – 2TSO – DMBSO(B). All remaining units have been facelifted with new trim, fluorescent lighting and PA. Units with express gear ratio (e) are classified Class 415/7.

Electrical Equipment: 1951-type.
Bogies: Mark 3C (Mk 3D*) bogies.
Gangways: Non-gangwayed.
Traction Motors: Two EE507 of 185 kW.
Dimensions: 19.50 x 2.82 m. (outer cars), 19.35 x 2.82 m (inner cars).
Maximum Speed: 75 mph (90 mph e).

DMBSO(A). Dia. EB271. Lot No. 30582 Eastleigh 1959 – 61. 82S. 41 t.
DMBSO(B). Dia. EB272. Lot No. 30582 Eastleigh 1959 – 61. 82S. 41 t.
TSO. Dia. EH271. Lot No. 30583 Eastleigh 1959 – 61. 102S. 29.5 t.

e Express gear ratio.

5601	*	**N**	NKSX	SG	61550	70409	70410	61551
5602		**N**	NKSX	SG	61582	70441	70442	61583
5603	*	**N**	NKSX	SG	61538	70397	70398	61539
5604		**N**	NKSX	SG	61588	70447	70448	61589
5605	*	**N**	NKSX	SG	61540	70399	70400	61541
5606	*	**N**	NKSX	SG	61536	70395	70396	61537
5610		**N**	NKSX	SG	61566	70425	70426	61567
5611		**N**	NKSX	SG	61570	70429	70430	61571
5612	*	**N**	NKSX	SG	61542	70401	70402	61543
5613	*	**N**	NKSX	SG	61532	70391	70392	61533
5614	*	**N**	NKSX	SG	61546	70405	70406	61547
5615		**N**	NKSX	SG	61612	70471	70472	61613
5616		**N**	NKSX	SG	61576	70435	70436	61577
5617		**N**	NKSX	SG	61592	70451	70452	61593
5619		**N**	NKSX	SG	61562	70421	70422	61563
5620		**N**	NKSX	SG	61602	70461	70462	61603
5621	*	**N**	NKSX	SG	61520	70380	70379	61521
5622		**N**	NKSX	SG	61560	70419	70420	61561
5623	e	**N**	NKCX	RE	61578	70437	70438	61584
5624	e	**N**	NKCX	RE	61572	70431	70432	61573
5625	e	**N**	NKCX	RE	61608	70455	70468	61609
5626	e	**N**	NKCX	RE	61590	70449	70450	61591
5627	e	**N**	NKCX	RE	61600	70460	70459	61601
5628	e	**N**	NKCX	RE	61604	70464	70463	61605

CLASS 455/7

DTSO – MSO – TSO – DTSO. Sliding doors. Disc brakes. Fluorescent lighting PA. Second series with TSOs originally in class 508. Pressure ventilation.

Bogies: BT13 (DTSO), BP27 (MSO), BX1 (TSO).
Gangways: Through gangwayed.
Traction Motors: Four EE507 of 185 kW.
Dimensions: 19.83 x 2.82 m. (outer cars), 19.92 x 2.82 m (inner cars).
Maximum Speed: 75 mph.

DTSO. Dia. EE218. Lot No. 30976 York 1984 – 85. 74S. 29.5 t.
MSO. Dia. EC203. Lot No. 30975 York 1984 – 85. 84S. 45 t.
TSO. Dia. EH219. Lot No. 30944 York 1977 – 80. 86S. 25.48 t.

5701	**N**	NSBX	WD	77727	62783	71545	77728
5702	**N**	NSBX	WD	77729	62784	71547	77730
5703	**N**	NSBX	WD	77731	62785	71540	77732
5704	**N**	NSBX	WD	77733	62786	71548	77734
5705	**N**	NSBX	WD	77735	62787	71565	77736
5706	**N**	NSBX	WD	77737	62788	71534	77738
5707	**N**	NSBX	WD	77739	62789	71536	77740
5708	**N**	NSBX	WD	77741	62790	71560	77742

5709	N	NSBX	WD	77743	62791	71532	77744
5710	N	NSBX	WD	77745	62792	71566	77746
5711	N	NSBX	WD	77747	62793	71542	77748
5712	N	NSBX	WD	77749	62794	71546	77750
5713	N	NSBX	WD	77751	62795	71567	77752
5714	N	NSBX	WD	77753	62796	71539	77754
5715	N	NSBX	WD	77755	62797	71535	77756
5716	N	NSBX	WD	77757	62798	71564	77758
5717	N	NSBX	WD	77759	62799	71528	77760
5718	N	NSBX	WD	77761	62800	71557	77762
5719	N	NSBX	WD	77763	62801	71558	77764
5720	N	NSBX	WD	77765	62802	71568	77766
5721	N	NSBX	WD	77767	62803	71553	77768
5722	N	NSBX	WD	77769	62804	71533	77770
5723	N	NSBX	WD	77771	62805	71526	77772
5724	N	NSBX	WD	77773	62806	71561	77774
5725	N	NSBX	WD	77775	62807	71541	77776
5726	N	NSBX	WD	77777	62808	71556	77778
5727	N	NSBX	WD	77779	62809	71562	77780
5728	N	NSBX	WD	77781	62810	71527	77782
5729	N	NSBX	WD	77783	62811	71550	77784
5730	N	NSBX	WD	77785	62812	71551	77786
5731	N	NSBX	WD	77787	62813	71555	77788
5732	N	NSBX	WD	77789	62814	71552	77790
5733	N	NSBX	WD	77791	62815	71549	77792
5734	N	NSBX	WD	77793	62816	71531	77794
5735	N	NSBX	WD	77795	62817	71563	77796
5736	N	NSBX	WD	77797	62818	71554	77798
5737	N	NSBX	WD	77799	62819	71544	77800
5738	N	NSBX	WD	77801	62820	71529	77802
5739	N	NSBX	WD	77803	62821	71537	77804
5740	N	NSBX	WD	77805	62822	71530	77806
5741	N	NSBX	WD	77807	62823	71559	77808
5742	N	NSBX	WD	77809	62824	71543	77810
5750	N	NSBX	WD	77811	62825	71538	77812

CLASS 455/8

DTSO – MSO – TSO – DTSO. Sliding doors. Disc brakes. Fluorescent lighting. PA. First series. Pressure ventilation.

Bogies: BP20 (MSO), BT13 (trailer cars).
Gangways: Through gangwayed.
Traction Motors: Four EE507 of 185 kW.
Dimensions: 19.83 x 2.82 m. (outer cars), 19.92 x 2.82 m (inner cars).
Maximum Speed: 75 mph.

DTSO. Dia. EE218. Lot No. 30972 York 1982 – 84. 74S. 29.5 t.
MSO. Dia. EC203. Lot No. 30973 York 1982 – 84. 84S. 45.6 t.
TSO. Dia. EH221. Lot No. 30974 York 1982 – 84. 84S. 27.1 t.

5800	N	NSLX	SU	77634	62736		77631
5801	N	NSLX	SU	77579	62709	71637	77580

5802	N	NSLX	SU	77581	62710	71664	77582
5803	N	NSLX	SU	77583	62711	71639	77584
5804	N	NSLX	SU	77585	62712	71640	77586
5805	N	NSLX	SU	77587	62713	71641	77588
5806	N	NSLX	SU	77589	62714	71642	77590
5807	N	NSLX	SU	77591	62715	71643	77592
5808	N	NSLX	SU	77593	62716	71644	77594
5809	N	NSLX	SU	77595	62717	71645	77596
5810	N	NSLX	SU	77597	62718	71646	77598
5811	N	NSLX	SU	77599	62719	71647	77600
5812	N	NSLX	SU	77601	62720	71648	77602
5813	N	NSLX	SU	77603	62721	71649	77604
5814	N	NSLX	SU	77605	62722	71650	77606
5815	N	NSLX	SU	77607	62723		77608
5816	N	NSLX	SU	77609	62724	71652	77633
5817	N	NSLX	SU	77611	62725	71653	77612
5818	N	NSLX	SU	77613	62726	71654	77614
5819	N	NSLX	SU	77615	62727	71655	77616
5820	N	NSLX	SU	77617	62728	71656	77618
5821	N	NSLX	SU	77619	62729	71657	77620
5822	N	NSLX	SU	77621	62730	71658	77622
5823	N	NSLX	SU	77623	62731	71659	77624
5824	N	NSLX	SU	77637	62732	71660	77626
5825	N	NSLX	SU	77627	62733	71661	77628
5826	N	NSLX	SU	77629	62734	71662	77630
5827	N	NSLX	SU	77610	62735	71663	77632
5829	N	NSLX	SU	77635	62737	71665	77636
5830	N	NSLX	SU	77625	62743	71666	77638
5831	N	NSLX	SU	77639	62739	71667	77640
5832	N	NSLX	SU	77641	62740	71668	77642
5833	N	NSLX	SU	77643	62741	71669	77644
5834	N	NSLX	SU	77645	62742	71670	77646
5835	N	NSLX	SU	77647	62738	71671	77648
5836	N	NSLX	SU	77649	62744	71672	77650
5837	N	NSLX	SU	77651	62745	71673	77652
5838	N	NSLX	SU	77653	62746	71674	77654
5839	N	NSLX	SU	77655	62747	71675	77656
5840	N	NSLX	SU	77657	62748	71676	77658
5841	N	NSLX	SU	77659	62749	71677	77660
5842	N	NSLX	SU	77661	62750	71678	77662
5843	N	NSLX	SU	77663	62751	71679	77664
5844	N	NSLX	SU	77665	62752	71680	77666
5845	N	NSLX	SU	77667	62753	71681	77668
5846	N	NSLX	SU	77669	62754	71682	77670
5847	N	NSBX	WD	77671	62755	71683	77672
5848	N	NSBX	WD	77673	62756	71684	77674
5849	N	NSBX	WD	77675	62757	71685	77676
5850	N	NSBX	WD	77677	62758	71686	77678
5851	N	NSBX	WD	77679	62759	71687	77680
5852	N	NSBX	WD	77681	62760	71688	77682
5853	N	NSBX	WD	77683	62761	71689	77684
5854	N	NSBX	WD	77685	62762	71690	77686

855	**N**	NSBX	WD	77687	62763	71691	77688
856	**N**	NSBX	WD	77689	62764	71692	77690
857	**N**	NSBX	WD	77691	62765	71693	77692
858	**N**	NSBX	WD	77693	62766	71694	77694
859	**N**	NSBX	WD	77695	62767	71695	77696
860	**N**	NSBX	WD	77697	62768	71696	77698
861	**N**	NSBX	WD	77699	62769	71697	77700
862	**N**	NSBX	WD	77701	62770	71698	77702
863	**N**	NSBX	WD	77703	62771	71699	77704
864	**N**	NSBX	WD	77705	62772	71700	77706
865	**N**	NSBX	WD	77707	62773	71701	77708
866	**N**	NSBX	WD	77709	62774	71702	77710
867	**N**	NSBX	WD	77711	62775	71703	77712
868	**N**	NSBX	WD	77713	62776	71704	77714
869	**N**	NSBX	WD	77715	62777	71705	77716
870	**N**	NSBX	WD	77717	62778	71706	77718
871	**N**	NSBX	WD	77719	62779	71707	77720
872	**N**	NSBX	WD	77721	62780	71708	77722
873	**N**	NSBX	WD	77723	62781	71709	77724
874	**N**	NSBX	WD	77725	62782	71710	77726
pare	**N**	NSLX	SU (U)			71651	

CLASS 455/9

TSO – MSO – TSO – DTSO. Sliding doors. Disc brakes. Fluorescent lighting. A. Third series. Convection heating.

ogies: BP20 (MSO), BT13 (trailer cars).
angways: Through gangwayed.
raction Motors: Four EE507 of 185 kW.
imensions: 19.83 x 2.82 m. (outer cars), 19.92 x 2.82 m (inner cars).
laximum Speed: 75 mph.

TSO. Dia. EE226. Lot No. 30991 York 1985. 74S. 29.5 t.
ISO. Dia. EC206. Lot No. 30992 York 1985. 84S. 45.6 t.
SO. Dia. EH224. Lot No. 30993 York 1985. 84S. 27.1 t.
SO n. Dia. EH224. Lot No. 30932 Derby 1981. 84S. 27.1 t.

Chopper control.
Tread brakes.
Class 455/8 TSO.
"Crossrail" interiors.

901	**N**	NSBX	WD	77813	62826	71714	77814
902	**N**	NSBX	WD	77815	62827	71715	77816
903	**N**	NSBX	WD	77817	62828	71716	77818
904	**N**	NSBX	WD	77819	62829	71717	77820
905	**N**	NSBX	WD	77821	62830	71718	77822
906	**N**	NSBX	WD	77823	62831	71719	77824
907	**N**	NSBX	WD	77825	62832	71720	77826
908	**N**	NSBX	WD	77827	62833	71721	77828
909	**N**	NSBX	WD	77829	62834	71722	77830
910	**N**	NSBX	WD	77831	62835	71723	77832
911	**N**	NSBX	WD	77833	62836	71724	77834

5912	*	**N**	NSBX	WD	77835	62837	71725	77836
5913	§	**N**	NSBX	WD	77837	62838	71726	77838
5914	§	**N**	NSBX	WD	77839	62839	71727	77840
5915	§	**N**	NSBX	WD	77841	62840	71728	77842
5916	*	**N**	NSBX	WD	77843	62841	71729	77844
5917	*	**N**	NSBX	WD	77845	62842	71730	77846
5918	*n	**N**	NSBX	WD	77847	62843	67400	77848
5919	*★	**N**	NSBX	WD	77849	62844	71638	77850
5920	*	**N**	NSBX	WD	77851	62845	71733	77852
Spare	c	**N**	NSBX	WD			71731	
Spare	c	**N**	NSBX	WD			71732	

CLASS 416/2 BR DESIGN 2 EP

DMBSO – DTSso.

Electrical Equipment: 1951-type.
Bogies: Mk. 3D.
Gangways: Non-gangwayed.
Traction Motors: Two EE507 of 185 kW.
Dimensions: 19.49 x 2.82 m.
Maximum Speed: 75 mph.

65301 – 65304. DMBSO. Dia. EB269. Lot No. 30114 Ashford/Eastleigh 1954 84S. 42 t.
65327 – 65341. DMBSO. Dia. EB269. Lot No. 30119 Ashford/Eastleigh 1954 84S. 42 t.
65344 – 65365. DMBSO. Dia. EB269. Lot No. 30167 Ashford/Eastleigh 1955 84S. 42 t.
65367 – 65392. DMBSO. Dia. EB269. Lot No. 30314 Ashford/Eastleigh 1956 – 58. 84S. 42 t.
77501 – 77504. DTSso. Dia. EE264. Lot No. 30115 Ashford/Eastleigh 1954 102S. 30.5 t.
77512 – 77526. DTSso. Dia. EE264. Lot No. 30120 Ashford/Eastleigh 1954 102S. 30.5 t.
77529 – 77550. DTSso. Dia. EE264. Lot No. 30168 Ashford/Eastleigh 1955 102S. 30.5 t.
77552 – 77577. DTSso. Dia. EE264. Lot No. 30315 Ashford/Eastleigh 1956 – 58. 102S. 30.5 t.

Note: 77537/9 are DTSO and seat 92S. (Dia. EE275).

6202	NKSX	SG	65301	77501
6203	NKSX	SG	65302	77502
6205	NKSX	SG	65304	77504
6213	NKSX	SG	65327	77512
6217	NKSX	SG	65331	77516
6221	NKSX	SG	65335	77520
6223	NKSX	SG	65337	77522
6224	NKSX	SG	65338	77523
6225	NKSX	SG	65339	77524
6226	NKSX	SG	65340	77525
6227	NKSX	SG	65341	77526
6230	NKSX	SG	65344	77529
6231	NKSX	SG	65345	77530

235	NKSX	SG	65349 77534
236	NKSX	SG	65350 77535
237	NKSX	SG	65351 77536
239	NKSX	SG	65353 77538
240	NKSX	SG	65354 77539
241	NKSX	SG	65355 77540
245	NKSX	SG	65359 77544
247	NKSX	SG	65361 77546
249	NKSX	SG	65363 77548
251	NKSX	SG	65365 77550
253	NKSX	SG	65367 77552
255	NKSX	SG	65369 77554
256	NKSX	SG	65370 77555
259	NKSX	SG	65373 77558
260	NKSX	SG	65374 77559
261	NKSX	SG	65375 77560
262	NKSX	SG	65376 77561
263	NKSX	SG	65377 77562
264	NKSX	SG	65378 77563
265	NKSX	SG	65379 77564
267	NKSX	SG	65381 77566
268	NKSX	SG	65382 77567
270	NKSX	SG	65384 77569
271	NKSX	SG	65385 77570
272	NKSX	SG	65386 77571
273	NKSX	SG	65387 77572
274	NKSX	SG	65388 77573
275	NKSX	SG	65389 77574
277	NKSX	SG	65391 77576
278	NKSX	SG	65392 77577

LASS 416/3 SR DESIGN 2 EPB

MBSO – DTSso. These units were made by producing new bodies for former Nol underframes. All have now been facelifted with new seat trim, fluores-ent lighting and PA.

lectrical Equipment: 1951-type.
ogies: Central 40'' motor bogies and SR standard trailer bogies.
angways: Non-gangwayed.
raction Motors: Two EE507 of 185 kW.
imensions: 19.05 x 2.82 m.
laximum Speed: 75 mph.

4283. DMBSO. Dia. EB269. Lot No. 4016 Eastleigh 1954 – 5. 82S. 40 t.
4542 – 14590. DMBSO. Dia. EB269. Lot No. 4281 Eastleigh 1957 – 9. 82S. 0 t.
TSO. Dia. EE269. Lot No. 4281 Eastleigh 1957 – 9. 92S. 30 t.

301	**N**	NSLX	SU	14577 16121
302	**N**	NSLX	SU	14580 16124
303	**N**	NSLX	SU	14576 16120
304	**N**	NSLX	SU	14589 16133

6305	N	NSLX	SU	14587	16131
6306	N	NSLX	SU	14571	16115
6307	N	NSLX	SU	14573	16117
6308	N	NSLX	SU	14564	16108
6309	N	NSLX	SU	14562	16106
6310	N	NSLX	SU	14574	16118
6311	N	NSLX	SU	14565	16109
6312	N	NSLX	SU	14579	16123
6313	N	NSLX	SU	14558	16102
6314	N	NSLX	SU	14586	16130
6315	N	NSLX	SU	14590	16134
6316	N	NSLX	SU	14559	16103
6317	N	NSLX	SU	14578	16122
6318	N	NSLX	SU	14566	16110
6319	N	NSLX	SU	14568	16112
6320	N	NSLX	SU	14561	16105
6321	N	NSLX	SU	14283	16128
6322	N	NSLX	SU	14488	16119
6323	N	NSLX	SU	14581	16125
6324	N	NSLX	SU	14560	16104
6325	N	NSLX	SU	14567	16111
6326	N	NSLX	SU	14585	16129
6327	N	NSLX	SU	14572	16116
6328	N	NSLX	SU	14582	16126
6329	N	NSLX	SU	14542	16114
6330	N	NSLX	SU	14588	16132
6331	N	NSLX	SU	14583	16127
6332		NSLX	SU	14569	16113
6333	N	NSLX	SU	14557	16101
6334	N	NSLX	SU	14546	16107

CLASS 416/4 FACELIFTED BR DESIGN 2 EP

DMBSO – DTSO. Facelifted units with new trim, fluorescent lighting and PA

Electrical Equipment: 1951-type.
Bogies: Mk. 3D.
Gangways: Non-gangwayed.
Traction Motors: Two EE507 of 185 kW.
Dimensions: 19.49 x 2.82 m.
Maximum Speed: 75 mph.

65305 – 65309. DMBSO. Dia. EB281. Lot No. 30114 Ashford/Eastleigh 1954 82S. 42 t.
65328 – 65334. DMBSO. Dia. EB281. Lot No. 30119 Ashford/Eastleigh 1954 82S. 42 t.
65342 – 65366. DMBSO. Dia. EB281. Lot No. 30167 Ashford/Eastleigh 1955 82S. 42 t.
65368 – 65372. DMBSO. Dia. EB281. Lot No. 30314 Ashford/Eastleig 1956 – 58. 79S. 42 t.
77113. DTSO. Dia. EE279. Lot No. 30117 Eastleigh 1955. Former Sout Tyneside trailer. 92s. 30.5 t.

etwork-SouthEast liveried Class 302 No. 302 203 passes Limehouse on 19th mber 1992. *Norman Barrington*

lass 303 No. 303 014 in Strathclyde PTE livery at Partick on 25th May 1991. *Norman Barrington*

▲ Class 304 No. 304 045 near Cliff Vale (Stoke) whilst working the 11.33 Man-chester Piccadilly – Stoke-on-Trent service on 6th December 1991.
Hugh Ballar

▼ Regional Railways liveried Class 305 No. 305 514 departing from Crew 29th August 1992 with a Manchester service. *John Augus*

Class 308 No. 308 150 pauses at Barking on 19th September 1991 whilst ning a Shoeburyness service. *Norman Barrington*

Class 309 Clacton Express unit No. 309 618 forms the 09.04 Liverpool et – Clacton at Marks Tay on 14th May 1992. *Brian Denton*

▲ Class 310 No. 310 087 at Barking with a London service on 17th July 19
Norman Barring

▼ Class 312 No. 312 792 at Barking with a London service on 31st March 19
Norman Barring

Dual voltage Class 313 No. 313 003 at Gospel Oak on 29th August 1992
lst forming the 13.03 Richmond – North Woolwich. *Kevin Conkey*

Class 314 No. 314 206 pauses at Dalmuir with the 15.54
:nsburgh – Airdrie on 21st May 1990. *Tom Heavyside*

▲ Class 317 No. 317 319 passing Great Chesterford as the 15.02 Liverp
Street – Cambridge on 25th March 1991. *Hugh Ballant*

▼ Class 318 No. 318 250 leaves Irvine with the 17.30 Glasgow Central –
on 2nd August 1990. *John August*

:lass 319/1 No. 319 174 at Cricklewood on 1st September 1992 whilst for-
] the 12.48 Bedford – Brighton. *Kevin Conkey*

:lass 321 No. 321 356 passing through Stratford on 17th October 1992 with
/erpool Street service. *Kevin Conkey*

▲ Also at Stratford Class 322 No. 322 482 forms the 10.30 Star
Airport – Liverpool Street service on 21st May 1992. *Brian De*

▼ Class 323 No. 323 201 in Centro livery stands outside the works of Hu
TPL. These units will enter service shortly on the Cross City line between Lic
and Redditch. *Hunslet*

Class 421/5 ('Greyhound 4 Cig') unit No. 1312 stands at Portsmouth Har-
ır on 29th August 1992. *Mervyn Turvey*

Refurbished Class 412 (4 Bep) unit No. 2305 forms the front portion of the
05 Portsmouth Harbour – Waterloo at Fratton on 3rd April 1992.
Brian Denton

60

:lass 413/4 (4 Cap) No. 3321 approaches Orpington whilst forming the 12.38 Victoria on 8th September 1992. *Chris Wilson*

:lass 423 (4 Vep) No. 3405 near Southampton with the 13.05 erloo – Southampton on 12th September 1992. *Chris Wilson*

▲ SR design Class 415/4 (4 EPB) No. 5486 with one blue and grey MBSO st
at Woolwich Arsenal with the 14.57 Charing Cross – Gillingham on
September 1992.
Chris W

▼ Class 455/7 No. 5702 leaves Wimbledon on 27th July 1992 with a Guil
train.
Hugh Ballan

? design Class 416/3 2 EPB No. 6301 forms the front portion of the 10.10 ria – East Grinstead at Clapham cutting on 27th March 1991.
Brain Denton

lass 456 No. 456 011 approaching Clapham Junction on 27th July 1992.
Hugh Ballantyne

B LECKMANN
465001
8

French Railways 'Sybic'-liveried Class 90 No. 90130 'Fretconnection' at Slindon with the Dover Town-Basford Hall company train on 7th September 1992.
Hugh Ballantyne

▲ Class 90 No. 90016 near Hest Bank on 6th August 1992 with the 05
Glasgow Central – Crewe empty vans. *Paul Shanr*

▼ Class 91 No. 91008 'Thomas Cook' pauses at York on 27th March 19
whilst working a Kings Cross – Newcastle train. *George Alls*

47344	a +	**FD**	MDDT	TI	
47345		**FR**	MDWT	TI	
47346		**C**	RBJI	IM	
47347	a	**FM**	MDAT	TI	
47348		**FO**	FPYI	IM	St. Christopher's Railway Home
47349		**FD**	MDYX	TI (U)	
47350		**FO**	MDWT	TI	
47351	+	**FD**	MDDT	TI	
47352		**C**	FIJI	IM	
47353		**C**	CEJC	CD	
47354		**FD**	MDAT	TI	
47355		**FD**	MDAT	TI	
47356		**FO**	CEJC	CD	
47357		**C**	CEJC	CD	The Permanent Way Institution
47358		**FO**	RCLC	CD	
47359		**FD**	MDWT	TI	
47360	a +	**FD**	MDCT	TI	
47361		**FD**	MDAT	TI	Wilton Endeavour
47362	a +	**FD**	MDCT	TI	
47363	+	**F**	MDDT	TI	
47364		**C**	NKJO	OC	
47365	+	**FD**	MDDT	TI	ICI Diamond Jubilee
47366		**FO**	IGJO	OC	
47367		**FR**	MDAT	TI	
47368		**FP**	FPFR	IM	Neritidae
47369		**FP**	FPFR	IM	
47370		**FO**	MDWT	TI	
47371		**FO**	MDWT	TI	
47372		**C**	CEJC	CD	
47375		**FD**	MDAT	TI	Tinsley Traction Depot (Quality Approved)
47376			MDAT	TI	
47377		**FD**	MDAT	TI	
47378	+	**FD**	MDDT	TI	
47379	+	**FP**	FPFR	IM	

Class 47/4. Equipped with train heating. RA7. Max Speed 95 (75§) mph.

47433	**BR**	PXLC	CD	
47439	**BR**	PXLC	CD	
47442	**BR**	PXLC	CD	
47443	**BR**	PXLC	CD	North Eastern
47449	**BR**	NXXB	OC	
47458	**R**	PXLC	CD	County of Cambridgeshire
47462	**R**	PXLC	CD	Cambridge Traction & Rolling Stock Depot
47463		PXLC	CD	
47467	**BR**	PXLC	CD	
47471	**IO**	PXLC	CD	Norman Tunna G.C.
47473	**BR**	IWJD	CD	
47474	**R**	PXLC	CD	Sir Rowland Hill
47475	**RX**	PXLC	CD	Restive
47476	**R**	PXLC	CD	Night Mail

47478				IWJD	CD	
47481			**BR**	PXLC	CD	
47482			**BR**	PXLC	CD	
47483			**M**	IMJC	CD	
47484			**G**	IGJW	OC	ISAMBARD KINGDOM BRUNEL
47485			**BR**	PXLC	CD	
47488			**BR**	PXLC	CD	
47489			**R**	PXLC	CD	Crewe Diesel Depot
47490		+	**RX**	PXLB	CD	
47491		+	**RX**	PXLB	CD	
47492			**IO**	PXLC	CD	
47500		+	**RX**	PXLB	CD	
47501			**R**	PXLC	CD	Craftsman
47503		+	**RX**	PXLB	CD	
47508			**M**	IXXS	BR (U)	
47513			**BR**	PXLC	CD	Severn
47517		+	**RX**	PXLB	CD	
47519			**BR**	PXLC	CD	
47520			**M**	IGJA	BR	
47521			**N**	PXLC	CD	
47522			**R**	PXLC	CD	Doncaster Enterprise
47523			**M**	PXLC	CD	
47524			**M**	PXLC	CD	
47525			**IO**	IWJD	CD	
47526			**BR**	NXXB	OC	
47528			**M**	PXLC	CD	The Queen's Own Mercian Yeomanry
47530			**RX**	PXLC	CD	
47531	(47974)	+	**RX**	PXLB	CD	
47532			**RX**	PXLC	CD	
47535			**R**	NXXB	OC	University of Leicester
47536			**BR**	PXLC	CD	
47537		+	**RX**	PXLB	CD	
47539			**RX**	PXLC	CD	
47541		+	**RX**	PXLB	CD	
47543			**R**	PXLC	CD	
47547			**N**	PXLC	CD	
47550			**M**	IEJI	IM	University of Dundee
47551	(47801)		**BR**	PXLC	CD	
47555	(47126)		**IO**	IMJC	CD	
47557	(47024)		**M**	PXLC	CD	
47558	(47027)		**M**	PXLC	CD	Mayflower
47559	(47028)		**RX**	PXLC	CD	
47562	(47672)	+	**RX**	PXLB	CD	
47564	(47038)		**BR**	PXLC	CD	
47565	(47039)		**M**	PXLC	CD	
47566	(47043)		**M**	PXLC	CD	
47567	(47044)		**M**	PXLC	CD	Red Star
47568	(47045)		**M**	PXLC	CD	Royal Engineers Postal & Courier Services
47569	(47047)		**R**	PXLC	CD	The Gloucestershire Regiment

47572	(47168)		**R**	PXLC	CD	Ely Cathedral
47573	(47173)		**RX**	PXLC	CD	
47574	(47174)		**R**	PXLC	CD	Benjamin Gimbert G.C.
47575	(47175)		**R**	PXLC	CD	City of Hereford
47576	(47176)		**RX**	PXLC	CD	
47578	(47181)	+	**RX**	PXLB	CD	
47579	(47183)		**N**	NTWE	OC	James Nightall G.C.
47580	(47167)		**BR**	PXLC	CD	County of Essex
47581	(47169)		**N**	PXLC	CD	
47582	(47170)		**R**	PXLC	CD	County of Norfolk
47583	(47172)		**N**	NTWE	OC	County of Hertfordshire
47584	(47180)		**M**	PXLC	CD	County of Suffolk
47587	(47263)		**N**	PXLC	CD	
47588	(47178)		**RX**	PXLC	CD	Resurgent
47592	(47171)		**BR**	PXLC	CD	County of Avon
47594	(47035)		**RX**	PXLC	CD	Resourceful
47596	(47255)		**N**	PXLC	CD	Aldeburgh Festival
47597	(47026)		**RX**	PXLC	CD	Resilient
47598	(47182)		**RX**	PXLC	CD	
47599	(47177)		**RX**	PXLC	CD	
47600	(47250)		**RX**	PXLC	CD	
47603	(47267)		**BR**	PXLC	CD	
47605	(47160)		**RX**	PXLC	CD	
47615	(47252)		**RX**	PXLC	CD	
47624	(47087)		**M**	PXLC	CD	
47625	(47076)		**RX**	PXLC	CD	Resplendent
47626	(47082)		**M**	PXLC	CD	ATLAS
47627	(47273)		**RX**	PXLC	CD	
47628	(47078)		**M**	PXLC	CD	
47630	(47041)	+	**RX**	PXLB	CD	
47631	(47059)	+	**RX**	PXLB	CD	
47634	(47158)		**R**	PXLC	CD	Holbeck
47635	(47029)		**R**	PXLC	CD	
47636	(47243)		**BR**	PXLD	CD	Sir John de Graeme
47640	(47244)		**R**	PXLC	CD	University of Strathclyde
47641	(47086)		**BR**	PXLD	CD (U)	
47642	(47040)	+	**RX**	PXLB	CD	Resolute
47644	(47246)		**BR**	PXLD	CD (U)	
47671	(47616)	§	**BR**	IGJA	BR	Y Ddraig Goch/ The Red Dragon
47673	(47593)	§	**IO**	IGJA	BR	Galloway Princess
47674	(47604)	§	**BR**	IMJK	CD	Women's Royal Voluntary Service
47675	(47595)	§	**M**	IGJA	BR	Confederation of British Industry
47676	(47586)	§	**I**	IEJI	IM	Northamptonshire
47677	(47617)	§	**I**	IGJA	BR	University of Stirling

Class 47/7. TDM fitted. RA6. Max speed. 100 mph.

47701	(47493)	+	**N**	NTWE	OC	Old Oak Common Traction & Rolling Stock Depot
47702	(47504)	+	**N**	NTWE	OC	Saint Cuthbert

47703	(47514)	+	**R**	NTWE	OC	The Queen Mother
47704	(47495)	+	**RX**	PXLD	CD	
47705	(47554)	+	**N**	NTWE	OC	
47706	(47494)	+	**PS**	NTWE	OC	
47707	(47506)	+	**N**	NTWE	OC	Holyrood
47708	(47516)	+	**N**	NTWE	OC	Templecombe
47709	(47499)	+	**N**	NTWE	OC	
47710	(47496)	+	**N**	NTWE	OC	Capital Radio's Help a London Child
47711	(47498)	+	**N**	NTWE	OC	
47712	(47505)	+	**R**	NTWE	OC	Lady Diana Spencer
47714	(47511)	+	**N**	NTWE	OC	
47715	(47502)	+	**N**	NTWE	OC	Haymarket
47716	(47507)	+	**N**	NTWE	OC	Duke of Edinburgh's Award
47717	(47497)	+	**R**	NTWE	OC	

Class 47/4 continued.

47802	(47552)	+	**I**	IMJK	CD	
47803	(47553)	+	**IO**	IMJK	CD	
47804	(47591)	+	**I**	IGJA	BR	Kettering
47805	(47650)	+	**I**	ILRA	BR	Bristol Bath Road
47806	(47651)	+	**I**	ILRA	BR	
47807	(47652)	+	**I**	ILRA	BR	
47808	(47653)	+	**I**	ILRA	BR	Samson
47809	(47654)	+	**I**	IBRA	BR	Finsbury Park
47810	(47655)	+	**I**	ILRA	BR	
47811	(47656)	+	**I**	ILRA	BR	
47812	(47657)	+	**I**	ILRA	BR	
47813	(47658)	+	**I**	ILRA	BR	
47814	(47659)	+	**I**	ILRA	BR	
47815	(47660)	+	**I**	ILRA	BR	
47816	(47661)	+	**I**	ILRA	BR	
47817	(47662)	+	**I**	ILRA	BR	
47818	(47663)	+	**M**	ILRA	BR	
47819	(47664)	+	**I**	IBRA	BR	
47820	(47665)	+	**I**	IBRA	BR	
47821	(47607)	+	**I**	IBRA	BR	Royal Worcester
47822	(47571)	+	**I**	ILRA	BR	
47823	(47610)	+	**I**	IBRA	BR	SS Great Britain
47824	(47602)	+	**M**	IBRB	BR (S)	Glorious Devon
47825	(47590)	+	**M**	ILRA	BR	Thomas Telford
47826	(47637)	+	**I**	ILRA	BR	
47827	(47589)	+	**I**	ILRA	BR	
47828	(47629)	+	**I**	ILRA	BR	
47829	(47619)	+	**M**	ILRA	BR	
47830	(47649)	+	**I**	ILRA	BR	
47831	(47563)	+	**M**	ILRA	BR	Bolton Wanderer
47832	(47560)	+	**M**	ILRA	BR	Tamar
47833	(47608)	+	**I**	IBRA	BR	
47834	(47609)	+	**I**	IBRA	BR	FIRE FLY
47835	(47620)	+	**I**	IBRA	BR	Windsor Castle
47836	(47618)	+	**I**	ILRA	BR	

47838	(47612)	+	**I**	IBRB	BR (U)	
47839	(47621)	+	**I**	ILRA	BR	
47840	(47613)	+	**I**	ILRA	BR	NORTH STAR
47841	(47622)	+	**I**	ILRA	BR	The Institution of Mechanical Engineers
47842	(47606)	+	**I**	IBRB	BR (U)	
47843	(47623)	+	**I**	ILRA	BR	
47844	(47556)	+	**I**	ILRA	BR	Derby & Derbyshire Chamber of Commerce & Industry
47845	(47638)	+	**I**	ILRA	BR	County of Kent
47846	(47647)	+	**I**	ILRA	BR	THOR
47847	(47577)	+	**I**	ILRA	BR	
47848	(47632)	+	**I**	ILRA	BR	
47849	(47570)	+	**M**	ILRA	BR	
47850	(47648)	+	**I**	ILRA	BR	
47851	(47639)	+	**I**	ILRA	BR	
47853	(47614)	+	**M**	ILRA	BR	
47971	(97480)	*	**BR**	CDJC	CD	Robin Hood
47972	(97545)		**BR**	CDJC	CD	
47973	(97561)		**M**	CDJC	CD	Derby Evening Telegraph
47975	(47540)	*	**C**	CDJC	CD	The Institution of Civil Engineers
47976	(47546)	*	**C**	CDJC	CD	Aviemore Centre

CLASS 50 ENGLISH ELECTRIC TYPE 4 Co – Co

Built: 1967 – 68 by English Electric Co. at Vulcan Foundry, Newton le Willows.
Engine: English Electric 16CVST of 2010 kW (2700 hp) at 850 rpm.
Main Generator: English Electric 840/4B.
Traction Motors: English Electric 538/5A.
Max. Tractive Effort: 216 kN (48500 lbf).
Cont. Tractive Effort: 147 kN (33000 lbf) at 23.5 mph.
Power At Rail: 1540 kW (2070 hp). **Length over Buffers:** 20.88 m.
Brake Force: 59 t. **Wheel Diameter:** 1092 mm.
Design Speed: 105 mph. **Weight:** 117 t.
Max. Speed: 100 mph. **RA:** 6.
Train Heating: Electric. **ETH Index:** 61.
Train Brakes: Air & vacuum.
Multiple Working: Orange Square coupling code. (Within class only).
Communication Equipment: Cab to shore radio-telephone.
All equipped with slow speed control.

Formerly numbered 407, 433, 400.

50007	**G**	NWXA	LA	SIR EDWARD ELGAR
50033	**N**	NWXA	LA	Glorious
50050		NWXA	LA	

CLASS 56 BRUSH TYPE 5 Co – Co

Built: 1976 – 84 by Electroputere at Craiova, Romania (as sub contractors for Brush) or BREL at Doncaster or Crewe Works.
Engine: Ruston Paxman 16RK3CT of 2460 kW (3250 hp) at 900 rpm.

56001 – 56038

Main Alternator: Brush BA1101A.
Traction Motors: Brush TM73-62.
Max. Tractive Effort: 275 kN (61800 lbf).
Cont. Tractive Effort: 240 kN (53950 lbf) at 16.8 mph.
Power At Rail: 1790 kW (2400 hp). **Length over Buffers:** 19.36 m.
Brake Force: 60 t. **Wheel Diameter:** 1143 mm.
Design Speed: 80 mph. **Weight:** 125 t.
Max. Speed: 80 mph. **RA:** 7.
Train Brakes: Air.
Multiple Working: Red Diamond coupling code.
Communication Equipment: Cab to shore radio-telephone.
All equipped with slow speed control.

§ Derated to 1790 kW (2400 hp).
* Derated to 2060 kW (2800 hp).

56001	**FA**	FASB	SL	Whatley
56003	**F**	FCBN	TO	
56004		FCBN	TO	
56005	**FC**	FCBN	TO	
56006	**FC**	FCBN	TO	
56007	**FC**	FCBN	TO	
56008		FCXX	TO (U)	
56009	**FC**	FCBN	TO	
56010		FCBN	TO	
56011	**FR**	FCBN	TO	
56012	**FC**	FCXX	TO (U)	
56013	**FC**	FCBN	TO	
56014	**FC**	FCXX	TO (S)	
56015	**FC**	FCXX	TO (U)	
56016	**FC**	FCXX	TO (U)	
56018	**FC**	FCBN	TO	
56019	**FR**	FCBN	TO	
56020		FCXX	TO (S)	
56021	**FC**	FCBN	TO	
56022		FCBN	TO	
56023	**FC**	FCDN	TO	
56024	**FO**	FCXX	TO (S)	
56025	**FC**	FCBN	TO	
56026		FCXX	TO (U)	
56027	**FC**	FCDN	TO	
56028	**FC**	FCXX	TO (U)	West Burton Power Station
56029	**FC**	FCDN	TO	
56030	**FC**	FCDN	TO	Eggborough Power Station
56031	**C**	NKJM	SL	Merehead
56032	**FM**	FMCK	CF	Sir De Morgannwg/ County of South Glamorgan
56033	**FA**	FASB	SL	
56034	**FA**	FASB	SL	Castell Ogwr/Ogmore Castle
56035	**FA**	FASB	SL	
56036	**C**	NKJM	SL	
56037	**FA**	FASB	SL	Richard Trevithick
56038	**FM**	FMCK	CF	Western Mail

56039	**FA**	FASB	SL	
56040	**FM**	FMCK	CF	Oystermouth
56041	**FA**	FASB	SL	
56043	**FA**	FASB	SL	
56044	**FM**	FMCK	CF	Cardiff Canton
56045	**FA**	FAXN	TO	
56046	**FA**	FMXX	CF (S)	
56047	**FC**	FCDN	TO	
56048	**FR**	FMCK	CF	
56049	**C**	NKJM	SL	
56050	**FA**	FASB	SL	
56051	**FA**	FASB	SL	
56052	**FA**	FMCK	CF	
56053	**FA**	FMCK	CF	Sir Morgannwg Ganol/ County of Mid Glamorgan
56054	**FC**	FAXN	TO	
56055	**FA**	FASB	SL	
56056	**FA**	FASB	SL	
56057	**FA**	FAXN	TO	
56058	**FA**	FAXN	TO	
56059	**FA**	FAXN	TO	
56060	**FA**	FMCK	CF	The Cardiff Rod Mill
56061	**FM**	FMTY	TE	
56062	**FA**	FAXN	TO	Mountsorrel
56063	**FA**	FMTY	TE	Bardon Hill
56064	**FA**	FMCK	CF	
56065	**FA**	FAXN	TO	
56066	**FC**	FCXX	TO (U)	
56067	**FC**	FCDN	TO	
56068	**FC**	FCDN	TO	
56069	§ **FM**	FMTY	TE	
56070	**FA**	FAXN	TO	
56071	**FC**	FCDN	TO	
56072	**FC**	FCDN	TO	
56073	**FM**	FMCK	CF	
56074	**FC**	FCDN	TO	Kellingley Colliery
56075	**FC**	FCDN	TO	West Yorkshire Enterprise
56076	**FC**	FCDN	TO	
56077	§ **FC**	FCDN	TO	Thorpe Marsh Power Station
56078	**FA**	FCEN	TO	
56079	**FC**	FCDN	TO	
56080	**FC**	FCDN	TO	Selby Coalfield
56081	**FC**	FCDN	TO	
56082	**FC**	FCDN	TO	
56083	* **FC**	FCDN	TO	
56084	* **FC**	FCDN	TO	
56085	**FC**	FCDN	TO	
56086	* **FC**	FCDN	TO	
56087	**FC**	FCDN	TO	
56088	**FC**	FCDN	TO	
56089	**FC**	FCDN	TO	Ferrybridge C Power Station
56090	**FC**	FCDN	TO	

56091	**FC**	FCDN	TO	Castle Donington Power Station
56092	**FC**	FCBN	TO	
56093	**FC**	FCDN	TO	The Institution of Mining Engineers
56094	**FC**	FCDN	TO	
56095	**FC**	FCDN	TO	Harworth Colliery
56096	**FC**	FCDN	TO	
56097	**FC**	FMTY	TE	
56098	**FC**	FCDN	TO	
56099	**FC**	FCDN	TO	Fiddlers Ferry Power Station
56100	**FC**	FCDN	TO	
56101	**FC**	FCDN	TO	Mutual Improvement
56102	**FC**	FCDN	TO	Scunthorpe Steel Centenary
56103	**FA**	FAXN	TO	
56104	**FC**	FCDN	TO	
56105	**FA**	FAXN	TO	
56106	**FC**	FCDN	TO	
56107	§ **FC**	FCDN	TO	
56108	**FR**	FCDN	TO	
56109	**FC**	FCDN	TO	
56110	**FA**	FAXN	TO	Croft
56111	**FC**	FCXX	TO (U)	
56112	**FC**	FCEN	TO	
56113	**FC**	FCEN	TO	
56114	**FC**	FCBN	TO	Maltby Colliery
56115	**FC**	FCBN	TO	
56116	**FC**	FMTY	TE	
56117	**FC**	FCEN	TO	Wilton-Coalpower
56118	**FC**	FCEN	TO	
56119	**FC**	FCEN	TO	
56120	**FC**	FCEN	TO	
56121	**FC**	FCBN	TO	
56123	**FC**	FCEN	TO	Drax Power Station
56124	**BR**	FCEN	TO	
56125	**FC**	FCEN	TO	
56126	**BR**	FCEN	TO	
56127	**FC**	FCEN	TO	
56128	**FC**	FCXX	TO (U)	
56129	**FC**	FCEN	TO	
56130	**FC**	FCEN	TO	Wardley Opencast
56131	**FC**	FCEN	TO	Ellington Colliery
56132	**FC**	FCEN	TO	
56133	**FC**	FCEN	TO	Crewe Locomotive Works
56134	**FC**	FCEN	TO	Blyth Power
56135	**FC**	FCEN	TO	Port of Tyne Authority

CLASS 58 BREL TYPE 5 Co – Co

Built: 1983 – 87 by BREL at Doncaster Works.
Engine: Ruston Paxman RK3ACT of 2460 kW (3300 hp) at 1000 rpm.
Main Alternator: Brush BA1101B.
Traction Motors: Brush TM73-62.
Max. Tractive Effort: 275 kN (61800 lbf).

Cont. Tractive Effort: 240 kN (53950 lbf) at 17.4 mph.
Power At Rail: 1780 kW (2387 hp). **Length over Buffers:** 19.13 m.
Brake Force: 62 t. **Wheel Diameter:** 1120 mm.
Design Speed: 80 mph. **Weight:** 130 t.
Max. Speed: 80 mph. **RA:** 7.
Train Brakes: Air.
Multiple Working: Red Diamond coupling code.
Communication Equipment: Cab to shore radio-telephone.
All equipped with slow speed control.

58001	**FC**	FCBN	TO	
58002	**FC**	FCBN	TO	Daw Mill Colliery
58003	**FC**	FCAN	TO	Markham Colliery
58004	**FC**	FCAN	TO	
58005	**FC**	FCAN	TO	
58006	**FC**	FCAN	TO	
58007	**FC**	FCBN	TO	Drakelow Power Station
58008	**FC**	FCAN	TO	
58009	**FC**	FCAN	TO	
58010	**FC**	FCAN	TO	
58011	**FC**	FCBN	TO	
58012	**FC**	FCBN	TO	
58013	**FC**	FCBN	TO	
58014	**FC**	FCBN	TO	Didcot Power Station
58015	**FC**	FCBN	TO	
58016	**FC**	FCBN	TO	
58017	**FC**	FCBN	TO	
58018	**FC**	FCBN	TO	High Marnham Power Station
58019	**FC**	FCBN	TO	Shirebrook Colliery
58020	**FC**	FCBN	TO	Doncaster Works
58021	**FC**	FCBN	TO	
58022	**FC**	FCBN	TO	
58023	**FC**	FCBN	TO	
58024	**FC**	FCBN	TO	
58025	**FC**	FCBN	TO	
58026	**FC**	FCBN	TO	
58027	**FC**	FCBN	TO	
58028	**FC**	FCBN	TO	
58029	**FC**	FCBN	TO	
58030	**FC**	FCBN	TO	
58031	**FC**	FCBN	TO	
58032	**FC**	FCBN	TO	
58033	**FC**	FCBN	TO	
58034	**FC**	FCBN	TO	Bassetlaw
58035	**FC**	FCBN	TO	
58036	**FC**	FCBN	TO	
58037	**FC**	FCBN	TO	
58038	**FC**	FCBN	TO	
58039	**FC**	FCBN	TO	Rugeley Power Station
58040	**FC**	FCDN	TO	Cottam Power Station
58041	**FC**	FCDN	TO	Ratcliffe Power Station
58042	**FC**	FCDN	TO	Ironbridge Power Station

58043	**FC**	FCBN	TO	
58044	**FC**	FCBN	TO	Oxcroft Opencast
58045	**FC**	FCBN	TO	
58046	**FC**	FCBN	TO	Thoresby Colliery
58047	**FC**	FCBN	TO	Manton Colliery
58048	**FC**	FCBN	TO	Coventry Colliery
58049	**FC**	FCBN	TO	Littleton Colliery
58050	**FC**	FCBN	TO	Toton Traction Depot

CLASS 59 GENERAL MOTORS TYPE 5 Co – Co

Built: 1985 (59001 – 4), 1989 (59005) by General Motors, La Grange, Illinois, U.S.A. or 1990 (59101 – 4) by General Motors, London, Ontario, Canada.
Engine: General Motors 645E3C two stroke of 2460 kW (3300 hp) at 900 rpm.
Main Alternator: General Motors AR11 MLD-D14A.
Traction Motors: General Motors D77B.
Max. Tractive Effort: 506 kN (113 550 lbf).
Cont. Tractive Effort: 291 kN (65 300 lbf) at 14.3 mph.
Power At Rail: 1889 kW (2533 hp).
Brake Force: 69 t.
Design Speed: 60 mph.
Max. Speed: 60 mph.
Length over Buffers: 21.35 m.
Wheel Diameter: 1067 mm.
Weight: 121 t.
RA: 7.

Class 59/0. Owned by Foster-Yeoman Ltd. Blue/silver/blue livery with white lettering and cast numberplates.

59001	**0**	XYPO	FY	YEOMAN ENDEAVOUR
59002	**0**	XYPO	FY	YEOMAN ENTERPRISE
59003	**0**	XYPO	FY	YEOMAN HIGHLANDER
59004	**0**	XYPO	FY	YEOMAN CHALLENGER
59005	**0**	XYPO	FY	KENNETH J. PAINTER

Class 59/1. Owned by ARC Limited. Yellow/grey with grey lettering.

59101	**0**	XYPA	AR	Village of Whatley
59102	**0**	XYPA	AR	Village of Chantry
59103	**0**	XYPA	AR	Village of Mells
59104	**0**	XYPA	AR	Village of Great Elm

Class 59/2. Under construction for National Power.

59201

CLASS 60 BRUSH TYPE 5 Co – Co

Built: 1989 onwards by Brush Traction.
Engine: Mirrlees MB275T of 2310 kW (3100 hp) at 1000 rpm.
Main Alternator: Brush .
Traction Motors: Brush separately excited.
Max. Tractive Effort: 500 kN (106500 lbf).
Cont. Tractive Effort: 336 kN (71570 lbf) at 17.4 mph.
Power At Rail: 1800 kW (2415 hp).
Brake Force: 74 t.
Design Speed: 62 mph.
Max. Speed: 60 mph.
Length over Buffers: 21.34 m.
Wheel Diameter: 1118 mm.
Weight: 129 t.
RA: 7.

Multiple Working: Within class.
Communication Equipment: Cab to shore radio-telephone.
All equipped with slow speed control.

60001	FA	FASB	SL	Steadfast
60002	FP	FPDI	IM	Capability Brown
60003	FP	FPDI	IM	Christopher Wren
60004	FC	FCJN	TO	Lochnagar
60005	FA	FPDI	IM	Skiddaw
60006	FA	FAXN	TO	Great Gable
60007	FP	FXXB		Robert Adam
60008	FM	FMYI	IM	Moel Fammau
60009	FA	FXXA		Carnedd Dafydd
60010	FA	FAXN	TO	Pumlumon Plynlimon
60011	FA	FAXN	TO	Cader Idris
60012	FA	FAXN	TO	Glyder Fawr
60013	FP	FXXA		Robert Boyle
60014	FP	FXXB		Alexander Fleming
60015	FA	FXXA		Bow Fell
60016	FA	FXXB		Langdale Pikes
60017	FA	FASB	SL	Arenig Fawr
60018	FA	FASB	SL	Moel Siabod
60019	FA	FASB	SL	Wild Boar Fell
60020	FM	FMEK	CF	Great Whernside
60021	FM	FPTY	TE	Pen-y-Ghent
60022	FM	FPTY	TE	Ingleborough
60023	FM	FMMY	TE	The Cheviot
60024	FP	FPEK	CF	Elizabeth Fry
60025	FP	FPEK	CF	Joseph Lister
60026	FP	FPDI	IM	William Caxton
60027	FP	FPDI	IM	Joseph Banks
60028	FP	FMYI	IM	John Flamsteed
60029	FM	FMEK	CF	Ben Nevis
60030	FM	FMMY	TE	Cir Mhor
60031	FM	FMMY	TE	Ben Lui
60032	FC	FCJN	TO	William Booth
60033	FP	FPEK	CF	Anthony Ashley Cooper
60034	FM	FMEK	CF	Carnedd Llewelyn
60035	FM	FMEK	CF	Florence Nightingale
60036	FM	FMEK	CF	Sgurr Na Ciche
60037	FM	FMXX	TE	Helvellyn
60038	FM	FMMY	TE	Bidean Nam Bian
60039	FA	FPDI	IM	Glastonbury Tor
60040	FA	FASB	SL	Brecon Beacons
60041	FA	FASB	SL	High Willhays
60042	FA	FABI	IM	Dunkery Beacon
60043	FA	FABI	IM	Yes Tor
60044	FM	FCHN	TO	Ailsa Craig
60045	FC	FCHN	TO	Josephine Butler
60046	FC	FCJN	TO	William Wilberforce
60047	FC	FCHN	TO	Robert Owen
60048	FA	FAXN	TO	Saddleback

60049	**FM**	FMMY	TE	Scafell
60050	**FM**	FMYI	IM	Roseberry Topping
60051	**FP**	FPEK	CF	Mary Somerville
60052	**FM**	FMMY	TE	Goat Fell
60053	**FP**	FPDI	IM	John Reith
60054	**FP**	FPDI	IM	Charles Babbage
60055	**FC**	FCHN	TO	Thomas Barnardo
60056	**FC**	FCJN	TO	William Beveridge
60057	**FC**	FCHN	TO	Adam Smith
60058	**FC**	FCJN	TO	John Howard
60059	**FC**	FMMY	TE	Samuel Plimsoll
60060	**FC**	FCHN	TO	James Watt
60061	**FC**	FCHN	TO	Alexander Graham Bell
60062	**FP**	FPEK	CF	Samuel Johnson
60063	**FP**	FPEK	CF	James Murray
60064	**FP**	FPDI	IM	Back Tor
60065	**FP**	FPEK	CF	Kinder Low
60066	**FC**	FCHN	TO	John Logie Baird
60067	**FC**	FPDI	IM	James Clerk-Maxwell
60068	**FC**	FCJN	TO	Charles Darwin
60069	**FC**	FCHN	TO	Humphry Davy
60070	**FC**	FCHN	TO	John Loudon McAdam
60071	**FC**	FCJN	TO	Dorothy Garrod
60072	**FC**	FCJN	TO	Cairn Toul
60073	**FC**	FCJN	TO	Cairn Gorm
60074	**FC**	FCJN	TO	Braeriach
60075	**FC**	FCJN	TO	Liathach
60076	**FC**	FCJN	TO	Suilven
60077	**FC**	FCJN	TO	Canisp
60078	**FC**	FCJN	TO	Stac Pollaidh
60079	**FC**	FCJN	TO	Foinaven
60080	**FA**	FABI	IM	Kinder Scout
60081	**FA**	FPDI	IM	Bleaklow Hill
60082	**FA**	FPDI	IM	Mam Tor
60083	**FA**	FAXN	TO	Shining Tor
60084	**FA**	FXXB		Cross Fell
60085	**FA**	FABI	IM	Axe Edge
60086	**FC**	FMMY	TE	Schiehallion
60087	**FC**	FCJN	TO	Slioch
60088	**FC**	FCJN	TO	Buachaille Etive Mor
60089	**FC**	FCJN	TO	Arcuil
60090	**FC**	FCJN	TO	Quinag
60091	**FC**	FCJN	TO	An Teallach
60092	**FC**	FCHN	TO	Reginald Munns
60093	**FC**	FCJN	TO	John Stirk
60094	**FA**	FASB	SL	Tryfan
60095	**FA**	FABI	IM	Crib Goch
60096	**FA**	FABI	IM	Ben Macdui
60097	**FA**	FABI	IM	Pillar
60098	**FA**	FABI	IM	Charles Francis Brush
60099	**FA**	FAXN	TO	Ben More Assynt
60100	**FA**	FAXN	TO	Boar of Badenoch

1.2. BR ELECTRIC LOCOMOTIVES

CLASS 73/0 ELECTRO – DIESEL Bo – Bo

Built: 1962 by BR at Eastleigh Works.
Supply System: 660 – 850 V d.c. from third rail.
Engine: English Electric 4SRKT of 447 kW (600 hp) at 850 rpm.
Main Generator: English Electric 824/3D.
Traction Motors: English Electric 542A.
Max. Tractive Effort: Electric 187 kN (42000 lbf). Diesel 152 kN (34100 lbf).
Continuous Rating: Electric 1060 kW (1420 hp) giving a tractive effort of 43 kN (9600 lbf) at 55.5 mph.
Cont. Tractive Effort: Diesel 72 kN (16100 lbf) at 10 mph.
Maximum Rail Power: Electric 1830 kW (2450 hp) at 37 mph.
Brake Force: 31 t. **Length over Buffers:** 16.36 m.
Design Speed: 80 mph. **Weight:** 76.5 t.
Max. Speed: 60 mph. **RA:** 6.
Wheel Diameter: 1016 mm. **ETH Index (Elec. power):** 66
Train Brakes: Air, Vacuum and electro-pneumatic.
Multiple Working: Within each sub-class and with Class 33/1 and also various SR EMUs.
Communication Equipment: All equipped with driver – guard telephone.
Couplings: Drop-head buckeye.
Formerly numbered E 6001 – /3/5/6.

Non-standard Livery: 73005 is Network SouthEast blue.

73001		NKJR	SL	
73002	**BR**	NKJR	SL	
73003	**BR**	NKJR	SL	
73005	**0**	NKJR	SL	Mid Hants WATERCRESS LINE
73006	**BR**	NKFE	SL	

CLASS 73/1 & 73/2 ELECTRO – DIESEL Bo – Bo

Built: 1965 – 67 by English Electric Co. at Vulcan Foundry, Newton le Willows.
Engine: English Electric 4SRKT of 447 kW (600 hp) at 850 rpm.
Main Generator: English Electric 824/5D.
Traction Motors: English Electric 546/1B.
Supply System: 660 – 850 V d.c. from third rail.
Max. Tractive Effort: Electric 179 kN (40000 lbf). Diesel 160 kN (36000 lbf).
Continuous Rating: Electric 1060 kW (1420 hp) giving a tractive effort of 35 kN (7800 lbf) at 68 mph.
Cont. Tractive Effort: Diesel 60 kN (13600 lbf) at 11.5 mph.
Maximum Rail Power: Electric 2350 kW (3150 hp) at 42 mph.
Brake Force: 31 t. **Length over Buffers:** 16.36 m.
Design Speed: 90 mph. **Weight:** 77 t.
Max. Speed: 60 (90*) mph. **RA:** 6.
Wheel Diameter: 1016 mm. **ETH Index (Elec. power):** 66
Train Brakes: Air, Vacuum and electro-pneumatic.

Multiple Working: Within each sub-class and with Class 33/1 and also various SR EMUs.
Communication Equipment: All equipped with driver – guard telephone.
Couplings: Drop-head buckeye.

Non-standard Livery: 73101 is Pullman umber & Cream.
Formerly numbered E 6001 – 20/22 – 26/28 – 49 (not in order).

Class 73/2 are locos dedicated to InterCity and Network SouthEast services.

73101		**0**	NKJL	SL	The Royal Alex'
73103		**IO**	NKJL	SL	
73104		**IO**	NKFE	SL	
73105		**C**	NKJL	SL	
73106		**D**	NKFE	SL	
73107		**C**	NKJL	SL	
73108		**C**	NKJL	SL	
73109		* **N**	NWXB	SL	Battle of Britain 50th Anniversary
73110		**C**	NKJL	SL	
73112		**N**	NKFE	SL	University of Kent at Canterbury
73114		**IO**	NKJL	SL	
73117		**IO**	NKJL	SL	University of Surrey
73118		**N**	NKJL	SL	The Romney Hythe and Dymchurch Railway
73119		**C**	NKJL	SL	Kentish Mercury
73126		**N**	NKJL	SL	Kent & East Sussex Railway
73128		**C**	NKJL	SL	OVS BULLIED C.B.E. 1937 1949 C.M.E. SOUTHERN RAILWAY
73129		**N**	NKJL	SL	City of Winchester
73130		**N**	NKJL	SL	City of Portsmouth
73131		**C**	NKJL	SL	County of Surrey
73132		**IO**	NKJL	SL	
73133		**N**	NKJL	SL	The Bluebell Railway
73134		**IO**	NKJL	SL	Woking Homes 1885 – 1985
73136		**N**	NKFE	SL	Kent Youth Music
73138		**C**	NKJL	SL	
73139		**IO**	NKJR	SL	
73140		**IO**	NKJR	SL	
73141		**IO**	NKJR	SL	
73201	(73142)	* **I**	IVGA	SL	Broadlands
73202	(73137)	* **I**	IVGA	SL	Royal Observer Corps
73203	(73127)	* **I**	IVGA	SL	
73204	(73125)	* **I**	IVGA	SL	Stewarts Lane 1860 – 1985
73205	(73124)	* **M**	IVGA	SL	London Chamber of Commerce
73206	(73123)	* **I**	IVGA	SL	Gatwick Express
73207	(73122)	* **I**	IVGA	SL	County of East Sussex
73208	(73121)	* **I**	IVGA	SL	Croydon 1883 – 1983
73209	(73120)	* **I**	IVGA	SL	
73210	(73116)	* **I**	IVGA	SL	Selhurst
73211	(73113)	* **I**	IVGA	SL	
73212	(73102)	* **I**	IVGA	SL	Airtour Suisse
73235	(73135)	* **I**	IVGA	SL	

CLASS 86/1 BR DESIGN Bo – Bo

Built: 1965 – 66 by English Electric Co. at Vulcan Foundry, Newton le Willows or BR at Doncaster Works. Rebuilt with Class 87 type bogies and motors. Tap changer control.
Supply System: 25 kV a.c. from overhead equipment.
Traction Motors: GEC G412AZ frame mounted.
Max. Tractive Effort: 258 kN (58000 lbf).
Continuous Rating: 3730 kW (5000 hp) giving a tractive effort of 95 kN (21300 lbf) at 87 mph.
Maximum Rail Power: 5860 kW (7860 hp) at ?? mph.
Brake Force: 40 t.
Design Speed: 110 mph.
Max. Speed: 110 mph.
ETH Index: 74
Train Brakes: Air & Vacuum.
Length over Buffers: 17.83 m.
Weight: 87 t.
RA: 6.
Wheel Diameter: 1150 mm.
Electric Brake: Rheostatic.
Communication Equipment: Driver – guard telephone and cab to shore radio-telephone.
Note: Class 86 were formerly numbered E 3101 – 3200 (not in order).

86101	(86201)	**M**	IWPA	WN	Sir William A Stanier FRS
86102	(86202)	**IO**	IWPA	WN	Robert A Riddles
86103	(86203)	**I**	IWPA	WN	André Chapelon

CLASS 86/2 BR DESIGN Bo – Bo

Built: 1965 – 66 by English Electric Co. at Vulcan Foundry, Newton le Willows or BR at Doncaster Works. Later rebuilt with resilient wheels and flexicoil suspension. Tap changer control.
Supply System: 25 kV a.c. from overhead equipment.
Traction Motors: AEI 282BZ.
Max. Tractive Effort: 207 kN (46500 lbf).
Continuous Rating: 3010 kW (4040 hp) giving a tractive effort of 85 kN (19200 lbf) at 77.5 mph.
Maximum Rail Power: 4550 kW (6100 hp) at 49.5 mph.
Brake Force: 40 t.
Design Speed: 125 mph.
Max. Speed: 100 (110§) mph.
ETH Index: 74
Train Brakes: Air & Vacuum.
Length over Buffers: 17.83 m.
Weight: 85 t – 86 t.
RA: 6.
Wheel Diameter: 1156 mm.
Electric Brake: Rheostatic.
Communication Equipment: Driver – guard telephone and cab to shore radio-telephone.
Multiple Working: Time division multiplex system.

86204		**I**	IWPA	WN	City of Carlisle
86205	(86503)	**I**	ICCA	LG	City of Lancaster
86206		**M**	ICCA	LG	City of Stoke on Trent
86207		**I**	IWPA	WN	City of Lichfield
86208		**I**	IWPA	WN	City of Chester
86209		§ **M**	IWPA	WN	City of Coventry
86210		**I**	IWPA	WN	City of Edinburgh
86212		**M**	ICCA	LG	Preston Guild 1328 – 1992

86213		**IO**	IWPA	WN	Lancashire Witch
86214		**I**	ICCA	LG	Sans Pareil
86215		**M**	IANA	NC	Joseph Chamberlain
86216		**I**	ICCA	LG	Meteor
86217	(86504)	**I**	IANA	NC	Halley's Comet
86218		**I**	IANA	NC	Planet
86219		**I**	IWPA	WN	Phoenix
86220		**I**	IANA	NC	The Round Tabler
86221		**M**	IANA	NC	B.B.C. Look East
86222	(86502)	**I**	ICCA	LG	LLOYD'S LIST 250th ANNIVERSARY
86223		**I**	IANA	NC	Norwich Union
86224		§**I**	IWPA	WN	Caledonian
86225		§**I**	IWPA	WN	Hardwicke
86226		**M**	IWPA	WN	Royal Mail Midlands
86227		**M**	ICCA	LG	Sir Henry Johnson
86228		**I**	ICCA	LG	Vulcan Heritage
86229		**I**	ICCA	LG	Sir John Betjeman
86230		**M**	IANA	NC	The Duke of Wellington
86231		§**I**	IWPA	WN	Starlight Express
86232		**I**	IANA	NC	Norwich Festival
86233	(86506)	**I**	ICCA	LG	Laurence Olivier
86234		**I**	ICCA	LG	J B Priestley OM
86235		**I**	IANA	NC	Crown Point
86236		**I**	IWPA	WN	Josiah Wedgwood MASTER POTTER 1736 – 1795
86237		**I**	IANA	NC	Sir Charles Hallé
86238		**I**	IANA	NC	European Community
86239	(86507)	**R**	PXLE	CE	L S Lowry
86240		**I**	IWPA	WN	Bishop Eric Treacy
86241	(86508)	**R**	PXLE	CE	Glenfiddich
86242		**M**	IWPA	WN	James Kennedy GC
86243		**IO**	PXLE	CE	The Boys' Brigade
86244		**I**	ICCA	LG	The Royal British Legion
86245		**I**	IWPA	WN	Dudley Castle
86246	(86505)	**I**	IANA	NC	Royal Anglian Regiment
86247		**I**	IWPA	WN	Abraham Darby
86248		**I**	IWPA	WN	Sir Clwyd/County of Clwyd
86249		**M**	IWPA	WN	County of Merseyside
86250		**I**	IANA	NC	The Glasgow Herald
86251		**M**	IWPA	WN	The Birmingham Post
86252		**IO**	ICCA	LG	The Liverpool Daily Post
86253	(86044)	**I**	IWPA	WN	The Manchester Guardian
86254	(86047)	**RX**	PXLE	CE	
86255	(86042)	**I**	ICCA	LG	Penrith Beacon
86256	(86040)	**M**	ICCA	LG	Pebble Mill
86257	(86043)	**I**	IWPA	WN	Snowdon
86258	(86501)	**I**	IWPA	WN	Talyllyn – The First Preserved Railway
86259	(86045)	**I**	ICCA	LG	Peter Pan
86260	(86048)	**I**	ICCA	LG	Driver Wallace Oakes G.C.
86261	(86041)	**RX**	PXLE	CE	

CLASS 86/4 & 86/6 BR DESIGN Bo – Bo

Built: 1965 – 66 by English Electric Co. at Vulcan Foundry, Newton le Willows or BR at Doncaster Works. Later rebuilt with resilient wheels and flexicoil suspension. Tap changer control.
Supply System: 25 kV a.c. from overhead equipment.
Traction Motors: AEI 282AZ.
Max. Tractive Effort: 258 kN (58000 lbf).
Continuous Rating: 2680 kW (3600 hp) giving a tractive effort of 89 kN (20000 lbf) at 67 mph.
Maximum Rail Power: 4400 kW (5900 hp) at 38 mph.
Brake Force: 40 t.
Design Speed: 100 mph.
Max. Speed: 100 (75*) mph.
ETH Index: 74
Train Brakes: Air & Vacuum.
Length over Buffers: 17.83 m.
Weight: 83 t – 84 t.
RA: 6.
Wheel Diameter: 1156 mm.
Electric Brake: Rheostatic.
Multiple Working: Time division multiplex system.
Communication Equipment: Driver – guard telephone and cab to shore radio-telephone.

Note: 86405/11/4/5/28/31 have recently been renumbered from 86/6.

Class 86/4. ETH equipment operative.

86401	(86001)	**RX**	PXLE	CE	
86405	(86605)	**FD**	PXLE	CE	Intercontainer
86411	(86611)	**FD**	PXLE	CE	Airey Neave
86414	(86614)	**FD**	PXLE	CE	Frank Hornby
86415	(86615)	**FD**	PXLE	CE	Rotary International
86416	(86316)	**RX**	PXLE	CE	
86417	(86317)	**M**	PXLE	CE	The Kingsman
86419	(86319)	**R**	PXLE	CE	Post Haste 150 YEARS OF TRAVELLING POST OFFICES
86424	(86324)	**R**	PXLE	CE	
86425	(86325)	**R**	PXLE	CE	
86426	(86326)	**RX**	PXLE	CE	
86428	(86628)	**FD**	PXLE	CE	Aldaniti
86430	(86030)	**RX**	PXLE	CE	
86431	(86631)	**FD**	PXLE	CE	

Class 86/6. ETH equipment isolated.

86602	(86402)	* **FD**	MDNC	CE	
86603	(86403)	* **FD**	MDNC	CE	
86604	(86404)	* **FD**	MDNC	CE	
86606	(86406)	* **FD**	MDNC	CE	
86607	(86407)	* **FD**	MDNC	CE	The Institution of Electrical Engineers
86608	(86408)	* **FD**	MDNC	CE	St. John Ambulance
86609	(86409)	* **FD**	MDNC	CE	
86610	(86410)	* **FD**	MDNC	CE	
86612	(86412)	* **FD**	MDNC	CE	Elizabeth Garrett Anderson
86613	(86413)	* **FD**	MDNC	CE	County of Lancashire
86618	(86418)	* **FD**	MDNC	CE	

86620	(86420)	* **FD**	MDNC	CE	
86621	(86421)	* **FD**	MDNC	CE	London School of Economics
86622	(86422)	* **FD**	MDNC	CE	
86623	(86423)	* **FD**	MDNC	CE	
86627	(86427)	* **FD**	MDNC	CE	The Industrial Society
86632	(86432)	* **FD**	MDNC	CE	Brookside
86633	(86433)	* **FD**	MDNC	CE	Wulfruna
86634	(86434)	* **FD**	MDNC	CE	University of London
86635	(86435)	* **FD**	MDNC	CE	
86636	(86436)	* **FD**	MDNC	CE	
86637	(86437)	* **FD**	MDNC	CE	
86638	(86438)	* **FD**	MDNC	CE	
86639	(86439)	* **FD**	MDNC	CE	

CLASS 87 BR DESIGN Bo – Bo

Built: 1973 – 75 by BREL at Crewe Works. Class 87/1 has thyristor control instead of HT tap changing.
Supply System: 25 kV a.c. from overhead equipment.
Traction Motors: GEC G412AZ frame mounted (87/0), G412BZ (87/1).
Max. Tractive Effort: 258 kN (58000 lbf).
Continuous Rating: 3730 kW (5000 hp) giving a tractive effort of 95 kN (21300 lbf) at 87 mph (Class 87/0), 3620 kW (4850 hp) giving a tractive effort of 96 kN (21600 lbf) at 84 mph (Class 87/1).
Maximum Rail Power: 5860 kW (7860 hp) at ?? mph.
Brake Force: 40 t.
Design Speed: 110 mph
Max. Speed: 110 (75*) mph.
ETH Index: 95
Train Brakes: Air.
Length over Buffers: 17.83 m.
Weight: 83.5 t.
RA: 6.
Wheel Diameter: 1150 mm.
Electric Brake: Rheostatic.
Multiple Working: Time division multiplex system.
Communication Equipment: All equipped with driver – guard telephone and cab to shore radio-telephone.

Class 87/0. Standard Design. Tap Changer Control.

87001	**I**	IWSA	WN	Royal Scot
87002	**I**	IWSA	WN	Royal Sovereign
87003	**I**	IWSA	WN	Patriot
87004	**I**	IWSA	WN	Britannia
87005	**I**	IWSA	WN	City of London
87006	**IO**	IWSA	WN	City of Glasgow
87007	**I**	IWSA	WN	City of Manchester
87008	**I**	IWSA	WN	City of Liverpool
87009	**M**	IWSA	WN	City of Birmingham
87010	**I**	IWCA	WN	King Arthur
87011	**M**	IWCA	WN	The Black Prince
87012	**M**	IWCA	WN	The Royal Bank of Scotland
87013	**I**	IWCA	WN	John O' Gaunt
87014	**I**	IWCA	WN	Knight of the Thistle
87015	**IO**	IWCA	WN	Howard of Effingham
87016	**I**	IWCA	WN	Willesden Intercity Depot
87017	**IO**	IWCA	WN	Iron Duke

87018	**M**	IWCA	WN	Lord Nelson
87019	**IO**	IWCA	WN	Sir Winston Churchill
87020	**IO**	IWCA	WN	North Briton
87021	**IO**	IWCA	WN	Robert the Bruce
87022	**M**	IWCA	WN	Cock o' the North
87023	**IO**	IWCA	WN	Velocity
87024	**IO**	IWCA	WN	Lord of the Isles
87025	**IO**	IWCA	WN	County of Cheshire
87026	**IO**	IWCA	WN	Sir Richard Arkwright
87027	**IO**	IWCA	WN	Wolf of Badenoch
87028	**M**	IWCA	WN	Lord President
87029	**IO**	IWCA	WN	Earl Marischal
87030	**IO**	IWCA	WN	Black Douglas
87031	**M**	IWCA	WN	Hal o' the Wynd
87032	**IO**	IWCA	WN	Kenilworth
87033	**M**	IWCA	WN	Thane of Fife
87034	**IO**	IWCA	WN	William Shakespeare
87035	**M**	IWCA	WN	Robert Burns

Class 87/1. Thyristor Control.

87101 *	**FD**	MDNC	CE	STEPHENSON

CLASS 90 GEC DESIGN Bo – Bo

Built: 1987 – 90 by BREL at Crewe Works. Thyristor control.
Supply System: 25 kV a.c. from overhead equipment.
Traction Motors: GEC G412CY separately excited frame mounted.
Max. Tractive Effort: 192 kN (43150 lbf).
Continuous Rating: 3730 kW (5000 hp) giving a tractive effort of 95 kN (21300 lbf) at 87 mph.
Maximum Rail Power: 5860 kW (7860 hp) at ?? mph.
Brake Force: 40 t.
Design Speed: 110 mph.
Max. Speed: 110 (75*) mph.
ETH Index: 95
Train Brakes: Air.
Length over Buffers: 18.80 m.
Weight: 84.5 t.
RA: 7.
Wheel Diameter: 1156 mm.
Electric Brake: Rheostatic.
Couplings: Drop-head buckeye.
Multiple Working: Time division multiplex system.
Communication Equipment: Driver – guard telephone and cab to shore radio-telephone.

Non-standard Liveries:

90128 is in SNCB/NMBS (Belgian Railways) electric loco livery.
90129 is in DB (German Federal Railways) 'neurot' livery.
90130 is in SNCF (French Railways) 'Sybic' livery.
90136 is in livery "FD", but with yellow ends and roof.

Class 90/0. As built.

90001	**I**	IWCA	WN	BBC Midlands Today
90002	**I**	IWCA	WN	
90003	**I**	IWCA	WN	
90004	**I**	IWCA	WN	The D' Oyly Carte Opera Company

90005		**I** IWCA	WN	Financial Times
90006		**I** IWCA	WN	High Sheriff
90007		**I** IWCA	WN	Lord Stamp
90008		**I** IWCA	WN	The Birmingham Royal Ballet
90009		**I** IWCA	WN	Royal Show
90010		**I** IWCA	WN	275 Railway Squadron (Volunteers)
90011		**I** IWCA	WN	The Chartered Institute of Transport
90012		**I** IWCA	WN	Glasgow 1990 Cultural Capital of Europe
90013		**I** IWCA	WN	The Law Society
90014		**I** IWCA	WN	''The Liverpool Phil''
90015		**I** IWCA	WN	BBC North West
90016		**RX** PXLA	CE	
90017		**RX** PXLA	CE	
90018		**RX** PXLA	CE	
90019		**RX** PXLA	CE	Penny Black
90020		**RX** PXLA	CE	Colonel Bill Cockburn CBE TD
90021		**FD** PXLA	CE	
90022		**FD** MDLC	CE	Freightconnection
90023		**FD** MDLC	CE	
90024		**FD** MDLC	CE	
90025		**FD** MDLC	CE	

Class 90/1. ETH equipment isolated.

90126	*	**FD** MDMC	CE	
90127	*	**M** MDMC	CE	
90128	*	**0** MDMC	CE	Vrachtverbinding
90129	*	**0** MDMC	CE	Frachtverbindungen
90130	*	**0** MDMC	CE	Fretconnection
90131	*	**M** MDMC	CE	
90132	*	**M** MDMC	CE	
90133	*	**M** MDMC	CE	
90134	*	**M** MDMC	CE	
90135	*	**M** MDMC	CE	
90136	*	**0** MDMC	CE	
90137	*	**FD** MDMC	CE	
90138	*	**FD** MDMC	CE	
90139	*	**FD** MDMC	CE	
90140	*	**FD** MDMC	CE	
90141	*	**FD** MDMC	CE	
90142	*	**FD** MDMC	CE	
90143	*	**FD** MDMC	CE	
90144	*	**FD** MDMC	CE	
90145	*	**FD** MDMC	CE	
90146	*	**FD** MDMC	CE	
90147	*	**FD** MDMC	CE	
90148	*	**FD** MDMC	CE	
90149	*	**FD** MDMC	CE	
90150	*	**FD** MDMC	CE	

CLASS 91 GEC DESIGN Bo – Bo

Built: 1988 onwards by BREL at Crewe Works. Thyristor control.
Supply System: 25 kV a.c. from overhead equipment.
Traction Motors: GEC G426AZ.
Max. Tractive Effort: .
Continuous Rating: 4540 kW (6090 hp).
Maximum Rail Power: 4700 kW (6300 hp).
Brake Force: 45 t.
Design Speed: 140 mph.
Max. Speed: 140 mph.
ETH Index: 95
Train Brakes: Air.
Length over Buffers: 19.40 m.
Weight: 84 t.
RA: 7.
Wheel Diameter: 1000 mm.
Electric Brake: Rheostatic.
Couplings: Drop-head buckeye.
Multiple Working: Time division multiplex system.
Communication Equipment: Driver – guard telephone and cab to shore radio-telephone.

91001	I	IECA	BN	Swallow
91002	I	IECA	BN	
91003	I	IECA	BN	
91004	I	IECA	BN	The Red Arrows
91005	I	IECA	BN	Royal Air Force Regiment
91006	I	IECA	BN	
91007	I	IECA	BN	Ian Allan
91008	I	IECA	BN	Thomas Cook
91009	I	IECA	BN	Saint Nicholas
91010	I	IECA	BN	
91011	I	IECA	BN	Terence Cuneo
91012	I	IECA	BN	
91013	I	IECA	BN	Michael Faraday
91014	I	IECA	BN	Northern Electric
91015	I	IECA	BN	
91016	I	IECA	BN	
91017	I	IECA	BN	
91018	I	IECA	BN	
91019	I	IECA	BN	Scottish Enterprise
91020	I	IECA	BN	
91021	I	IECA	BN	
91022	I	IECA	BN	
91023	I	IECA	BN	
91024	I	IECA	BN	
91025	I	IECA	BN	BBC Radio One FM
91026	I	IECA	BN	
91027	I	IECA	BN	
91028	I	IECA	BN	Guide Dog
91029	I	IECA	BN	Queen Elizabeth II
91030	I	IECA	BN	Palace of Holyroodhouse
91031	I	IECA	BN	Sir Henry Royce

CLASS 92 GEC DESIGN Co – Co

Built: 1993 onwards by Brush Traction. Thyristor control. Full details not yet available. Fitted with TVM430 cab signalling for Channel Tunnel.
Supply System: 25 kV a.c. from overhead equipment and 750 V d.c. third rail.
Multiple Working: Time division multiplex system.
Communication Equipment: Driver – guard telephone and cab to shore radio-telephone.

92001
92002
92003
92004
92005
92006
92007
92008
92009
92010
92011
92012
92013
92014
92015
92016
92017
92018
92019
92020
92021
92022
92023
92024
92025
92026
92027
92028
92029
92030
92031
92032
92033
92034
92035
92036
92037

1.3. BR DEPARTMENTAL LOCOMOTIVES

CLASS 97/2 BR TYPE 2 Bo – Bo

Built: 1966 by Beyer Peacock, Manchester (97251), BR at Derby Loco Works (97252). Converted to ETH generator vehicles (non self-propelled) to work with steam locomotives.
Engine: Sulzer 6LDA28-B of 930 kW (1250 hp) at 750 rpm.
Main Generator: AEI RTB 15656.
Brake Force: 38 t.
Weight: 71.7 t.
Max. Speed: 90 mph.
ETH Index: 66.
Length over Buffers: 15.39 m.
Wheel Diameters: 1143 mm.
RA: 5.

97251 (25305)	**M**	RAIS	IS
97252 (25314)	**M**	RAIS	IS

CLASS 97/6 RUSTON SHUNTER 0 – 6 – 0

Built: 1959 by Ruston & Hornsby at Lincoln.
Engine: Ruston 6VPH of 123 kW (165 hp).
Main Generator: British Thomson Houston RTB6034.
Traction Motor: One British Thomson Houston RTA5041.
Max. Tractive Effort: 75 kN (17000 lbf).
Brake Force: 16 t.
Weight: 31 t.
Max. Speed: 20 mph.
Train Brakes: Vacuum.
Length over Buffers: 7.62 m.
Wheel Diameter: 978 mm.
RA: 1.

Non-Standard Livery: Departmental Yellow.

97651 (PWM 651)	v	**0**	REJK	CF
97654 (PWM 654)	v	**0**	IGJK	RG

CLASS 97/7 BATTERY LOCOS Bo – Bo

Built: 1973 – 80 by BREL at Doncaster and Wolverton Works. Converted from Class 501 EMU cars.
Supply System: 750 V d.c. third rail or 320 V d.c. batteries.
Traction Motors: GEC WT344A.
Max. Tractive Effort: 73 kN (16400 lbf).
Brake Force: 45 t.
Weight: 59 t.
Max. Speed: 25 mph.
Length over Buffers: 18.44 m.
Wheel Diameter: 1071 mm.
RA: 4.
Multiple Working: Work in pairs.
Non-Standard Livery: Bright blue with yellow stripe.

97701	(61136)	a	**0**	RCBD	BD
97702	(61139)	a	**0**	RCBD	BD
97703	(61182)	a		NKFH	HE
97704	(61185)	a		NKFH	HE
97705	(61184)	a		NKFH	HE

97706	(61189)	a		NKFH	HE
97707	(61166)	a	N	NKFH	HE
97708	(61173)	a	N	NKFH	HE
97709	(61172)	a		NKFH	HE (S)
97710	(61175)	a		NKFH	HE (S)

Note: 97701/2 carry DB 977363/2 in error.

CLASS 97/8 EE SHUNTER 0–6–0

For details see Class 09. Severn Tunnel emergency train locomotive.

Non-Standard Livery: BR blue with grey cab.

97806	(09017) xo	0	IGJK	CF	Normally kept at Sudbrook.

DB 968xxx SERIES

This number series was introduced in 1969 and is for former capital stock locomotives which no longer operate under their own power.

Non-standard Livery: 968021 is British Rail Research red/blue/white.

ADB 968021	(84009)	x	CE	Mobile load bank.
TDB 968030	(33018)	x		Moreton-in-Marsh training loco.

1.4. EUROTUNNEL LOCOMOTIVES

CLASS 0 MaK Bo – Bo

These general purpose diesel locomotives are the same basic design as the Netherlands Railways 6400 Class.
Built: 1992 – 3 by Krupp-MaK/ABB at Kiel, Germany. (Type DE1004)
Engine: MaK 940 kW (1280 hp) at 1800 r.p.m.
Traction Motor: Four ABB three-phase traction motors.
Max. Tractive Effort: 305 kN.
Continuous Tractive Effort: 140 kN at 20 m.p.h.
Power at Rail: 750 kW.
Brake Force: 120 kN.
Weight: 84 tonnes
Max. Speed: 60 mph.
Length over Buffers: 15.90 m.
Wheel Diameter: 1000 mm.
Train Brakes: Air.
Communication Equipment: Cab to shore radio.
Couplings: High and Low level Sharfenberg plus UIC screw.
Cab Signalling: TVM 430.
Livery: Standard NS grey and yellow (Netherlands Railways).

0001	
0002	CQ
0003	CQ
0004	
0005	CQ

CLASS 9 BRUSH EUROSHUTTLE Bo – Bo – Bo

A.C. electric locomotives which will be used on the Eurotunnel shuttle trains between Cheriton and Coquelles.
Built: 1992 – 3 by Brush/ABB at Loughborough.
Supply System: 25 kV a.c. from overhead equipment.
Traction Motors:
Max. Tractive Effort: 400 kN (90 000 lbf).
Continuous Rating: 5760 kW (7725 hp) giving a tractive effort of 310 kN at 65 km/h.
Brake Force: 50 t.
Design Speed: 110 mph.
Max. Speed: 100 mph.
ETH Index: 95
Train Brakes: Air.
Length over Buffers: 22.00 m.
Weight: 132 t.
RA: Channel Tunnel only.
Wheel Diameter: 1250 mm.
Electric Brake: Regenerative.
Multiple Working: Time division multiplex system.
Couplings: High and Low level Sharfenburg plus UIC screw.
Communication Equipment: Cab to shore radio.
Cab Signalling: TVM 430.
Livery: Metallic silver.

9001	CQ
9002	CQ
9003	
9004	

EUROTUNNEL 9005 – 9038

9005
9006
9007
9008
9009
9010
9011
9012
9013
9014
9015
9016
9017
9018
9019
9020
9021
9022
9023
9024
9025
9026
9027
9028
9029
9030
9031
9032
9033
9034
9035
9036
9037
9038

1.5. BR LOCOMOTIVES AWAITING DISPOSAL

03084	March Whitemoor Yard
03158	March Whitemoor Yard
08222	Bounds Green T&RSMD
08224	Doncaster TMD
08239	Neville Hill T&RSMD
08254	Gateshead
08285	Doncaster TMD
08295	Thornaby TMD
08305	Healey Mills
08308	Hull Botanic Gardens
08309 **F**	Knottingley TMD
08367	Doncaster TMD
08375	Cardiff Canton T&RSMD
08385	Doncaster TMD
08399	Crewe Diesel TMD
08416	RFS Kilnhurst
08420	Doncaster TMD
08427	March TMD
08434	Derby T&RSMD
08436	Doncaster TMD
08439	Immingham TMD
08468	Springs Branch
08473	Leicester
08478	Immingham TMD
08479	Cardiff Canton T&RSMD
08496	Cambridge T&RSMD
08508	Scunthorpe Yard
08515	Gateshead
08518	March TMD
08533	Stratford TMD
08537 **FO**	Bescot TMD
08539	ABB Crewe
08544	Heaton T&RSMD
08556	Willesden TMD
08570 **M**	Eastfield TMD
08579	Healey Mills
08584	ABB Crewe
08589	Cardiff Canton T&RSMD
08608	Gateshead
08618	Gateshead
08626	Allerton TMD
08631 **N**	March TMD
08637	Ashford TMD
08638 **BS**	Reading T&RSMD
08652	Cardiff Canton T&RSMD
08654	Cardiff Canton T&RSMD
08657	York
08659	Healey Mills
08660	Cardiff Canton T&RSMD
08667	Neville Hill T&RSMD
08671	Gateshead
08672	Bescot TMD
08680	Eastfield TMD
08684	Bletchley TMD
08686	Allerton TMD
08688	Allerton TMD
08700	Bescot TMD
08708	Stratford TMD
08712	Motherwell TMD
08719	Bletchley TMD
08725	Eastfield TMD
08729	BRML Doncaster
08741	BRML Doncaster
08744	ABB Crewe
08747	BRML Doncaster
08760	BRML Eastleigh
08761 **O**	Eastfield TMD
08771	Heaton T&RSMD
08777	Hull Dairycoates
08778 **D**	Cardiff Canton T&RSMD
08787	ABB Crewe
08791 **F**	Eastfield TMD
08794	Neville Hill T&RSMD
08796	Ashford TMD
08797	Thornaby TMD
08803 **D**	Reading T&RSMD
08814	Derby T&RSMD
08821	Laira T&RSMD
08831	Eastleigh T&RSMD
08838	Derby T&RSMD
08839	Laira T&RSMD
08840	Allerton TMD
08841	ABB Crewe
08848	Cardiff Canton T&RSMD
08850	Reading T&RSMD
08857	ABB Crewe
08858	Allerton TMD
08859	March TMD
08868	March TMD
08874	RFS Kilnhurst
08875	RFS Kilnhurst
08876	RFS Kilnhurst
08889	Peterborough
08898	Bescot TMD
08916	Allerton TMD
08917	Allerton TMD
08929	Old Oak Common TMD
08936	March TMD

09002 Selhurst T&RSMD
20008**BS** Thornaby TMD
20009 Thornaby TMD
20010**FR** Toton TMD
20011 Derby T&RSMD
20013 Toton TMD
20019 Toton TMD
20025 Scunthorpe Yard
20028**BS** Toton TMD
20029 Thornaby TMD
20042 Scunthorpe Yard
20043 Scunthorpe Yard
20058 Toton TMD
20061 Scunthorpe Yard
20068 Immingham TMD
20078 Toton TMD
20080 BRML Doncaster
20089 Immingham TMD
20099 Toton TMD
20112 Thornaby TMD
20119 Toton TMD
20122**FR** BRML Glasgow
20124 BRML Glasgow
20141**FR** Toton TMD
20143 Toton TMD
20144 Thornaby TMD
20148 Toton TMD
20156**FR** BRML Glasgow
20160 Bescot Yard
20163**FR** Toton TMD
20170**FR** Toton TMD
20172 Toton TMD
20174 Thornaby TMD
20176 Scunthorpe Yard
20181 Bescot Yard
20182 Toton TMD
20185 Thornaby TMD
20188 Ilford T&RSMD
20197 Toton TMD
20198 BRML Glasgow
20199 BRML Glasgow
20202 Toton TMD
20205 Scunthorpe Yard
20211 BRML Glasgow
20212 BRML Glasgow
20220 Kingmoor Yard
20221 Kingmoor Yard
20223 Kingmoor Yard
25080 Basford Hall Yard
25194 Bescot Yard
25205 Bescot Yard
25206 BRML Doncaster
25211 Bescot Yard
25259 Bescot Yard
26002**FC** Inverness T&RSMD
26004**C** Inverness T&RSMD
26010 Eastfield
26011**C** Inverness T&RSMD
26014 Inverness T&RSMD
26015 Eastfield TMD
26021 Eastfield TMD
26024 Inverness T&RSMD
26026**C** Inverness T&RSMD
26027 Perth
26035**C** Inverness T&RSMD
26038**FR** Inverness T&RSMD
26039 MC Metals Glasgow
26040**C** Inverness T&RSMD
26041**FR** Inverness T&RSMD
26042 Inverness T&RSMD
26046 Eastfield TMD
31108**FO** Scunthorpe Yard
31120**FC** CF Booth Rotherham
31123 Bescot Yard
31156 Scunthorpe Yard
31162 Immingham TMD
31168 Bescot Yard
31210**FO** Scunthorpe Yard
31212 Immingham TMD
31220 Stratford TMD
31221 Scunthorpe Yard
31223 Immingham TMD
31240**FO** Stratford TMD
31243**FO** Stratford TMD
31249 Scunthorpe Yard
31264 Thornaby TMD
31283**O** Stratford TMD
31286 Bescot Yard
31289 Bescot Yard
31293 Stratford TMD
31299**FO** Stratford TMD
31305 Bescot Yard
31400 CF Booth Rotherham
31402 Bescot Yard
31404 Holbeck
31425 CF Booth Rotherham
31428 Basford Hall Yard
31429 Crewe Diesel TMD
31970**O** ABB Crewe
33006 BRML Eastleigh
33009**C** BRML Eastleigh
33038 Stratford TMD
33058 BRML Eastleigh
33102 Eastleigh T&RSMD

33110		Stewarts Lane T&RSMD
33111		Eastleigh Yard
33113		Stewarts Lane T&RSMD
33205	**FD**	Stewarts Lane T&RSMD
37008	**FR**	Stratford Major Depot
37273	**FP**	Cardiff Canton T&RSMD
37681	**FA**	BRML Doncaster
45013		March Whitemoor Yard
45015		Toton TMD
45041		Thornaby TMD
45058		March Whitemoor Yard
45062		March Whitemoor Yard
45076		March Whitemoor Yard
45105		March Whitemoor Yard
45114		March Whitemoor Yard
45119		March Whitemoor Yard
45121		Derby T&RSMD
45122		March Whitemoor Yard
45127		March Whitemoor Yard
45137		March Whitemoor Yard
45139		March Whitemoor Yard
45142		March Whitemoor Yard
45143		March Whitemoor Yard
46010		Doncaster TMD
46023		Basford Hall Yard
47001		Basford Hall Yard
47002		Doncaster Belmont Yard
47005		CF Booth Rotherham
47006	**FA**	Tinsley TMD
47007	**FA**	Doncaster Belmont Yard
47008		Stratford TMD
47010	**FP**	Immingham TMD
47011		ABB Crewe
47015		Basford Hall Yard
47018	**FO**	Doncaster TMD
47054	**FP**	Immingham TMD
47094	**FP**	Immingham TMD
47096		Tinsley TMD
47098		Eastleigh Yard
47099	**FO**	Doncaster Belmont Yard
47100		Doncaster Belmont Yard
47101		Basford Hall Yard
47102		Tinsley TMD
47107	**FO**	Doncaster Belmont Yard
47110		Thornaby TMD
47112	**FO**	Old Oak Common TMD
47115		Scunthorpe Yard
47116		ABB Crewe
47117		Doncaster Belmont Yard
47118	**BR**	Doncaster Belmont Yard
47119	**FP**	Thornaby TMD
47120	**BR**	Doncaster Belmont Yard
47123		Doncaster TMD
47143		Doncaster TMD
47159		Thornaby TMD
47191		Springs Branch
47195	**FP**	Tinsley TMD
47198		Cardiff Canton T&RSMD
47199		Kingmoor Yard
47215	**FO**	Eastleigh Yard
47233	**FP**	Scunthorpe Yard
47311	**FD**	Tinsley TMD
47324	**FP**	Immingham TMD
47373	**FP**	Immingham TMD
47374	**FO**	Immingham TMD
47380	**FP**	Immingham TMD
47381	**FP**	Immingham TMD
47401	**G**	Immingham TMD
47402		Immingham TMD
47403		Moreton-on-Lugg
47406	**IO**	Scunthorpe Yard
47407	**BR**	Scunthorpe Yard
47411	**BR**	Scunthorpe Yard
47413	**BR**	Immingham TMD
47418		Scunthorpe Yard
47421		Crewe Diesel TMD
47422	**BR**	CF Booth Rotherham
47423		Old Oak Common TMD
47424	**BR**	ABB Crewe
47425		Old Oak Common TMD
47426	**BR**	Old Oak Common TMD
47430	**FA**	Old Oak Common TMD
47431	**BR**	Old Oak Common TMD
47432	**BR**	Gresty Lane
47434	**BR**	Basford Hall Yard
47435		Basford Hall Yard
47436	**BR**	Inverness T&RSMD
47438	**BR**	Old Oak Common TMD
47440	**BR**	Old Oak Common TMD
47441	**BR**	Old Oak Common TMD
47444	**BR**	Basford Hall Yard
47445	**FD**	Doncaster Belmont Yard
47446	**BR**	Old Oak Common TMD
47447	**BR**	Doncaster Belmont Yard
47448	**BR**	Holbeck
47450	**BR**	Doncaster Belmont Yard
47451	**BR**	Doncaster Belmont Yard
47452	**BR**	Old Oak Common TMD
47453	**BR**	Old Oak Common TMD
47454	**BR**	Doncaster Belmont Yard
47455	**BR**	ABB Crewe
47456	**BR**	CF Booth Rotherham
47457	**BR**	Old Oak Common TMD
47459	**BR**	CF Booth Rotherham

47460**BR** Crewe Diesel TMD
47461**PS** Basford Hall Yard
47465**BR** Old Oak Common TMD
47466**BR** Holbeck
47470**M** ABB Crewe
47472 Old Oak Common TMD
47477 CF Booth Rotherham
47479**R** CF Booth Rotherham
47509**I** Bristol Bath Road TMD
47512**BR** Crewe Diesel TMD
47515**M** Holbeck
47527**M** Bristol Bath Road TMD
47533**R** Old Oak Common TMD
47534**BR** ABB Crewe
47538**BR** Devonport Dockyard
47542 Stratford TMD
47549**IO** Crewe Diesel TMD
47585**BR** Holbeck
47633**BR** Eastfield TMD
47643**IO** Inverness T&RSMD
47837**I** Crewe Diesel TMD
47852**O** CF Booth Rotherham
50029**N** Laira T&RSMD
50030**N** Laira T&RSMD
56002**FC** Doncaster TMD
56017**FC** Toton TMD
56042**F** Toton TMD
56122**FC** Toton TMD
73004**O** Stewarts Lane T&RSMD
73111**IO** Selhurst TMD
82003 Crewe Electric TMD
82005 Crewe Electric TMD
83009 Crewe Electric TMD
83015 Crewe Electric TMD
85005 Crewe Electric TMD
85008 Crewe Electric TMD
85013 Crewe Electric TMD
85017 Crewe Electric TMD
85020 Crewe Electric TMD
85022 Crewe Electric TMD
85026 Crewe Electric TMD
85028 Crewe Electric TMD
85029 Crewe Electric TMD
85034 Crewe Electric TMD
85040 Crewe Electric TMD
85101 Crewe Electric TMD
85107 Crewe Electric TMD
85112 Crewe Electric TMD
85113 Crewe Electric TMD
85114 Crewe Electric TMD
97250**O** Inverness T&RSMD
97653**O** Cardiff Canton T&RSMD

Non-Standard Liveries:

08761 Provincial grey light blue, white and dark blue
31283 Blue with large numbers
31970 Research light grey, dark grey, white and red
47852 BR blue, but with yellow cabsides and silver roof
73004 NSE blue
97250 BR carriage blue & grey
97653 Departmental yellow

2. LOCO-HAULED PASSENGER STOCK

This book contains full details and differences of all BR locomotive-hauled coaching stock. Coaches are listed in batches, according to their class, with lot number information for the various batches being shown above the listings. Where a coach has been renumbered, the former number is shown in parentheses. If the coach has been renumbered more than once, the original number is shown in parentheses, with the intermediate numbers being given in the text. Where the old number of a coach due to be converted or renumbered is known and the conversion or renumbering has not yet taken place, the coach is listed both under its old number with its depot allocation, and under its new number without an allocation

We regret that it has not proved possible to include a list of HST formations in this issue, due to the present variability of the sets. It may be possible to reintroduce this in future.

NUMBERING SYSTEMS

Six different numbering systems were in use on BR. These were the BR series the four pre-nationalisation companies' series' and the Pullman Car Company' series. Only BR number series loco-hauled coaches now exist in stock.

All coaching stock vehicles have now been given depot allocations, regiona prefixes not now being used.

The format used is number, old number(s) if applicable, notes, livery, secto depot allocation.

DETAILED INFORMATION AND CODES

After the heading, the following details are shown:

(1) Diagram code. This consists of the first three characters of the TOPS cod followed by two numbers which relate to the particular design of vehicle.
(2) 'Mark' of coach (see below).
(3) Number of first class seats , standard class seats and lavatory compartment shown as nF nS nL respectively.
(4) Bogie type (see below).
(5) Brake type. (see below).
(6) Heating type. (see below).
(7) Additional features.
(8) ETH Index.

BOGIE TYPES

BR Mk 1 (BR1). Standard double bolster leaf spring bogie. Generally 90 m.p.h but certain vehicles were allowed to run at 100 m.p.h. with special maintenance Weight: 6.1 t.
BR Mk 1 (heavy duty). Similar to above. Weight 6.5 t.
BR Mk 2 (BR2). Later variant of BR Mark 1 used on certain vans.
COMMONWEALTH (C). Heavy, cast steel soil spring bogie. 100 m.p.h. Weigh 6.75 t.
B4. Coil spring fabricated bogie for 100 m.p.h. Certain BGs (classified NHA are allowed to run at 110 m.p.h. with special maintenance. Weight: 5.2 t.
B5. Heavy duty version of B4. 100 m.p.h. Weight: 5.3 t.
BT10. A fabricated bogie designed for 125 m.p.h. Air suspension.
T4. The latest 125 m.p.h. bogie from BREL.
The new Mark 4 vehicles are fitted with bogie from the Swiss firm of SIG.

BRAKE TYPE CODES.

a Air braked.
v Vacuum braked.
x Dual braked (air and vacuum).

HEATING TYPE CODES.

d Dual heated (steam & electric).
e electric heated
o No heating apparatus.

Steam piped & electric wired.
UIC/BR electric heat.
Electric wired.

lote: All BR train heating nowadays is electric, but dual heated vehicles still fften retain the steam heating equipment, albeit isolated.

DDITIONAL FEATURE CODES.

Facelifted or fluorescent lighting provided.
Composition brake blocks (instead of cast iron).
Day/night lighting.
Fitted with public telephone.
a Public address speakers installed.
g Public address transmission and driver – guard communication.
t Public address transmission and speakers.
Fitted with catering staff to shore telephone.
o Public address transmission only.
v Fitted with wheelchair space.
Fitted with wheelchair space and disabled persons' toilet.

IOTES ON ETH INDICES.

The sum of ETH indices in a train must not be more than that of the locomotive. uffix 'S' was used to denote SR 750 V heaters, the usual voltage on BR being 000, and suffix 'X' denotes 600 amp wiring instead of 400 amp. Trains whose TH index comes to more than 66 must be formed completely with 600 amp vired stock. There are now no loco-hauled vehicles in BR capital stock with R heaters.

'OPS CODES

OPS (Total operations processing system) codes are allocated to all coaching tock. For passenger stock the code consists of:

1) Two letters denoting the layout of the vehicle as follows:

A Gangwayed Corridor
B Gangwayed Corridor Brake
C Gangwayed Open (2+2 seating)
D Gangwayed Open (2+1 seating)
E Gangwayed Open Brake
F Gangwayed Driving Open Brake
G Micro-Buffet
H Brake Micro-Buffet
I As 'AC' but fitted with drop-head buckeye and no gangway at one end.
J Restaurant Buffet with Kitchen
K Kitchen Car
L As 'AC' but with disabled person's toilet (Mark 4 only)
N Miniature Buffet
O Privately-owned
S Sleeping Car
T Royal Train Coach
U Sleeping Car with Pantry

(2) A digit for the class of passenger accommodation:

1 first
2 standard (formerly second)
3 Composite
4 Unclassified
5 None

(3) A suffix relating to the build of coach.

1 Mark 1	A Mark 2A	C Mark 2C	E Mark 2E	G Mark 3 or	H Mark 3B
Z Mark 2	B Mark 2B	D Mark 2D	F Mark 2F	Mark 3A	J Mark 4

For non-passenger carrying coaching stock, the suffix denotes the brake type

A Air braked
V Vacuum braked
X Dual braked

OPERATOR CODES

The normal operator codes are given in brackets after the TOPS codes. These are as follows:

F First
S standard (formerly known as 'second')
C Composite
B Brake
O Open
K Side corridor with lavatory

Various other letters are in use and the meaning of these can be ascertained by referring to the titles at the head of each class.

ABBREVIATIONS:

DMU Diesel multiple unit
GER Great Eastern Railway
GWR Great Western Railway
LMS London Midland and Scottish Railway
LNER London & North Eastern Railway
LNWR London & North Western Railway

THE DEVELOPMENT OF BR STANDARD COACHES

The standard BR coach built from 1951 to 1963 is the mark 1. This has separate underframe and body. The underframe is normally 64'6'' long, but certain vehicles were built on short (57') frames. Tungsten lighting is standard and until 1961, BR mark 1 bogies were generally provided. In 1959 TSOs to lot No 30525 appeared with fluorescent lighting and melamine interior panels and from 1961 onwards Commonwealth bogies were fitted in an attempt to improve the quality of ride which became very poor when the tyre profiles on the wheels of the Mark 1 bogies became worn. The further batches of TSO and BSOs retained the features of lot 30525, but the BSKs, SKs, BCKs and CKs, whilst utilising melamine panelling in standard class, still retained tungsten lighting. Wooden interior finish was retained in first class compartments. The FOs had fluorescent lighting with wooden panelling except for lot No. 30648 which had tungsten lighting. In later years many mark 1s had their mark 1 bogies replaced by B4s.

In 1964, a new train was introduced. Known as "XP64", it featured new seat designs, pressure ventilation, aluminium compartment doors and corridor partitions, foot pedal operated toilets, and B4 bogies. The vehicles were on standard mark 1 underframes. Folding doors were fitted but these proved troublesome and were later replaced with hinged doors. All XP64 coaches have now been withdrawn, but some have been preserved.

The prototype mark 2 vehicle (W 13252) was produced in 1963. This was an FK of semi-integral construction and was pressure ventilated. Tungsten lighting was provided and B4 bogies. This vehicle has been preserved by the National Railway Museum. The production build was similar, but wider windows were used. The standard class open vehicles used the new seat design similar to that in the XP64 and fluorescent lighting was provided. Interior finish reverted to wood. MK 2s were built from 1964–66.

The mark 2As, built 1967–68, incorporated the rest of the novel features first used in the XP64 set, i.e. foot pedal operated toilets (except BSOs), new first class seat design, aluminium compartment doors and partitions together with fluorescent lighting in first class compartments. Folding gangway doors (lime green coloured) were used instead of the traditional variety. The following list summarises the changes made in the later Mk 2 variants:

Mk 2B: Wide wrap round doors, no centre doors, slightly longer body. In standard class, one toilet at each end instead of two at one end as previously . Red gangway doors.
Mk 2C: Lowered ceiling with twin strips of fluorescent lighting, ducting for air conditioning, but no air conditioning.
Mk 2D: Air conditioning. No opening lights in windows.
Mk 2E: Smaller toilets with luggage racks opposite. Fawn gangway doors.
Mk 2F: Plastic interior panels. Inter-City 70 seats. Modified air conditioning system.

The Mark 3 coach has BT10 bogies, is 75' long and is of fully integral construction with Inter-City 70 seats. Gangway doors are yellow (red in RFB). Loco-hauled coaches are classified Mark 3A, Mark 3 being reserved for HST trailers. A new batch of FOs and BFOs classified Mark 3B was built in 1985 with APT style seating and revised lighting. The last vehicles in the Mark 3 series are the driving brake vehicles (officially called driving van trailers) which have been built for West Coast Main Line services.

The Mark 4 coach built by Metro-Cammell for the East Coast Main Line electrification scheme features a body profile suitable for tilting trains, although tilt is not fitted, and is not intended to be. They are suitable for 140 m.p.h. running, although initially they are restricted to 125 m.p.h. pending the installation of automatic train protection (ATP) on the East Coast Main Line.

2.1. LOCO-HAULED PASSENGER STOCK

AJ11 (RF) RESTAURANT FIRST

Dia. AJ106. Mark 1. Gas cooking. 24F. B5 bogies. ETH 2. This coach spent most of its life as a Royal train vehicle 2907.

Lot No. 30633 Swindon 1961. 41 t.

325	I	ICHV	BN

AJ1F(RFB) BUFFET OPEN FIRST

Dia. AJ104. Mark 2F. Air conditioned. Converted 1988 – 9/91 at BREL, Derby from Mark 2F FOs. 1200/1/3/6/11/14 – 17/20/21/50/2/5/6/9 have Stones equipment, others have Temperature Ltd. 26F 1L. B4 bogies. ae. pt. payphone. Catering staff – shore telephone. ETH 6X.

1200/3/6/11/14/16/20/52/5/6. Lot No. 30845 Derby 1973. 33 t.
1201/4/5/7/8/10/12/13/15/17 – 9/21/50/1/4/7/9. Lot No. 30859 Derby 1973 – 4. 33 t.
1202/9/53/8. Lot No. 30873 Derby 1974 – 5. 33 t.

Note: 1200 – 2/5/7/9/10/2/4/7/20 were also numbered 6459/45/56/38/22/57/62/53/33/44/32 respectively when declassified prior to conversion.

1200 (3287)	I	ICCX	MA
1201 (3361)	I	ICCX	PC
1202 (3436)	I	ICCX	PC
1203 (3291)	I	ICCX	MA
1204 (3401)	I	ICCX	PC
1205 (3329)	I	ICCX	PC
1206 (3319)	I	ICCX	PC
1207 (3328)	I	ICCX	PC
1208 (3393)	I	ICCX	PC
1209 (3437)	I	ICCX	PC
1210 (3405)	I	ICCX	PC
1211 (3305)	I	ICCX	PC
1212 (3427)	I	ICCX	PC
1213 (3419)	I	ICCX	PC
1214 (3317)	I	ICCX	MA
1215 (3377)	I	ICCX	PC
1216 (3302)	I	ICCX	PC
1217 (3357)	I	ICCX	PC
1218 (3332)	I	ICCX	MA
1219 (3418)	I	ICCX	MA
1220 (3315)	I	ICCX	PC
1221 (3371)	I	ICCX	MA
1250 (3372)	I	ICCX	MA
1251 (3383)	I	ICCX	MA
1252 (3280)	I	ICCX	MA
1253 (3432)	I	ICCX	MA
1254 (3391)	I	ICCX	MA
1255 (3284)	I	ICCX	MA
1256 (3296)	I	ICCX	MA
1258 (3322)	I	ICCX	MA
1259 (3439)	I	ICCX	MA
1260 (3378)	I	ICCX	MA

AJ41 (RBR) RESTAURANT BUFFET

Dia. AJ403. Mark 1. Gas cooking. Built with 23 loose chairs (dia. AJ402). All remaining vehicles refurbished with 23 (21 w) fixed polypropylene chairs and fluorescent lighting. Commonwealth bogies. pt. ETH 2 (2X*).

Coaches with suffix 'R' in sector code have been further refurbished. 21 chairs, payphone, wheelchair space and carpets (Dia. AJ417).

Note: 1680 is on loan to Flying Scotsman Services (set BN91).

Lot No. 30628 Pressed Steel 1960 – 61. d. 39 t.

1644 a	I	ICHV	BN
1645 a	I	ICHV	BN
1646 a	I	IXXZ	OM
1647 a	I	IANR	NC
1649 aw	I	ICHH	BN
1650 aw	I	ICHH	BN
1652 aw	I	ICHH	BN
1653 aw	I	ICHV	OM
1655 a	I	ICHH	CL
1658 a	I	ICHV	BN
1659 a	I	ICHV	OM
1663 x*	I	ICHV	BN
1666 x*	I	ICHH	BN
1667 x	I	ICHV	BN
1670 x*w		ICHV	BN
1671 x* p	I	ICHX	CL
1672 x*	I	ICHV	BN
1673 aw		ICHH	BN
1674 a	I	ICHV	BN
1675 x*	I	ICHV	BN
1678 x*	I	ICHV	BN
1679 a	I	ICHV	BN
1680 x*w	M	ICHL	BN
1683 a p	I	IANR	NC
1684 x*		ICHH	CL
1686 a p	I	IANR	NC
1688 aw		ICHH	BN
1689 a p	I	IANR	NC
1691 a p	I	IANR	NC
1692 a p	I	IANR	NC
1693 x*	I	ICHV	BN
1696 a p	I	ICHX	BN
1697 a p	I	IANR	NC
1698 a	I	ICHV	OM
1699 a p	I	IANR	NC

AN21 (RMB) MINIATURE BUFFET CAR

Dia. AN203. Mark 1. Gas cooking. 44S 2L. These vehicles are basically an open standard with two full window spaces removed to accommodate a buffet counter, and four seats removed to for a stock cupboard. All remaining vehicles now have fluorescent lighting. All vehicles have Commonwealth bogies except 1850 (B5). d. ETH 3.

1832. Lot No. 30520 Wolverton 1960. 38 t.
1842 – 1850. Lot No. 30507 Wolverton 1960. 37 t (1850 is 36 t).
1853 – 1863. Lot No. 30670 Wolverton 1961 – 2. 38 t.
1871 – 1876. Lot No. 30702 Wolverton 1962. 38 t.

1842/50/71 have been been refurbished and are fitted with a microwave oven and payphone. Dia. AN208.

1832 x	I	ICHD	LL
1842 x pt	I	ICCR	DY
1850 v pt	I	ICCR	DY
1853 x	I	ICHD	LL
1860 x	I	IXXT	CL
1863 x pt		IXXT	CL
1871 x pt	I	ICCR	DY
1876 a	I	IXXT	CL

AJ41 (RBR) RESTAURANT BUFFET

Dia. AJ414. Mark 1. Gas cooking. These vehicles were built as unclassified restaurant (RU). All remaining vehicles were rebuilt with buffet counter and 21 fixed polypropylene chairs (RBS). They were then further refurbished by fitting fluorescent lighting and reclassified RBR. ad. w pt. ETH 2X.

Lot No. 30632 Ashford/Eastleigh 1960 – 61. Commonwealth bogies. 39 t.

1959	I	IXXZ	BN
1966	I	ICHH	BN
1971	I	IXXZ	BN
1972		IXXZ	BN
1984		IXXZ	BN

AU51 CHARTER TRAIN STAFF COACHES

Dia. AU501. Mark 1. Converted from BCKs. ETH 2.

Lot No. 30732 Derby 1964. Commonwealth bogies. ae. 37 t.

2833 (21270) **I**	ICHV	BN	
2834 (21267) **I**	ICHV	BN	

AT5 ROYAL SALOONS

Non-standard livery: All Royal vehicles are in Royal purple.

AT51. Royal Saloon (Royal family or household).

Dia AT501. Mark 1. This vehicle is a side corridor with a lounge, four bedrooms and a bathroom. Air conditioned. Converted 1977 from vs to ae and B5 bogies.

Lot No. 30130 Wolverton 1955. ETH 5X. 42 t.

2900 **0** ICHX ZN

AT51. Royal Saloon (Private secretary and Royal household).

Dia AT503. Mark 1. This vehicle is a side corridor with an attendant's compartment, three bedrooms two bathrooms and a lounge/office compartment. Air conditioned. Converted 1977 from vs to ae and B5 bogies.

Lot No. 30131 Wolverton 1957. ETH 5X. 42 t.

2901 **0** ICHX ZN

AT5G. The Queen's Saloon.

Dia. AT525. Mark 3. Converted from a mark 3 FO built 1972. Consists of a lounge, bedroom and bathroom for the Queen, and a combined bedroom and bathroom for the Queen's dresser. One entrance vestibule has double doors. Air conditioned. ae. BT10 bogies.

Lot No. 30886 Wolverton 1977. ETH 9X. 36 t.

2903 (11001) **0** ICHX ZN

AT5G. The Duke of Edinburgh's Saloon.

Dia. AT526. Mark 3. Converted from a mark 3 TSO built 1972. Consists of a combined lounge/dining room, a bedroom and a shower room for the Duke, a kitchen and a valet's bedroom and bathroom. Air conditioned. ae. BT10 bogies.

Lot No. 30887 Wolverton 1977. ETH 15X. 36 t.

2904 (12001) **0** ICHX ZN

AT5B. Staff Couchette/Power Brake.

Dia. AT527. Mark 2B. Converted from a Mk. 2B BFK built 1969. Consists of luggage accommodation, guard's compartment, 350 kW diesel generator and Staff sleeping accommodation. Pressure ventilated. ae. B5 bogies.

Lot No. 30888 Wolverton 1977. ETH 5X. 46 t.

2905 (14105) **0** ICHX ZN

AT5B. Staff Couchette.

Dia. AT528. Mark 2B. Converted from a Mk. 2B BFK built 1969. Pressure ventilated. ae. B5 bogies.

Lot No. 30889 Wolverton 1977. ETH 4X. 35.5 t.

2906 (14112) **0** ICHX ZN

AT5G. Royal Train Staff Sleeping Cars.

Dia. AT531. Mark 3A Details as for 10646 – 732 except that controlled emission toilets are not fitted. ETH11X.

Lot No. 31002 Derby/Wolverton 1985. 42.5 t 2915 is 44 t.

2914 **0** ICHX ZN | 2915 **0** ICHX ZN

AT5G Royal Dining Car.

Lot No. 31059 Wolverton 1986. Converted from HST TRUK. Dia. AT537.

2916 (40512) **0** ICHX ZN

AT5G New Royal Vehicles. Full details not available.

Lot Nos. 31083 Wolverton 1989. Dia. AT539. 43 t. ETH13X.

2917 (40514) **0** ICHX ZN

Lot Nos. 31084 Wolverton 1989. Dia. AT538. 41.05 t. ETH10X.

2918 (40515) **0** ICHX ZN

Lot Nos. 31085 Wolverton 1989. Dia. AT540.

2919 (40518) **0** ICHX ZN

AT5B. Royal Train Staff/Generator Vehicle. Dia. AT536. Mark 2B. B5 bogies. 48 t. ETH2X.

Lot Nos. 31044 Wolverton 1986.

2920 (17109) **0** ICHX ZN

AT5B. Royal Staff Couchette. Dia. AT541. Mark 2B. B4 bogies. Dia. AT541. 41.5 t. ETH7X.

Lot No. 31086 Wolverton 1990.

2921 (17107) **0** ICHX ZN

AT5G. Royal Sleeping Car.

Lot No. 31035 Derby/Wolverton 1987. Dia. AT534.

2922 **0** ICHX ZN

AT5G. The Prince of Wales's Saloon.

Lot No. 31036 Derby/Wolverton 1987. Dia. AT535.

2923 **0** ICHX ZN

AD11 (FO) OPEN FIRST

Dia. AD103. Mark 1. 42F 2L. ETH 3. d. Now fitted with table lights for use in first class charter trains. pa.

Lot No. 30576 BRCW 1959. B4 bogies. 33 t.

2922	I	ICHX	ZN	3098 a	I	ICHV	BN
2923	I	ICHX	ZN	3100 x	I	ICHV	BN
3097 a	I	ICHV	BN				

Later design with fluorescent lighting, aluminium window frames and Commonwealth bogies. pa.

3107 – 3127. Lot No. 30697 Swindon 1962 – 3. 36 t.
3131 – 3150. Lot No. 30717 Swindon 1963. 36 t.

Note: 3136/41/3/4/6/7/8 were renumbered 1060/3/5/6/8/9/70 when reclassified RUO, then 3605/8/9/2/6/4/10 when declassified, but have now regained their original numbers.

Note: 3131 – 3 are leased to Flying Scotsman Services (see 99190 – 2).

3107 x	I	ICHV	BN	3133 x	**M**	ICHL	BN
3111 x	I	ICHV	BN	3134 x	I	ICHV	BN
3114 x	I	ICHV	BN	3136 a	I	ICHV	BN
3115 x	I	ICHV	BN	3140 x	I	ICHV	BN
3118 x	I	ICHV	BN	3141 a	I	ICHV	BN
3119 x	I	ICHV	BN	3143 a	I	ICHV	BN
3120 x	I	ICHV	BN	3144 a	I	ICHV	BN
3121 a	I	ICHV	BN	3146 a	I	ICHV	BN
3123 a	I	ICHV	BN	3147 a	I	ICHV	BN
3124 a	I	ICHV	BN	3148 a	I	ICHV	BN
3127 a	I	ICHV	BN	3149 a	I	ICHV	BN
3131 x	**M**	ICHL	BN	3150 a	I	ICHV	BN
3132 x	**M**	ICHL	BN				

AD1D (FO) OPEN FIRST

Dia. AD105. Mark 2D. Air conditioned. 3172 – 88 have Stones equipment. 3192/3202 have Temperature Ltd and require at least 800 V train heating supply. 42F 2L. B4 bogies. ae. pa. ETH 5.

Lot No. 30821 Derby 1971 – 2. 32.5 t.

3172	I	ICHH	CL	3186	I	ICHH	CL
3174	I	ICHH	CL	3187	I	ICHH	CL
3178	I	ICHH	CL	3188	I	ICHH	CL
3181	I	ICHV	BN	3192	I	ICCL	DY
3182	I	ICHH	CL	3202	I	ICHH	CL

AD1E (FO) OPEN FIRST

Dia. AD106. Mark 2E. Air conditioned. Stones equipment. Require at least 800 V train heating supply. 42F 2L (41F 2L w). B4 bogies. ae. pa. ETH 5.

* Seats removed to accommodate catering module. 40F 1L.
§ Fitted with power supply for Mk. 1 RBR.

Lot No. 30843 Derby 1972 – 3. 32.5 t.

3221 w	I	IANR	NC
3223	I	ICHD	LL
3224	I	ICCX	DY
3225	I	ICHH	CL
3226	I	ICHH	CL
3227	I	ICHV	OM
3228 §	I	IANR	NC
3229	I	ICCX	DY
3230	I	ICHH	CL
3231	I	ICHV	OM
3232 w	I	ICHX	CL
3233		ICHH	CL
3234 w	I	ICHV	OM
3235 §	I	IANX	NC
3237	I	ICHV	OM
3239	I	ICHH	CL
3240	I	ICCX	DY
3241	I	ICCX	DY
3242 w§	I	IANX	NC
3244 w	I	IANR	NC
3245	I	ICHH	CL
3246 w	I	ICCX	DY
3247	I	ICHV	OM
3248	I	ICHH	CL
3249 *	I	IWCX	WB
3250 w	I	ICHV	OM
3251 *	I	IWCX	WB
3252 w	I	ICCX	DY
3256 w	I	ICCX	DY
3257 w	I	ICHH	CL
3258 n	I	ICHH	CL
3259 *	I	IWCX	WB
3261 w	I	ICCX	DY
3262	I	ICHX	BN
3263	I	ICHV	OM
3264	I	ICCX	DY
3265	I	ICHV	OM
3266 §	I	ICHX	BN
3267	I	ICHD	LL
3268	I	ICHH	CL
3269	I	ICCX	DY
3270	I	ICHV	OM
3272	I	ICHV	OM
3273	I	ICHH	CL
3275	I	ICHV	OM

AD1F (FO) OPEN FIRST

Dia. AD107. Mark 2F. Air conditioned. 3277 – 3318/58 – 81 have Stones equipment, others have Temperature Ltd. 42F 2L. All now refurbished with power-operated vestibule doors, new panels and new seat trim. B4 bogies. ae. pa. ETH 5X.

3277 – 3318. Lot No. 30845 Derby 1973. 33 t.
3325 – 3428. Lot No. 30859 Derby 1973 – 4. 33 t.
3429 – 3438. Lot No. 30873 Derby 1974 – 5. 33 t.

§ Fitted with power supply for Mk. 1 RBR.

3277	I	IANR	NC
3278	I	IWCR	MA
3279 §	I	IANR	NC
3285	I	IWCR	OY
3290	I	IANR	NC
3292	I	IANR	NC
3293	I	IWCR	MA
3295	I	IWCR	OY
3299	I	IWCR	OY
3300	I	IWCR	OY
3303	I	IANR	NC
3304	I	IWCR	OY
3309	I	IWCR	MA
3312	I	IWCR	MA
3313	I	IWCR	OY
3314	I	IWCR	MA
3318	I	IANR	NC
3325	I	IWCR	OY
3326	I	IWCR	OY
3330	I	IWCR	OY
3331	I	IANR	NC
3333	I	IWCR	OY
3334	I	IANR	NC
3336 §	I	IANR	NC

3337	I	IWCR	OY
3338 §	I	IANR	NC
3340	I	IWCR	OY
3344	I	IWCR	MA
3345	I	IWCR	OY
3348	I	IWCR	OY
3350	I	IWCR	MA
3351	I	IANR	NC
3352	I	IWCR	MA
3353	I	IWCR	OY
3354	I	IWCR	OY
3356	I	IWCR	MA
3358	I	IANR	NC
3359	I	IWCR	MA
3360	I	IWCR	OY
3362	I	IWCR	OY
3363	I	IWCR	OY
3364	I	IWCR	MA
3366	I	IWCR	OY
3368	I	IANR	NC
3369	I	IWCR	OY
3373	I	IWCR	MA
3374	I	IWCR	MA
3375	I	IANR	NC
3379 §	I	IANR	NC
3381	I	IWCR	OY
3384	I	IWCR	OY
3385	I	IWCR	OY
3386	I	IWCR	OY
3387	I	IWCR	OY
3388	I	IANR	NC
3389	I	IWCR	OY
3390	I	IWCR	MA
3392	I	IWCR	MA
3395	I	IWCR	OY
3397	I	IWCR	OY
3399 §	I	IANR	NC
3400	I	IANR	NC
3402	I	IWCR	OY
3403	I	IWCR	OY
3408	I	IWCR	MA
3411	I	IWCR	OY
3414	I	IANR	NC
3416	I	IANR	NC
3417	I	IANR	NC
3424	I	IWCR	OY
3425	I	IWCR	OY
3426	I	IWCR	OY
3428	I	IWCR	OY
3429	I	IWCR	OY
3431	I	IWCR	OY
3433	I	IWCR	OY
3434	I	IWCR	OY
3438	I	IWCR	OY

AG1E (FO) OPEN FIRST (TROLLEY

Dia. AG101. Mark 2E. Air conditioned. Converted from FO. 36F 1L. B4 bogies ae. pa. ETH 5X.

Lot No. 30843 Derby 1972 – 3. 32.5 t.

3520 (3253)	I	IWRX	OM
3521 (3271)	I	IWRX	OM
3522 (3236)	I	IWRX	OM
3523 (3238)	I	ICCX	PC
3524 (3254)	I	ICCX	PC
3525 (3255)	I	ICCX	PC

AC21 (TSO) OPEN STANDARD

Dia. AC204. Mark 1. These vehicles have 2 + 2 seating and are classified TS ('Tourist second open' – a former LNER designation). TSOs numbered belo 4098 have narrower seats than later vehicles. These narrow seats are also fi ted to the later batch adjacent to the vestibule end doors. The remaining vehicle are used in the Heaton football special set. 64S 2L. BR1 bogies. ETH 4.

3769/71. Lot No. 30079 York 1953. 32.5 t.
3958/61. Lot No. 30086 Ashford/Eastleigh 1954 – 5. 33 t.
4420. Lot No. 30226 BRCW 1956 – 7. 33 t.

3769	RBHT	HT
3771	RBHT	HT
3958	RBHT	HT
3961	RBHT	HT
4420	RBHT	HT

C21 (TSO) OPEN STANDARD

ia. AC201. Mark 1. Development of dia. AC204 with fluorescent lighting and odified design of seat headrest. Built with BR1 bogies but most rebuilt with 4 bogies. 64S 2L. ETH 4.

ote: 4860 and 5032/5 are leased to Flying Scotsman Services and 4856 and 028 sre leased to the SRPS at Bo'ness (shown as 'BO').

ot No. 30506 Wolverton 1959. xd. Commonwealth bogies. pa. 35 t.

830	**N**	NTCZ	OM

ot No. 30525 Wolverton 1959 – 60. d. B4 bogies. 33 t.

842 x	**I**	ICHD	LL
849 v pa	**N**	NWRX	OM
854 v pa	**N**	NWRX	OM
856 x		ICHL	BO
858 x	**I**	ICHH	BN
860 x	**M**	ICHL	BN
862 v pa	**N**	RDDY	DY
4866 v pa	**N**	RDDY	DY
4867 v pa	**N**	NWRX	OM
4869 x	**I**	ICHD	LL
4873 v pa	**N**	NWRX	OM
4875 v pa	**N**	RDDY	DY
4876 v pa	**N**	RDDY	DY
4880 v pa	**N**	RDDY	DY

ot No. 30646 Wolverton 1961. Built with Commonwealth bogies, but BR1 ogies substituted by the SR. Most now re-rebogied. BR1 bogies except where tated otherwise. d. 35 t. (34 t B4, 36 t C).

902 x B4	**I**	ICHH	CL
903 v		RBHT	HT
904 v		RBHT	HT
905 vCpa	**N**	RDDY	DY
906 v		RBHT	HT
4909 x B4	**I**	ICHD	LL
4910 vCpa	**N**	NWRX	OM
4915 x B4	**I**	ICHD	LL
4916 x B4	**I**	ICHD	LL
4917 vCpa	**RR**	RDDY	DY

ot No. 30690 Wolverton 1961 – 2. Commonwealth bogies and aluminium win- ow frames. d. 37 t.

– Facelifted with new laminate, new diffusers etc.

919 afpa	**I**	RDDY	DY
923 v pa	**N**	NWRX	OM
925 a pa	**I**	ICHD	LL
927 afpa	**I**	RDDY	DY
930 afpa	**I**	RCLL	LL
933 v	**N**	NWRX	OM
936 v pa	**N**	NWRX	OM
938 a pa	**I**	ICHD	LL
939 a pa	**I**	ICHD	LL
940 v pa	**N**	RDDY	DY
946 afpa	**I**	RCLL	LL
949 a pa	**I**	ICHD	LL
951 v pa	**N**	RDDY	DY
956 a pa	**I**	ICHD	LL
959 a pa	**I**	ICHD	LL
960 v	**E**	ICHH	CL
961 afpa	**I**	RDDY	DY
963 a pa	**I**	ICHH	CL
4966 afpa	**I**	RDDY	DY
4973 v pa	**N**	RDDY	DY
4977 a pa	**I**	ICHD	LL
4979 afpa	**I**	RCLL	LL
4984 v	**E**	ICHH	CL
4986 a pa	**I**	ICHD	LL
4990 v pa	**N**	NWRX	OM
4991 a pa	**I**	ICHD	LL
4993 a pa	**I**	ICHD	LL
4994 v pa	**N**	NWRX	OM
4996 afpa	**I**	RCLL	LL
4998 a pa	**I**	ICHD	LL
4999 a pa	**I**	ICHD	LL
5000 v pa	**N**	NWRX	OM
5001 afpa	**I**	RDDY	DY
5002 a pa	**I**	ICHD	LL
5005 a pa	**I**	ICHD	LL
5007 a pa	**I**	ICHD	LL

5008 afpa	I	RCLL	LL
5009 a pa	I	ICHH	CL
5010 a pa	I	ICHD	LL
5023 a pa	I	ICHD	LL
5025 a pa	I	ICHH	CL
5027 a pa	I	ICHD	LL
5028 x		ICHL	BO
5029 a pa	I	ICHH	CL
5030 a pa	I	ICHH	CL
5032 x	M	ICHL	BN
5033 a pa	I	ICHH	CL
5035 x	M	ICHL	BN
5037 a pa	I	ICHD	LL
5040 x	I	ICHH	CL
5041 a pa	I	ICHD	LL
5042 x	I	ICHH	CL
5044 a pa	I	ICHH	CL

AC2Z (TSO) OPEN STANDARD

Dia. AC205. Mark 2. Pressure ventilated. 64S 2L. B4 bogies. vd. ETH 4.

Lot No. 30751 Derby 1965 – 7. 32 t.

5085	N	RAIS	IS
5090	N	NWRX	OM
5104	N	RAIS	IS
5105	N	NWRX	OM
5132 pa	E	RAIS	IS
5133	RR	RAIS	IS
5135	RR	RAIS	IS
5138	RR	RAIS	IS
5139 pa	E	RAIS	IS
5140	N	NWRX	OM
5145 pa		RAIS	IS
5148 pa	RR	RAIS	IS
5149 pa		RAIS	IS
5154 pa	E	RAIS	IS
5156 pa	RR	RAIS	IS
5157	RR	RAIS	IS
5158	RR	RAIS	IS
5159	RR	RAIS	IS
5161	RR	RAIS	IS
5163	RR	RAIS	IS
5166 pa	E	RAIS	IS
5167	RR	RAIS	IS
5171	N	RAIS	IS
5173	RR	RAIS	IS
5174 pa	RR	RAIS	IS
5175	N	RAIS	IS
5177	RR	RAIS	IS
5179	RR	RAIS	IS
5180	RR	RDDY	DY
5183	RR	RAIS	IS
5184	RR	RAIS	IS
5186	RR	RAIS	IS
5191 pa	E	RAIS	IS
5193 pa	E	RAIS	IS
5194	RR	RAIS	IS
5198	RR	RAIS	IS
5200	N	NWRX	OM
5204	N	RAIS	IS
5207 pa	RR	RAIS	IS
5209	RR	RAIS	IS
5210	RR	RAIS	IS
5211	N	NWRX	OM
5212 pa	E	RAIS	IS
5213	RR	RAIS	IS
5215	N	NWRX	OM
5219	N	NWRX	OM
5220	N	NWRX	OM
5221 pa	RR	RAIS	IS
5222	N	NWRX	OM
5225	RR	RAIS	IS
5226	RR	RAIS	IS

Named vehicles:

5132 CLAN MUNRO
5139 CLAN ROSS
5154 CLAN FRASER
5166 CLAN MACKENZIE
5191 CLAN DONALD
5193 CLAN MACLEOD
5212 CAPERKAILZIE

AD2Z (SO) OPEN STANDARD

Dia. AD203. Mark 2. Pressure ventilated. 48S 2L. B4 bogies. Originally used as restaurant cars. d. pa. ETH 4.

* Converted to SO(T) seating 40S 1L.

Lot No. 30752 Derby 1966.

5230 v	**E**	RAIS	IS	5234 v	**E**	RAIS	IS
5232 v	**RR**	RAIS	IS	5255 a		NWXX	OM
5233 v	**RR**	RAIS	IS				

Named vehicles:

5230 CORRIEMOILLIE

5234 CLAN MACKINTOSH

AC2A (TSO) OPEN STANDARD

Dia. AC206. Mark 2A. Pressure ventilated. 64S 2L. B4 bogies. ad. ETH 4.

5259 – 5345. Lot No. 30776 Derby 1967 – 8. 32 t.
5349 – 5433. Lot No. 30787 Derby 1968. 32 t.

5259	**RR**	RDDY	DY	5349	**RR**	RDDY	DY
5261 pa	**N**	NWXX	OM	5350 pa	**N**	NWXX	OM
5264	**RR**	RDDY	DY	5353 pa	**RR**	RCLL	LL
5265 pa	**N**	NWXX	OM	5354	**RR**	RCLL	LL
5266	**RR**	RCLL	LL	5362	**RR**	RDDY	DY
5267	**RR**	RCLL	LL	5364	**RR**	RCLL	LL
5271 pa	**RR**	RCLL	LL	5365	**RR**	RCLL	LL
5272 pa	**RR**	RDDY	DY	5366	**RR**	RCLL	LL
5275	**N**	NWXX	OM	5373	**N**	NWXX	OM
5276 pa	**N**	NWXX	OM	5376	**N**	NWXX	OM
5277 pa		RDDY	DY	5378	**N**	NWXX	OM
5278 pa	**N**	NWXX	OM	5379	**RR**	NWXX	OM
5279 pa		RDDY	DY	5381 pa	**N**	NWXX	OM
5282 pa	**RR**	RCLL	LL	5384 pa	**N**	NWXX	OM
5290 pa	**N**	NWXX	OM	5385	**RR**	RCLL	LL
5291	**RR**	NWXX	OM	5386	**RR**	RCLL	LL
5292 pa	**RR**	RDDY	DY	5389 pa	**N**	NWXX	OM
5293	**N**	NWXX	OM	5391	**RR**	NWXX	OM
5300 pa		NWXX	OM	5392 pa		NWXX	OM
5301	**RR**	NWXX	OM	5393 pa	**RR**	RCLL	LL
5304	**RR**	RCLL	LL	5396	**RR**	RCLL	LL
5307 pa	**RR**	RDDY	DY	5401 pa	**RR**	RCLL	LL
5309	**N**	NWXX	OM	5402		RDDY	DY
5314		NWXX	OM	5404 pa	**N**	NWXX	OM
5316	**RR**	RCLL	LL	5408 pa	**N**	NWXX	EH
5322	**N**	NWXX	EH	5410	**N**	NWXX	EH
5323	**RR**	RDDY	DY	5412	**N**	NWXX	OM
5331 pa	**N**	NWXX	OM	5414	**RR**	RDDY	DY
5335	**N**	NWXX	EH	5418	**N**	NWXX	EH
5336 pa	**N**	NWXX	OM	5419 pa	**N**	NWXX	EH
5337		NWXX	OM	5420 pa	**N**	NWXX	OM
5341	**RR**	RCLL	LL	5432	**RR**	RCLL	LL
5345 pa	**N**	NWXX	OM	5433 pa	**N**	NWXX	OM

AC2B (TSO) OPEN STANDARD

Dia. AC207. Mark 2B. Pressure ventilated. 62S 2L. B4 bogies. ad. ETH 4.

Lot No. 30791 Derby 1969. 32 t.

5435	pa	N	NWXX	OM
5436	pa	N	NWXX	EH
5439		N	NWXX	EH
5443		N	NWXX	EH
5444	pa	N	NWXX	OM
5446	pa	N	NWXX	OM
5447	pa	N	NWXX	OM
5448	pa	N	NSWZ	OM
5449	pa	N	NWXX	OM
5450	pa	N	NWXX	OM
5453		RR	RDDY	DY
5454	pa	N	NWXX	OM
5455		N	NWXX	OM
5456	pa	N	NWXX	OM
5458		N	NWXX	EH
5462	pa	N	NWXX	OM
5463		RR	RDDY	DY
5464	pa	N	NWXX	EH
5465	pa	N	NWXX	OM
5468	pa	N	NWXX	OM
5470	pa	N	NWXX	OM
5471		N	NWXX	EH
5472	pa	N	NWXX	OM
5474	pa	N	NWXX	OM
5475	pa	N	NWXX	OM
5478			RDDY	DY
5480	pa	N	NWXX	OM
5482	pa	N	NWXX	OM
5484		N	NWXX	EH
5487			RDDY	DY
5491		RR	RCLL	LL
5492	pa	N	NWXX	OM
5494	pa	N	NWXX	OM
5495	pa	N	NWXX	OM
5497	pa	N	NWXX	OM

AC2C (TSO) OPEN STANDARD

Dia. AC208. Mark 2C. Pressure Ventilated. 62S 2L. B4 bogies. ad. pa. ETH 5.

Lot No. 30795 Derby 1969 – 70. 32.4 t.

5505	RR	RCLL	LL
5554	RR	RCLL	LL
5569		RDDY	DY
5586		RDDY	DY
5614	RR	RDDY	DY

AC2D (TSO) OPEN STANDARD

Dia. AC209. Mark 2D. Air conditioned. Stones (5653 has Temperature Ltd.) equipment. 62S 2L. B4 bogies. ae. pa. ETH 5.

LE – Stored at Landore.
MK – Stored at MoD Kineton.

Lot No. 30822 Derby 1971. 33 t.

5616	I	ICHX	BN
5617	I	ICCL	DY
5618	I	ICCR	PC
5620	I	ICCR	PC
5621	I	IXXT	MK
5623	I	ICCR	PC
5624	I	ICCR	PC
5625	I	IWCL	WB
5626	I	ICCR	PC
5628	I	IANR	NC
5629	I	ICCR	PC
5630	I	ICCL	DY
5631	I	ICCR	PC
5632	I	ICCR	PC
5633	I	ICCL	DY
5634	I	ICCR	PC
5636	I	ICCR	PC
5637	I	ICCL	PC

5638	I	ICCR	PC
5639	I	IXXB	LE
5640	I	IXXB	LE
5646	I	ICCR	PC
5647	I	ICHX	BN
5648	I	ICCL	DY
5650	I	ICCR	PC
5651	I	ICCR	PC
5652	I	ICCR	PC
5653	I	ICCR	PC
5654	I	IANR	NC
5657	I	ICCR	PC
5658	I	ICCR	PC
5659	I	ICCR	PC
5660	I	IXXB	LE
5661	I	IXXT	MK
5662	I	ICCR	PC
5663	I	IXXT	MK
5665	I	ICCR	PC
5669	I	IANR	NC
5671	I	ICCR	PC
5673	I	ICCR	PC
5674	I	IXXT	MK
5675	I	ICCL	DY
5676	I	ICCR	PC
5679	I	IANR	NC
5682	I	ICCR	PC
5685	I	ICCR	PC
5686	I	ICCR	PC
5687	I	IXXT	MK
5689	I	ICHX	BN
5690	I	ICCR	PC
5692	I	ICCR	PC
5693	I	IANR	NC
5694	I	IXXT	MK
5695	I	IANR	NC
5699	I	IXXB	LE
5700	I	ICCR	PC
5701	I	IXXT	MK
5703	I	ICCR	PC
5705	I	IWCL	WB
5706	I	IXXX	ZA
5710	I	ICCR	PC
5711	I	ICCR	PC
5713	I	IXXZ	BN
5715	I	ICCR	PC
5716	I	IXXT	MK
5717	I	IXXT	MK
5718	I	IXXT	MK
5719	I	ICCL	DY
5722	I	ICCL	DY
5723	I	ICCR	PC
5724	I	ICCR	PC
5726	I	ICCR	PC
5728	I	IANR	NC
5729	I	ICCX	PC
5730	I	ICCR	PC
5731	I	IXXT	MK
5732	I	ICHD	LL
5734	I	IXXB	LE
5735	I	IANR	NC
5737	I	IANR	NC
5738	I	IXXT	MK
5739	I	ICHD	LL
5740	I	ICCR	PC
5742	I	IXXX	ZA
5743	I	IANR	NC

AC2E (TSO) OPEN STANDARD

Dia. AC210. Mark 2E. Air conditioned. Stones equipment. 64S 2L (62S 2L w). B4 bogies. Require at least 800 V train heat supply. ae. pa. ETH 5.

5744 – 5803. Lot No. 30837 Derby 1972. 33.5 t.
5810 – 5907. Lot No. 30844 Derby 1972 – 3. 33.5 t.

LE – Stored at Landore.
MK – Stored at MoD Kineton.

5744	I	ICCX	MA
5745	I	IXXT	MK
5746	I	ICCR	PC
5747	I	ICCX	PC
5748 w	I	ICCR	PC
5750	I	IXXT	MK
5751 w	I	ICCR	PC
5752 w	I	ICCX	PC
5754 w	I	ICCR	PC
5755	I	ICCX	PC
5759	I	IWCL	MA
5760	I	ICCR	PC
5761	I	ICHD	LL
5762	I	ICHD	LL

5763	I	IXXT	MK
5764	I	ICCX	MA
5766	I	ICCX	MA
5768	I	IXXT	MK
5769	I	ICCR	PC
5770	I	ICHX	BN
5772 w	I	ICCR	PC
5773	I	IXXT	MK
5774	I	IXXB	PC
5775	I	IXXT	MK
5776	I	ICCR	PC
5777	I	ICCX	MA
5778 w	I	ICCR	PC
5779	I	ICCX	MA
5780 w	I	ICCR	PC
5781 w	I	ICCX	MA
5784	I	ICCR	PC
5785	I	IXXT	MK
5786	I	IWCL	OY
5787	I	IXXT	MK
5788 w	I	ICCX	MA
5789	I	ICCR	PC
5791 w	I	ICCR	PC
5792	I	ICCR	PC
5793	I	ICCR	PC
5794 w	I	ICCR	PC
5795	I	IXXT	MK
5796 w	I	ICCR	PC
5797	I	ICCR	PC
5799	I	ICCX	PC
5800	I	ICCX	MA
5801	I	ICCR	PC
5803	I	ICCX	MA
5810	I	IXXT	MK
5811	I	ICHD	LL
5812 w	I	ICCR	PC
5814	I	ICCR	PC
5815	I	IXXB	LE
5816	I	ICCR	PC
5818	I	ICCX	MA
5820	I	ICCX	MA
5821	I	ICCR	PC
5822	I	ICCX	MA
5823	I	IXXX	ZA
5824 w	I	ICCR	PC
5826	I	ICCR	PC
5827 w	I	ICCX	MA
5828 w	I	ICCX	MA
5829	I	ICHD	LL
5831	I	ICCX	MA
5832	I	IXXX	ZA
5833	I	ICCX	MA
5834	I	IXXT	MK
5835	I	ICHD	LL
5836	I	IXXT	WB
5837	I	ICHD	LL
5838	I	IXXT	MK
5840	I	ICCX	MA
5841	I	IXXX	DY
5842 w	I	ICCX	MA
5843 w	I	ICCR	PC
5844	I	IXXB	LE
5845 w	I	ICCX	MA
5846	I	IXXX	DY
5847 w	I	ICCR	PC
5849	I	IXXT	MK
5851	I	ICCX	MA
5852	I	ICCX	MA
5853	I	ICCX	MA
5854	I	ICCX	MA
5858	I	ICCL	DY
5859	I	ICCX	MA
5860 w	I	ICCL	DY
5861	I	ICCX	MA
5863	I	ICHX	BN
5866	I	ICCX	MA
5868	I	ICCR	PC
5869	I	ICCR	PC
5870	I	IXXT	MK
5871	I	ICCX	MA
5872 n	I	IXXT	MK
5873	I	ICHD	LL
5874 w	I	ICCX	MA
5875	I	ICCX	MA
5876	I	ICCR	PC
5878	I	ICCX	MA
5879	I	ICCX	MA
5881	I	IXXT	MK
5883	I	IWCL	OY
5884	I	IXXB	LE
5885	I	ICCL	PC
5886	I	IXXT	MK
5887 w	I	ICCR	PC
5888 w	I	ICCR	PC
5889	I	ICCR	PC
5890	I	ICCX	MA
5891	I	ICCX	MA
5892	I	ICCR	PC
5893	I	ICCR	PC
5897	I	ICCR	PC
5898	I	IXXZ	PC
5899	I	ICCR	PC
5900	I	ICCR	PC
5901	I	IXXT	MK

5902	I	ICCX	MA
5903	I	ICCX	MA
5904	I	ICHX	BN
5905	I	ICCR	PC
5906	I	ICCR	PC
5907	I	ICHD	LL

AC2F (TSO) OPEN STANDARD

Dia. AC211. Mark 2F. Air conditioned. Temperature Ltd. equipment. 64S 2L (62S 1L w). Inter-City 70 seats. All now refurbished with power-operated vestibule doors, new panels and new seat trim. B4 bogies. ae. pa. ETH 5X.

* – Early Mark 2 style seats.

5908 – 5958. Lot No. 30846 Derby 1973. 33 t.
5959 – 6170. Lot No. 30860 Derby 1973 – 4. 33 t.
6171 – 6184. Lot No. 30874 Derby 1974 – 5. 33 t.

w Wheelchair space. 62S 2L.

5908	I	IWCR	OY
5910 w	I	IWCR	OY
5911	I	IWCR	MA
5912	I	ICCR	DY
5913	I	ICCR	MA
5914	I	IWCR	MA
5915	I	IWCR	OY
5916 w	I	ICCR	DY
5917	I	ICCR	MA
5918 w	I	ICCR	DY
5919	I	IWCR	MA
5920	I	IWCR	OY
5921	I	IANR	NC
5922	I	IWCR	MA
5924	I	IANR	NC
5925 w	I	ICCR	MA
5926	I	IWCR	MA
5927	I	IANR	NC
5928	I	IANR	NC
5929	I	IANR	NC
5930 w	I	ICCR	MA
5931 w	I	IWCR	MA
5932	I	IWCR	MA
5933	I	IWCR	OY
5934	I	IWCR	MA
5935	I	IWCR	MA
5936	I	IANR	NC
5937	I	IWCR	OY
5939	I	IWCR	OY
5940 w	I	IWCR	MA
5941	I	IWCR	OY
5943 w	I	IWCR	OY
5944 w	I	IWCR	OY
5945 w	I	IWCR	MA
5946	I	IWCR	OY
5947	I	ICCR	MA
5948 w	I	IWCR	OY
5949 w	I	IWCR	MA
5950	I	IANR	NC
5951	I	ICCR	MA
5952	I	IWCR	MA
5953	I	IWCR	MA
5954	I	IANR	NC
5955	I	IWCR	OY
5956	I	IANR	NC
5957	I	IWCR	MA
5958	I	IWCR	OY
5959 n	I	IANR	NC
5960	I	IWCR	MA
5961	I	ICCR	MA
5962	I	ICCR	DY
5963	I	IWCR	OY
5964	I	IANR	NC
5965 w	I	ICCR	DY
5966	I	IANR	NC
5967 w	I	ICCR	MA
5968	I	IANR	NC
5969 w	I	IWCR	OY
5971	I	ICCR	DY
5973	I	IANR	NC
5975 *	I	ICCR	DY
5976 w	I	ICCR	DY
5977	I	IWCR	MA
5978 *	I	IWCR	MA
5980	I	IWCR	OY
5981	I	ICCR	MA
5983	I	ICCR	MA
5984 *	I	IWCR	OY
5985	I	IWCR	OY
5986	I	IWCR	OY
5987 *	I	IWCR	OY
5988 w	I	IWCR	MA

5989 w	I	ICCR	MA
5991	I	ICCR	DY
5993 *w	I	ICCR	MA
5994 *	I	ICCR	MA
5995	I	ICCR	DY
5996	I	IWCR	MA
5997	I	IWCR	OY
5998	I	IANR	NC
5999	I	ICCR	MA
6000	I	IWCR	MA
6001 w	I	IWCR	OY
6002	I	IWCR	OY
6005 *	I	ICCR	MA
6006	I	IWCR	MA
6008	I	ICCR	MA
6009	I	IWCR	OY
6010 n	I	ICCR	MA
6011	I	ICCR	MA
6012 *	I	IWCR	OY
6013 *	I	ICCR	DY
6014	I	IWCR	MA
6015 w	I	ICCR	DY
6016	I	IWCR	MA
6018 *	I	IWCR	MA
6021	I	IWCR	MA
6022 w	I	ICCR	DY
6024	I	ICCR	MA
6025 *w	I	ICCR	MA
6026 *	I	ICCR	MA
6027 w	I	IWCR	OY
6028	I	IWCR	OY
6029	I	IWCR	OY
6030 w	I	ICCR	MA
6031	I	IWCR	OY
6034	I	IWCR	OY
6035 w	I	ICCR	DY
6036 *	I	IANR	NC
6037	I	IWCR	MA
6038	I	ICCR	DY
6041	I	ICCR	MA
6042	I	IWCR	MA
6043	I	IWCR	MA
6045 w	I	IWCR	OY
6046	I	IWCR	MA
6047 *n	I	IWCR	MA
6049	I	IWCR	MA
6050	I	ICCR	MA
6051 *	I	IWCR	OY
6052 w	I	ICCR	MA
6053 *	I	IANR	NC
6054	I	IWCR	OY
6055	I	IWCR	OY
6056	I	IWCR	OY
6057	I	IWCR	OY
6059	I	ICCR	MA
6060 *	I	IWCR	OY
6061 *	I	IWCR	MA
6062 *	I	IWCR	OY
6063 w	I	IWCR	OY
6064	I	IWCR	OY
6065	I	IWCR	OY
6066	I	ICCR	MA
6067	I	IWCR	OY
6073	I	ICCR	MA
6100 *	I	IWCR	MA
6101	I	IWCR	OY
6102	I	IWCR	MA
6103	I	IANR	NC
6104	I	IWCR	OY
6105	I	ICCR	DY
6106	I	IWCR	MA
6107	I	IWCR	MA
6110 w	I	IWCR	MA
6111	I	IWCR	OY
6112	I	ICCR	MA
6113	I	IWCR	OY
6115	I	ICCR	MA
6116	I	IWCR	OY
6117 w	I	ICCR	MA
6119 w	I	ICCR	DY
6120	I	ICCR	MA
6121	I	IWCR	MA
6122	I	IWCR	OY
6123	I	IANR	NC
6124	I	ICCR	MA
6134	I	IWCR	MA
6135	I	ICCR	DY
6136	I	IWCR	MA
6137	I	ICCR	DY
6138	I	IWCR	MA
6139 *n	I	IANR	NC
6141 w	I	IWCR	OY
6142 *	I	IWCR	MA
6144 *	I	IWCR	MA
6145 *	I	ICCR	MA
6146 *	I	IWCR	OY
6147 *	I	IWCR	MA
6148 *	I	ICCR	DY
6149 *w	I	IWCR	OY
6150 *	I	ICCR	DY
6151 *	I	IWCR	MA
6152 *	I	IANR	NC
6153 *	I	IWCR	MA
6154 *	I	ICCR	MA

6155 *	I	IANR	NC
6157 *	I	ICCR	MA
6158 *	I	IWCR	OY
6159 *n	I	ICCR	MA
6160 *	I	IANR	NC
6161 *	I	IWCR	OY
6162	I	ICCR	MA
6163	I	IWCR	MA
6164	I	IWCR	OY
6165	I	IWCR	MA
6166	I	IANR	NC
6167	I	IANR	NC
6168	I	ICCR	DY
6170	I	IWCR	OY
6171	I	IWCR	OY
6172	I	ICCR	MA
6173	I	IWCR	OY
6174	I	IANR	NC
6175	I	IWCR	OY
6176 w	I	ICCR	DY
6177	I	ICCR	DY
6178 w	I	IWCR	OY
6179	I	IWCR	MA
6180 w	I	IWCR	MA
6181 wn	I	IWCR	MA
6182	I	ICCR	DY
6183	I	ICCR	DY
6184 *	I	ICCR	MA

AC2D (TSO) OPEN STANDARD

Dia. AC217. Mark 2D. Air conditioned. Stones. 58S 2L. (58S 1L*). B4 bogies. ae. pa. ETH 5X. Rebuilt from FO with new style 2+2 seats.

Lot No. 30821 Derby 1971 – 2. 33.5 t.

6200 (3198)	I	IWRX	OM
6201 (3210) *	I	IWCX	WB
6202 (3191) *	I	IWCX	WB
6203 (3180)	I	IWCX	WB
6204 (3216)	I	ICHX	BN
6205 (3193)	I	ICCX	DY
6206 (3183)	I	IWRX	OM
6207 (3204)	I	ICCX	DY
6208 (3205)	I	IWCX	WB
6209 (3177)	I	ICHX	BN
6210 (3196) *	I	IWCX	WB
6211 (3215)	I	IWCX	WB
6212 (3176)	I	ICCX	DY
6213 (3208)	I	IWRX	OM
6214 (3211)	I	IWCX	WB
6215 (3170)	I	ICCX	DY
6216 (3179)	I	ICCX	DY
6217 (3184)	I	IWCX	WB
6218 (3209)	I	IWCX	WB
6219 (3213)	I	IWCX	WB
6220 (3175)	I	ICCX	DY
6221 (3173)	I	IWCX	WB
6222 (3171)	I	IWCX	WB
6223 (3194)	I	ICCX	DY
6224 (3195) *	I	IWCX	WB
6225 (3200)	I	ICHX	BN
6226 (3203)	I	IWRX	OM
6227 (3197)	I	ICCX	DY
6228 (3201) *	I	IWCX	WB
6229 (3212)	I	IWCX	WB
6230 (3185)	I	ICCX	DY
6231 (3189)	I	ICHX	BN
6232 (3199) *	I	IWCX	WB
6233 (3206)	I	ICCX	DY
6234 (3207)	I	IWCX	WB
6235 (3190)	I	ICHX	BN

AD4Z (OC) OBSERVATION CAR

Dia.AD401. Converted 1987 from DMU DTCL. DMU bogies. 42U 1L. v. pa.

Lot No. 30468 Metro-Cammell 1958. 25.5 t.

6300 (54356)	E	RAIS	IS	HEBRIDEAN

GX51 GENERATOR VAN

Dia. GX501. Renumbered 1989 from BR departmental series. Three-phase supply generator van for use with HST trailers. Often used at times of low availability of HST power cars. Rebuilt from NDA 81448. B5 bogies.

Lot No. 30400 Pressed Steel 1958. t.

6310 (ADB 975325) I IXXB PM

AX51 GENERATOR VAN

Dia. AX501. Converted to generator vans for use with pairs of Class 37s in Scotland. B5 bogies.

6311. Lot No. 30162 Pressed Steel 1958. t.
6312. Lot No. 30224 Cravens 1956. t.
6313. Lot No. 30484 Pressed Steel 1958. t.

6311 (80903, 92011, 92911)	I	IWCX	IS
6312 (81023, 84023, 92025, 92925)	I	IWCX	IS
6313 (81553, 84553, 92167)	I	IWCX	IS

AZ5Z SPECIAL SALOON

Dia. AZ501. Renumbered 1989 from LMR departmental series. Formerly the LMR General Manager's saloon. Rebuilt from LMS period 1 BFK M 5033 M to dia. 1654 and mounted on the underframe of BR suburban BS M 43232. B5 bogies. This vehicle has a maximum speed of 100 mph, but is restricted to 60 mph when carrying passengers with screw coupling operative.

LMS Lot No. 326 Derby 1927. t.

6320 (TDM 395707) I ICHV BN

GS5(HSBV) HST BARRIER VEHICLE

Various diagrams. Renumbered from departmental stock, or converted from various types. ae. B4 bogies (Commonwealth bogies *).

6330/9. Lot No. 30786 Derby 1968. 32 t.
6332/43. Lot No. 30795 Derby 1969/70. 32 t.
6334. Lot No. 30400 Pressed Steel 1957 – 8. 31.5 t.
6335. Lot No. 30775 Derby 1967 – 8. 32 t.
6336/8. Lot No. 30715 Gloucester 1962. 31 t.
6340. Lot No. 30669 Swindon 1962. 36 t.
6341/2. Lot No. 30632 Ashford/Swindon 1961. 38 t.
6343. Lot No. 30091 Doncaster 1954. 33 t.
6344. Lot No. 30163 Pressed Steel 1957. 31.5 t.
6345. Lot No. 30796 Derby 1970. 32.5 t.
6346. Lot No. 30777 Derby 1967. 31.5 t.
6347. Lot No. 30787 Derby 1968. 31.5 t.

6330 (14084, ADB 975629)	GS503		IWRG	OO
6332 (5594)	GS508	I	ICCG	EC
6334 (81478, 92128)	GS507	I	IMLG	NL
6335 (14065, ADB 975655)	GS503	I	ICCG	EC
6336 (81591, 92185)	GS507	I	IECG	BN
6338 (81551, 92180)	GS507	I	IWRG	PM
6339 (14078, ADB 975666)	GS503	I	ICCG	PM
6340 (21251, ADB 975678)	GS504*	I	IWRG	LA

6341 (1967, ADB 975980)	GS505*	I	IWRG	OO
6342 (1983, ADB 975981)	GS505*	I	IWRG	OO
6343 (5522)	GS508	I	IMLG	NL
6344 (81263, 92080)	GS507	I	IECG	HT
6345 (14137, 17137)	GS510	I	IECG	BN
6346 (9422)	GS511	I	ICCG	EC
6347 (5395)	GS509	I	IWRG	PM

GF5 (HSBV) MARK 4 BARRIER VEHICLE

Various diagrams. Renumbered from departmental stock, or converted from FK or BSO. ae. B4 bogies.

6350. Lot No. 30472 BRCW 1959. 33 t.
6351. Lot No. 30091 Doncaster 1954. 33 t.
6352/3. Lot No. 30774 Derby 1968. 33 t.
6354 – 6. Lot No. 30820 Derby 1970. 32 t.
6357. Lot No. 30798 Derby 1970. 32 t.
6358 – 9. Lot No. 30788 Derby 1968. 31.5 t.

6350 (3088, ADB 977434)	AV501	I	IECG	BN
6351 (3050, ADB 977435)	AV501		IECG	EC
6352 (13465, 19465)	AV502		IECG	BN
6353 (13478, 19478)	AV503		IECG	EC
6354 (9459)	AV504	I	IECG	BN
6355 (9477)	AV504		IECG	BN
6356 (9455)	AV504		IECG	BN
6357 (9443)	AV504		IECG	BN
6358 (9432)	AV505		IECG	BN
6359 (9429)	AV505		IECG	BN

GF5 (HSBV) DMU/EMU* BARRIER VEHICLE

Various diagrams. Converted from BFK, BSO or BG. ae. B4 bogies.

6360. Lot No. 30777 Derby 1967. 31.5 t.
6361 – 2. Lot No. 30820 Derby 1970. 32 t.
6363. Lot No. 30796 Derby 1970. 32 t.
6364. Lot No. 30039 Derby 1954. 32 t.
6365. Lot No. 30323 Pressed Steel 1957. 32 t.

6360 (9420)	**RR**	RFXX
6361 (9460)	**RR**	RFXX
6362 (9467)	**RR**	RFXX
6363 (17117)	**RR**	RFXX
6364 (80565)	**RR**	RFXX
6365 (84296)	**RR**	RFXX

AG2C (TSOT) OPEN STANDARD (TROLLEY)

Dia. AG201. Mark 2C. Converted from TSO by removal of one seating bay and replacing this by a counter with a space for a trolley. Adjacent toilet removed and converted to steward's washing area/store. Pressure ventilated. 54S 1L. B4 bogies. ad. pa. ETH 4.

Lot No. 30795 Derby 1969 – 70. 32.5 t.

6500 (5603)	pt	**N**	NWXX	OM
6501 (5547)	pt	**N**	NWXX	OM

6521 (5558)	N	NWXX	OM	6527 (5563) pt	N NWXX	OM
6523 (5568)		RDDY	DY	6528 (5592)	RDDY	DY

AG2D (TSOT) OPEN STANDARD (TROLLEY)

Dia. AG202. Mark 2D. Converted from TSO by removal of one seating bay and replacing this by a counter with a space for a trolley. Adjacent toilet removed and converted to steward's washing area/store. Air conditioned. Stones equipment. 54S 1L. B4 bogies. ae. pa. ETH 5.

MK – Stored at MoD Kineton.

Lot No. 30822 Derby 1971. 33 t.

6605 (5741)	I	IXXT	MK	6614 (5725)	I	IXXT	MK
6607 (5635)	I	IXXB	ZH	6618 (5644)	I	IXXB	PC
6608 (5696)	I	IXXT		6619 (5655)	I	IXXT	MK
6609 (5698)	I	IXXT					

AN2D (RMBT) MINIATURE BUFFET CAR

Dia. AN207. Mark 2D. Converted from TSOT by the removal of another seating bay and fitting a proper buffet counter with boiler and microwave oven. Air conditioned. Stones equipment. 46S 1L. B4 bogies. ae. pa. q. ETH 5.

Lot No. 30822 Derby 1971. 33 t.

Note: Original numbers shown in parentheses. These vehicles carried 6602/10 – 2/5 when they were TSOTs.

6652 (5622)	I	ICCX	DY	6662 (5641)	I	ICCX	DY
6660 (5627)	I	ICCX	DY	6665 (5721)	I	ICCX	DY
6661 (5736)	I	ICCX	DY				

AN1F (RLO) SLEEPER RECEPTION CAR

Dia. AN101 (AN102*). Mark 2F. Converted from FO, these vehicles consist of pantry, microwave cooking facilities, seating area for passengers, telephone booth and staff toilet. 6703 – 8 also have a bar. Converted at RTC, Derby (6700), Ilford (6701 – 5) and Derby (6706 – 8). Air conditioned. ae. pa. q. B4 bogies. Fitted with payphone. 26F 1L.

6701 – 2/4/8. Lot No. 30859 Derby 1973 – 4. 33.5 t.
6703/5 – 7. Lot No. 30845 Derby 1973. 33.5 t.

Note: 6705 – 7 were also numbered 6430/21/18 when declassified prior to conversion.

6700 (3347)	I	IWCX	WB	6705 (3310)	I	IWCX	WB
6701 (3346)	*I	IWCX	WB	6706 (3283)	I	IWCX	WB
6702 (3421)	*I	IWCX	WB	6707 (3276)	I	IWCX	WB
6703 (3308)	I	IWCX	WB	6708 (3370)	I	IWCX	WB
6704 (3341)	I	IWCX	WB				

AC2F (TSO) OPEN STANDARD

Dia. AC224. Mark 2F. Renumbered 1985 – 6 from FO. Converted 1990 to TSO with mainly unidirectional seating and power-operated sliding doors. Air conditioned. B4 bogies. 74S 2L + one tip-up seat. 6800 – 14 were converted by BREL Derby and have Temperature Ltd. air conditioning. 6815 – 29 were converted by RFS Industries Doncaster and have Stones air conditioning. ae. pa. ETH 5X. The coaches were also numbered 6435/42/39/43/9/36/40/52/4/5/1/37/48/63/65 and 6420/61/31/27/46/34/58/47/24/29/60/25/8/64/23 respectively.

6800 – 07. 6810 – 12. 6813 – 14. 6819/22/28. Lot No. 30859 Derby 1973 – 4. 33 t.
6808 – 6809. Lot No. 30873 Derby 1974 – 5. 33.5 t.
6815 – 18. 6820 – 21. 6823 – 27. 6829. Lot No. 30845 Derby 1973. 33 t.

6800 (3323)	I	IANR	NC	6815 (3282)	I	IANR	NC
6801 (3349)	I	IANR	NC	6816 (3316)	I	IANR	NC
6802 (3339)	I	IANR	NC	6817 (3311)	I	IANR	NC
6803 (3355)	I	IANR	NC	6818 (3298)	I	IANR	NC
6804 (3396)	I	IANR	NC	6819 (3365)	I	IANR	NC
6805 (3324)	I	IANR	NC	6820 (3320)	I	IANR	NC
6806 (3342)	I	IANR	NC	6821 (3281)	I	IANR	NC
6807 (3423)	I	IANR	NC	6822 (3376)	I	IANR	NC
6808 (3430)	I	IANR	NC	6823 (3289)	I	IANR	NC
6809 (3435)	I	IANR	NC	6824 (3307)	I	IANR	NC
6810 (3404)	I	IANR	NC	6825 (3301)	I	IANR	NC
6811 (3327)	I	IANR	NC	6826 (3294)	I	IANR	NC
6812 (3394)	I	IANR	NC	6827 (3306)	I	IANR	NC
6813 (3410)	I	IANR	NC	6828 (3380)	I	IANR	NC
6814 (3422)	I	IANR	NC	6829 (3288)	I	IANR	NC

AA31 (CK) CORRIDOR COMPOSITE

Mark 1. There were two variants: those built for the Eastern, London Midland, North Eastern or Scottish regions which have 6-seater standard class compartments with armrests (24F 18S 2L. Dia. AA301) and those built for the Southern and Western regions which have 8-seater standard class compartments without armrests (24F 24S 2L. dia AA302). The remaining vehicle seats 24F 18S, was renumbered from 16168 and was built with Commonwealth bogies, metal window frames and melamine finish in the standard class sections. Facelifted with fluorescent lighting, wide mirrors, blinds removed. vd. ETH 4.

Lot No. 30665 Derby 1961. 37 t.

7168	**N**	NWRX	OM

AH2Z (BSOT) OPEN BRAKE STANDARD (MICRO-BUFFET)

Dia. AH203. Mark 2. Converted from BSO by removal of one seating bay and replacing this by a counter with a space for a trolley. Adjacent toilet removed and converted to a steward's washing area/store. 23S 0L. ETH 4.

Lot No. 30757 Derby 1966.

9100 (9405)	**RR**	RAIS	IS
9101 (9398)	**RR**	RAIS	IS
9105 (9404) pt	**RR**	RAIS	IS

AE2Z (BSO) OPEN BRAKE STANDARD

Dia. AE203. Mark 2. These vehicles use the same body shell as the mark 2 BFK and have first class seat spacing and wider tables. Pressure ventilated. 31S 1L. B4 bogies. vd. pt. ETH 4.

Lot No. 30757 Derby 1966. 31.5 t.

9384	**N**	NWRX	OM
9385	**E**	RAIS	IS
9388	**E**	RAIS	IS
9390	**N**	RDDY	DY
9396	**N**	RDDY	DY
9409	**N**	NWRX	OM
9414	**E**	RAIS	IS

Named vehicles:

9385 BALMACARA
9388 BAILECHAUL
9414 BRAHAN SEER

AE2A (BSO) OPEN BRAKE STANDARD

Dia. AE204. Mark 2A. These vehicles use the same body shell as the mark 2A BFK and have first class seat spacing and wider tables. Pressure ventilated. 31S 1L. B4 bogies. ad. ETH 4.

9417 – 9424. Lot No. 30777 Derby 1967. 31.5 t.
9428 – 9438. Lot No. 30788 Derby 1968. 31.5 t.

9417	**RR**	RCLL	LL
9418 pt	**RR**	RDDY	DY
9419	**RR**	RCLL	LL
9421	**RR**	RCLL	LL
9424 pt	**RR**	RCLL	LL
9428 pt		RDDY	DY
9431 pt	**RR**	RDDY	DY
9434 pt	**RR**	RDDY	DY
9435	**RR**	RCLL	LL
9438	**I**	RDDY	DY

AE2C (BSO) OPEN BRAKE STANDARD

Dia. AE205. Mark 2C. Pressure ventilated. 31S 1L. B4 bogies. ad. ETH 4.

9440 – 9448. Lot No. 30798 Derby 1970. 32 t.
9458. Lot No. 30820 Derby 1970. 32 t.

9440 pt		RDDY	DY
9448		RDDY	DY
9458	**RR**	RCLL	LL

AE2D (BSO) OPEN BRAKE STANDARD

Dia. AE206. Mark 2D. Air conditioned (Stones). 31S 1L. B4 bogies. ae. pg. ETH 5.

Lot No. 30824 Derby 1971. 33 t.

9479	**I**	ICCX	MA
9480	**I**	ICCX	DY
9481	**I**	ICCX	MA
9482	**I**	ICCX	MA

483	I	IXXX	DY	9490	I	ICCX	DY
484	I	ICCX	MA	9492	I	IWRX	OM
485	I	ICCX	MA	9493	I	ICCX	MA
486	I	IWRX	OM	9494	I	IWRX	OM
488	I	ICCX	DY	9495	I	IECX	BN
489	I	ICCX	MA				

E2E (BSO) OPEN BRAKE STANDARD

ia. AE207. Mark 2E. Air conditioned (Stones). 32S 1L. B4 bogies. ae. pg. TH 5.

ɔt No. 30838 Derby 1972. 33 t.

496	I	ICCX	MA	9503	I	IXXX	DY
497	I	ICCX	MA	9504	I	ICCX	MA
498	I	ICCX	MA	9505	I	IXXX	DY
499	I	IXXX	DY	9506	I	ICCX	MA
500	I	ICCX	MA	9507	I	ICCX	MA
501	I	IWRX	OM	9508	I	ICCX	MA
502	I	ICCX	MA	9509	I	ICCX	MA

E2F (BSO) OPEN BRAKE STANDARD

ia. AE208. Mark 2F. Air conditioned (Temperature Ltd.). 32S 1L. B4 bogies. ɘ. pg. ETH 5X. All now r efurbished with power-operated vestibule doors, new anels and seat trim.

ɔt No. 30861 Derby 1974. 34 t.

513	I	ICCR	DY	9526 n	I	ICCR	DY
516 n	I	ICCR	DY	9527	I	ICCR	DY
520 n	I	ICCR	DY	9529	I	ICCR	DY
521	I	ICCR	DY	9531	I	ICCR	MA
522	I	ICCR	MA	9533	I	ICCR	MA
523	I	ICCR	MA	9537 n	I	ICCR	DY
524 n	I	ICCR	DY	9538	I	ICCR	MA
525	I	ICCR	MA	9539	I	ICCR	DY

F2F (DBSO) DRIVING OPEN BRAKE STANDARD

a. AF201. Mark 2F. Air conditioned (Temperature Ltd.). Push & pull (t.d.m. stem). Converted from BSO, these vehicles originally had half cabs at the brake d. They have since been refurbished and have had their cabs widened and e outer gangways removed. Fitted with cowcatchers. 32S 0L. B4 bogies. ae. ı. Cab to shore communication. BR Cellnet phone and data transmitter. H 5X.

701 – 9710. Lot No. 30861 Derby 1974. Converted 1979. Disc brakes. 34 t.
711 – 9713. Lot No. 30861 Derby 1974. Converted Glasgow 1985. 34 t.
714. Lot No. 30861 Derby 1974. Converted Glasgow 1986. Disc brakes. 34 t.

701 (9528)	I	IANR	NC	9704 (9512)	I	IANR	NC
702 (9510)	I	IANR	NC	9705 (9519)	I	IANR	NC
703 (9517)	I	IANR	NC	9707 (9511)	I	IANR	NC

9708 (9530)	I	IANR	NC	9712 (9534)	I	IANR	NC
9709 (9515)	I	IANR	NC	9713 (9535)	I	IANR	NC
9710 (9518)	I	IANR	NC	9714 (9536)	I	IANR	NC
9711 (9532)	I	IANR	NC				

AJ1G (RFM) RESTAURANT BUFFET FIRST (MODULAR

Dia. AJ103 (10200/1 are Dia. AJ101). Mark 3A. Air conditioned. Converte from HST TRFKs, RFBs and FOs. 22F (24F*). BT10 bogies. ae. pt. q. Fitte with payphone. ETH 14X.

10200 – 10211. Lot No. 30884 Derby 1977.
10212 – 10229. Lot No. 30878 Derby 1975 – 6. 39.80 t.
10230 – 10260. Lot No. 30890 Derby 1979. 39.80 t.

10200 (40519) *	I	IWCX	WB	10229 (11059)	I	IWCX	MA
10201 (40520) *	I	IWCX	WB	10230 (10021)	I	IWCX	PC
10202 (40504)	I	IWCX	MA	10231 (10016)	I	IWCX	PC
10203 (40506)	I	IANX	NC	10232 (10027)	I	IWCX	OY
10204 (40502)	I	IWCX	OY	10233 (10013)	I	IWCX	MA
10205 (40503)	I	IWCX	OY	10234 (10004)	I	IWCX	WB
10206 (40507)	I	IWCX	OY	10235 (10015)	I	IWCX	OY
10207 (40516)	I	IWCX	WB	10236 (10018)	I	IWCX	PC
10208 (40517)	I	IWCX	WB	10237 (10022)	I	IWCX	WB
10209 (40508)	I	IWCX	WB	10238 (10017)	I	IWCX	OY
10210 (40509)	I	IWCX	WB	10240 (10003)	I	IWCX	OY
10211 (40510)	I	IWCX	PC	10241 (10009)	I	IWCX	WB
10212 (11049)	I	IWCX	PC	10242 (10002)	I	IWCX	WB
10213 (11050)	I	IWCX	MA	10245 (10019)	I	IWCX	WB
10214 (11034)	I	IANX	NC	10246 (10014)	I	IWCX	MA
10215 (11032)	I	IWCX	WB	10247 (10011)	I	IANX	NC
10216 (11041)	I	IANX	NC	10248 (10005)	I	IWCX	OY
10217 (11051)	I	IWCX	MA	10249 (10012)	I	IWCX	WB
10218 (11053)	I	IWCX	WB	10250 (10020)	I	IWCX	OY
10219 (11047)	I	IWCX	OY	10251 (10024)	I	IWCX	MA
10220 (11056)	I	IWCX	OY	10252 (10008)	I	IWCX	MA
10221 (11012)	I	IWCX	PC	10253 (10026)	I	IWCX	WB
10222 (11063)	I	IWCX	MA	10254 (10006)	I	IWCX	OY
10223 (11043) s	I	IANX	NC	10255 (10010)	I	IWCX	OY
10224 (11062)	I	IWCX	MA	10256 (10028)	I	IWCX	MA
10225 (11014)	I	IWCX	OY	10257 (10007)	I	IWCX	WB
10226 (11015)	I	IWCX	MA	10258 (10023)	I	IWCX	WB
10227 (11057)	I	IWCX	MA	10259 (10025)	I	IWCX	OY
10228 (11035)	I	IANX	NC	10260 (10001)	I	IWCX	WB

AJ1J (RFM) RESTAURANT BUFFET FIRST (MODULA

Dia. AJ105. Mark 4. Air conditioned. 20F 1L. SIG bogies (BT41). ae. p ETH X.

Lot No. 31045 Metro-Cammell 1989 onwards. 45.5 t.

10300	I	IECX	BN	10302	I	IECX	BN
10301	I	IECX	BN	10303	I	IECX	BN

0304	I	IECX	BN	10319	I	IECX	BN
0305	I	IECX	BN	10320	I	IECX	BN
0306	I	IECX	BN	10321	I	IECX	BN
0307	I	IECX	BN	10322	I	IECX	BN
0308	I	IECX	BN	10323	I	IECX	BN
0309	I	IECX	BN	10324	I	IECX	BN
0310	I	IECX	BN	10325	I	IECX	BN
0311	I	IECX	BN	10326	I	IECX	BN
0312	I	IECX	BN	10327	I	IECX	BN
0313	I	IECX	BN	10328	I	IECX	BN
0314	I	IECX	BN	10329	I	IECX	BN
0315	I	IECX	BN	10330	I	IECX	BN
0316	I	IECX	BN	10331	I	IECX	BN
0317	I	IECX	BN	10332	I	IECX	BN
0318	I	IECX	BN	10333	I	IECX	BN

U4G (SLEP) SLEEPING CAR WITH PANTRY

a. AU401. Mark 3A. Air conditioned. 12 compartments with a fixed lower rth and a hinged upper berth, plus an attendants compartment with 2L (con-olled emission). BT10 bogies. ae. ETH 7X.

K – Stored at MoD Kineton.

t No. 30960 Derby 1981 – 3.

0500	I	ICHV	BN	10536	I	IWCR	WB
0501	I	IWCR	WB	10537	I	ICCR	PC
0502	I	IWCR	WB	10538	I	IWCX	WB
0503	I	ICHV	BN	10539	I	IWRX	LA
0504	I	IWCR	WB	10540	I	IWRX	LA
0506	I	IWCR	WB	10541	I	IWCX	WB
0507	I	IWCR	WB	10542	I	IWCR	WB
0508	I	IWCR	WB	10543	I	IWCR	WB
0510	I	IWCR	WB	10544	I	IWCR	WB
0512	I	IWCR	WB	10546	I	ICCR	PC
0513	I	IWCR	WB	10547	I	IWCR	WB
0514	I	ICHV	BN	10548	I	IWCR	WB
0515	I	IWCR	WB	10549	I	ICCX	PC
0516	I	IWCR	WB	10550	I	IXXT	MK
0519	I	IWCR	WB	10551	I	IWCR	WB
0520	I	IWCR	WB	10553	I	IWCR	WB
0522	I	IWCR	WB	10554	I	ICCR	PC
0523	I	IWCR	WB	10555	I	IWCR	WB
0526	I	IWCR	WB	10556	I	IWRX	LA
0527	I	IWCR	WB	10557	I	IXXC	ZN
0529	I	IWCR	WB	10558	I	IWCX	WB
0530	I	ICCR	PC	10559	I	IWCR	WB
0531	I	ICCR	PC	10560	I	IWCX	WB
0532	I	ICCR	PC	10561	I	IWCR	WB
0533	I	ICHX	BN	10562		IWCR	WB
0534	I	IWRR	LA	10563	I	ICCR	PC
0535	I	ICCR	PC	10565	I	IWCR	WB

10566	I	ICCX	PC
10567	I	IECT	BN
10569	I	IWCX	WB
10570	I	IXXT	MK
10571	I	IXXC	ZN
10572	I	ICCR	PC
10573	I	IWCX	WB
10574	I	ICHV	BN
10575	I	ICHV	BN
10576		IXXH	WB
10577		IXXX	ZA
10578	I	IXXT	MK
10579		IXXT	MK
10580	I	ICCR	PC
10581		IXXH	WB
10582	I	IECT	BN
10583	I	IWRX	LA
10584	I	IWRR	LA
10586	I	IWCX	WB
10588	I	IWRR	LA
10589	I	IWCR	WB
10590	I	IWCR	WB
10591	I	IXXT	MK
10592	I	IXXT	MK
10593	I	IWCX	WB
10594	I	ICCR	PC
10595		IXXT	MK
10596	I	IWRR	LA
10597	I	IWCR	WB
10598	I	IWCR	WB
10599	I	IXXT	MK
10600	I	IWCR	WB
10601	I	ICCR	PC
10602	I	IWCX	PC
10603	I	IXXH	MK
10604	I	IWCX	WB
10605	I	IWRX	LA
10606	I	IXXH	MK
10607	I	IWCR	WB
10609		IXXT	MK
10610	I	IWCR	WB
10612	I	IWRR	LA
10613	I	IWCR	WB
10614	I	IWCR	WB
10616	I	IWRX	LA
10617	I	IWCR	WB

AS4G (SLE) SLEEPING CA

Dia. AS403. Mark 3A. Air conditioned. 13 compartments with a fixed low berth and a hinged upper berth. 2L (controlled emission). BT10 bogies. a ETH 6X.

MK – Stored at MoD Kineton.

Lot No. 30961 Derby 1980 – 4.

10646	I	ICHV	BN
10647	I	IWCR	WB
10648	I	IWCR	WB
10649	I	IWCR	WB
10650	I	IWCR	WB
10651	I	IWCR	WB
10653	I	IWCR	WB
10654	I	IWCR	WB
10655	I	ICHV	BN
10656	I	IXXT	MK
10657	I	ICHV	BN
10658	I	IWCR	WB
10660	I	IWCR	WB
10661	I	ICHV	BN
10662	I	ICHV	BN
10663	I	IWCR	WB
10665	I	IECT	BN
10666	I	IWCR	WB
10668	I	IWCR	WB
10670	I	IXXT	MK
10672	I	IWCR	WB
10673		IXXH	WB
10674	I	IWCR	WB
10675	I	IWCR	WB
10678		IXXH	WB
10679		IXXH	MK
10680	I	IWCR	WB
10682	I	IWCR	WB
10683	I	IWCR	WB
10684		IXXT	MK
10685	I	IWCR	WB
10686	I	IWCR	WB
10687	I	IWCR	WB
10688	I	IWCR	WB
10689	I	IWCR	WB
10690	I	IWCR	WB
10691	I	IWCR	WB
10692	I	IWCR	WB

0693	I	IWCR	WB
0696	I	IWCR	WB
0697	I	IWCR	WB
0699	I	IWCR	WB
0700		IXXH	MK
0701	I	IWCR	WB
0702	I	IXXC	ZN
0703	I	IWCR	WB
0704	I	IXXC	ZN
0705	I	IECT	BN
0706	I	IWCR	WB
0707	I	IECT	BN
0708	I	IWCR	WB
0709	I	IWCR	WB
0710		IWCR	WB
0711	I	IWCR	WB
0712	I	IWCR	WB
0713	I	IECX	BN
10714	I	IWCR	WB
10715	I	IXXC	ZN
10716	I	IWCR	WB
10717	I	IWCR	WB
10718	I	IWCR	WB
10719	I	IWCR	WB
10720	I	IXXH	WB
10722	I	IWCR	WB
10723	I	IWCR	WB
10724	I	ICHV	BN
10725	I	ICHV	BN
10726	I	ICHV	BN
10727	I	ICHV	BN
10728	I	ICHV	BN
10729	I	ICHV	BN
10730	I	IWCR	WB
10731	I	IWCR	WB
10732	I	IWCR	WB

.D1G (FO) OPEN FIRST

ia. AD108. Mark 3A. Air conditioned. 48F 2L. BT10 bogies (BT15 b). ae. pa. TH 6X. All now facelifted with new upholstery, carpets etc. 11005 – 7 have gained their original numbers, having being converted back from open com- osites 11905 – 7.

ot No. 30878 Derby 1975 – 6. 34.30 t.

1005	I	IWCX	WB
1006	I	IWCX	WB
1007	I	IWCX	WB
1011 z	I	IWCX	WB
1013	I	IWCX	WB
1016	I	IWCX	PC
1017	I	IWCX	PC
1018	I	IWCX	WB
1019	I	IWCX	PC
1020	I	IWCX	WB
1021 b	I	IWCX	WB
1023	I	IWCX	PC
1024	I	IWCX	WB
1026	I	IWCX	WB
1027	I	IWCX	PC
1028	I	IWCX	WB
1029	I	IWCX	WB
1030	I	IWCX	WB
11031	I	IWCX	WB
11033	I	IWCX	WB
11036	I	IWCX	WB
11037	I	IWCX	PC
11038	I	IWCX	PC
11039	I	IWCX	PC
11040	I	IWCX	PC
11042	I	IWCX	WB
11044	I	IWCX	WB
11045	I	IWCX	PC
11046	I	IWCX	WB
11048	I	IWCX	PC
11052	I	IWCX	WB
11054	I	IWCX	WB
11055	I	IWCX	PC
11058	I	IWCX	WB
11060	I	IWCX	WB

.D1H (FO) OPEN FIRST

ia. AD109. Mark 3B. Air conditioned. 48F 2L. BT10 bogies. ae. pa. ETH 6X. ter-City 80 seats. Some of these coaches were named, but the names are ow being removed.

Lot No. 30982 Derby 1985. 36.46 t.

11064		I	IWCX	OY		
11065		I	IWCX	MA		
11066		I	IWCX	MA		
11067		I	IWCX	WB		
11068		I	IWCX	WB		
11069		I	IWCX	MA		
11070		I	IWCX	MA		
11071		I	IWCX	OY		
11072		I	IWCX	WB		
11073		I	IWCX	MA		
11074		I	IWCX	WB		
11075		I	IWCX	WB		
11076		I	IWCX	OY		
11077		I	IWCX	WB		
11078		I	IWCX	OY		
11079		I	IWCX	OY		
11080		I	IWCX	WB		
11081		I	IWCX	WB		
11082		I	IWCX	WB		
11083	p	I	IWCX	WB		
11084	p	I	IWCX	WB		
11085	p	I	IWCX	MA		
11086	p	I	IWCX	WB		
11087	p	I	IWCX	OY		
11088	p	I	IWCX	WB		
11089	p	I	IWCX	MA		
11090	p	I	IWCX	WB		
11091	p	I	IWCX	MA		
11092	p	I	IWCX	WB		
11093	p	I	IWCX	MA		
11094	p	I	IWCX	MA		
11095	p	I	IWCX	WB		
11096	p	I	IWCX	MA		
11097	p	I	IWCX	WB		
11098	p	I	IWCX	WB		
11099	p	I	IWCX	WB		
11100	p	I	IWCX	MA		
11101	p	I	IWCX	MA		

AD1J (FO) OPEN FIRS

Dia. AD111. Mark 4. Air conditioned. Known as 'Pullman open' by BR. 46F 1 SIG bogies (BT41). ae. pa. ETH 6.

Note: 11264 – 71 have now been cancelled.

Lot No. 31046 Metro-Cammell 1989 onwards. 39.70 t.

11200		I	IECX	BN
11201	p	I	IECX	BN
11202		I	IECX	BN
11203	p	I	IECX	BN
11204	p	I	IECX	BN
11205		I	IECX	BN
11206		I	IECX	BN
11207	p	I	IECX	BN
11208		I	IECX	BN
11209		I	IECX	BN
11210		I	IECX	BN
11211	p	I	IECX	BN
11212		I	IECX	BN
11213	p	I	IECX	BN
11214	p	I	IECX	BN
11215		I	IECX	BN
11216		I	IECX	BN
11217	p	I	IECX	BN
11218		I	IECX	BN
11219	p	I	IECX	BN
11220		I	IECX	BN
11221	p	I	IECX	BN
11222	p	I	IECX	BN
11223		I	IECX	BN
11224		I	IECX	BN
11225	p	I	IECX	BN
11226		I	IECX	BN
11227	p	I	IECX	BN
11228	p	I	IECX	BN
11229	p	I	IECX	BN
11230		I	IECX	BN
11231	p	I	IECX	BN
11232		I	IECX	BN
11233	p	I	IECX	BN
11234		I	IECX	BN
11235	p	I	IECX	BN
11236		I	IECX	BN
11237	p	I	IECX	BN
11238		I	IECX	BN
11239	p	I	IECX	BN
11240		I	IECX	BN
11241		I	IECX	BN
11242	p	I	IECX	BN
11243	p	I	IECX	BN
11244		I	IECX	BN
11245	p	I	IECX	BN

1246 p	I	IECX	BN
1247 p	I	IECX	BN
1248	I	IECX	BN
1249 p	I	IECX	BN
1250	I	IECX	BN
1251 p	I	IECX	BN
1252	I	IECX	BN
1253 p	I	IECX	BN
1254	I	IECX	BN
1255 p	I	IECX	BN
1256	I	IECX	BN
1257 p	I	IECX	BN
11258	I	IECX	BN
11259 p	I	IECX	BN
11260	I	IECX	BN
11261 p	I	IECX	BN
11262	I	IECX	BN
11263 p	I	IECX	BN
11272	I	IECX	BN
11273	I	IECX	BN
11274	I	IECX	BN
11275	I	IECX	BN
11276	I	IECX	BN

C2G (TSO) OPEN STANDARD

ia. AC213 (AC220 z). Mark 3A. Air conditioned. All now refurbished with odified seat backs and new layout. 76S 2L (74S 2L z). BT10 (BREL T4*, BT15) bogies. ae. pa. ETH 6X. 12169 – 72 have been converted from open composites 11908 – 10/22, formerly FOs 11008 – 10/22.

ot No. 30877 Derby 1975 – 7. 34.30 t.

2004	I	IWCX	WB
2005	I	IWCX	WB
2007	I	IWCX	WB
2008	I	IWCX	WB
2009	I	IWCX	WB
2010 b	I	IWCX	WB
2011	I	IWCX	WB
2012	I	IWCX	WB
2013	I	IWCX	WB
2014	I	IWCX	WB
2015	I	IWCX	WB
2016	I	IWCX	WB
2017	I	IWCX	WB
2019	I	IWCX	WB
2020	I	IWCX	WB
2021	I	IWCX	WB
2022	I	IWCX	WB
2023	I	IWCX	WB
2024	I	IWCX	OY
2025	I	IWCX	WB
2026 w	I	IWCX	OY
2027	I	IWCX	WB
2028	I	IWCX	WB
2029	I	IWCX	PC
2030	I	IWCX	WB
2031	I	IWCX	OY
2032	I	IWCX	PC
2033 z	I	IWCX	WB
2034	I	IWCX	MA
2035	I	IWCX	OY
2036 s	I	IWCX	MA
12037	I	IWCX	WB
12038	I	IWCX	MA
12040	I	IWCX	PC
12041	I	IWCX	PC
12042 w	I	IWCX	WB
12043	I	IWCX	WB
12044	I	IWCX	WB
12045	I	IWCX	WB
12046	I	IWCX	PC
12047 z	I	IWCX	PC
12048	I	IWCX	WB
12049	I	IWCX	PC
12050 w	I	IWCX	OY
12051	I	IWCX	OY
12052	I	IWCX	WB
12053	I	IWCX	WB
12054 z	I	IWCX	WB
12055	I	IWCX	WB
12056	I	IWCX	MA
12057	I	IWCX	WB
12058	I	IWCX	WB
12059 w	I	IWCX	WB
12060	I	IWCX	MA
12061 w	I	IWCX	WB
12062	I	IWCX	MA
12063	I	IWCX	PC
12064	I	IWCX	PC
12065	I	IWCX	PC
12066	I	IWCX	WB
12067	I	IWCX	WB
12068	I	IWCX	WB

12069		I IWCX	WB
12070		I IWCX	WB
12071		I IWCX	WB
12072		I IWCX	WB
12073		I IWCX	WB
12075		I IWCX	OY
12076		I IWCX	WB
12077		I IWCX	WB
12078		I IWCX	PC
12079		I IWCX	OY
12080		I IWCX	OY
12081		I IWCX	PC
12082		I IWCX	PC
12083		I IWCX	WB
12084		I IWCX	WB
12085	w	I IWCX	WB
12086	w	I IWCX	WB
12087	w	I IWCX	OY
12088	z	I IWCX	PC
12089		I IWCX	PC
12090		I IWCX	WB
12091		I IWCX	WB
12092		I IWCX	OY
12093		I IWCX	WB
12094		I IWCX	WB
12095		I IWCX	PC
12096		I IWCX	PC
12097		I IWCX	PC
12098		I IWCX	WB
12099		I IWCX	PC
12100	z	I IWCX	PC
12101	w	I IWCX	WB
12102		I IWCX	WB
12103	z	I IWCX	WB
12104		I IWCX	PC
12105		I IWCX	MA
12106		I IWCX	WB
12107		I IWCX	MA
12108	w	I IWCX	WB
12109	w	I IWCX	MA
12110		I IWCX	MA
12111		I IWCX	WB
12112	z	I IWCX	WB
12113		I IWCX	WB
12114		I IWCX	OY
12115		I IWCX	PC
12116		I IWCX	PC
12117		I IWCX	WB
12118		I IWCX	WB
12119		I IWCX	PC
12120		I IWCX	MA
12121		I IWCX	WB
12122	z	I IWCX	WB
12123		I IWCX	WB
12124		I IWCX	WB
12125		I IWCX	MA
12126		I IWCX	WB
12127		I IWCX	WB
12128	w	I IWCX	MA
12129		I IWCX	WB
12130		I IWCX	WB
12131		I IWCX	MA
12132		I IWCX	WB
12133		I IWCX	PC
12134		I IWCX	WB
12135		I IWCX	PC
12136		I IWCX	WB
12137		I IWCX	PC
12138		I IWCX	WB
12139		I IWCX	MA
12140	*z	I IWCX	PC
12141		I IWCX	WB
12142	z	I IWCX	PC
12143		I IWCX	WB
12144	z	I IWCX	WB
12145		I IWCX	PC
12146		I IWCX	MA
12147		I IWCX	PC
12148		I IWCX	PC
12149		I IWCX	OY
12150		I IWCX	OY
12151		I IWCX	PC
12152		I IWCX	WB
12153		I IWCX	PC
12154		I IWCX	MA
12155		I IWCX	WB
12156		I IWCX	WB
12157		I IWCX	MA
12158		I IWCX	WB
12159		I IWCX	MA
12160	w	I IWCX	MA
12161	z	I IWCX	PC
12163		I IWCX	WB
12164		I IWCX	OY
12165		I IWCX	PC
12166		I IWCX	PC
12167		I IWCX	MA
12168	w	I IWCX	PC
12169	z	I IWCX	WB
12170	z	I IWCX	WB
12171	z	I IWCX	WB
12172	z	I IWCX	WB

Mark 1 Stock. Resturant first (RF) No. 325 is seen at York on 1st May 1992. is the only BR traffic vehicle to be renumbered from Royal train stock.
John Augustson

Open first (FO) No. 3149 in InterCity livery at Carlisle Upperby on 29th ember 1992.
Kevin Conkey

Corridor first (FK) No. 13225 in Regional Railways livery at Grosmont on 19th
ember 1992. This vehicle is fitted with composition brake blocks which can
dentified due to them being painted yellow. *John Augustson*

Corridor brake standard (BSK) No. 35317 in Network-SouthEast livery at
ord on 30th August 1990. *John Augustson*

C1
SCOTRAIL
BUFFET
9100
C1

Open brake standard (BSO) No. 9388 'BAILECHAUL' at Kyle of Lochalsh on 26th September 1992. This vehicle carries LNER tourist livery. *John Augustson*

▲ **Mark 2A Stock.** TSO No. 5410 at Exeter on 19th August 1988 in Netw
SouthEast livery. *John August*

▼ Corridor brake first (BFK) No. 17064 at Inverness on 26th September 19
John August

Mark 2C Stock. Regional Railways liveried TSO No. 5505 at Hartlepool on :h April 1992. *John Augustson*

Mark 2E Stock. TSO No. 5899 in InterCity livery at Carlisle on 22nd August ʔ2. *Kevin Conkey*

Network
13575
1
C1
AA1D

Mark 2F Stock. InterCity buffet open first (RFB) No. 1253 at Carlisle on 19th e 1992. *Kevin Conkey*

Driving open brake standard (DBSO) No. 9703 at Ipswich on the rear of the)5 Norwich – Liverpool Street on 13th September 1991. *John Augustson*

▲ **Mark 3 Stock.** HST trailer guards standard (TGS) No. 44045 at Newca
on 28th July 1992. *John August*

▼ **Mark 3A Stock.** TSO No. 12026 leaving Glasgow Central on 1st Au
1990. *John August*

Mark 3B Stock. Open brake first (BFO) No. 17174 at Carlisle on 7th March
)2. *John Augustson*

Mark 4 Stock. Restaurant buffet first (RFM) No. 10319 at Durham on 14th
y 1992. *John Augustson*

▲ FO No. 11245 at Durham on 14th May 1992. *John Augusts*

▼ **Non-passenger-carrying Coaching Stock.** Courier van No. 80221 in b
and grey livery at Newcastle on 18th August 1992. *John Augusts*

Mark 3 DVT No. 82127 heads the 14.25 Carlisle – Euston on 13th September
92. *Kevin Conkey*

Mark 4 DVT No. 82225 leaving Darlington at the head of a Newcastle – Kings
oss service on 1st May 1992. *John Augustson*

▲ NHA No. 92928 at York on 21st May 1992. *John Augusts*

▼ NCX No. 95229 in Rail Express Systems livery leaves Carlisle on the rea
the Edinburgh – Bristol vans on 10th July 1992. *Kevin Con*

Isle of Wight Class 483 units Nos. 483 004 & 438 008 leave Ryde Pier Head with a Shanklin service on 31st July 1992.
John Augustson

▲ Class 507 No. 507 005 pauses at Kirkdale on 13th October 1992 wit
Kirkby service. *Norman Barring*

▼ Class 508 No. 508 134 arrives at Kirkdale with a Liverpool Central serv
on 19th June 1992. *Hugh Ballant*

7505. DTSO. Dia. EE274. Lot No. 30115 Ashford/Eastleigh 1954. 92S. 30.5 t.
7513 – 77519. DTSO. Dia. EE274. Lot No. 30120 Ashford/Eastleigh 1954. 2S. 30.5 t.
7527 – 77551. DTSO. Dia. EE274. Lot No. 30168 Ashford/Eastleigh 1955. 2S. 30.5 t.
7553 – 77557. DTSO. Dia. EE274. Lot No. 30315 Ashford/Eastleigh 956 – 58. 92S. 30.5 t.

– Modified for working Maidstone service. Doors fitted between saloon and uards compartment in motor car and between saloon and cab in trailer. DMBSO eats 79S (dia. EB280) and DTSO seats 90S (dia. EE271).

401	*	**N**	NKSX	SG	65346	77531
402	*	**N**	NKSX	SG	65362	77547
403	*	**N**	NKSX	SG	65356	77541
404	*	**N**	NKSX	SG	65329	77514
405	*	**N**	NKSX	SG	65347	77532
406	*	**N**	NKSX	SG	65305	77505
407	*	**N**	NKSX	SG	65330	77515
408	*	**N**	NKSX	SG	65342	77527
409	*	**N**	NKSX	SG	65309	77113
410		**N**	NKSX	SG	65334	77519
411		**N**	NKSX	SG	65333	77518
412		**N**	NKSX	SG	65364	77549
413		**N**	NKSX	SG	65372	77557
414		**N**	NKSX	SG	65368	77553
415		**N**	NKSX	SG	65348	77533
416		**N**	NKSX	SG	65328	77513
417		**N**	NKSX	SG	65366	77551
418		**N**	NKSX	SG	65360	77545

:LASS 488 VICTORIA – GATWICK TRAILER SETS

FOLH – TSOL (Class 488/3 only) – TSOLH. Converted 1983 – 84 from loco-auled Mk. 2F FOs and TSOs for Victoria – Gatwick service. Express stock. Air onditioned. Fluorescent lighting. PA. Conversion consisted of a modified seating yout and the removal of one toilet to provide additional luggage space.

ogies: B4.
angways: Throughout.
imensions: 20.12 x 2.82 m.
laximum Speed: 90 mph.

2500 – 72509. TFOLH. Dia. EP101. Lot No. 30859 Derby 1973 – 74. 41F 1L. 5 t.
2602 – 72647. TSOLH. Dia. EP201. Lot No. 30860 Derby 1973 – 74. 48S L. 35 t.
2701 – 72718. TSOL. Dia. EH285. Lot No. 30860 Derby 1973 – 74. 48S 1L. 5 t.

LASS 488/2. Note: TFOLH fitted with public telephone.

201	I	IVGX	SL	72500 (3413)	72638 (6068)
202	I	IVGX	SL	72501 (3382)	72617 (6086)

8203	I	IVGX	SL	72502 (3321)	72640 (6097)
8204	I	IVGX	SL	72503 (3407)	72641 (6079)
8205	I	IVGX	SL	72504 (3406)	72628 (6058)
8206	I	IVGX	SL	72505 (3415)	72629 (6048)
8207	I	IVGX	SL	72506 (3335)	72642 (6076)
8208	I	IVGX	SL	72507 (3412)	72643 (6040)
8209	I	IVGX	SL	72508 (3409)	72644 (6039)
8210	I	IVGX	SL	72509 (3398)	72635 (6128)

CLASS 488/3. TSOLH – TSOL – TSOLH.

8302	I	IVGX	SL	72602 (6130)	72701 (6088)	72604 (6087)
8303	I	IVGX	SL	72603 (6093)	72702 (6099)	72608 (6077)
8304	I	IVGX	SL	72606 (6084)	72703 (6075)	72611 (6083)
8305	I	IVGX	SL	72605 (6082)	72704 (6132)	72609 (6080)
8306	I	IVGX	SL	72607 (6020)	72705 (6032)	72610 (6074)
8307	I	IVGX	SL	72612 (6156)	72706 (6143)	72613 (6126)
8308	I	IVGX	SL	72614 (6090)	72707 (6127)	72615 (5938)
8309	I	IVGX	SL	72616 (6007)	72708 (6095)	72639 (6070)
8310	I	IVGX	SL	72618 (6044)	72709 (5982)	72619 (5909)
8311	I	IVGX	SL	72620 (6140)	72710 (6003)	72621 (6108)
8312	I	IVGX	SL	72622 (6004)	72711 (6109)	72623 (6118)
8313	I	IVGX	SL	72624 (5972)	72712 (6091)	72625 (6085)
8314	I	IVGX	SL	72626 (6017)	72713 (6023)	72627 (5974)
8315	I	IVGX	SL	72636 (6071)	72714 (6092)	72645 (5942)
8316	I	IVGX	SL	72630 (6094)	72715 (6019)	72631 (6096)
8317	I	IVGX	SL	72632 (6072)	72716 (6114)	72633 (6129)
8318	I	IVGX	SL	72634 (6089)	72717 (6069)	72637 (6098)
8319	I	IVGX	SL	72646 (6078)	72718 (5979)	72647 (6081)

CLASS 489 VICTORIA – GATWICK GL

Converted 1983 – 84 from class 414/3 (2 Hap) DMBSOs to work with clas 488. **Bogies:** Mk 4.
Gangways: Gangwayed at inner end only.
Traction Motors: Two EE507 of 185 kW.
Dimensions: 19.49 x 2.82 m.
Maximum Speed: 90 mph.

DMLV. Dia. EX561. Lot No. 30452 Ashford/Eastleigh 1959. 40.5 t.

9101	I	IVGX	SL	68500 (61269)
9102	I	IVGX	SL	68501 (61281)
9103	I	IVGX	SL	68502 (61274)
9104	I	IVGX	SL	68503 (61277)
9105	I	IVGX	SL	68504 (61286)
9106	I	IVGX	SL	68505 (61299)
9107	I	IVGX	SL	68506 (61292)
9108	I	IVGX	SL	68507 (61267)
9109	I	IVGX	SL	68508 (61272)
9110	I	IVGX	SL	68509 (61280)

CLASS 456

DMSO – DTSO. Sliding doors. Disc brakes. Fluorescent lighting. PA.

Bogies: P7 (motor) and T3 trailer.
Gangways: Within set.
Traction Motors: Two EE507 of 185 kW.

Dimensions: 19.83 x 2.82 m.
Maximum Speed: 75 mph.

DMSO. Dia. EA267. Lot No. 31073 York 1990 – 1. 79S. 41.1 t.
DTSO. Dia. EE276. Lot No. 31074 York 1990 – 1. 51S. 31.4 t.

456 001	**N** NSLX	SU	64735	78250
456 002	**N** NSLX	SU	64736	78251
456 003	**N** NSLX	SU	64737	78252
456 004	**N** NSLX	SU	64738	78253
456 005	**N** NSLX	SU	64739	78254
456 006	**N** NSLX	SU	64740	78255
456 007	**N** NSLX	SU	64741	78256
456 008	**N** NSLX	SU	64742	78257
456 009	**N** NSLX	SU	64743	78258
456 010	**N** NSLX	SU	64744	78259
456 011	**N** NSLX	SU	64745	78260
456 012	**N** NSLX	SU	64746	78261
456 013	**N** NSLX	SU	64747	78262
456 014	**N** NSLX	SU	64748	78263
456 015	**N** NSLX	SU	64749	78264
456 016	**N** NSLX	SU	64750	78265
456 017	**N** NSLX	SU	64751	78266
456 018	**N** NSLX	SU	64752	78267
456 019	**N** NSLX	SU	64753	78268
456 020	**N** NSLX	SU	64754	78269
456 021	**N** NSLX	SU	64755	78270
456 022	**N** NSLX	SU	64756	78271
456 023	**N** NSLX	SU	64757	78272
456 024	**N** NSLX	SU	64758	78273

CLASS 465 NETWORKER

DMSO – TSO – TSOL – DMSO. New units with Aluminium bodies. Sliding doors. Disc, rheostatic and regenerative brakes. PA.

Electrical Equipment: Networker.
Bogies:
Gangways: Within set.
Traction Motors:
Dimensions:
Maximum Speed: 75 mph.

64759 – 64808. DMSO(A). Dia. EA268. Lot No. 31100 BREL York 1991 – 2. 86S. t.
64809 – 64858. DMSO(B). Dia. EA268. Lot No. 31100 BREL York 1991 – 2. 86S. t.
65700 – 65749. DMSO(A). Dia. EA269. Lot No. 31103 Metro-Cammell 1991 – 2. 86S. t.
65750 – 65799. DMSO(B). Dia. EA269. Lot No. 31103 Metro-Cammell 1991 – 2. 86S. t.
72028 – 72126 (even Nos.). TSO. Dia. EH293. Lot No. 31102 BREL York 1991 – 2. 86S. t.

72029 – 72127 (odd Nos.). TSOL. Dia. EH292. Lot No. 31101 BREL York 1991 – 2. 86S. t.
72719 – 72817 (odd Nos.). TSOL. Dia. EH294. Lot No. 31104 Metro-Cammell 1991 – 2. 86S. t.
72720 – 72818 (even Nos.). TSO. Dia. EH295. Lot No. 31105 Metro-Cammell 1991 – 2. 86S. t.

Class 465/0. Built by ABB.

465 001	**N**	NKSX	SG	64759	72028	72029	64809
465 002	**N**	NKSX	SG	64760	72030	72031	64810
465 003	**N**	NKSX	SG	64761	72032	72033	64811
465 004	**N**	NKSX	SG	64762	72034	72035	64812
465 005	**N**	NKSX	SG	64763	72036	72037	64813
465 006	**N**	NKSX	SG	64764	72038	72039	64814
465 007	**N**	NKSX	SG	64765	72040	72041	64815
465 008	**N**	NKSX	SG	64766	72042	72043	64816
465 009	**N**	NKSX		64767	72044	72045	64817
465 010	**N**	NKSX		64768	72046	72047	64818
465 011	**N**	NKSX		64769	72048	72049	64819
465 012	**N**	NKSX		64770	72050	72051	64820
465 013	**N**	NKSX		64771	72052	72053	64821
465 014	**N**	NKSX		64772	72054	72055	64822
465 015	**N**	NKSX		64773	72056	72057	64823
465 016	**N**	NKSX		64774	72058	72059	64824
465 017	**N**	NKSX		64775	72060	72061	64825
465 018	**N**	NKSX		64776	72062	72063	64826
465 019	**N**	NKSX		64777	72064	72065	64827
465 020	**N**	NKSX		64778	72066	72067	64828
465 021	**N**	NKSX		64779	72068	72069	64829
465 022	**N**	NKSX		64780	72070	72071	64830
465 023	**N**	NKSX		64781	72072	72073	64831
465 024	**N**	NKSX		64782	72074	72075	64832
465 025	**N**	NKSX		64783	72076	72077	64833
465 026	**N**	NKSX		64784	72078	72079	64834
465 027	**N**	NKSX		64785	72080	72081	64835
465 028	**N**	NKSX		64786	72082	72083	64836
465 029	**N**	NKSX		64787	72084	72085	64837
465 030	**N**	NKSX		64788	72086	72087	64838
465 031	**N**	NKSX		64789	72088	72089	64839
465 032	**N**	NKSX		64790	72090	72091	64840
465 033	**N**	NKSX		64791	72092	72093	64841
465 034	**N**	NKSX		64792	72094	72095	64842
465 035	**N**	NKSX		64793	72096	72097	64843
465 036	**N**	NKSX		64794	72098	72099	64844
465 037	**N**	NKSX		64795	72100	72101	64845
465 038	**N**	NKSX		64796	72102	72103	64846
465 039	**N**	NKSX		64797	72104	72105	64847
465 040	**N**	NKSX		64798	72106	72107	64848
465 041	**N**	NKSX		64799	72108	72109	64849
465 042	**N**	NKSX		64800	72110	72111	64850
465 043	**N**	NKSX		64801	72112	72113	64851
465 044	**N**	NKSX		64802	72114	72115	64852

465 045	N	NKSX		64803	72116	72117	64853
465 046	N	NKSX		64804	72118	72119	64854
465 047	N	NKSX		64805	72120	72121	64855
465 048	N	NKSX		64806	72122	72123	64856
465 049	N	NKSX		64807	72124	72125	64857
465 050	N	NKSX		64808	72126	72127	64858

Class 465/2. Built by Metro-Cammell.

465 201	N	NKSX	SG	65700	72719	72720	65750
465 202	N	NKSX	SG	65701	72721	72722	65751
465 203	N	NKSX	SG	65702	72723	72724	65752
465 204	N	NKSX	SG	65703	72725	72726	65753
465 205	N	NKSX	SG	65704	72727	72728	65754
465 206	N	NKSX	SG	65705	72729	72730	65755
465 207	N	NKSX	SG	65706	72731	72732	65756
465 208	N	NKSX	SG	65707	72733	72734	65757
465 209	N	NKSX	SG	65708	72735	72736	65758
465 210	N	NKSX	SG	65709	72737	72738	65759
465 211	N	NKSX	SG	65710	72739	72740	65760
465 212	N	NKSX	SG	65711	72741	72742	65761
465 213	N	NKSX	SG	65712	72743	72744	65762
465 214	N	NKSX	SG	65713	72745	72746	65763
465 215	N	NKSX	SG	65714	72747	72748	65764
465 216	N	NKSX	SG	65715	72749	72750	65765
465 217	N	NKSX	SG	65716	72751	72752	65766
465 218	N	NKSX	SG	65717	72753	72754	65767
465 219	N	NKSX	SG	65718	72755	72756	65768
465 220	N	NKSX	SG	65719	72757	72758	65769
465 221	N	NKSX		65720	72759	72760	65770
465 222	N	NKSX		65721	72761	72762	65771
465 223	N	NKSX		65722	72763	72764	65772
465 224	N	NKSX		65723	72765	72766	65773
465 225	N	NKSX		65724	72767	72768	65774
465 226	N	NKSX		65725	72769	72770	65775
465 227	N	NKSX		65726	72771	72772	65776
465 228	N	NKSX		65727	72773	72774	65777
465 229	N	NKSX		65728	72775	72776	65778
465 230	N	NKSX		65729	72777	72778	65779
465 231	N	NKSX		65730	72779	72780	65780
465 232	N	NKSX		65731	72781	72782	65781
465 233	N	NKSX		65732	72783	72784	65782
465 234	N	NKSX		65733	72785	72786	65783
465 235	N	NKSX		65734	72787	72788	65784
465 236	N	NKSX		65735	72789	72790	65785
465 237	N	NKSX		65736	72791	72792	65786
465 238	N	NKSX		65737	72793	72794	65787
465 239	N	NKSX		65738	72795	72796	65788
465 240	N	NKSX		65739	72797	72798	65789
465 241	N	NKSX		65740	72799	72800	65790
465 242	N	NKSX		65741	72801	72802	65791
465 243	N	NKSX		65742	72803	72804	65792
465 244	N	NKSX		65743	72805	72806	65793

465 245	N	NKSX	65744 72807 72808 65794
465 246	N	NKSX	65745 72809 72810 65795
465 247	N	NKSX	65746 72811 72812 65796
465 248	N	NKSX	65747 72813 72814 65797
465 249	N	NKSX	65748 72815 72816 65798
465 250	N	NKSX	65749 72817 72818 65799

CLASS 466 NETWORKER

DMSO – DTSO. New units with Aluminium bodies. Sliding doors. Disc, rheostatic and regenerative brakes. PA.

Electrical Equipment: Networker.
Bogies:
Gangways: Within set.
Traction Motors:
Dimensions:
Maximum Speed: 75 mph.

DMSO. Dia. EA271. Lot No. 31128 Metro-Cammell 1992 – 3. 86S. t.
DTSO. Dia. EE279. Lot No. 31129 Metro-Cammell 1991 – 2. 82S. t.

466 001	N	NKSX	64860 78312
466 002	N	NKSX	64861 78313
466 003	N	NKSX	64862 78314
466 004	N	NKSX	64863 78315
466 005	N	NKSX	64864 78316
466 006	N	NKSX	64865 78317
466 007	N	NKSX	64866 78318
466 008	N	NKSX	64867 78319
466 009	N	NKSX	64868 78320
466 010	N	NKSX	64869 78321
466 011	N	NKSX	64870 78322
466 012	N	NKSX	64871 78323
466 013	N	NKSX	64872 78324
466 014	N	NKSX	64873 78325
466 015	N	NKSX	64874 78326
466 016	N	NKSX	64875 78327
466 017	N	NKSX	64876 78328
466 018	N	NKSX	64877 78329
466 019	N	NKSX	64878 78330
466 020	N	NKSX	64879 78331
466 021	N	NKSX	64880 78332
466 022	N	NKSX	64881 78333
466 023	N	NKSX	64882 78334
466 024	N	NKSX	64883 78335
466 025	N	NKSX	64884 78336
466 026	N	NKSX	64885 78337
466 027	N	NKSX	64886 78338
466 028	N	NKSX	64887 78339
466 029	N	NKSX	64888 78340
466 030	N	NKSX	64889 78341
466 031	N	NKSX	64890 78342

466 032	**N**	NKSX	64891	78343
466 033	**N**	NKSX	64892	78344
466 034	**N**	NKSX	64893	78345
466 035	**N**	NKSX	64894	78346
466 036	**N**	NKSX	64895	78347
466 037	**N**	NKSX	64896	78348
466 038	**N**	NKSX	64897	78349
466 039	**N**	NKSX	64898	78350
466 040	**N**	NKSX	64899	78351
466 041	**N**	NKSX	64900	78352
466 042	**N**	NKSX	64901	78353
466 043	**N**	NKSX	64902	78354

4.3. SOUTHERN REGION TUBE STOCK

These classes are tube stock used on the Isle of Wight or for the Waterloo and City line in London (known colloquially as the ''Drain'').

CLASS 482 NEW WATERLOO & CITY STOCK

DMSO – MSO. Built 1983. New sets under construction. Aluminium bodies. Fluorescent lighting. Run as pairs of sets.

System: 630 V d.c. third rail.
Gangways:
Traction Motors:
Dimensions:
Maximum Speed: 60 mph.

DMSO. Dia. E . ABB Derby 1993. 36S. t.
MSO. Dia. E . ABB Derby 1993. 36S. t.

482 051	**N**	NKSX	65501	67501
482 052	**N**	NKSX	65502	67502
482 053	**N**	NKSX	65503	67503
482 054	**N**	NKSX	65504	67504
482 055	**N**	NKSX	65505	67505
482 056	**N**	NKSX	65506	67506
482 057	**N**	NKSX	65507	67507
482 058	**N**	NKSX	65508	67508

CLASS 483 'NEW' ISLE OF WIGHT STOCK

DMBSO(A) – DMBSO(B). Built 19 for LTE. Converted 1989 – 90 for Isle of Wight Line. Sliding doors. End doors. dg. pa. Former London Underground numbers are shown in parentheses.

System: 660 V d.c. third rail.
Gangways: Non-gangwayed.
Traction Motors: Two of 130 kW.
Dimensions: 15.95 x 2.69 m.
Maximum Speed: 45 mph.

DMSO (A). Lot No. 31071. Dia. EA265. 42S. 27.5 t.
DMSO (B). Lot No. 31072. Dia. EA266. 42S. 27.5 t.

483 001	**N**	NSSX	RY	121	(10184)	221	(11184)
483 002	**N**	NSSX	RY	122	(10221)	222	(11221)
483 003	**N**	NSSX	RY	123	(10116)	223	(11116)
483 004	**N**	NSSX	RY	124	(10205)	224	(11205)
483 005	**N**	NSSX	RY	125	(10142)	225	(11142)
483 006	**N**	NSSX	RY	126	(10297)	226	(11297)
483 007	**N**	NSSX	RY	127	(10291)	227	(11291)
483 008	**N**	NSSX	RY	128	(10255)	228	(11255)
483 009	**N**	NSSX	RY	129	(10289)	229	(11229)

CLASSES 485 & 486 ISLE OF WIGHT STOCK

DMBSO – 2TSO – DTSO. Built 1923 – 31 for London Electric Railway (later LT). Converted 1967 for Isle of Wight Line. Sliding doors. End doors. Former London Underground numbers are shown in parentheses. Deicing unit.

System: 660 V d.c. third rail.
Gangways: Non-gangwayed.
Traction Motors: Two EE507 of 178 kW.
Dimensions: 15.16 x 2.64 m.
Maximum Speed: 45 mph.

DMBSO. Dia. EB261. Metro-Cammell 1932 – 5. 26S. 32 t.
TSO. Dia. EH261. Cammell-Laird 1924. 42S. 19 t.
DTSO. Dia. EE260. Metro-Cammell 1926 – 9. 38S. 17 t.

485 **N** NXXZ RY 5 (3185) 31 (5283) 28 (5304)

CLASS 487 WATERLOO & CITY

Built 1940. Do not run in permanent sets. Run as single motor cars or as pairs of motors with up to three trailers in between.

System: 630 V d.c. third rail.
Gangways: Non-gangwayed. End doors.
Traction Motors: Two EE500 of 140 kW.
Dimensions: 14.33 x 2.64 m.
Maximum Speed: 35 mph.

DMBSO. Dia. EB260. English Electric 1940. 40S. 29 t.
TSO. Dia. EH260. English Electric 1940. 52S. 19 t.

DMBSO

51 **N** NKSX WC
53 **N** NKSX WC
54 **N** NKSX WC
56 **N** NKSX WC
57 **N** NKSX WC
59 **N** NKSX WC
60 **N** NKSX WC
61 **N** NKSX WC
62 **N** NKSX WC

TSO

72 **N** NKSX WC
73 **N** NKSX WC
74 **N** NKSX WC
75 **N** NKSX WC
76 **N** NKSX WC
77 **N** NKSX WC
78 **N** NKSX WC
80 **N** NKSX WC
81 **N** NKSX WC
83 **N** NKSX WC
84 **N** NKSX WC
85 **N** NKSX WC
86 **N** NKSX WC

MERSEYRAIL 750 V d.c. EMUs

CLASS 507

BDMSO – TSO – DMSO. Tightlock couplers. Sliding doors. Disc and rheostatic brakes. PA.

System: 750 V d.c. third rail.
Bogies: BX1.
Gangways: Gangwayed within unit. End doors.
Traction Motors: Four GEC G310AZ of 82.125 kW.
Dimensions: 19.80 x 2.82 m (outer cars), 19.92 x 2.82 m (inner cars).
Maximum Speed: 75 mph.

BDMSO. Dia. EI202. Lot No. 30906 York 1978 – 80. 74S. 37.06 t.
TSO. Dia. EH205. Lot No. 30907 York 1978 – 80. 82S. 25.60 t.
DMSO. Dia. EA201. Lot No. 30908 York 1978 – 80. 74S. 35.62 t.

507 001		RCHR	HR	64367	71342	64405
507 002		RCHR	HR	64368	71343	64406
507 003		RCHR	HR	64369	71344	64407
507 004		RCHR	HR (S)	64388	71345	64426
507 005		RCHR	HR	64371	71346	64409
507 006		RCHR	HR	64372	71347	64410
507 007		RCHR	HR	64373	71348	64411
507 008		RCHR	HR	64374	71349	64412
507 009		RCHR	HR	64375	71350	64413
507 010		RCHR	HR	64376	71351	64414
507 011		RCHR	HR	64377	71352	64415
507 012		RCHR	HR	64378	71353	64416
507 013	**MT**	RCHR	HR	64379	71354	64417
507 014	**MT**	RCHR	HR	64380	71355	64418
507 015		RCHR	HR	64381	71356	64419
507 016		RCHR	HR	64382	71357	64420
507 017		RCHR	HR	64383	71358	64421
507 018		RCHR	HR	64384	71359	64422
507 019		RCHR	HR	64385	71360	64423
507 020	**MT**	RCHR	HR	64386	71361	64424
507 021	**MT**	RCHR	HR	64387	71362	64425
507 022		RFXX	HR (S)	64370	71363	64408
507 023		RCHR	HR	64389	71364	64427
507 024		RCHR	HR	64390	71365	64428
507 025		RCHR	HR	64391	71366	64429
507 026		RCHR	HR	64392	71367	64430
507 027		RCHR	HR	64393	71368	64431
507 028	**MT**	RCHR	HR	64394	71369	64432
507 029		RCHR	HR	64395	71370	64433
507 030		RCHR	HR	64396	71371	64434
507 031		RCHR	HR	64397	71372	64435
507 032		RCHR	HR	64398	71373	64436
507 033		RCHR	HR	64399	71374	64437

:LASS 508

MSO – TSO – BDMSO. Tightlock couplers. Sliding doors. Disc and rheostatic 'akes. PA. Originally built as four car units and numbered 508 001 – 043. One ailer removed and used for class 455/7 on transfer from the SR.

ystem: 750 V d.c. third rail.
ogies: BX1.
angways: Gangwayed within unit. End doors.
raction Motors: Four GEC G310AZ of 82.125 kW.
imensions: 19.80 x 2.82 m (outer cars), 19.92 x 2.82 m (inner cars).
aximum Speed: 75 mph.

4649 – 64691. DMSO. Dia. EA208. Lot No. 30979 York 1979 – 80. 74S. 6.15 t.
1483 – 71525. TSO. Dia. EH218. Lot No. 30980 York 1979 – 80. 82S. 26.72

4692 – 64734. BDMSO. Dia. EI203. Lot No. 30981 York 1979 – 80. 74S. 6.61 t.

08 101		RCBD	BD	64649	71483	64692
08 102		RCBD	BD	64650	71484	64693
08 103	**MT**	RCBD	BD	64651	71485	64694
08 104		RCBD	BD	64652	71486	64695
08 105		RCBD	BD (S)	64653	71487	64696
08 106		RCBD	BD (S)	64654	71488	64697
08 107		RCBD	BD	64655	71489	64698
08 108		RCBD	BD	64656	71490	64699
08 109		RCBD	BD (S)	64657	71491	64700
08 110		RCBD	BD	64658	71492	64701
08 111		RCBD	BD	64659	71493	64702
08 112		RCBD	BD	64660	71494	64703
08 113		RCBD	BD	64661	71495	64704
08 114	**MT**	RCBD	BD	64662	71496	64705
08 115		RCBD	BD	64663	71497	64706
08 116		RCBD	BD	64664	71498	64707
08 117		RCBD	BD	64665	71499	64708
08 118		RCBD	BD	64666	71500	64709
08 119		RCBD	BD	64667	71501	64710
08 120		RCBD	BD	64668	71502	64711
08 121		RCBD	BD	64669	71503	64712
08 122		RCBD	BD	64670	71504	64713
08 123		RCBD	BD	64671	71505	64714
08 124		RCBD	BD	64672	71506	64715
08 125		RCBD	BD	64673	71507	64716
08 126		RCBD	BD	64674	71508	64717
08 127		RCBD	BD	64675	71509	64718
08 128		RCBD	BD	64676	71510	64719
08 129		RCBD	BD	64677	71511	64720
08 130		RCBD	BD	64678	71512	64721
08 131		RCBD	BD	64679	71513	64722
08 132		RCBD	BD	64680	71514	64723
08 133		RCBD	BD	64681	71515	64724

508 134	RCBD	BD	64682	71516	64725
508 135	RCBD	BD	64683	71517	64726
508 136	RCBD	BD	64684	71518	64727
508 137	RCBD	BD	64685	71519	64728
508 138	RCBD	BD	64686	71520	64729
508 139	RCHR	HR	64687	71521	64730
508 140	RCHR	HR	64688	71522	64731
508 141	RCHR	HR	64689	71523	64732
508 142	RCHR	HR	64690	71524	64733
508 143	RCHR	HR	64691	71525	64734

4.5. DEPARTMENTAL EMUs

Denotes departmental numbers not carried.

Individual vehicles.

ADB 975032	(75165)	SH	SR class 932 experimental stock. 'Mars'.
DB 977335	(76277)	ZA	MTA Pool Generator coach for DB999550.
ADB 977362	(10392)	SU	SR class 930 deicing trailer.
ADB 977364	(10400)	SU	SR class 930 deicing trailer.
ADB 977578	(77101)	HE	Sandite car. (work with Class 317/319).
ADB 977579	(77109)	SU	Sandite car. (work with Class 317/319).
ADB 977601	(75211)	IL	Sandite car.
DB 999602	(62483)	ZA	Ultrasonic test train instrumentation car. MTA pool.

Complete Units

750 V d.c. Class 930 De-icing and Sandite units.

930 003	SU	ADB	975594 (12658)	ADB	975595 (10994)
930 004	EH	ADB	975586 (10907)	ADB	975587 (10908)
930 005	WD	ADB	975588 (10981)	ADB	975589 (10982)
930 006	WD	ADB	975590 (10833)	ADB	975591 (10834)
930 007	GI	ADB	975592 (10993)	ADB	975593 (12659)
930 008	AF	ADB	975596 (10844)	ADB	975597 (10987)
930 009	BI	ADB	975598 (10989)	ADB	975599 (10990)
930 010	BI	ADB	975600 (10988)	ADB	975601 (10843)
930 011	RE	ADB	975602 (10991)	ADB	975603 (10992)
930 012	BM	ADB	975604 (10939)	ADB	975605 (10940)
930 013	RE	ADB	975896 (11387)	ADB	975897 (11388)
930 014	EH	ADB	977609 (65414)	ADB	977207 (61658)
930 015	WD	ADB	977531 (14047)	ADB	977532 (14048)
930 016	AF	ADB	977533 (14273)	ADB	977534 (14384)
930 017	EH	ADB	977566 (65312)	ADB	977567 (65314)
930 030	AF		977804 (65336)		977805 (65357)

750 V d.c. Class 931 Carriage Cleaning Fluid Unit:

931 062	SG	ADB	977559 (65313)	ADB	977560 (65320)

750 V d.c. Class 932 Tractor Units:

932 021	WD	ADB	977304 (65317)	ADB	977305 (65322)
932 080*	SL	ADB	977395 (61035)	ADB	977396 (61392)
932 081*	SL	ADB	977397 (61388)	ADB	977398 (61389)

750 V d.c. Test Units:

932 050	SH	ADB	977296 (65319)	ADB	977297 (77108)
930 053	SH	ADB	977505 (65321)	ADB	977507 (77110)
930 054	SH	ADB	977506 (65323)	ADB	977508 (77112)

DEPARTMENTAL EMUS

Class 438 6 TC Unit:

8007	SL	ADB	977684 (76282)	ADB 977685 (70818)
		ADB	977763 (70871)	ADB 977764 (70866)
		ADB	977686 (70850)	ADB 977687 (76281)

Class 302 three-car Sandite Units:

937 996	CC	ADB	977598 (75080)	ADB 977599 (61073)
		ADB	977600 (75061)	Carries 302 996
937 998	EM	ADB	977604 (75077)	ADB 977605 (61056)
		ADB	977606 (75070)	Carries 302 998
305 908	IL	ADB	977741 (75469)	ADB 977742 (61436)
		ADB	977743 (75521)	

Demonstration Unit:

303 999	CC	TDB	977711 (75759)	TDB 977712 (61825)
		TDB	977713 (75815)	

InterCity Instruction Unit:

305 935	HQ	ADB	977639 (75548)	ADB 977640 (61463)
		ADB	977641 (75214)	

Note: 977641 of 305 935 is a former Class 302 car.

Test unit awaiting conversion.

316 999*	ZA		977708 (75018)	977709 (61018)
			977710 (75118)	

Merseyrail Sandite Units:

936 001	BD	ADB	977345 (61178)	ADB 977346 (75178)
936 002	BD	ADB	977347 (61180)	ADB 977348 (75180)
936 003	BD	ADB	977349 (61183)	ADB 977350 (75183)

Emergency training units.

930 997	SG		977777 (14303)	977778 (15230)
			977779 (15285)	977780 (14356)

Note: Most units do not carry '93x' numbers.

CLASS 419 1957 type MLV

DMLV. Built 1959 – 61. Dual braked.These units are now officially in departmental stock, but they retain their capital stock side numbers.

Electrical Equipment: 1957-type.
Bogies: Mk 3B.
Gangways: Non-gangwayed.
Traction Motors: Two EE507 of 185 kW.
Dimensions: 19.64 x 2.82 m.
Maximum Speed: 90 mph.

68001 – 2. DMLV. Dia. EX560. Lot No. 30458 Ashford./Eastleigh. 1959. 45.5 t.
68003 – 10. DMLV. Dia. EX560. Lot No. 30623 Ashford./Eastleigh. 1960 – 61. 45.5 t.

931090	(9010)	**J**	NBTX	RE	68010
931091	(9001)	**N**	NBTX	RE	68001
931092	(9002)	**N**	NBTX	RE	68002
931093	(9003)	**N**	NBTX	RE	68003
931094	(9004)	**N**	NBTX	RE	68004
931095	(9005)	**N**	NBTX	RE	68005
931096	(9006)	**J**	NBTX	RE	68006
931097	(9007)	**N**	NBTX	RE	68007
931098	(9008)	**N**	NBTX	RE	68008
931099	(9009)	**N**	NBTX	RE	68009

5. NON-PASSENGER-CARRYING COACHING STOCK

Please note that in this section, that where vehicles have been renumbered more than once, both the original number and the most recent former number are shown in brackets (except when the original number can easily be deduced).

AK51 (RK) KITCHEN CAR

Dia. AK503. Mark 1. Gas cooking. Converted from RBR. Fluorescent lighting. xd*. ETH 2X.

Note: Kitchen cars have traditionally been numbered in the NPCCS series, but have passenger coach diagram numbers!

Lot No. 30628 Pressed Steel 1960 – 61. 39 t.

80041 (1690)	**I**	ICHV	BN

NN COURIER VEHICLE

Dia. NN504. Converted 1986 – 7 from Mark 1 BSKs. One compartment retained for courier use. Roller shutter doors. xd. ETH 2.

80204 – 6/8/11 – 14/16 – 17/21 – 23/25. Lot No. 30699 Wolverton 1962. Commonwealth bogies. 37 t.
80203/9 – 10/15/20/24. Lot No. 30573 Gloucester 1960. B4 bogies. 35 t.
80218. Lot No. 30427 Wolverton 1958 – 9. B4 bogies. ETH 2. 35 t.
80219. Lot No. 31027 Wolverton 1958. B4 bogies. ETH 2. 35 t.

80204 (35297)	**P**	P	HT
80206 (35304)	**P**	P	OM
80207 (35466)	**P**	P	HT
80208 (35341)	**P**	P	NC
80211 (35296)	**P**	P	HT
80212 (35307)	**RX**	P	CA
80213 (35316)	**P**	P	OM
80214 (35323)	**P**	P	HT
80215 (35292)	**P**	P	MA
80216 (35295)	**R**	P	MA
80217 (35299)		P	CA
80218 (35197)		P	HT
80219 (35201)		P	CA
80220 (35276)	**P**	P	HT
80221 (35328)		P	HT
80222 (35315)	**P**	P	OM
80223 (35331)	**P**	P	EC
80224 (35291)		P	MA
80225 (35327)	**P**	P	HT

NPX POST OFFICE GUV

Dia. NP502. Converted 1991 onwards from newspaper vans. Mark 1. Short frames (57'). Originally converted from GUV. Fluorescent lighting, toilets and gangways fitted. Load 14 t. ETH 3X. These vehicles were originally renumbered 85500 – 85534. xd. B5 bogies.

Lot No. 30922 Wolverton or Doncaster 1977 – 8. xe. 31 t (33 t*).

80250 (94008)	**P**	P	OM
80251 (94017)	**P**	P	OM
80252 (94022)	**P**	P	OM
80253 (94018)	**P**	P	OM
80254 (94012)	**P**	P	OM
80255 (94019)	**P**	P	OM

80256 (94013)	**P**	P	OM	
80257 ( )				
80258 ( )				
80259 ( )				

NS (POS) POST OFFICE SORTING VAN

Used in travelling post office (TPO) trains. Mark 1. Various diagrams.

The following lots are vd and have Mark 1 bogies except * – B5 bogies. xd. (subtract 2 t from weight).

80300 – 80305. Lot No. 30486 Wolverton 1959. Dia. NS501. Originally built with nets for collecting mail bags in motion. Equipment now removed. ETH 3X. 36 t.
80306 – 80308. Lot No. 30487 Wolverton 1959. Dia. NS502. ETH 3. 36 t.
80309 – 80314. Lot No. 30661 Wolverton 1961. Dia. NS501. ETH 3. 37 t.
80315 – 80316. Lot No. 30662 Wolverton 1961. Dia. NS501. ETH 3X. 36 t.
80318. Lot No. 30663 Wolverton 1961. Dia. NS501. ETH 3X. 35 t.

80300		**P**	P	MA
80301		**P**	P	MA
80303	*	**P**	P	HT
80305		**P**	P	NC
80306		**P**	P	CA
80308	*	**P**	P	HT
80309	*	**P**	P	HT
80310		**P**	P	NC
80312		**P**	P	NC
80313		**P**	P	NC
80314	*	**P**	P	HT
80315		**P**	P	NC
80316	*	**P**	P	EC
80318	*	**P**	P	HT

The following lots are pressure ventilated and have B5 bogies. xd. ETH4.

80319 – 80327. Dia. NS504. Lot No. 30778 York 1968 – 9. xd. ETH 4. 35 t.
80328 – 80338. Dia. NS505. Lot No. 30779 York 1968 – 9. xd. ETH 4. 35 t.
80339 – 80355. Dia. NS506. Lot No. 30780 York 1968 – 9. xd. ETH 4. 35 t.

80319	**P**	P	CA
80320	**P**	P	CA
80321	**P**	P	CA
80322	**P**	P	CA
80323	**P**	P	HT
80324	**P**	P	HT
80325	**P**	P	DY
80326	**P**	P	DY
80327	**P**	P	DY
80328	**P**	P	EN
80329	**P**	P	MA
80330	**P**	P	HT
80331	**P**	P	HT
80332	**P**	P	HT
80333	**P**	P	HT
80334	**P**	P	MA
80335	**P**	P	HT
80336	**P**	P	HT
80337	**P**	P	HT
80338	**P**	P	EN
80339	**P**	P	EN
80340	**P**	P	MA
80341	**P**	P	EN
80342	**P**	P	EN
80343	**P**	P	MA
80344	**P**	P	EN
80345	**P**	P	HT
80346	**P**	P	HT
80347	**P**	P	EN
80348	**P**	P	EN
80349	**P**	P	DY
80350	**P**	P	HT
80351	**P**	P	DY
80352	**P**	P	HT
80353	**P**	P	EN
80354	**P**	P	EN
80355	**P**	P	MA

Name: 80320 The Borders Mail

80356 – 80380. Lot No. 30839 York 1972 – 3. Dia. NS501. Pressure ventilated. Fluorescent lighting. B5 bogies. xd. ETH 4X. 37 t.

80356	**P**	P	EN
80357	**P**	P	EN
80358	**P**	P	HT
80359	**P**	P	HT
80360	**P**	P	HT
80361	**P**	P	HT
80362	**P**	P	HT
80363	**P**	P	HT
80364	**P**	P	HT
80365	**P**	P	HT
80366	**P**	P	EN
80367	**P**	P	EN
80368	**P**	P	EN
80369	**P**	P	EN
80370	**P**	P	EN
80371	**P**	P	EN
80372	**P**	P	EN
80373	**P**	P	EN
80374	**P**	P	MA
80375	**P**	P	MA
80376	**P**	P	EN
80377	**P**	P	EN
80378	**P**	P	EN
80379	**P**	P	OM
80380	**P**	P	MA

80381 – 80395. Lot No. 30900 Wolverton 1977. Dia NS531. Converted from SK. Pressure ventilated. Fluorescent lighting. B5 bogies. xd. ETH 4X. 38 t.

80381	(25112)	**P**	P	OM
80382	(25109)	**P**	P	OM
80383	(25033)	**P**	P	OM
80384	(25078)	**P**	P	OM
80385	(25083)	**P**	P	OM
80386	(25099)	**P**	P	OM
80387	(25045)	**P**	P	OM
80388	(25088)	**P**	P	OM
80389	(25103)	**P**	P	OM
80390	(25047)	**P**	P	OM
80391	(25089)	**P**	P	OM
80392	(25082)	**P**	P	OM
80393	(25118)	**P**	P	OM
80394	(25156)	**P**	P	OM
80395	(25056)	**P**	P	MA

NT (POT) POST OFFICE STOWAGE VAN

Mark 1. Open vans used for stowage of mail bags in conjunction with POS. Various diagrams.

Lot No. 30488 Wolverton 1959. Dia. NT502. Originally built with nets for collecting mail bags in motion. Equipment now removed. B5 bogies. xd. ETH 3. 35 t.

80400	**P**	P	EN
80401	**P**	P	EN
80402	**P**	P	EN

The following twelve vehicles were converted at York from BSK to lot 30143 (80403) and 30229 (80404 – 80414). No new lot number was issued. Dia. NT503. B5 bogies. xd. 35 t. (*dia. NT501 BR2 bogies 38 t. ETH 3 (3X*).

80403	(34361)	**P**	P	MA
80404	(35014)	**P**	P	MA
80405	(35009)	**P**	P	MA
80406	(35022)	**P**	P	MA
80411	(35003)	***P**	P	CA
80412	(35002)	***P**	P	MA
80413	(35004)	***P**	P	CA
80414	(35005)	***P**	P	MA

Lot No. 30781 York 1968. Dia. NT505. Pressure ventilated. B5 bogies. xd. ETH 4. 34 t.

80415	**P**	P	EN
80416	**P**	P	EN
80417	**P**	P	EN
80418	**P**	P	EN
80419	**P**	P	EN
80420	**P**	P	HT
80421	**P**	P	HT
80422	**P**	P	HT
80423	**P**	P	CA
80424	**P**	P	EN

Lot No. 30840 York 1973. Dia. NT504. Pressure ventilated. fluorescent lighting. B5 bogies. xd. ETH 4X. 35 t.

80425	**P**	P	EN	80428	**P**	P	EN
80426	**P**	P	HT	80429	**P**	P	EN
80427	**P**	P	HT	80430	**P**	P	EN

Lot No. 30901 Wolverton 1977. converted from SK. Dia. NT521. Pressure ventilated. Fluorescent lighting. B5 bogies. xd. ETH 4X. 35 t.

80431	(25104)	**P**	P	DY	80436	(25077)	**P**	P	OM
80432	(25071)	**P**	P	HT	80437	(25068)	**P**	P	OM
80433	(25150)	**P**	P	HT	80438	(25139)	**P**	P	DY
80434	(25119)	**P**	P	HT	80439	(25127)	**P**	P	DY
80435	(25117)	**P**	P	OM					

NU (BPOT) BRAKE POST OFFICE STOWAGE VAN

As NT but with brake. Mark 1.

Lot No. 30782 York 1968. Dia. NU502. Pressure ventilated. B5 bogies. xd. ETH 4. 36 t.

80456	**P**	P	EN	80458	**P**	P	EN
80457	**P**	P	EN				

NB/NC/ND (BG) GANGWAYED BRAKE VAN (90 mph)

These vans are built on short frames (57′). Load 10t. BR1 bogies. There are a number of variants:

NDV or NDX (x) (Dia ND501). BG dual heated. ETH 1 (1X*).
NBV (b) (Dia. NB501). High security letter mail van. Converted at WB from BG 1985. Gangways removed. vd. 84382/7/461/77 formerly renumbered 80460 – 3, but since given original number to prevent identification by potential train robbers!
NCV (c) (Dia. NC501). Newspaper packing van. Fluorescent lighting. ETH 3X. Not now used for newspapers.

80501 – 80529. Lot No. 30009 Derby 1952 – 3. 31 t.
80537 – 80565. Lot No. 30039 Derby 1954. 31 t.
80570 – 80596. Lot No. 30040 Wolverton 1954 – 5. 32 t.
80597 – 80671. Lot No. 30046 York 1954. 31.5 t.
80672 – 80724. Lot No. 30136 Metro-Cammell 1955. 31.5 t.
80726 – 80802. Lot No. 30140 BRCW 1955 – 6. 31.5 t.
80803 – 80852. Lot No. 30144 Cravens 1955. 31.5 t.
80855 – 80962. Lot No. 30162 Pressed Steel 1956 – 7. 32 t.
80965 – 80999. Lot No. 30173 York 1956. 31.5 t.

80592	*		P	BK	80782	c*	**B**	P	BK
80654	*		P	BK	80794	c*		P	BK
80709	*		P	BK	80886	x*		P	BK
80730			NXXZ	BK	80889	x*	**P**	P	BK
80768	c*	**B**	P	BK	80926	x		P	BK
80775	c*	**B**	P	BK	80976	*		P	BK

NZ (DLV) DRIVING BRAKE VAN (110 mph)

Dia. NZ501. Mark 3B. Air conditioned. T4 bogies. ae. dg. Cab to shore communication. ETH 5X.

Lot No. 31042 Derby 1988. 45.18 t.

82101	I	IWCX	MA
82102	I	IWCX	OY
82103	I	IWCX	OY
82104	I	IWCX	PC
82105	I	IWCX	OY
82106	I	IWCX	PC
82107	I	IWCX	PC
82108	I	IWCX	WB
82109	I	IWCX	MA
82110	I	IWCX	WB
82111	I	IWCX	PC
82112	I	IWCX	WB
82113	I	IWCX	OY
82114	I	IWCX	WB
82115	I	IWCX	WB
82116	I	IWCX	WB
82117	I	IWCX	MA
82118	I	IWCX	WB
82119	I	IWCX	WB
82120	I	IWCX	WB
82121	I	IWCX	MA
82122	I	IWCX	OY
82123	I	IWCX	OY
82124	I	IWCX	OY
82125	I	IWCX	WB
82126	I	IWCX	MA
82127	I	IWCX	WB
82128	I	IWCX	MA
82129	I	IWCX	PC
82130	I	IWCX	WB
82131	I	IWCX	WB
82132	I	IWCX	OY
82133	I	IWCX	MA
82134	I	IWCX	WB
82135	I	IWCX	MA
82136	I	IWCX	OY
82137	I	IWCX	WB
82138	I	IWCX	OY
82139	I	IWCX	OY
82140	I	IWCX	WB
82141	I	IWCX	MA
82142	I	IWCX	WB
82143	I	IWCX	MA
82144	I	IWCX	PC
82145	I	IWCX	OY
82146	I	IWCX	MA
82147	I	IWCX	MA
82148	I	IWCX	OY
82149	I	IWCX	WB
82150	I	IWCX	WB
82151	I	IWCX	OY
82152	I	IWCX	OY

NZ (DLV) DRIVING BRAKE VAN (140 mph)

Dia. NZ502. Mark 4. Air conditioned. Swiss-built (SIG) bogies. ae. dg. Cab to shore communication. ETH 6X.

Lot No. 31043 Metro-Cammell 1988. 45.18 t.

82200	I	IECX	BN
82201	I	IECX	BN
82202	I	IECX	BN
82203	I	IECX	BN
82204	I	IECX	BN
82205	I	IECX	BN
82206	I	IECX	BN
82207	I	IECX	BN
82208	I	IECX	BN
82209	I	IECX	BN
82210	I	IECX	BN
82211	I	IECX	BN
82212	I	IECX	BN
82213	I	IECX	BN
82214	I	IECX	BN
82215	I	IECX	BN
82216	I	IECX	BN
82217	I	IECX	BN
82218	I	IECX	BN
82219	I	IECX	BN
82220	I	IECX	BN
82221	I	IECX	BN
82222	I	IECX	BN
82223	I	IECX	BN

82224	I	IECX	BN	82228	I	IECX	BN
82225	I	IECX	BN	82229	I	IECX	BN
82226	I	IECX	BN	82230	I	IECX	BN
82227	I	IECX	BN	82231	I	IECX	BN

NZ (DLV) DRIVING BRAKE VAN (Exptl.)

Dia. NZ503. This is in effect locomotive 33115 with its traction equipment isolated which has been fitted with TGV bogies with third-rail pick-up shoes. It works coupled to a Class 73 locomotive which has its shoegear removed.

83301 (33115)	I	GPSG	SL

NB/NC/ND (BG) GANGWAYED BRAKE VAN (90 mph)

Class continued from 80994. Note: All 84XXX vehicles were renumbered from the 81XXX series by adding 3000 to the original number.

84000 – 84014. Lot No. 30173 York 1956. 31.5 t.
84015 – 84053. Lot No. 30224 Cravens 1956. 31.5 t.
84055 – 84179. Lot No. 30228 Metro-Cammell 1957 – 8. 31.5 t.
84180 – 84204. Lot No. 30234 Cravens 1956 – 7. 31.5 t.
84205 – 84265. Lot No. 30163 Pressed Steel 1957. 31.5 t.
84266 – 84312. Lot No. 30323 Pressed Steel 1957. 32 t.
84313 – 84497. Lot No. 30400 Pressed Steel 1957 – 8. 32 t.
84498 – 84572. Lot No. 30484 Pressed Steel 1958. 32 t.
84573 – 84592. Lot No. 30715 Gloucester 1962. 31 t.
84594 – 84612. Lot No. 30716 Gloucester 1962. 31 t.
84613 – 84628. Lot No. 30725 Gloucester 1962 – 3. 31 t.

84016	*		P	BK
84044	x		P	BK
84100	c	**B**	P	BK
84119	c	**B**	P	BK
84129	c	**B**	P	BK
84133			P	BK
84135	c	**B**	P	BK
84181	c*	**B**	P	BK
84185			P	BK
84195	*		P	BK
84197			P	BK
84202			P	BK
84203			P	BK
84204			P	BK
84215	x*		P	BK
84234	x*	**P**	P	BK
84298			P	BK
84302			P	BK
84356			P	BK
84371			P	BK
84382	b		P	EN
84386			P	BK
84387	b		P	EN
84399	x		P	BK
84406			P	BK
84419	x		P	BK
84420	x	**P**	P	BK
84428			P	BK
84435			P	BK
84439			P	BK
84445	x		P	BK
84456	x		P	BK
84461	b		P	EN
84467			P	BK
84477	b		P	EN
84499	x		P	BK
84510	x	**P**	P	BK
84519			P	BK
84531	x*		P	BK
84577	x		P	BK

NE/NH (BG) 100/110 mph GANGWAYED BRAKE VAN

As ND but rebogied with B4 bogies suitable for 100 mph – NE (110 mph with special maintenance – NH). d. ETH 1 (1X* and NHA). For lot numbers refer to original number series. Deduct 1.5t from weights. All NHA are a*pg.

92100	(81391) a to	**I**	ICCX	PC
92101	(81392) a to		P	CA
92103	(81400) x to		P	BK
92105	(81405) a to	**P**	P	CA
92106	(81409) x to	**P**	P	CA
92107	(81410) x to		P	CA
92110	(81426) x*to	**RX**	P	EN
92111	(81432) NHA	**I**	ICCX	PC
92112	(81440) x to	**P**	P	BK
92113	(81442) a to	**I**	P	EN
92114	(81443) NHA	**I**	ICCX	PC
92116	(81450) a to	**I**	ICCX	PC
92117	(81451) x	**P**	P	CA
92118	(81452) a to	**I**	P	CA
92119	(81454) x to	**P**	P	EN
92120	(81455) x to		P	CA
92121	(81457) x*to	**I**	P	EN
92122	(81459) x*to	**P**	P	BK
92123	(81460) a to	**P**	P	CA
92124	(81465) x	**P**	P	BK
92125	(81470) a to	**I**	ICCX	PC
92126	(81471) a pg	**I**	ICCX	PC
92127	(81473) x*pg	**RX**	P	CA
92130	(81480) a to		P	EN
92131	(81481) a to	**P**	P	CA
92132	(81482) a to	**P**	P	CA
92133	(81484) a to		P	CA
92134	(81485) a to		P	CA
92135	(81486) a to		P	CA
92136	(81487) a to	**P**	P	CA
92137	(81488) a to	**P**	P	HT
92138	(81490) a to		P	EN
92139	(81491) a to	**P**	P	CA
92140	(81492) a to		P	EN
92142	(81494) a to		P	CA
92143	(81495) a to	**P**	P	CA
92144	(81496) a to	**P**	P	HT
92146	(81498) NHA	**I**	IWCX	WB
92147	(81500) a to	**I**	P	EN
92148	(81506) a to	**P**	ICCX	MA
92149	(81509) x		P	LL
92152	(81518) a to		P	CA
92153	(81520) x*to	**I**	P	EN
92154	(81522) x to	**P**	P	CA
92155	(81525) a*pg	**I**	ICCX	PC
92156	(81529) x*to	**I**	P	BK

92157	(81532)	x*pg	**RX**	P	EN
92158	(81533)	a to		P	CA
92159	(81534)	NHA	**I**	IWCX	WB
92160	(81537)	x to	**P**	P	CA
92161	(81538)	a to	**P**	P	CA
92162	(81539)	a to	**P**	P	CA
92164	(81541)	a to		P	EN
92165	(81546)	a to		P	CA
92166	(81550)	a to		P	CA
92168	(81555)	a to	**P**	P	HT
92169	(81556)	x	**P**	P	BK
92170	(81559)	x to		P	BK
92172	(81562)	a pg	**I**	P	EN
92173	(81565)	x to	**P**	P	CA
92174	(81567)	NHA	**I**	IWCX	PC
92175	(81568)	a pg	**I**	ICCX	MA
92176	(81569)	x to	**P**	P	BK
92177	(81572)	a to	**P**	P	CA
92178	(81574)	x		P	BK
92179	(81580)	x to	**P**	P	CA
92181	(81582)	x to		P	BK
92182	(81585)	x to	**P**	P	BK
92183	(81588)	a*pg	**I**	ICCX	PC
92184	(81589)	a to	**P**	P	CA
92186	(81595)	a to	**I**	P	EN
92187	(81597)	a to	**P**	P	CA
92188	(81598)	a to		ICCX	PC
92190	(81600)	a to	**I**	ICCX	MA
92192	(81602)	x to		P	BK
92193	(81604)	a pg	**I**	P	EN
92194	(81606)	a to	**I**	IWRX	LA
92195	(81607)	a to	**I**	ICCX	MA
92196	(81609)	a to	**I**	IWRX	LA
92197	(81610)	a to	**I**	IWRX	LA
92198	(81613)	a to		P	CA
92200	(81615)	x to	**P**	P	BK
92203	(81621)	a to	**I**	P	EN
92204	(81622)	a to	**P**	P	HT
92205	(81623)	a to	**P**	P	CA
92206	(81624)	x		P	BK
92207	(81627)	x to	**P**	P	BK
92208	(84403)	x		P	BK
92209	(80873)	x		P	BK
92210	(84466)	x		P	BK
92211	(81267)	x	**P**	P	BK
92212	(80937)	x	**P**	P	BK
92213	(81321)	x		P	EC
92214	(84504)	x		P	CA
92215	(80911)	x		P	CA
92216	(81376)	x	**P**	P	CA
92217	(80877)	x	**P**	P	CA
92218	(84314)	x	**P**	P	CA

92219 (84285) x		P	CA
92220 (80924) x	**P**	P	CA
92221 (80888) x	**P**	P	BK
92222 (80887) x		P	CA
92224 (84277) x	**P**	P	CA
92225 (80891) x		P	CA
92226 (80879) x	**P**	P	BK
92227 (84337) x		P	CA
92228 (80921) x	**P**	P	CA
92229 (80902) x	**P**	P	CA
92230 (81423) x	**P**	P	CA
92231 (80860) x		P	CA
92232 (80870) x		P	CA
92233 (80890) x	**P**	P	CA
92234 (84336) x	**RX**	P	CA
92235 (80908) x		P	CA
92236 (80909) x	**RX**	P	BK
92237 (80738) x		P	EN
92238 (84563) x	**P**	P	CA
92239 (81170) x	**P**	P	EN
92240 (80703) x	**P**	P	BK
92241 (80943) x		P	BK
92242 (80857) x	**RX**	P	CA
92243 (84489) x	**P**	P	EN
92244 (84248) x	**P**	P	EN
92245 (80939) x		P	BK
92247 (84536) x	**P**	P	CA
92248 (80935) x	**P**	P	EN
92249 (84511) x	**P**	P	EN
92250 (81235) x		P	CA
92251 (84425) x		P	CA
92252 (80959) x	**P**	P	EN
92253 (80936) x	**P**	P	EN
92254 (80894) x	**P**	P	CA
92255 (80871) x	**P**	P	CA
92256 (84424) x		P	CA
92257 (80955) x	**P**	P	BK
92258 (84346) x	**P**	P	CA
92259 (84313) x	**P**	P	BK
92260 (84104) x	**P**	P	BK
92261 (80988) x*	**P**	P	MA
92262 (84240) x*	**P**	P	BK
92263 (84325) x		P	CA
92264 (84239) x*	**P**	P	BK
92265 (80945) x	**P**	P	CA
92266 (84515) x	**P**	P	BK
92267 (84404) x		P	CA
92268 (84352) x		P	DY
92269 (84010) x		P	CA
92270 (84289) x	**RX**	P	CA
92271 (80962) x*	**P**	P	LL
92272 (84262) x*	**P**	P	MA

NE (BG) 100 mph GANGWAYED BRAKE VAN

As ND but rebogied with Commonwealth bogies suitable for 100 mph. xe. ETH 1 (1X*). For lot numbers refer to original number series. Add 1.5 t to weights to allow for the increased weight of the Commonwealth bogies.

92301	(80737) x		P	CA
92302	(84501) x	**RX**	P	CA
92303	(84427) x		P	EN
92304	(84339) x		P	CA
92306	(84217) x*	**P**	P	EN
92307	(80805) *		P	CA
92309	(84043) x*	**RX**	P	EN
92311	(84453) x	**P**	P	EN
92312	(84548) x	**RX**	P	EN
92313	(80992) x*		P	CA
92314	(80777) x*	**P**	P	CA
92316	(80980) x*	**P**	P	EN
92317	(80836) x*	**RX**	P	DY
92318	(80847) x*		P	CA
92319	(84055) x*	**P**	P	EN
92320	(84166) x		P	BK
92321	(84566) x	**P**	P	BK
92322	(80771) x*	**RX**	P	CA
92323	(80832) x*	**P**	P	CA
92324	(84087) x	**P**	P	EN
92325	(80791) x	**P**	P	CA
92326	(84270) x		P	BK
92327	(80842) x*		P	BK
92328	(80999) x*	**P**	P	CA
92329	(84001) x*	**P**	P	BK
92330	(80995) x*	**P**	P	CA
92331	(84365) x		P	CA
92332	(80845) x*	**RX**	P	CA
92333	(80982) x*	**P**	P	BK
92334	(80983) x*	**P**	P	BK
92335	(80973) x*		P	CA
92336	(84045) x*		P	EN
92337	(84140) x*	**RX**	P	CA
92338	(84524) x		P	HQ
92339	(84530) x	**P**	P	BK
92340	(84059) x*	**P**	P	BK
92341	(84316) x	**P**	P	EN
92342	(84397) x	**P**	P	EN
92343	(84505) x	**P**	P	EN
92344	(84154) x*	**P**	P	EN
92345	(84083) x*	**P**	P	EN
92346	(84091) x	**P**	P	EN
92347	(84326) x	**RX**	P	CA
92348	(84075) x*	**P**	P	LL
92349	(84178) x	**P**	P	EN
92350	(84049) x*	**P**	P	EN

92351 (84174) x	**RX**	P	CA
92353 (84323) x	**P**	P	EC
92354 (84353) x	**P**	P	BK
92355 (84517) x	**RX**	P	CA
92356 (84535) x		P	BK
92357 (84136) x	**RX**	P	BK
92358 (84393) x	**RX**	P	EN
92360 (84431) x		P	EN
92362 (84188) x	**P**	P	EN
92363 (84294) x	**P**	P	EN
92364 (84030) x*	**P**	P	BK
92365 (84122) x	**RX**	P	EN
92366 (84551) x	**RX**	P	CA
92368 (84334) x	**RX**	P	CA
92369 (80960) x*		P	CA
92370 (84324) x	**RX**	P	CA
92371 (80856) x*		P	CA
92372 (84362) x	**P**	P	CA
92373 (84528) x	**P**	P	CA
92374 (84317) x		P	CA
92375 (84335) x		P	CA
92377 (80928) x*	**RX**	P	CA
92379 (80914) x*	**RX**	P	CA
92380 (84247) x*	**P**	P	EN
92381 (84476) x	**RX**	P	CA
92382 (84561) x	**RX**	P	EN
92383 (84429) x		P	EN
92384 (80893) x	**P**	P	LL
92385 (84261) x*	**P**	P	CA
92386 (80843) x*	**RX**	P	EN
92387 (84380) x		P	CA
92388 (80868) x*	**P**	P	EN
92389 (84026) x	**P**	P	BK
92390 (80834) x*		P	CA
92391 (80790) x	**P**	P	CA
92392 (80861) x*	**P**	P	EN
92393 (80701) x	**P**	P	BK
92395 (84274) x		P	BK
92396 (84430) x		P	CA
92397 (80700) x*	**P**	P	CA
92398 (80859) x*	**P**	P	CA
92399 (80781) x*	**P**	P	CA
92400 (84211) x*		P	BK
92401 (84280) x		P	CA
92402 (84099) x*	**P**	P	BK
92403 (84273) x	**P**	P	CA
92404 (84051) x*		P	CA
92405 (84320) x	**P**	P	EN
92406 (84475) x	**P**	P	CA
92407 (84363) x		P	CA
92408 (84351) x		P	CA
92409 (84370) x*		P	CA

²410 (84469) x		P		CA
²411 (84252) x*	**P**	P		BK
²412 (84354) x	**P**	P		CA
²413 (84472) x	**P**	P		CA
²414 (84458) x		P		CA
²415 (84388) x	**RX**	P		BK
²416 (84250) x*	**P**	P		BK
²417 (80885) x*	**RX**	P		BK
²418 (84512) x	**RX**	P		BK
²419 ( )				
²420 ( )				

F (BG) 100/110 mph GANGWAYED BRAKE VAN

ehicles with emergency equipment removed. For details and lot numbers refer original number series.

2518 (80941, 92918) x*to	**I**	P	CA
2542 (81207, 92942) a to	**P**	P	CA
2547 (81216, 92947) a to	**RX**	P	CA
2551 (81221, 92951) a to	**P**	P	HT
2584 (81268, 92984) a to	**P**	P	HT
2602 (81394, 92102) a to		P	CA
2604 (81401, 92104) a to	**P**	P	CA
2608 (81411, 92108) a to	**P**	P	CA
2609 (81413, 92109) a to	**RX**	P	CA
2615 (81444, 92115) a to		P	CA
2629 (81479, 92129) a to	**P**	P	HT
2641 (81493, 92141) a to	**RX**	P	CA
2645 (81497, 92145) a to	**P**	P	CA
2650 (81514, 92150) x to	**P**	P	EN
2651 (81516, 92151) a to	**I**	P	CA
2663 (81540, 92163) a to		P	CA
2723 (80932, 92223) x	**RX**	P	CA
2746 (80929, 92246) x	**P**	P	EN
2800 (81200, 92300) x	**RX**	P	BK
2805 (81590, 92305) x	**RX**	P	CA
2808 (80784, 92308) x*	**RX**	P	EN
2810 (81105, 92310) x	**P**	P	EN
2815 (80848, 92315) x*	**P**	P	EN
2852 (81182, 92352) x	**RX**	P	EN
2859 (81275, 92359) x	**RX**	P	EN
2861 (81463, 92361) x	**P**	P	BK
2867 (81293, 92367) x	**RX**	P	CA
2876 (81374, 92376) x	**RX**	P	EN
2894 (81322, 92394) x	**RX**	P	BK

NE/NH (BG) 100/110 mph GANGWAYED BRAKE VA

Renumbered from 92xxx series by adding 900 to number to avoid conflict w
Class 92 locos.

92900	(80723) a pg	**I**	ICCX	PC
92901	(80855) NHA	**I**	IWCX	WB
92902	(80858) x*to	**I**	P	EN
92903	(80864) x*to	**P**	P	EN
92904	(80867) x*to	**I**	P	EN
92905	(80876) x*to	**I**	P	EN
92906	(80878) NHA	**I**	ICCX	PC
92907	(80880) x*pg	**RX**	P	CA
92908	(80895) NHA	**I**	IWCX	WB
92909	(80897) x*to	**I**	P	EN
92910	(80900) x*to	**I**	P	EN
92912	(80910) a*pg	**I**	ICCX	PC
92913	(80916) x*pg	**I**	P	BK
92914	(80923) x*pg	**I**	P	EN
92915	(80927) x*to	**P**	P	CA
92916	(80930) x*pg	**P**	P	EN
92917	(80940) x*to	**RX**	P	CA
92919	(80944) x*pg	**I**	P	EN
92920	(80950) x*pg	**I**	P	CA
92921	(80956) x*to	**I**	P	BK
92922	(80958) x*pg	**RX**	P	BK
92923	(80971) a*pg	**I**	IWCX	WB
92926	(81060) NHA	**I**	ICCX	PC
92927	(81061) NHA	**I**	IWCX	WB
92928	(81064) NHA	**I**	ICCX	PC
92929	(81077) NHA	**I**	ICCX	PC
92931	(81102) NHA	**I**	IWCX	PC
92932	(81117) NHA	**I**	IWCX	WB
92933	(81123) NHA	**I**	IWCX	MA
92934	(81142) NHA	**I**	IWCX	WB
92935	(81150) a*pg	**I**	IWCX	WB
92936	(81158) NHA	**I**	IWCX	WB
92937	(81165) NHA	**I**	IWCX	WB
92938	(81173) NHA	**I**	IWCX	WB
92939	(81175) NHA	**I**	IWCX	WB
92940	(81186) a pg	**I**	ICCX	PC
92941	(81205) a to		P	CA
92943	(81208) a to	**P**	P	HT
92944	(81209) a to	**I**	P	CA
92945	(81210) a to		P	EN
92946	(81214) NHA	**I**	IWCX	WB
92948	(81218) NHA	**I**	IWCX	WB
92949	(81219) a to		P	CA
92950	(81220) a pg	**I**	P	EN
92952	(81222) a to	**P**	P	CA
92953	(81223) a to	**P**	P	CA
92954	(81224) a to	**P**	P	HT

955	(81225) a to	**RX**	P	CA
956	(81226) a to	**P**	P	HT
957	(81227) a to	**I**	ICCX	PC
958	(81228) a to	**P**	P	CA
959	(81229) a to	**P**	P	EN
960	(81230) a to	**P**	P	HT
961	(81231) a	**I**	IANX	NC
962	(81232) a to		P	CA
963	(81233) a*pg	**I**	ICCX	PC
964	(81236) a to	**RX**	P	CA
965	(81237) a		P	EN
966	(81238) a to		P	CA
967	(81243) a to	**I**	P	EN
968	(81244) a to		P	HT
969	(81245) a to	**RX**	P	CA
970	(81246) a		P	CA
971	(81249) a to		P	CA
972	(81253) a to		P	CA
973	(81254) a to	**P**	P	EN
974	(81255) a to	**P**	P	CA
975	(81256) a to	**P**	P	CA
976	(81257) a to		P	HT
977	(81258) a to		P	EN
978	(81259) a to	**RX**	P	CA
979	(81260) a to	**P**	P	HT
981	(81264) a to	**P**	P	CA
982	(81265) a to	**P**	P	CA
983	(81266) a to	**RX**	P	HT
986	(81282) a to	**I**	IANX	NC
987	(81283) x*to	**I**	P	EN
988	(81284) a to	**I**	ICCX	PC
989	(81303) a to	**I**	ICCX	PC
990	(81305) a to		P	CA
991	(81308) a to	**I**	IANX	NC
992	(81309) a to	**I**	P	CA
993	(81312) a*to		P	EN
994	(81367) a to	**I**	ICCX	PC
995	(81375) a to	**P**	P	CA
996	(81377) a to		P	CA
997	(81378) a to		P	CA
998	(81381) NHA	**I**	IWCX	WB
999	(81383) x*pg	**I**	P	BK

J/NK/NX (GUV) GENERAL UTILITY VAN

ark 1. Short frames. Load 14 t. All vehicles are through steam piped only (Dia. <501) unless otherwise stated. Screw couplings. Electric wired vehicles or eam piped and electric wired vehicles are Dia. NJ501. All vehicles have BR ark 2 bogies. ETH 0 or 0X.

3078 – 93499. Lot No. 30417 Pressed Steel 1958 – 9. 30 t.
3501 – 93519. Lot No. 30343 York 1957. 30 t.
3521 – 93654. Lot No. 30403 York/Glasgow 1958 – 60. 30 t.

93655 – 93834. Lot No. 30565 Pressed Steel 1959. 30 t.
93835 – 93984. Lot No. 30616 Pressed Steel 1959 – 60. 30 t.

93078		**B**	P	BK
93105		**B**	P	BK
93117		**B**	P	BK
93131	vr*	**P**	P	BK
93135	vr*	**B**	P	BK
93163	vr*	**B**	P	BK
93176	vr*	**B**	P	BK
93185	vr*	**B**	P	BK
93187		**B**	GPSM	HQ
93195	vr*	**B**	P	BK
93207		**B**	P	BK
93210	xy*	**B**	P	BK
93236	vr*	**B**	P	BK
93251	vr*	**B**	P	BK
93258	vr*	**B**	P	BK
93267	vr*	**P**	P	BK
93273	xr*	**B**	P	BK
93278	vr*	**B**	P	BK
93284	vr*	**B**	P	BK
93291		**B**	P	BK
93292	vr*	**B**	P	BK
93295		**B**	GPSM	HQ
93345	vr	**B**	P	BK
93349	vr	**B**	P	BK
93367	vr*	**B**	P	BK
93370	vr*	**P**	P	BK
93375	vr*	**B**	P	BK
93379	vr*	**P**	P	BK
93386		**B**	GPSM	HQ
93388	vr*	**B**	P	BK
93394	vr*	**P**	P	BK
93401	vr*	**B**	P	BK
93411	xy*	**B**	P	BK
93429	xy*	**RX**	P	BK
93431	vr*	**B**	P	BK
93446	vr	**B**	P	BK
93450	vr*	**B**	P	BK
93464		**B**	P	BK
93474	vr*	**P**	P	BK
93478	vr	**B**	P	BK
93490	vr	**B**	P	BK
93495	vr*		P	BK
93508	vr*	**B**	P	BK
93511	vr*	**P**	P	BK
93515	vr*	**B**	P	BK
93525	vr*	**B**	P	BK
93529	vr*	**B**	P	BK
93536	vr*	**B**	P	BK
93541	vr*	**P**	P	BK
93556	vr*	**B**	P	BK
93557	vr*	**B**	P	BK
93562	vr*	**B**	P	BK
93563	vr*	**B**	P	BK
93585	vr*	**P**	P	BK
93622	vr*	**B**	P	BK
93630	vr*	**B**	P	BK
93633	vr*	**B**	P	BK
93635		**B**	P	BK
93643	vr	**P**	P	BK
93656			P	BK
93660	vr*	**P**	P	BK
93664		**B**	GPSM	HQ
93677	vr*	**B**	P	BK
93683	vr*	**B**	P	BK
93701	vr*	**B**	P	BK
93706	vy	**B**	P	BK
93710	vy	**B**	P	BK
93711	vy	**B**	P	BK
93713	vy	**P**	P	BK
93714	vy	**B**	P	BK
93715	vy	**B**	P	BK
93717	vy	**B**	P	BK
93720	vy	**P**	P	BK
93722	vy	**P**	P	BK
93725	vy	**B**	P	BK
93726	vy	**P**	P	BK
93728	vy	**B**	P	BK
93823	vr	**B**	P	BK
93830	vr	**B**	P	BK
93847	vr*	**P**	P	BK
93849	vr*	**P**	P	BK
93854	vr*	**B**	P	BK
93855	vr*	**B**	P	BK
93857	vr*	**B**	P	BK
93859	vr*	**B**	P	BK
93881	vr*	**B**	P	BK
93886	vr*	**P**	P	BK
93889	vr*	**B**	P	BK
93893	vr*	**B**	P	BK
93905	vr*	**P**	P	BK
93911	vr*	**B**	P	BK
93915	vr*	**B**	P	BK
93930		**B**	P	BK
93935	vr*	**P**	P	BK
93950	vr*	**B**	P	BK
93952	vr*	**B**	P	BK
93955		**B**	P	BK
93962	vr*	**B**	P	BK

93973 vr*	**B**	P	BK	93982 vr*	**P**	P	BK
93979 vr*	**B**	P	BK				

NLX NEWSPAPER VAN

Dia. NL501. Mark 1. Short frames (57'). Converted from GUV. Fluorescent lighting, toilets and gangways fitted. Load 14 t. ETH 3X. These vehicles were originally renumbered 85500 – 85534. Not now used for News traffic. B5 bogies.

Lot No. 30922 Wolverton or Doncaster 1977 – 8. xe. 31 t (33 t*).

94002 (86651)	**P**	P	OM	94023 (86221)	**P**	P	OM
94003 (93999)	**RX**	P	OM	94024 (86106)	**B**	P	OM
94004 (86156)	**P**	P	OM	94025 (86377)	**P**	P	OM
94005 (86845)	**P**	P	OM	94026 (86703)	**P**	P	BK
94006 (86202)	**B**	P	BK	94027 (86732)	**P**	P	BK
94007 (86572)	**B**	P	OM	94028 (86733)	**B**	P	BK
94009 (86144)	**P**	P	OM	94029 (86740)	**P**	P	BK
94010 (86151)	**RX**	P	OM	94030 (86746)	**B**	P	OM
94011 (86437)	**B**	P	OM	94031 (86747)	**B**	P	OM
94015 (86484)	**B**	P	BK	94032 (86730)	**B**	P	OM
94016 (86317)	**B**	P	OM	94033 (86731)	**P**	P	BK
94020 (86220)	**P**	P	OM	94034 (86200)	**B**	P	OM
94021 (86204)	**B**	P	OM				

NMV NEWSPAPER VAN

Dia. NM501/2. Mark 1. Standard GUVs modified as newspaper vans. vd or vd*. ETH 3 (3X*). For lot numbers see old number series. Formerly NLV. Not now used for News traffic.

94050 (93771) d*	**B**	P	BK	94062 (93803) d*	**B**	P	BK
94051 (93708) e	**B**	P	BK	94068 (93424) d*	**B**	P	BK
94052 (93709) e	**B**	P	BK	94071 (93544) d*	**B**	P	BK
94056 (93804) e	**B**	P	BK	94077 (93862) d*	**B**	P	BK
94058 (93530) d*	**B**	P	BK	94078 (93971) d*	**B**	P	BK
94061 (93763) d*	**B**	P	BK				

NOX (GUV) GENERAL UTILITY VAN (100 MPH ETH WIRED)

Dia. NO513. xy. ETH 0 (0X*). Commonwealth bogies. For lot Nos. see GUV section. Add 2 t to weight.

95100 (93668)	**B**	P	CA	95106 (93353)	**RX**	P	CA
95101 (93142)	**B**	P	CA	95107 (93576)	**RX**	P	CA
95102 (93762)	**B**	P	CA	95108 (93600)	**B**	P	CA
95103 (93956)	**B**	P	CA	95109 (93269)	**B**	P	CA
95104 (93942)	**B**	P	CA	95110 (93393)	**B**	P	CA
95105 (93126)	**RX**	P	CA	95111 (93578)	**B**	P	CA

95112 (93673)	B	P	CA
95113 (93235)	B	P	CA
95114 (93081)	B	P	CA
95115 (93174)	B	P	CA
95116 (93426)	B	P	CA
95117 (93534)	B	P	CA
95118 (93675)	B	P	CA
95119 (93167)	P	P	CA
95120 (93468)	P	P	CA
95121 (93518)	B	P	CA
95122 (93864)	B	P	CA
95123 (93376)	B	P	CA
95124 (93836)	P	P	CA
95125 (93143)	B	P	CA
95126 (93692)	B	P	CA
95127 (93323)	P	P	CA
95128 (93764)	P	P	CA
95129 (93347)	P	P	CA
95130 (93263)	P	P	CA
95131 (93860)	B	P	CA
95132 (93607)	P	P	CA
95133 (93604)	RX	P	CA
95134 (93462)	RX	P	CA
95135 (93249)	P	P	CA
95136 (93396)	RX	P	CA
95137 (93160)	RX	P	CA
95138 (93212)	RX	P	CA
95139 (93172)	P	P	CA
95140 (93571)	P	P	CA
95141 (93362)	RX	P	CA
95142 (93844)	RX	P	CA
95143 (93485)	B	P	CA
95144 (93165)	P	P	CA
95145 (93293)	RX	P	CA
95146 (93648)	RX	P	CA
95147 (93091)	P	P	CA
95148 (93416)	RX	P	CA
95149 (93265)	P	P	CA
95150 (93560)	P	P	CA
95151 (93606)	RX	P	CA
95152 (93969)	P	P	CA
95153 (93798)	P	P	CA
95154 (93897)	P	P	CA
95155 (93820)	P	P	CA
95156 (93160)	RX	P	CA
95157 (93523)	B	P	CA
95158 (93499)	RX	P	CA
95159 (93084)	RX	P	CA
95160 (93581)	RX	P	CA
95161 (93205)	RX	P	BK
95162 (93122)	P	P	BK
95163 (93407)	RX	P	BK
95164 (93104)	RX	P	BK
95165 (93262)	RX	P	BK
95166 (93112)	RX	P	BK
95167 (93255)	RX	P	BK
95168 (93914)	RX	P	BK
95169 (93277)	RX	P	BK
95170 (93395)	P	P	BK
95171 (93110)	RX	P	BK
95172 ( )			
95173 (94076)	RX	P	BK
95174 (93852)	RX	P	BK
95175 (93521)	RX	P	BK
95176 ( )			
95177 ( )			
95178 ( )			
95179 ( )			
95180 ( )			
95181 ( )			
95182 ( )			
95183 ( )			
95184 ( )			
95185 ( )			
95186 ( )			
95187 ( )			
95188 ( )			
95189 ( )			
95190 ( )			
95191 ( )			
95192 ( )			
95193 (93694)	RX	P	BK
95194 (93192)	RX	P	BK
95195 (93539)	RX	P	CA
95196 (93775)	RX	P	BK
95197 (93590)	RX	P	CA
95198 (93134)	RX	P	CA
95199 (93141)	RX	P	CA

NCX NEWSPAPER VAN (100 mph)

Dia. NC501. BGs modified to carry newspapers. xe. ETH 3 (3X*). Commonwealth bogies. For lot Nos. see BG section. Add 2 t to weight. Not now used for News traffic. 95227/8/9/30 also carried 95310/32/29/21.

95200 (81019) *	P	P	BK
95201 (80875)	P	P	NC

5202	(80667)	*	**B**	P	BK	95216	(81542)			P	OM
5204	(80947)	*	**RX**	P	HT	95217	(81385)		**B**	P	BK
5205	(80620)	*	**B**	P	BK	95218	(80675)	*		P	BK
5206	(80561)		**P**	P	NC	95219	(80946)		**B**	P	BK
5207	(80560)	*	**P**	P	HT	95220	(80717)	*	**B**	P	BK
5208	(80660)	*	**P**	P	BK	95221	(81153)	*		P	BK
5209	(81047)		**RX**	P	BK	95222	(80774)		**RX**	P	HT
5210	(80731)		**RX**	P	BK	95223	(80933)	*	**P**	P	NC
5211	(80949)		**P**	P	OM	95227	(81292)		**RX**	P	OM
5212	(81179)		**B**	P	BK	95228	(81014)		**RX**	P	BK
5214	(81360)		**B**	P	BK	95229	(81381)		**RX**	P	BK
5215	(80643)	*	**B**	P	BK	95230	(80525)		**RX**	P	BK

ICV NEWSPAPER VAN (100 mph)

ia. NC501. ve. Commonwealth bogies. For lot Nos. see BG section. Add 2t o weight. Not now used for News traffic.

5300	(80689)	**B**	P	BK	95305	(80863)	**B**	P	BK
5303	(80614)	**B**	P	BK	95308	(81161)	**B**	P	BK
5304	(81345)	**P**	P	BK	95312	(80503)	**B**	P	BK

IOV (GUV) GENERAL UTILITY VAN (100 MPH ETH WIRED)

ia. NO513. xy. ETH 0X*. Commonwealth (B4*) bogies. For lot Nos. see GUV ection. Add 2 t to weight for Commonwealth bogies.

5350	(93624)	**B**	P	BK	95373	( )		
5351	(93596)	**B**	P	BK	95374	( )		
5352	(93727)	**B**	P	BK	95375	( )		
5353	(93514)	**B**	P	BK	95376	( )		
5354	( )				95377	( )		
5355	( )				95378	( )		
5356	( )				95379	( )		
5357	( )				95380	( )		
5358	( )				95381	( )		
5359	( )				95382	( )		
5360	( )				95383	( )		
5361	( )				95384	( )		
5362	( )				95385	( )		
5363	( )				95386	( )		
5364	( )				95387	( )		
5365	( )				95388	( )		
5366	( )				95389	( )		
5367	( )				95390	( )	*	
5368	( )				95391	( )	*	
5369	( )				95392	( )	*	
5370	( )				95393	( )	*	
5371	( )				95394	( )	*	
5372	( )				95395	( )	*	

NRX BAA CONTAINER VAN (100 mph)

Dia. NR503. Modified for carriage of British Airports Authority containers with roller shutter doors and roller floors and gangways removed. xe. ETH 3 (3X*). Commonwealth bogies. For lot Nos. see BG section. Add 2 t to weight. Also carried 95203/13 respectively.

95400	(80621)	**RX**	P	DY
95410	(80826)	**RX**	P	DY

NX (GUV) MOTORAIL VAN

Mark 1. Dia. NX501. Renumbered from 93XXX series. For details and lot numbers see 93XXX series. ETH 0 (0X*).

96100	(93734)	a*B5	**I**	IWCX	EN
96101	(93741)	a*B5	**I**	IWCX	EN
96103	(93744)	a*B5	**I**	IWCX	EN
96104	(93745)	a*B5	**I**	IWCX	EN
96110	(93738)	a*C	**I**	IWCX	EN
96111	(93742)	a*C	**I**	IWCX	EN
96112	(93750)	a*C	**I**	ICCX	EC
96130	(93736)	a*C	**I**	IWCX	EN
96131	(93737)	a*C	**I**	IWCX	EN
96132	(93754)	a*C	**I**	ICCX	EC
96133	(93685)	a C	**I**	IXXH	EC
96134	(93691)	a C	**I**	IXXH	EC
96135	(93755)	a C	**I**	ICCX	EC
96136	(93735)	a C	**I**	IXXH	EC
96137	(93748)	a C	**B**	IXXH	WB
96138	(93749)	a C	**I**	IXXH	EC
96139	(93751)	a C	**I**	ICCX	EC
96141	(93753)	a C	**B**	IXXH	EC
96150	(93097)	x*B5	**I**	IWCX	EN
96151	(93286)	x*B5	**I**	ICCX	EC
96152	(93324)	x*B5	**I**	IWCX	EN
96153	(93327)	x*B5	**I**	IWCX	EN
96154	(93331)	x*B5	**I**	IWCX	EN
96155	(93334)	x*B5	**I**	IWCX	EN
96156	(93337)	x*B5	**I**	IWCX	EN
96157	(93344)	x*B5	**I**	IWCX	EN
96158	(93351)	x*B5	**I**	IWCX	EN
96159	(93355)	x*B5	**I**	IWCX	EN
96160	(93385)	x*B5	**I**	IWCX	EN
96161	(93443)	x*B5	**I**	IWCX	EN
96162	(93647)	a*C	**I**	IWCX	EN
96163	(93646)	a*C	**I**	IWCX	EN
96164	(93880)	a*C	**I**	IWCX	EN
96165	(93784)	a*C	**I**	IWCX	EN
96166	(93834)	a*C	**I**	IWCX	EN
96167	(93756)	a*C	**I**	IWCX	EN
96168	(93978)	a*C	**I**	IWCX	EN
96169	(93937)	a*C	**I**	IWCX	EN
96170	(93159)	x*C	**I**	IWCX	EN
96171	(93326)	x*C	**I**	IWCX	EN
96172	(93363)	x*C	**I**	IWCX	EN
96173	(93440)	x*C	**I**	IWCX	EN
96174	(93453)	x*C	**I**	ICCX	EC
96175	(93628)	x*C	**I**	IWCX	EN
96176	(93641)	x*C	**I**	IWCX	EN
96177	(93980)	a*C	**I**	IWCX	EN
96178	(93782)	a*C	**I**	IWCX	EN
96179	(93910)	a*C	**I**	IWCX	EN
96181	(93875)	a*C	**I**	IWCX	EN
96182	(93944)	a*C	**I**	IWCX	EN
96185	(93083)	x*C	**I**	IWCX	EN
96186	(93087)	x*C	**I**	ICCX	EC
96187	(93168)	x*C	**I**	ICCX	EC
96188	(93320)	x*C	**I**	IWCX	EN
96189	(93447)	x*C	**I**	IWCX	EN
96190	(93448)	x*C	**I**	IWCX	EN
96191	(93665)	x*C	**I**	IWCX	EN
96192	(93669)	x*C	**I**	IWCX	EN
96193	(93874)	x*C	**I**	IWCX	EN
96194	(93949)	x*C	**I**	IWCX	EN
96195	(93958)	x*C	**I**	IWCX	EN

NY EXHIBITION VAN

Various interiors. Converted from various vehicle types. Electric heating from shore supply. In some cases new lot numbers were issued for conversions, but not always. Non-standard livery – varies according to job being undertaken.

Lot 30842 Swindon 1972–3. Dia. NY503. Converted from BSK to Lot No. 30156 Wolverton 1955.

99621	(34697) x	BR1	**0**	ICHH	BN	Exhibition Coach.
99625	(34693) x	Mk4	**0**	ICHH	BN	Generator Van.

Converted Salisbury 1981 from RB to Lot No. 30636 Pressed Steel 1962. Dia NY523/4 respectively.

99645	(1765) v	C	**0**	ICHH	BN	Club Car.
99646	(1766) v	C	**0**	ICHH	BN	Club Car.

6. TRANS-MANCHE SUPER TRAINS

The Trans-Manche Super Trains (TMSTs) are on order for the Channel Tunnel services between London and Paris and Brussels. They are based on the French TGV design concept, and the individual cars are numbered like French TGVs.

Each train consists of two 9-coach sets back-to-back with a power car at the outer end. BR sets will be allocated to North Pole (London), Belgian Railways (SNCB/NMBS) sets will be allocated to Bruxelles Forest/Brussel Vorst and French Railways (SNCF) sets will be allocated to Le Landy (Paris). In addition there are trains for North of London which consist of two 7-coach half-sets.

All sets are articulated with an extra motor bogie on the coach next to the power car. Coaches are numbered R1–R9 (and in traffic R10–R18 in the second set). Coaches R18–R10 are identical to R1–R9.

BR Sets.

3001	730010	730011	730012
3002	730020	730021	730022
3003	730030	730031	730032
3004	730040	730041	730042
3005	730050	730051	730052
3006	730060	730061	730062
3007	730070	730071	730072
3008	730080	730081	730082
3009	730090	730091	730092
3010	730100	730101	730102
3011	730110	730111	730112
3012	730120	730121	730122
3013	730130	730131	730132
3014	730140	730141	730142
3015	730150	730151	730152
3016	730160	730161	730162
3017	730170	730171	730172
3018	730180	730181	730182
3019	730190	730191	730192
3020	730200	730201	730202
3021	730210	730211	730212
3022	730220	730221	730222

SNCB/NMBS Sets.

3101	731010	731011	731012
3102	731020	731021	731022
3103	731030	731031	731032
3104	731040	731041	731042
3105	731050	731051	731052
3106	731060	731061	731062
3107	731070	731071	731072
3108	731080	731081	731082

Systems: 25 kV a.c. overhead, 3000 V d.c. overhead and 750 V d.c. third rail.

Built: 1992–3 by GEC Alsthom at various works.
Wheel Arrangement: Bo–Bo + Bo–2–2–2–2–2–2–2–2–2.
Traction Motors: 6.
Length: 22.15 + 21.845 + [7 x 18.70] + 21.845 m.
Max. Speed: 300 km/h (187.5 mph).
Livery: White with yellow window band.
Details:

Car	*Type*	*Seats*	*Lot No.*	*Car*	*Type*	*Seats*	*Lot No.*
M	DM		31118	R5	TSOL	60S 2L	31123
R1	MSOL	52S 1L	31119	R6	Kitchen/bar		31124
R2	TSOL	60S 1L	31120	R7	TFOL	39F 1L	31125
R3	TSOL	60S 2L	31121	R8	TFOL	39F 1L	31126
R4	TSOL	60S 1L	31122	R9	TBFOL	27F 1L	31127

730013	730014	730015	730016	730017	730018	730019
730023	730024	730025	730026	730027	730028	730029
730033	730034	730035	730036	730037	730038	730039
730043	730044	730045	730046	730047	730048	730049
730053	730054	730055	730056	730057	730058	730059
730063	730064	730065	730066	730067	730068	730069
730073	730074	730075	730076	730077	730078	730079
730083	730084	730085	730086	730087	730088	730089
730093	730094	730095	730096	730097	730098	730099
730103	730104	730105	730106	730107	730108	730109
730113	730114	730115	730116	730117	730118	730119
730123	730124	730125	730126	730127	730128	730129
730133	730134	730135	730136	730137	730138	730139
730143	730144	730145	730146	730147	730148	730149
730153	730154	730155	730156	730157	730158	730159
730163	730164	730165	730166	730167	730168	730169
730173	730174	730175	730176	730177	730178	730179
730183	730184	730185	730186	730187	730188	730189
730193	730194	730195	730196	730197	730198	730199
730203	730204	730205	730206	730207	730208	730209
730213	730214	730215	730216	730217	730218	730219
730223	730224	730225	730226	730227	730228	730229

731013	731014	731015	731016	731017	731018	731019
731023	731024	731025	731026	731027	731028	731029
731033	731034	731035	731036	731037	731038	731039
731043	731044	731045	731046	731047	731048	731049
731053	731054	731055	731056	731057	731058	731059
731063	731064	731065	731066	731067	731068	731069
731073	731074	731075	731076	731077	731078	731079
731083	731084	731085	731086	731087	731088	731089

SNCF Sets.

3201	732010	732011	732012
3202	732020	732021	732022
3203	732030	732031	732032
3204	732040	732041	732042
3205	732050	732051	732052
3206	732060	732061	732062
3207	732070	732071	732072
3208	732080	732081	732082
3209	732090	732091	732092
3210	732100	732101	732102
3211	732110	732111	732112
3212	732120	732121	732122
3213	732130	732131	732132
3214	732140	732141	732142
3215	732150	732151	732152
3216	732160	732161	732162
3217	732170	732171	732172
3218	732180	732181	732182
3219	732190	732191	732192
3220	732200	732201	732202
3221	732210	732211	732212
3222	732220	732221	732222
3223	732230	732231	732232
3224	732240	732241	732242
3225	732250	732251	732252
3226	732260	732261	732262
3227	732270	732271	732272
3228	732280	732281	732282
3229	732290	732291	732292
3230	732300	732301	732302
3231	732310	732311	732312
3232	732320	732321	732322

BR "North of London" Sets.

These are 7-coach sets consisting of PC + R1/3/2/5/6/7/9 only.

3301	733010	733011	733013
3302	733020	733021	733023
3303	733030	733031	733033
3304	733040	733041	733043
3305	733050	733051	733053
3306	733060	733061	733063
3307	733070	733071	733073
3308	733080	733081	733083
3309	733090	733091	733093
3310	733100	733101	733103
3311	733110	733111	733113
3312	733120	733121	733123
3313	733130	733131	733133
3314	733140	733141	733143

32013	732014	732015	732016	732017	732018	732019
32023	732024	732025	732026	732027	732028	732029
32033	732034	732035	732036	732037	732038	732039
32043	732044	732045	732046	732047	732048	732049
32053	732054	732055	732056	732057	732058	732059
32063	732064	732065	732066	732067	732068	732069
32073	732074	732075	732076	732077	732078	732079
32083	732084	732085	732086	732087	732088	732089
32093	732094	732095	732096	732097	732098	732099
32103	732104	732105	732106	732107	732108	732109
32113	732114	732115	732116	732117	732118	732119
32123	732124	732125	732126	732127	732128	732129
32133	732134	732135	732136	732137	732138	732139
32143	732144	732145	732146	732147	732148	732149
32153	732154	732155	732156	732157	732158	732159
32163	732164	732165	732166	732167	732168	732169
32173	732174	732175	732176	732177	732178	732179
32183	732184	732185	732186	732187	732188	732189
32193	732194	732195	732196	732197	732198	732199
32203	732204	732205	732206	732207	732208	732209
32213	732214	732215	732216	732217	732218	732219
32223	732224	732225	732226	732227	732228	732229
32233	732234	732235	732236	732237	732238	732239
32243	732244	732245	732246	732247	732248	732249
32253	732254	732255	732256	732257	732258	732259
32263	732264	732265	732266	732267	732268	732269
32273	732274	732275	732276	732277	732278	732279
32283	732284	732285	732286	732287	732288	732289
32293	732294	732295	732296	732297	732298	732299
32303	732304	732305	732306	732307	732308	732309
32313	732314	732315	732316	732317	732318	732319
32323	732324	732325	732326	732327	732328	732329

33012	733015	733016	733017	733019
33022	733025	733026	733027	733029
33032	733035	733036	733037	733039
33042	733045	733046	733047	733049
33052	733055	733056	733057	733059
33062	733065	733066	733067	733069
33072	733075	733076	733077	733079
33082	733085	733086	733087	733089
33092	733095	733096	733097	733099
33102	733105	733106	733107	733109
33112	733115	733116	733117	733119
33122	733125	733126	733127	733129
33132	733135	733136	733137	733139
33142	733145	733146	733147	733149

7.1. PRIVATELY OWNED COACHES

This list comprises privately owned coaches which are "plated" to run on BR. The PO number is carried on a yellow plate affixed to the solebar. Coaches have to be passed by BR each year and this is denoted by a white equilateral triangle painted on the solebar with the year painted in black. In the following list, the original number is shown in column 3. It should be noted that other numbers may also have been carried. It should be noted that there are other vehicles not at present registered for running, which also have BR private-owner numbers allocated.

Number		*Old No.*	*Type*	*Base*	
PWDS	99030	34666	BR Mark 1 BSK	SMC	5407 support coach
BLC	99035	35322	BR Mark 1 BSK	GWD	70000 support coach
MRC	99040	21232	BR Mark 1 BCK	MRC	80080 support coach
MRC	99041	35476	BR Mark 1 BSK	MRC	46203 support coach
SGM	99045	34625	BR Mark 1 BSK	MRC	44932 support coach
MCA	99050	1	GER insp'n saloon	SRC	Sir W.H.Mcalpine's sal.
RHE	99052	484	WCJS dining saloon	QOS	'Queen of Scots' train
RFM	99053	9004	GWR first saloon	SMC	Railfilms Ltd saloon
SPG	99070	35123	BR Mark 1 BSK	BKR	44871 support coach
SNG	99080	21096	BR Mark 1 BCK	SMC	4498 support coach
PES	99090	35131	BR Mark 1 BSK	SMC	46201 support coach
SGST	99108	14018	BR Mark 1 BFK	BRM	Locos support coach
SVR	99120	21236	BR Mark 1 BCK	SVR	SVR locos supp. coach
WDS	99121	3105	BR Mark 1 FO	SMC	Carnforth maroon set
FSS	99122	3106	BR Mark 1 FO	FSS	BN91 set
FSS	99123	3109	BR Mark 1 FO	FSS	BN91 set
FSS	99124	3110	BR Mark 1 FO	FSS	BN91 set
WDS	99127	3117	BR Mark 1 FO	SMC	Carnforth maroon set
FSS	99129	21272	BR Mark 1 BCK	FSS	BN91 set
GSWR	99131	1531	LNER prototype first	GSW	'Royal Scotsman' train
FSS	99132	1861	BR Mark 1 RMB	FSS	BN91 set
CHEL	99140	796	GWR third	GWD	Reb. as dynamometer car
CHEL	99141	14041	BR Mark 2 BFK	GWD	71000 support coach
SU	99180	35333	BR Mark 1 BSK	GWD	6024 support coach
FSS	99190	3131	BR Mark 1 FO	FSS	On lease from BR. BN91
FSS	99191	3132	BR Mark 1 FO	FSS	On lease from BR. BN91
FSS	99192	3133	BR Mark 1 FO	FSS	On lease from BR. BN91
FSS	99193	4860	BR Mark 1 TSO	FSS	On lease from BR. BN91
FSS	99194	5032	BR Mark 1 TSO	FSS	On lease from BR. BN91
FSS	99195	5035	BR Mark 1 TSO	FSS	On lease from BR. BN91
SVR	99241	35449	BR Mark 1 BSK	SRC	34027 support coach
SVR	99242	35467	BR Mark 1 BSK	SVR	SVR locos supp. coach
WDS	99302	13323	BR Mark 1 FK	SMC	Carnforth maroon set
WDS	99303	13317	BR Mark 1 FK	SMC	Carnforth maroon set
WDS	99304	21256	BR Mark 1 BCK	SMC	Carnforth maroon set
WDS	99311	1882	BR Mark 1 RMB	SMC	Carnforth maroon set
WDS	99312	35463	BR Mark 1 BSK	SMC	48151 support coach
DRC	99313	35451	BR Mark 1 BSK	KWV	45596 support coach
WDS	99314	25729	BR Mark 1 SK	SMC	Carnforth maroon set

WDS	99315	25955	BR Mark 1 SK	SMC	Carnforth maroon set
WDS	99316	13321	BR Mark 1 FK	SMC	Carnforth maroon set
WDS	99317	3766	BR Mark 1 TSO	SMC	Carnforth maroon set
WDS	99318	4912	BR Mark 1 TSO	SMC	Carnforth maroon set
WDS	99319	14168	BR Mark 2D BFK	SMC	Carnforth maroon set
WDS	99321	5299	BR Mark 2A TSO	SMC	Carnforth maroon set
WDS	99322	5600	BR Mark 2C TSO	SMC	Carnforth maroon set
FSS	99357	3112	BR Mark 1 FO	FSS	BN91 set
JBC	99405	35486	BR Mark 1 BSK	JBC	60009 support coach
HLPG	99420	21214	BR Mark 1 BSK	HLG	5305 support coach
HLPG	99423	4828	BR Mark 1 SO	HLG	
HLPG	99424	4823	BR Mark 1 SO	HLG	
HLPG	99425	4822	BR Mark 1 SO	HLG	
HLPG	99426	4786	BR Mark 1 SO	HLG	
HLPG	99427	35204	BR Mark 1 BSK	SRC	777 support coach
GWS	99512	34671	BR Mark 1 BSK	GWD	5029 support coach
VSOE	99530	301	Pullman parlour first	SCL	'PERSEUS'
VSOE	99531	302	Pullman parlour first	SCL	'PHOENIX'
VSOE	99532	308	Pullman parlour first	SCL	'CYGNUS'
VSOE	99533	70741	LNER BGP	SCL	'BAGGAGE CAR No. 7'
VSOE	99534	245	Pullman kitchen first	SCL	'IBIS'
VSOE	99535	213	Pullman Brake First	SCL	'MINERVA'
VSOE	99536	254	Pullman parlour first	SCL	'ZENA'
VSOE	99537	280	Pullman kitchen first	SCL	'AUDREY'
VSOE	99538	34991	BR Mark 1 BSK	SCL	'BAGGAGE CAR No. 9'
VSOE	99539	255	Pullman kitchen first	SCL	'IONE'
VSOE	99540	3069	BR Mark 1 FO	SCL	'SALOON CAR No. 1'
VSOE	99541	243	Pullman kitchen first	SCL	'LUCILLE'
VSOE	99542		Ex Ferry van 889202	SCL	'BAGGAGE CAR No. 8'
VSOE	99543	284	Pullman kitchen first	SCL	'VERA'
MANC	99670	546	Pullman parlour first	SMC	'CITY OF MANCHESTER'*
MANC	99671	548	Pullman parlour first	SMC	'ELIZABETHAN'*
MANC	99672	549	Pullman parlour first	SMC	'PRINCE RUPERT'*
MANC	99673	550	Pullman parlour first	SMC	'GOLDEN ARROW'*
MANC	99674	551	Pullman parlour first	SMC	'CALEDONIAN'*
MANC	99675	552	Pullman parlour first	SMC	'SOUTHERN BELLE'*
MANC	99676	553	Pullman parlour first	SMC	'KING ARTHUR'*
MANC	99677	586	Pullman brake first	SMC	'TALISMAN'*
MANC	99678	504	Pullman kitchen first	SMC	'THE WHITE ROSE'*
MANC	99679	506	Pullman kitchen first	SMC	'THE RED ROSE'*
MANC	99680	14102	BR Mark 2A BFK	SMC	'ATTENDANT'S CAR'*
TRTS	99710	25767	BR Mark 1 SK	SMC	Pilkington K glass set
TRTS	99712	25893	BR Mark 1 SK	SMC	Pilkington K glass set
TRTS	99713	26013	BR Mark 1 SK	SMC	Pilkington K glass set
TRTS	99714	16187	BR Mark 1 CK	SMC	Pilkington K glass set
TRTS	99716	25808	BR Mark 1 SK	SMC	Pilkington K glass set
TRTS	99717	25837	BR Mark 1 SK	SMC	Pilkington K glass set
TRTS	99718	25862	BR Mark 1 SK	SMC	Pilkington K glass set
TRTS	99719	16191	BR Mark 1 CK	SMC	Pilkington K glass set
TRTS	99720	35461	BR Mark 1 BSK	SMC	Pilkington K glass set
TRTS	99721	25806	BR Mark 1 SK	SMC	Pilkington K glass set
TRTS	99722	25756	BR Mark 1 SK	SMC	Pilkington K glass set

TRTS	99723	35459	BR Mark 1 BSK	SMC	Pilkington K glass set
NELP	99760	34557	BR Mark 1 BSK	NEL	44767 support coach
COWS	99792	14019	BR Mark 1 BSK	KWV	Locos support coach
SCR	99818	1730	BR Mark 1 RB	BKR	SRPS set
SCR	99820	4871	BR Mark 1 TSO	BKR	SRPS set
SCR	99821	9227	BR Mark 1 BSO	BKR	SRPS set
SCR	99822	1859	BR Mark 1 RMB	BKR	SRPS set
SCR	99823	4832	BR Mark 1 TSO	BKR	SRPS set
SCR	99824	4831	BR Mark 1 TSO	BKR	SRPS set
SCR	99825	13228	BR Mark 1 FK	BKR	SRPS set
SCR	99826	13229	BR Mark 1 FK	BKR	SRPS set
SCR	99827	3096	BR Mark 1 FO	BKR	SRPS set
SCR	99828		BR Mark 1	BKR	SRPS set
SCR	99829		BR Mark 1	BKR	SRPS set
SCR	99830		BR Mark 1	BKR	SRPS set
RHE	99880	5159	LNWR dining saloon	QOS	On loan to GSW
RHE	99881	807	GNR family saloon	QOS	'Queen of Scots' train
RHE	99886	35407	BR Mark 1 BSK	QOS	'Queen of Scots' train
GSWR	99887	2127	BR Mark 1 SLF	GSW	'Royal Scotsman' train
NRMY	99951	10656	SR DMBTK (EMU)	BI	National collection
NRMY	99952	12123	SR DTCK (2 Bil)	BI	National collection
NRMY	99953	35468	BR Mark 1 BSK	NRM	NRM Locos supp. coach
GSWR	99961	324	Pullman parlour first	GSW	'Royal Scotsman' train
GSWR	99962	329	Pullman parlour first	GSW	'Royal Scotsman' train
GSWR	99963	331	Pullman parlour first	GSW	'Royal Scotsman' train
GSWR	99964	313	Pullman kitchen first	GSW	'Royal Scotsman' train
GSWR	99965	319	Pullman kitchen first	GSW	'Royal Scotsman' train
GSWR	99966	34525	BR Mark 1 BSK	GSW	'Royal Scotsman'

*Manchester Pullman set.

Note: 13321 carries 13320 in error.

8. CODES

8.1. LIVERY CODES

All locomotives are blue unless otherwise indicated. The colour of the lower half of the bodyside is stated first. Minor variations to these liveries are ignored.

LOCOMOTIVES:

BR Revised blue (large numbers and full height BR logo)
BS Blue with red solebar stripe
C Civil Engineers (grey and yellow)
D Departmental (plain grey with black cab doors)
F New Railfreight (two-tone grey sides-no sub-sector markings) or sub-sector markings unknown.
FA Trainload Construction – As 'F' with markings as on page 33.
FC Trainload Coal – As 'F' with markings as on page 33.
FD Railfreight Distribution – As 'F' with markings as on page 33.
FM Trainload Metals – As 'F' with markings as on page 33.
FO Old Railfreight (grey sides, yellow cabsides, red bufferbeams and full height BR logo).
FP Trainload Petroleum – As 'F' with markings on page 33.
FR As FO but with red solebar stripe.
G BR or GWR green.
I InterCity (white and dark grey with red stripe and swallow motif)
IO Old InterCity (light grey and dark grey with red stripe and yellow lower cab sides).
M Mainline (As old Intercity but without the yellow cabsides).
N Network SouthEast (grey/white/red/white/blue/white).
O Other livery (non-Standard – refer to text).
PS Scotrail (light grey/light blue/white/dark grey).
P Parcels (post office red and dark grey).
RR Regional Railways (grey/light blue/white/dark blue).
RX Rail Express Systems (post office red with blue/black markings.

COACHING STOCK:

All coaching stock vehicles are in the old blue & grey livery unless otherwise indicated. The colour of the lower half of the bodyside is stated first. Please note that although the former Provincial Services sector is now known as Regional Railways, the former name is used for its original liveries.

B Plain Blue
CE Centro (WMPTE) (grey/light blue/white/green)
E LNER Tourist Green and Cream.
G Old Greater Manchester PTE (orange/brown)
GM New Greater Manchester PTE (dark grey/red/white/light grey)
I InterCity (light grey white on DVTs/red stripe/dark grey)
MT Merseyside PTE (yellow/white)
N Network SouthEast (grey/white/red/white/blue/white)
O Other livery (non-standard – refer to text)

P	Parcels (red) (EMUs and hauled stock)
P	Provincial Services (grey/light blue/white/dark blue) (DMUs)
PM	Provincial Midline. As 'P' but with grey and cream stripes
PN	Provincial Network NorthWest. As 'P' but grey and red stripe
PR	Provincial Services railbus variant (dark blue/white/light blue)
RE	Regional Railways Express (buff/light grey/dark grey/light grey/buff, with dark blue, white and light blue stripes)
RR	Regional Railways (grey/light blue/white/dark blue with three black and white stripes under cabs
RX	Rail Express Systems (Red and grey with blue/black markings)
S	Strathclyde PTE (orange and black)
T	Tyne & Wear PTE (yellow/light blue/white/yellow)
SG	Southern green
Y	West Yorkshire PTE (red and cream)

8.2. POOL AND SECTOR CODES

LOCOMOTIVE POOL CODES:

CDJC	Research. CD.
CDJN	Research. TO.
CDJX	Research. Stored.
CEJB	Civil Link. BS.
CEJC	Civil Link. CD.
FABI	Trainload Construction. IM Class 37 & 60 (based at Buxton).
FALY	Trainload Construction. TE Class 37.
FASB	Trainload Construction. SL Class 56 & 60.
FAXN	Trainload Construction. TO Class 56 & 60 (based at Leicester).
FCAN	Power Station Coal. TO Class 58 (West Midlands).
FCBK	Trainload Coal. CF Class 37.
FCBN	Power Station Coal. TO Class 56 & 58 (East Midlands).
FCCI	Trainload Coal. IM Class 47.
FCDN	Power Station Coal. TO Class 56 & 58 (Yorkshire).
FCEN	Power Station Coal. TO Class 56 (North East).
FCFN	Trainload Coal. TO Class 31 (Nuclear flask traffic).
FCGN	Power Station Coal. TO Class 20 (North West).
FCHN	Power Station Coal. TO Class 60 (North West).
FCJN	Power Station Coal. TO Class 60 (East Midlands).
FCKK	Power Station Coal. CF Class 37.
FCPM	Power Station Coal. ML Class 37.
FCXX	Power Station Coal. Stored.
FIJI	Trainload Freight – Infrastructure. IM.
FIJW	Trainload Freight – Infrastructure. IM (weekend work).
FMAK	Trainload Metals. CF Class 37.
FMCK	Trainload Metals. CF Class 56.
FMEK	Trainload Metals. CF Class 60.
FMHK	Trainload Metals. CF Class 37/7 & 37/9.
FMMY	Trainload Metals. TE Class 60.
FMTY	Trainload Metals. TE Class 37 & 56.
FMXX	Trainload Metals. Stored.
FMYI	Trainload Metals. IM Class 37 & 60.
FPAG	Trainload Petroleum. IM Class 37 (based at Grangemouth).

FPCI Trainload Petroleum. IM Class 37 & 47.
FPDI Trainload Petroleum. IM Class 60.
FPEK Trainload Petroleum. CF Class 37 & 60.
FPFR Trainload Petroleum. IM Class 37 & 47 (based at Ripple Lane).
FPTY Trainload Petroleum. TE Class 37 & 60.
FPYI Trainload Petroleum. IM Class 37 & 47 (restricted use).
FPYX Trainload Petroleum. Stored.
FSCD Doncaster Shunters.
FSCK Knottingley Shunters.
FSCN Toton Shunters.
FSNH Heaton Shunters.
FSNI Immingham Shunters.
FSNL Neville Hill Shunters.
FSNT Tinsley Shunters.
FSNX Selhurst Shunters.
FSNY Thornaby Shunters.
FSSA Ayr Shunters.
FSSB Aberdeen Shunters.
FSSG Grangemouth Shunters.
FSSI Inverness Shunters.
FSSM Motherwell Shunters.
FSWK Cardiff Canton Shunters.
FSWL Landore Shunters.
FXXA Trainload Freight New Class 60. Not accepted.
FXXB Trainload Freight New Class 60.
IANA InterCity Anglia Services Locos.
IBRA InterCity Bristol Class 47/4. Special Use.
IBRB InterCity Bristol Class 47/4. General Hire.
ICCA InterCity Cross Country Electrics.
ICCP InterCity Cross Country Class 43. LA or PM.
ICCS InterCity Cross Country Class 43. EC.
IECA InterCity ECML Electrics.
IECP InterCity ECML Class 43.
IEJI InterCity Infrastructure. ECML. IM.
IEJW InterCity Infrastructure. ECML. IM. (weekend work).
IGJA InterCity Infrastructure. GWML BR.
IGJK InterCity Infrastructure. GWML. CF.
IGJO InterCity Infrastructure. GWML. OC.
IGJW InterCity Infrastructure. GWML. OC. (weekend work).
IHFB InterCity M&EE. Overhead Line Maintenance. BS.
IHRB InterCity M&EE. Fleet Maintenance. BS.
IISA InterCity Inverness Class 37.
ILRA InterCity Bristol Class 47/4 Extended Range Locos.
IMJB InterCity Infrastructure. Midland/Cross Country. BS.
IMJC InterCity Infrastructure. Midland/Cross Country Civil engineer. CD.
IMJK InterCity Infrastructure. Midland/Cross Country S&T. CD.
IMJW InterCity Infrastructure. Midland/Cross Country. BS. (weekend work).
IMLP InterCity Midland Line Class 43.
IVGA InterCity Gatwick Express Services.
IWCA InterCity WCML Electric Locos.
IWCP InterCity WCML Class 43.
IWJB InterCity Infrastructure. WCML. BS.

SECTOR CODES

IWJC	InterCity Infrastructure. WCML. CD Class 31.
IWJD	InterCity Infrastructure. WCML. CD Class 47.
IWPA	InterCity Euston – West Midlands Services Locos.
IWRP	InterCity GWML Class 43.
IWSA	InterCity WCML CLass 87. (100 mph maximum).
IXXS	InterCity Stored.
MDAT	Distribution Tinsley Class 47.
MDCT	Distribution Tinsley Class 47 (based at Saltley).
MDDT	Distribution Tinsley Class 47 (extended range).
MDIB	Distribution Dover Train Ferry Class 33/2.
MDLC	Distribution Class 90/0.
MDMC	Distribution Class 90/1.
MDNC	Distribution Class 86/6 and 87/1 Locos.
MDRL	Distribution Laira Refurbished Class 37 (based at St. Blazey).
MDRM	Distribution Motherwell Refurbished Class 37.
MDRT	Distribution Tinsley Refurbished Class 37.
MDTT	Distribution Tinsley Unrefurbished Class 37 (extended range).
MDWT	Distribution Tinsley Class 37 & 47. (restricted use).
MDYX	Distribution Stored.
MSNA	Allerton Shunters.
MSNB	Bescot Shunters.
MSNC	Crewe Shunters.
MSNE	Derby Etches Park Shunters.
MSNL	Longsight Shunters.
MSNU	Carlisle Upperby Shunters.
MSSA	Bristol Bath Road Shunters.
MSSB	Bletchley Shunters.
MSSC	Cambridge Shunters.
MSSL	Laira Shunters.
MSSM	March Shunters.
MSSN	Norwich Shunters.
MSSO	Old Oak Common Shunters.
MSSR	Reading Shunters.
MSSS	Stratford Shunters.
MSSW	Willesden Shunters.
NKFE	Infrastructure. South electrification. EH.
NKFH	Infrastructure. North electrification. HE.
NKJD	Infrastructure. South. EH & RY Shunters.
NKJE	Infrastructure. South. EH.
NKJH	Infrastructure. South. AF & SU Shunters.
NKJL	Infrastructure. South. SL.
NKJM	Infrastructure. Meldon Quarry duties. EH.
NKJO	Infrastructure. Thames & Chiltern. OC.
NKJR	Infrastructure. South (restricted use).
NKJS	Infrastructure. North. SF.
NKJW	Infrastructure. North (weekend work).
NTWE	West of England/North Downs Services Class 47.
NWXA	Class 50 (special use). .
NWXB	West of England/North Downs Services Class 33 & 73.
NXXB	Class 47 (restricted use).
PXLA	Crewe Class 90.
PXLB	Crewe Class 47. (extended range).

PXLC Crewe Class 47.
PXLD Parcels Reserve and Stored Locos.
PXLE Crewe Class 86.
RAIS IS Class 97/2.
RAJE Infrastructure. Scotrail. IS.
RAJV Infrastructure. Scotrail. IS.
RBJI Infrastructure. North East. IM.
RBJW Infrastructure. North East (weekend work).
RCBD Infrastructure. North West. BD Class 97/7.
RCJC Infrastructure. North West. CD Class 31.
RCKC Infrastructure. North West. CD Class 31/4.
RCLC Infrastructure. North West. CD Class 47.
RCMC Infrastructure. North West. CD Class 37/4.
RDDJ Infrastructure. Central. SF (RETB fitted).
RDJB Infrastructure. Central. BS.
RDJS Infrastructure. Central. SF.
RDJW Infrastructure. Central. BS (weekend work).
REJK Infrastructure. South Wales & West. CF Class 37.
RFJX Infrastructure. Stored.
TAKX BR Telecoms Class 20 Stored.
XYPA ARC Class 59/1.
XYPD Hunslet-Barclay Class 20/9.
XYPO Foster-Yeoman Class 59/0.

COACHING STOCK SECTOR CODES:

GPSG European Passenger Services Ltd. DVT.
GPSM European Passenger Services Ltd. Vans.
IANL Inter-City: Anglia. On loan.
IANR Inter-City: Anglia. Refurbished.
IANX Inter-City: Anglia.
ICCE Inter-City: Cross Country. HST.
ICCL Inter-City: Cross Country. On loan.
ICCR Inter-City: Cross Country. Refurbished.
ICCT Inter-City: Cross Country. HST EC.
ICCX Inter-City: Cross Country.
ICHC Inter-City: Charter and Special Services (vacuum not refurb).
ICHD Inter-City: Charter and Special Services (air not refurb).
ICHH Inter-City: Charter and Special Services (held for re-use).
ICHL Inter-City: Charter and Special Services (for loan).
ICHP Inter-City: Charter and Special Services (PO loan).
ICHS Inter-City: Charter and Special Services (steam specials).
ICHV Inter-City: Charter and Special Services (VIP).
ICHX Inter-City: Charter and Special Services.
IECD Inter-City: East Coast Main Line. Class 92 Endurance Testing.
IECG Inter-City: East Coast Main Line. Barrier Vehicles.
IECX Inter-City: East Coast Main Line.
ILAG Inter-City: HST Barrier Vehicles LA.
IMLR Inter-City: Midland Main Line Refurbished.
IMLX Inter-City: Midland Main Line.
IWCD Inter-City: West Coast Main Line HSTs.
IWCL Inter-City: West Coast Main Line. On loan.
IWCR Inter-City: West Coast Main Line. Refurbished.

SECTOR CODES

IWCW	Inter-City: West Coast Main Line. WR HSTs.
IWCX	Inter-City: West Coast Main Line.
IWRG	Inter-City: Great Western Main Line. Barrier Vehicles.
IWRL	Inter-City: Great Western Main Line. On loan.
IWRR	Inter-City: Great Western Main Line. Refurbished.
IWRX	Inter-City: Great Western Main Line.
IXXB	Inter-City: Held for bogie reuse.
IXXH	Inter-City: Held for further use.
IXXT	Inter-City: Awaiting transfer.
IXXX	Inter-City: General.
IXXZ	Inter-City: Authorised for Withdrawal.
NGBX	Network SouthEast: Gospel Oak – Barking.
NGEX	Network SouthEast: Great Eastern.
NGNX	Network SouthEast: Great Northern.
NKCX	Network SouthEast: Kent Coast.
NKSX	Network SouthEast: Kent Suburban.
NMLX	Network SouthEast: Midland Line.
NMYX	Network SouthEast: Marylebone Line services.
NNDX	Network SouthEast: North-East London services.
NNLX	Network SouthEast: North London Line.
NNWX	Network SouthEast: London & North Western.
NSBX	Network SouthEast: Surrey and Berkshire suburban.
NSLX	Network SouthEast: Sussex local sevices.
NSSX	Network SouthEast: Solent and Sarum.
NSXX	Network SouthEast: Sussex.
NTCZ	Network SouthEast: Thames & Chiltern. Authorised for withdrawal.
NTSX	Network SouthEast: London Tilbury and Southend Line.
NWRX	Network SouthEast: Western Region.
NWXX	Network SouthEast: West of England/North Downs services.
NXXX	Network SouthEast: General.
NXXZ	Network SouthEast: Authorised for withdrawal.
P	Rail Express Systems: General.
RACK	Regional Railways Scotrail: Corkerhill.
RAGW	Regional Railways Scotrail: Glasgow Shields.
RAHA	Regional Railways Scotrail: Haymarket.
RAIS	Regional Railways Scotrail: Inverness.
RBHT	Regional Railways North-East: Heaton.
RBNL	Regional Railways North-East: Neville Hill.
RCBD	Regional Railways North-West: Birkenhead North.
RCHR	Regional Railways North-West: Hall Road.
RCLG	Regional Railways North-West: Longsight.
RCLL	Regional Railways North-West: Edge Hill.
RCLO	Regional Railways North-West: Longsight.
RCNH	Regional Railways North-West: Newton Heath.
RDBY	Regional Railways Central: Bletchley.
RDDY	Regional Railways Central: Derby.
RDLG	Regional Railways Central: Longsight.
RDNC	Regional Railways Central: Norwich Crown Point.
RDTS	Regional Railways Central: Tyseley.
RECF	Regional Railways South Wales and West: Cardiff Canton.
RELA	Regional Railways South Wales and West: Laira.

RFXX Regional Railways General.

Note: Sub-sector codes for Parcels vehicles are not shown, since BR official lists no longer show them, and since they do not convey any more information than can be learnt from the class heading information.

8.3. DEPOT CODES

AB	Aberdeen T&RSMD
AF	Ashford Chart Leacon TMD
AL	Aylesbury TMD
AN	Allerton TMD (Liverpool)
AR	ARC Limited (Whatley)
AY	Ayr TMD
BD	Birkenhead North T&RSMD
BI	Brighton T&RSMD
BK	Bristol Bardon Hill WRD
BM	Bournemouth EMUD
BN	Bounds Green T&RSMD (London)
BP	Blackpool Carriage Sidings
BR	Bristol Bath Road TMD
BS	Bescot TMD (Walsall)
BY	Bletchley TMD
CA	Cambridge T&RSMD
CC	Clacton EMUD
CD	Crewe TMD (D)
CE	Crewe TMD (E)
CF	Cardiff Canton T&RSMD
CK	Corkerhill SD (Glasgow)
CL	Carlisle Upperby T&RSMD
CQ	Coquelles T&RSMD (Eurotunnel)
DR	Doncaster TMD
DY	Derby Etches Park T&RSMD
EC	Craigentinny T&RSMD (Edinburgh)
FF	Bruxelles Forest/Brussel Vorst (SNCB/NMBS)
EH	Eastleigh T&RSMD
EM	East Ham EMUD (London)
EN	Euston Downside CARMD (London)
FY	Merehead (Foster Yeoman)
GI	Gillingham EMUD
GM	Grangemouth SD
GW	Glasgow Shields TMD
HA	Haymarket TMD (Edinburgh)
HB	Kilmarnock (Hunslet – Barclay)
HE	Hornsey TMD (London)
HR	Hall Road EMUD
HT	Heaton T&RSMD (Newcastle)
IL	Ilford T&RSMD (London)
IM	Immingham TMD (S. Humberside)
IS	Inverness T&RSMD
KY	Knottingley TMD

LA	Laira T&RSMD (Plymouth)
LE	Landore T&RSMD (Swansea)
LG	Longsight TMD (E) (Manchester)
LL	Liverpool Edge Hill CARMD
LO	Longsight TMD (D) (Manchester)
LP	Le Landy TMST Depot, Paris (SNCF)
MA	Manchester Longsight CARMD
ML	Motherwell TMD
MR	March TMD
NC	Norwich Crown Point T&RSMD
NH	Newton Heath T&RSMD (Leeds)
NL	Neville Hill T&RSMD (Leeds)
NP	North Pole International Depot (London)
OC	Old Oak Common TMD (D) (London)
OM	Old Oak Common CARMD (London)
OO	Old Oak Common TMD (HST) (London)
OY	Oxley CARMD (Wolverhampton)
PC	Polmadie CARMD (Glasgow)
PM	St. Phillips Marsh T&RSMD (Bristol)
RE	Ramsgate T&RSMD
RG	Reading TMD
RY	Ryde (Isle of Wight) T&RSMD
SA	Salisbury TMD
SF	Stratford TMD (London)
SG	Slade Green T&RSMD
SH	Strawberry Hill EMUD (London)
SL	Stewarts Lane T&RSMD (London)
SU	Selhurst TMD (London)
TE	Thornaby TMD
TI	Tinsley TMD (Sheffield)
TO	Toton TMD (Notts)
TS	Tyseley TMD (Birmingham)
WB	Wembley InterCity CARMD (London)
WC	Waterloo EMUD (Waterloo & City)
WD	East Wimbledon EMUD (London)
WN	Willesden TMD (London)
ZA	Railway Technical Centre, Derby
ZF	Doncaster Works BRML
ZG	Eastleigh Works BRML
ZH	Springburn Works BRML (Glasgow)
ZN	Wolverton Works BRML

Note: The code HQ denotes a BR headquarters responsibility. Not all vehicles shown by BR as HQ are so denoted in this book, the actual location of stores vehicles generally being shown.

8.4. GENERAL CODES

BRML	British Rail Maintenance Ltd.
CARMD	Carriage Maintenance depot.
CSD	Carriage Servicing depot.
CWMD	Carriage and wagon maintenance depot.
EMUD	Electric Multiple Unit Depot.
SD	Servicing depot.
TMD	Traction Maintenance Depot.
TMD (D)	Traction Maintenance Depot (Diesel).
TMD (E)	Traction Maintenance Depot (Electric).
TMD (HST)	HST Maintenance Depot.
T&RSMD	Traction and rolling stock maintenance depot.
WRD	Wagon Repair Depot.
GER	Great Eastern Railway
GWR	Great Western Railway
LNER	London & North Eastern Railway
LMS	London Midland & Scottish Railway
SR	Southern Railway

8.5. PRIVATE OPERATOR BASE CODES

BKR	Bo'Ness & Kinneil Railway, Bo'Ness Station, West Lothian.
BRC	Bulmers Railway Centre, Hereford, Herefordshire.
BRM	Birmingham Railway Museum, Tyseley, Birmingham, West Mids.
FSS	Flying Scotsman Services, BR Bounds Green T&RSMD., London.
GRT	Grampian Railtours, BR Inverness CS, Highland Region.
GSW	Great Scottish & Western Railway Company, BR Millerhill Royal Scotsman Siding, Edinburgh, Lothian.
GWD	Great Western Society, Didcot Railway Centre, Didcot, Oxfordshire.
HLG	Humberside Locomotive Group, Dairycoates Depot, Hull, Humbs.
KWV	Keighley & Worth Valley Railway, Ingrow, Keighley, West Yorkshire.
NEL	North Eastern Locomotive Preservation Group, ICI Wilton, Cleveland.
JBC	J.B. Cameron, Thornton Junction, Fife.
MRC	Midland Railway Centre, Butterley Station, Derbyshire.
NRM	National Railway Museum, Leeman Road, York, North Yorkshire.
NYM	North Yorkshire Moors Railway, Grosmont, North Yorkshire.
QOS	Queen of Scots Train, St. Leonards Depot, St. Leonards, East Sussex.
SCL	Sea Containers Ltd (VSOE), BR Stewarts Lane T&RSMD, London.
SMC	Steamtown Railway Centre, Carnforth, Lancashire.
SRC	Southall Railway Centre, Old Southall Diesel Depot, Southall, Greater London.
SVR	Severn Valley Railway, The Railway Station, Bewdley, Worcs.

Notes: We would like to thank Mr. P. Hall for information on preserved coaches. The above codes are not official BR codes.

9. OTHER RAILWAYS

9.1. BLACKPOOL & FLEETWOOD TRAMWAY

System: 660 V d.c. overhead. **Depot:** Rigby Road.
Livery: Cream and green. (many in advertising livery).

Note: Numbers in brackets are pre-1968 numbers.

ONE-MAN CARS

Rebuilt 1972 – 76 from English Electric railcoaches built 1934 – 5. Radio fitted. 13 converted (1 – 13).
Seats: 48U.
Traction Motors: Two EE305 of 40 kW.

Note: First numbers in brackets are post 1968 numbers prior to conversion.

5 (609, 221) | 10 (614, 267) | 11 (615, 268)

OPEN BOAT CARS

Built 1934 – 5 by English Electric. 12 built (225 – 236).
Seats: 56U.
Traction Motors: Two EE327 of 30 kW.

600* (225)
602★ (227)
604§ (230)
605 (233)(U)
606b (235)
607 (236)

* On loan to Heaton Park Tramway, Manchester.
★ Yellow and black livery.
§ Red and white livery.
b Blue & yellow livery.

REPLICA VANGUARD

Built 1987 on underframe of one man car No. 7.(619 – 282).
Seats: U.
Traction Motors: Two EE327 of 30 kW.

619

BRUSH RAILCOACHES

Built 1937 by Brush. 20 built (284 – 303).
Seats: 48U.
Traction Motors: Two EE305 of 40 kW. (EE327 of 30 kW*).

621 (284)
622* (285)
623 (286)
625 (288)
626 (289)
627 (290)
630 (293)
631 (294)
632 (295)
633 (296)
634 (297)
635 (299)
637 (300)

CENTENARY CLASS

Built 1984 – 7. Body by East Lancs. Coachbuilders, Blackburn. One man operated. Radio fitted.
Seats: 52U.
Traction Motors: Two EE305 of 40 kW.

* Rebuilt from GEC car 651.

641	644	647
642	645	648*
643	646	

CORONATION CLASS

Built 1953 by Charles Roberts & Co. Resilient wheels. 25 built (304 – 328).
Seats: 56U.
Traction motors: Four Crompton-Parkinson 92 of 34 kW.

660 (324)

PROGRESS TWIN CARS

Motor cars (671 – 677) rebuilt 1958 – 60 from English Electric railcoaches.
Seats: 53U.
Traction Motors: Two EE305 of 40 kW.
Driving trailers (681 – 687) built 1960 by Metro-Cammell.
Seats: 53U.

671 + 681 (281 + T1)	674 + 684 (284 + T4)	676 + 686 (286 + T6)
672 + 682 (282 + T2)	675 + 685 (285 + T5)	677 + 687 (287 + T7)
673 + 683 (283 + T1)		

SINGLE CARS

Rebuilt 1958 – 60 from English Electric railcoaches. Originally ran with trailers.
Seats: 48U.
Traction Motors: Two EE305 of 40 kW.

678 (278)	679 (279)	680 (280)

"BALLOON" DOUBLE DECKERS

Built 1934 – 5 by English Electric. 700 – 712 were originally built with open tops, and 706 has now reverted to that condition and is named 'PRINCESS ALICE'.
Seats: 94U.
Traction Motors: Two EE305 of 40 kW.

700 (237)	706 (243)	711 (248)
701§ (238)	707 (244)	712 (249)
702 (239)	708 (245)	713 (250)
703 (240)	709 (246)	715 (252)
704 (241)	710 (247)	716 (253)

§ Red and white livery.

717 (254)	720 (257)	723 (260)
718 (255)	721 (258)	724 (261)
719 (256)	722 (259)	726 (263)

ILLUMINATED CARS

732 (168)	Rocket	Seats: 47U
733 (209)	Western Train loco. & tender	Seats: 35U
734 (174)	Western Train coach	Seats: 60U
735 (222)	Hovertram	Seats: 99U
736 (170)	HMS Blackpool	Seats: 71U

WORKS CARS

259 (748, 624)	PW gang towing car.
260 (751, 628, 291)	Crane car and rail carrier.
749 (S)	Tower wagon trailer.
750	Cable drum trailer.
752 (2, 1)	Rail grinder and snowplough.
	New works car (unnumbered).

JUBILEE CLASS DOUBLE DECKERS

Rebuilt 1979/82 from Balloon cars. Standard bus ends, thyristor control and stairs at each end. 761 has one door per side whereas 762 has two. Radio fitted.
Seats: 100U.
Traction Motors: Two EE305 of 40 kW.

761 (725, 262)	762 (714, 251)

PRESERVED CARS

Blackpool & Fleetwood 40	Box car. Bogie single decker built 1914
Bolton 66	Bogie double-decker built 1901

9.2. DOCKLANDS LIGHT RAILWAY

This is a light rail line running in London's East End from ank, Tower Gateway and Stratford to Island Gardens. It is being extended to Beckton and Lewisham. Originally owned by London Transport, it is now owned by the London Docklands Development Corporation.

System: 750 V d.c. third rail (bottom contact).
Depot: Poplar.

CLASS P89 B – 2 – B

Built 1990 by BREL Ltd., York Works. 28.00 x 2.65 m. Inward Folding plug doors. Chopper control. Scharfenberg Couplers.

Weight: 39 t.
Seats: 84U.
Traction Motors: Two GEC of 185 kW.
Max. Speed: 80 km/h.
Electric Brake: Rheostatic.

12	15	18	20
13	16	19	21
14	17		

SIX-AXLE ARTICULATED CARS B – 2 – B

Built 1991 – 2 by BN Construction, Bruges, Belgium. (now Bombardier Eurorail). 28.8 x 2.65 m. Sliding doors. End doors for staff use. Chopper control. Scharfenberg Couplers

Weight: 36 t.
Seats: 66U + 4 tip-up.
Traction Motors: Two Brush of 140 kW.
Max. Speed: 80 km/h.
Electric Brake: Rheostatic.

22	28	34	40
23	29	35	41
24	30	36	42
25	31	37	43
26	32	38	44
27	33	39	

9.3. GREATER MANCHESTER METROLINK

This new light rail system runs from Bury to Altrincham through the streets of Manchester, with a spur to Piccadilly.

System: 750 V d.c. overhead.
Depot: Queens Road.

SIX-AXLE ARTICULATED CARS Bo – 2 – Bo

Built 1991 – 2 by Firema, Italy. Power operated sliding doors. Chopper control. Scharfenberg Couplers.

Weight: 45 t.
Seats: 84U.
Dimensions: 29.00 x 2.65 m.
Traction Motors: Four GEC of 130 kW.
Braking: Rheostatic, regenerative,disc and emergency track brakes.

1001
1002 MANCHESTER ARNDALE VOYAGER
1003 THE ROBERT OWEN
1004
1005
1006
1007 THE GUINNESS RECORD BREAKER
1008
1009 CIS 125 SPECIAL
1010 THE MANCHESTER CHAMPION
1011
1012
1013
1014
1015
1016
1017
1018
1019
1020
1021
1022
1023
1024 JOHN GREENWOOD
1025 THE CHRISTIE METRO CHALLENGER
1026

SPECIAL PURPOSE VEHICLES

Built 1991 by RFS Industries, Kilnhurst and Brown Root. Used for shunting and track maintenance. Includes a crane.

Unnumbered.

9.4. SOUTH YORKSHIRE SUPERTRAM

This new light rail system is due to open towards the end of 1993 between Sheffield City Centre and Meadowhall. Future phases under construction will take the system to Mosborough and Middlewood (Hillsborough). Because of the severe gradients in Sheffield (up to 1 in 12), all axles are powered on the vehicles under construction, the first of which should arrive in the summer.

System: 750 V d.c. overhead.
Depot: Nunnery.

EIGHT-AXLE ARTICULATED UNITS B–B–B–B

Built 1993 onwards by Siemens–Duewag, Düsseldorf, Germany.

Weight: 46 t.
Seats: 82U.
Dimensions: 34.75 x 2.65 m.
Traction Motors: Four monomotors.
Braking: Rheostatic, regenerative,disc and emergency track brakes.

25 vehicles are on order, but the numbers are not yet allocated.

Front Cover Photograph: Class 37/4 No. 37417 'Highland Region' in Mainline livery with the 17.30 Manchester Victoria – Southport on 12th June 1992 formed of six Regional Railways-liveried Mark 2a/b/c coaches. *L.A. Nixon*

Back Cover Photograph: Class 142 No. 142 020 recently repainted in Tyne & Wear PTE livery leaves Gateshead Metrocentre with the 13.32 to Sunderland on Christmas Eve 1992. *John Augustson*

9.5. STRATHCLYDE PTE UNDERGROUND

This circular 4′ gauge underground line in Glasgow is generally referred to as the ''Subway''.

System: 750 V d.c. third rail.
Depot: Broomloan.

SINGLE CARS Bo – Bo

Built 1978 – 9 by Metro-Cammell. Power-operated sliding doors. 12.58 x 2.34 m.

Seats: 36U.
Traction Motors: Two GEC G312AZ.

101	110	118	126
102	111	119	127
103	112	120	128
104	113	121	129
105	114	122	130
106	115	123	131
107	116	124	132
108	117	125	133
109			

INTERMEDIATE TRAILERS 2 – 2

Built 1992 by Metro-Cammell. Power-operated sliding doors. 12.58 x 2.34 m. No details available.

201	203	205	207
202	204	206	208

9.6. TYNE AND WEAR METRO

System: 1500 V d.c. overhead.
Depot: South Gosforth.

BATTERY/OVERHEAD ELECTRIC LOCOS

Built: 1989 – 80 by Hunslet, Leeds. BSI couplers.
Traction Motors: Hunslet-Greenbat T9-4P.
Weight: 26 t.

BL1 BL2 BL3

SIX-AXLE ARTICULATED UNITS B – 2 – B

Built 1976, 1978 – 81 by Metro-Cammell. 27.80 x 2.65m. BSI couplers.
Weight: 39 t.
Seats: 84U.
Traction Motors: Two 187 kW monomotor bogies.

4001
4002
4003
4004
4005
4006
4007
4008
4009
4010
4011
4012
4013
4014
4015
4016
4017
4018
4019
4020
4021
4022
4023
4024
4025
4026
4027
4028
4029
4030
4031
4032
4033
4034
4035
4036
4037
4038
4039
4040
4041
4042
4043
4044
4045
4046
4047
4048
4049
4050
4051
4052
4053
4054
4055
4056
4057
4058
4059
4060
4061
4062
4063
4064
4065
4066
4067
4068
4069
4070
4071
4072
4073
4074
4075
4076
4077
4078
4079
4080
4081
4082
4083
4084
4085
4086
4087
4088
4089
4090

Names:

4041 HARRY COWANS
4044 Director
4051 Times

Standard livery is yellow and white.

4044 is painted yellow.
4051 is painted claret.
4054/5 are painted in 'Metroland' advertising livery.

THE PLATFORM 5 TRANSPORT BOOK CLUB
MEMBERSHIP APPLICATION FORM

To enrol for one year's membership in the PLATFORM 5 TRANSPORT BOOK CLUB, please complete this form (or a photocopy) and send it with your cheque/postal order for £1.50 made payable to 'Platform 5 Publishing Limited' to:

The Platform 5 Transport Book Club, Wyvern House, Old Forge Business Park, Sark Road, SHEFFIELD, S2 4HG.

BLOCK CAPITALS PLEASE

Name: . . . .

Address: . . . .

. . . .

Post Code: . . . .

Telephone: . . . .

Please accept my application and enrol me as a member of the Platform 5 Transport Book Club.

As a member I will receive four issues of the club newsletter, each containing a number of new books at prices of at least 15% less than the published cover price (exclusive of postage and packing).

I understand I am not obliged to buy any of the books offered, and there is no limit to the number of copies of each book that may be ordered.

I enclose my cheque/postal order for £1.50 payable to Platform 5 Publishing Limited.

Signed: . . . .

Date: . . . .

Office Use Only: . . . .

PLATFORM 5 PUBLISHING LTD. MAIL ORDER LIST

NEW TITLES	Price
British Railways Locomotives & Coaching Stock 1993	7.25
Light Rail Review 4 **MARCH 93**	7.50
German Railways Locomotives & MUs 3rd edition **SPRING 93**	12.50
6203 'Princess Margaret Rose'	19.95
British Baltic Tanks	6.95
British Rail Track Diagrams 1 – ScotRail (Quail)	5.00
Scenes from the Past 16 – Midland from Manchester (Foxline)	9.95
LNWR Branch Lines of West Leics. & East Warwicks. (Milepost)	7.50
Bus Review 8 (Bus Enthusiast)	4.95
Modern British Railway Titles	
Motive Power Pocket Book Spring 1993	1.80
Coaching Stock Pocket Book 1993	1.80
Diesel Unit Pocket Book 1993	1.80
Electric Unit Pocket Book 1993	1.80
Preserved Locomotives of British Railways 7th Edition	5.50
Departmental Coaching Stock 4th Edition	4.95
On-Track Plant on British Railways 4th Edition	5.50
The Fifty 50s in Colour	5.95
Blood, Sweat and Fifties (Class 50 Society)	2.95
British Rail Internal Users (SCTP)	7.95
British Rail Wagon Fleet – Air Braked Stock (SCTP)	6.95
RIV Wagon Fleet (SCTP)	5.95
British Rail Track Diagrams 3 – Western (Quail)	5.00
British Rail Track Diagrams 4 – London Midland (Quail)	6.95
London Railway Map (Quail)	5.95
London Transport Track Map (Quail)	1.30
Miles & Chains Volume 2 – London Midland (Milepost)	1.40
Miles & Chains Vol. 3 – Scottish, Vol. 5 – Southern (Milepost)	each 1.00
Overseas Railways	
Swiss Railways/Chemins de Fer Suisses	9.95
French Railways/Chemins de Fer Francais 2nd Edition	9.95
ÖBB/Austrian Federal Railways 2nd Edition	6.95
Benelux Locomotives & Coaching Stock 2nd Edition	6.95
A Guide to Portuguese Railways (Fearless)	4.95
Railways of Southern Africa Locomotive Guide 1992 (Beyer-Garratt)	4.00
Historical Railway Titles	
Midland Railway Portrait	12.95
Steam Days on BR 1 – The Midland Line in Sheffield	4.95
Rails along the Sea Wall (Dawlish – Teignmouth Pictorial)	4.95
The Rolling Rivers	6.95
The Railways of Winchester	6.95
British Railways Mark 1 Coaches (Atlantic)	19.95
Register of Closed Railways 1948 – 91 (Milepost)	5.95
Private Owner Wagons Volume 3 (Headstock)	6.95
Private Owner Wagons Volume 4 (Headstock)	7.95
Political	
The Battle for the Settle & Carlisle	6.95

Rambling	**Price**
Rambles by Rail 1 – The Hope Valley Line	1.95
Rambles by Rail 2 – Liskeard-Looe	1.95
Light Rail Transit, Trams, Buses & Ships	
Light Rail Review 1 (Reprint)	6.95
Light Rail Review 2 & Light Rail Review 3	each 7.50
UK Light Rail Systems No.1: Manchester Metrolink	8.50
Blackpool & Fleetwood By Tram	7.50
Tramways in and around Stockport (Foxline)	6.95
London Buses in Exile 2nd Edition (Bus Enthusiast)	4.95
60 Years of A1 Service (Bus Enthusiast)	5.95
Edinburgh's Trams & Buses (Bus Enthusiast)	4.95
Speed Bonny Boat (The Story of Caledonian MacBrayne 1969-1990)	4.95
Scenes from the Past (Foxline Publishing)	
Scenes from the Past 11 – Nottingham	8.95
Scenes from the Past 12 – Conwy Valley	7.95
Scenes from the Past 13 – Stockport Tiviot Dale	5.95
Scenes from the Past 14 – Bangor	7.95
Scenes from the Past 15 – Denbigh/Mold Line	9.95
A few copies of earlier Scenes from the Past titles are still available Please send SAE to the address below for details	
PVC Book Covers	
A6 Pocket Book Covers in Blue, Red, Green or Grey	0.80
Locomotives & Coaching Stock Covers in Blue, Red, Green or Grey	1.00
A5 Book Covers in Blue, Red, Green or Grey	1.40
Back Numbers	
Locomotives & Coaching Stock 1985	2.95
Locomotives & Coaching Stock 1986	3.30
Locomotives & Coaching Stock 1987	3.30
Locomotives & Coaching Stock 1988	3.95
Locomotives & Coaching Stock 1989	4.95
Locomotives & Coaching Stock 1990	5.95
Locomotives & Coaching Stock 1991	6.60
British Railways Locomotives & Coaching Stock 1992	7.00
Reduced Price Titles	
Today's Railways Review of the Year Volume 1 (was 11.95)	5.95
Today's Railways Review of the Year Volume 2 (was 11.95)	5.95
Today's Railways Review of the Year Volume 3 (was 13.95)	6.95
Today's Railways Review of the Year Volume 4 (was 14.95)	6.95
The Handbook of British Railways Steam Motive Power Depots	
Volume 1 – Southern England (was 7.95)	3.95
Volume 2 – Central England, East Anglia & Wales (was 8.95)	3.95
Volume 3 – North Midlands, Lancashire & Yorkshire (was 8.95)	3.95
Volume 4 – Northern England & Scotland (was 9.95)	3.95
North West Rails in Colour (was 8.50)	4.25
Along LMS Routes Vol. 1. (Headstock) (was 14.95)	6.95

Postage: 10% (UK), 20% (Overseas). Minimum 30p. Please Note: Postage on reduced price titles must be based on original price.

All these publications are available from shops, bookstalls or direct from: Mail Order Department, Platform 5 Publishing Ltd., Wyvern House, Old Forge Business Park, Sark Road, SHEFFIELD, S2 4HG, ENGLAND. For a full list of titles available by mail order, please send SAE to the above address.